The Morality of War

THE MORALITY
OF WAR

Brian Orend

broadview press

Library and Archives Canada Cataloguing in Publication

Orend, Brian, 1971-
    The morality of war / Brian Orend.

Includes bibliographical references and index.
ISBN 1-55111-727-4

    1. War—Moral and ethical aspects—Textbooks. 2. War (International law)—Textbooks. 3. Just war doctrine—Textbooks. I. Title.

U22.0728 2006   172'.42   C2006-902534-7

Broadview Press is an independent, international publishing house, incorporated in 1985. Broadview believes in shared ownership, both with its employees and with the general public; since the year 2000 Broadview shares have traded publicly on the Toronto Venture Exchange under the symbol BDP.

We welcome comments and suggestions regarding any aspect of our publications—please feel free to contact us at the addresses below or at broadview@broadviewpress.com.

North America
PO Box 1243, Peterborough, Ontario, Canada K9J 7H5
PO Box 1015, 3576 California Road, Orchard Park, NY, USA 14127
Tel: (705) 743-8990; Fax: (705) 743-8353
email: customerservice@broadviewpress.com

UK, Ireland, and continental Europe
NBN International, Estover Road, Plymouth, UK PL6 7PY
Tel: 44 (0) 1752 202300; Fax: 44 (0) 1752 202330
email: enquiries@nbninternational.com

Australia and New Zealand
UNIREPS, University of New South Wales
Sydney, NSW, Australia 2052
Tel: 61 2 9664 0999; Fax: 61 2 9664 5420
email: info.press@unsw.edu.au

www.broadviewpress.com
Consulting Editor for Philosophy: John Burbidge
Broadview Press gratefully acknowledges the financial support of the Government of Canada through the Book Publishing Industry Development Program for our publishing activities.

Printed in Canada

For Mom

Contents

Acknowledgements

Thanks to everyone at Broadview, especially Julia Gaunce, for their strong support and enthusiastic commitment to this project. Particular gratitude must go to John Burbidge, who read and improved the entire manuscript, as did several very helpful anonymous reviewers. Judith Earnshaw and Tania Therien also provided important and appreciated help.

I've had much feedback on many of the ideas presented here, from lots of colleagues, students and audiences around the world. Thanks to everyone for sharing their thoughts, at institutions ranging from West Point to the Carnegie Council, from RIT to two TALs and three PROBUSes, and from Oklahoma State and Simon Fraser to the Universities of Wales, Montreal and Lyons. Merci beaucoup, aussi, to my many "just war" friends around the world who correspond with me on these issues: Christian Barry, Martin Cook, Mark Evans, Mo al-Hakim, Patrick Hayden, Larry Hinman, Brett Kessler, Alex Moseley, Jan Narveson, Al Pierce, Danny Statman, Michael Walzer and Dan Zupan. Enduring thanks to John English, Rhoda Howard-Hassmann and Thomas Pogge.

My department at Waterloo remains as supportive as ever, and I'm grateful. Thanks to my chair, Richard Holmes, and to all the boys and girls in the lunch lounge for camaraderie and various emergency services. Debbie Dietrich, too. Linda Daniel helped prepare parts of the manuscript with marvellous efficiency, even when my software codes tried to prevent her.

Appreciation goes to the University of Wales Press for allowing me to make amended use of some material from my earlier work, *Michael Walzer on War and Justice* (2000), which was also published by McGill-Queen's University Press. Thanks, too, to the Carnegie Council on Ethics and International Affairs in NYC for similar permission regarding "Justice After War," an article I published in 2002 in their fine journal, *Ethics and International Affairs*. The supreme emergency chapter saw previous life, in amended form, in M. Evans, ed. *Just War Theory: A Reappraisal* (Edinburgh: Edinburgh University Press, 2005).

This book was written during a difficult time of my life, and I'm glad to see something positive came out of it. Many people offered me help and support during that period: my department and university colleagues, my students, eternal friends like Pat Kennedy and of course my family, including my grandparents Al and Leo and my cousin Michelle and her family. Deepest thanks to my super-sister, Krista, my fab-father-in-law Barry and my marvellous mother, Mary Lou, to whom this book is dedicated with love. Special thanks to my sweet son Sammy, who fills my every minute with him with energy and adventure. *Let's go build a fort and save our friends!!!*

Introduction

Imagine that you are the President of the United States, and it's the morning of September 11, 2001. You are enjoying a public relations session, reading to school children in Florida. Up rushes a Secret Service Agent who whispers into your ear about the attacks in New York, Washington and Pennsylvania. You close your eyes, briefly, and your mind reels. The full weight—the incredible responsibility—of the presidency suddenly seems to push you down into the ground. You finish your session with the children politely, but your thoughts are detached, swirling around the questions of what you should do, and whether more attacks are coming ...

Well, what would *you* do? Your country has just experienced the most dramatic strikes against it since Pearl Harbor. Indeed, these attacks seem deliberately modelled after that explosive "Day of Infamy" in 1941. The attacks on the World Trade Center were terrorist acts, deliberately killing random civilians with the motive of spreading fear throughout the American people. But the strike on the Pentagon seems to be more a classical act of war, deliberately striking an official military target. Put them together and you have got a powerful case that your country is under attack by a deadly force with malevolent intent: armed self-defence seems the order of the day.

But is it? Are you letting your anger and desire for revenge affect your judgement? What about your fear and uncertainty? How do you find out who did this—and how do you know that you can trust that source of knowledge? How do you balance the views of those "hawkish" advisors urging a muscular military response—perhaps even invoking martial law—against those "doves" saying that terrorism is best dealt with by using police investigations, not the armed forces? Do you project an angry and forceful exterior so as to convey strength, or do you rather remain measured and cautious, so you won't panic your people? Do you strike now to prevent possible further attacks, or wait for more evidence and a cooler head?

How might your private beliefs mix with your public responsibilities here? Say you are an intensely religious person ... a pacifist by faith. Should you let your personal attitudes affect your official choices, which will have an impact upon the lives of millions? Say, by contrast, that you're a cynic, thinking it's a dog-eat-dog world out there. Will you let that cynicism rule your deliberations on grounds that "we've got to get them before they get us again"? Finally, what if you're a moralist, and you are outraged by the huge injustice dealt to your country by the attackers? Should you turn that outrage outward, using military force like a flaming sword, crusading on behalf of righteousness?

These are all difficult questions, they push different buttons, and only one person had to confront them for real that day. We should, to an extent, empathize with those who have to make such seemingly impossible decisions. On the other hand, we must still insist that such decision-makers *explain* their choices to us—their fellow citizens—and enumerate *their reasons* for doing, and ordering, what they do. For warfare, in all its forms, is serious business. Its very gravity, its degree of consequence, its cost and its impact on peoples' lives demand that we reflect intelligently upon its nature and the choices surrounding it.

War should be understood as an *actual, intentional* and *widespread* armed conflict between political communities. Thus, fisticuffs between individual persons do not count as war, nor does a gang fight, nor does a feud on the order of the Hatfields versus the McCoys. War is a phenomenon which occurs *only* between political communities, defined as those entities which either are states or intend to become states (in order to allow for civil war). Classical war is international war, a war between different states, like the two World Wars. But just as present—and apparently growing in incidence[1]—is war within a state between rival groups or communities, like the American Civil War. I suppose that certain political pressure groups, like terrorist organizations, might also be considered "political communities," in that they are associations of people with a political purpose and, indeed, many of them aspire to statehood or to influence the development of statehood in certain lands.

What's statehood? People often use "nation" and "state" interchangeably but we'll need to keep them conceptually distinct for our purposes. Most people follow Max Weber's distinction between nation and state. A nation is a group which thinks of itself as "a people," usually because they all share many things in common, such as ethnicity, language, culture, historical experience, a set of ideals and values, habitat, cuisine, fashion and so on. The state, by contrast, refers much more narrowly to the machinery of government which organizes life in a given territory.[2] Thus, we can distinguish between the American state and the American people, or between the government of France and the French nation. At the same time, you have probably heard the term "nation-state." "Nation-state" refers to the relatively recent phenomenon wherein a nation wants its own state, and moves to form one. This started out as a very European trend—an Italian state for the Italian nation, a German state for the German people, etc.—but it has spread throughout the world. Note that in some countries, such as America, Australia and Canada, the state actually presides over many nations, and you hear of "multi-national societies." Most societies with heavy immigration are multi-national. Multi-national countries are sometimes prone to civil wars between the different groups. This has been especially true of central Africa in recent years, as different peoples struggle over control of the one state, or else move to separate themselves from the existing arrangement (itself often having been put in place by distant imperial powers insensitive to local group and ethnic differences). All these distinctions will come in handy as we proceed. For now, we note how central the issue of statehood is to the essence of warfare. Indeed, I would argue that *all warfare is precisely, and ultimately, about governance.* War is a violent way for determining who gets to say what goes on in a given territory regarding, for example, who gets power, who gets wealth and resources, whose ideals prevail, who is a member and who is not, which laws get made, what gets taught in schools, where the border rests, how much tax is levied, and so on. War is the ultimate means for deciding these issues if a peaceful process or resolution can't be found.

The mere *threat* of war and the presence of mutual disdain between political communities do not suffice as indicators of war. The conflict of arms must be actual, and not merely latent, for it to count as war. Further, the actual armed conflict must be both intentional and widespread: isolated clashes between rogue officers, or border patrols, do not count as acts of war. The onset of war requires a conscious commitment and a significant mobilization on the part of the belligerents in question. There's no real war, so to speak, until the fighters *intend* to go to war and until they do so with a heavy *quantum* of force. Let us here cite, by way of support, the views of the one and only (so-called) "philosopher of war," Carl von Clausewitz. Clausewitz famously suggested that war is "the continuation of policy by other means." Surely, as a description, this conception is both powerful and plausible: war is about governance, using violence instead of peaceful measures to resolve policy (which organizes life in a land). This notion fits in nicely with Clausewitz's own general definition of war as "an act of violence intended to compel our opponent to fulfil our will." War, he says, is like a duel, but on "an extensive scale."[3] As Michael Gelven has written recently, war is intrinsically vast, communal (or political) and violent.[4] It is a widespread and deliberate armed conflict between political communities, motivated by a sharp disagreement over governance. In fact, we might say that Clausewitz was right, but not quite deep enough: it's not just that war is the continuation of policy by other means; it's that war is *about the very thing which creates policy* (i.e., governance itself). War is the intentional use of mass force to resolve disputes over governance. War is, indeed, governance by bludgeon. Ultimately, war is profoundly anthropological: it is about which group of people gets to say what goes on in a given territory.

War is a brutal and ugly enterprise. Yet it remains central to human history and social change. These two facts together might seem paradoxical and inexplicable, or they might reveal deeply disturbing facets of the human character. What is certainly true, in any event, is that war and its threat continue to be driving forces in our lives. Recent events graphically demonstrate this proposition, whether we think of the 9/11 attacks, the counter-attack on Afghanistan, the overthrow of Iraq's Saddam Hussein, the Darfur crisis in Sudan, or the ongoing "war on terror." We all had high hopes going into the new millennium in 2000; alas, this new century has already been savagely scarred with warfare.

War's violent nature and controversial social effects raise troubling moral questions for any thoughtful person. Is war always wrong? Might there be situations when it can be a justified, or even a smart, thing to do? Will war always be part of human experience, or can we do something to make it disappear? Is there a fair and sensible way to wage war, or is it all hopeless, barbaric slaughter? When wars end, how should post-war reconstruction proceed, and who should be in charge? What are our rights and responsibilities when our own society makes the move to go to war?

This book will explore all these questions and more. It is designed to be an introduction to the ethics of war and peace which is clear, comprehensive and informed by modern history. It guides the reader through all the controversies and competing values, and it discusses in detail cases ranging from World War II to the Persian Gulf War, from Vietnam and 9/11 to the overthrow of Saddam Hussein and the "war on terror." This text, it is hoped, will offer a very strong foundation on war's essential moral questions to any interested and reflective reader.

The book is split into two sections, and it *does* recommend a particular way of best understanding these issues. This way is framed by current international law and just war theory. This way is, in my view, both the most important and influential perspective in today's world, as well as the one most solidly grounded ethically. Hence the extended first section on this perspective. Just war theory is a connected body of ideas and values which considers when war can be ethically justified. It offers a set of moral rules which societies should follow during the beginning, middle and end of war. We shall examine and explain these rules, with depth and insight, in the first section. It is especially important to do so, since so many of these rules have made their way into the international laws of armed conflict, contained in such famous documents as the United Nations' Charter and the Geneva Conventions. This is not, however, a dusty book devoted to painstaking analysis of such laws; it is, rather, a "big picture" book centrally focused on the more important ethical principles behind them and how such principles apply to actual cases of armed conflict.

Just war theory's core premise is that sometimes countries can be morally justified in going to war. Pacifism, by contrast, is best understood as the view that war is never morally justified. Realism, the third big perspective on this issue, disagrees with both pacifism and just war theory by suggesting that war has nothing to do with morality—it is all about naked self-interest, survival and the pursuit of power over one's rivals. Almost all opinions of war's morality can be slotted into one of these three fundamental attitudes, based on these definitions.

Realism and pacifism are examined and evaluated in the second section and, where appropriate, I do describe the historical context and delve behind each body of thought. While, in the end, I do argue for and endorse just war theory, I make an effort to be fair and charitable to realism and pacifism. *They each have something substantial to contribute to the debate.* In the final analysis, though, I do believe that realism and pacifism should be, on the whole, rejected as somewhat extreme doctrines, whereas just war theory appeals as occupying the sensible middle ground. This is *not* to say that just war theory is perfect or fully satisfying. It is neither of these things, and it probably needs constant redevelopment in light of new events, ideas and technology, but it remains more satisfying than the alternatives.

This text has a number of distinctive features which commend it to the reader. First, it has moved into the twenty-first century, and analyzes the latest issues that have recently emerged, such as terrorism and preventive self-defence against it, as well as recent cases, such as the 2003 Iraq attack and the subsequent reconstruction and ongoing insurrection. Second, the book includes two appendices: the first offering lists of (and websites for finding) the most important laws of armed conflict; and the second offering a handy listing of just war theory sources most frequently cited. Third, this book connects just war theory to deeper issues of ethics and politics, such as human rights protection. Too often, just war theory is portrayed as a somewhat quaint, self-standing structure at the margins of applied ethics—instead of being a consistent, important and integral part of a human rights-based approach to some of the most pressing political issues of our time.

This book goes well beyond conventional treatments of just war theory by examining: 1) its main rivals, realism and pacifism, in detail; 2) both just war theory's history *and* its current concepts and applications; 3) the interconnections between the just war rules and categories; 4) new demands for *international* authorization for resorting to force; 5) supreme emergencies, including genocide; 6) the justice of peace settlements, occupations and postwar reconstruction; and 7) the complex issue of how governments should treat their own citizens—be they civilians or soldiers—during wartime. This last issue concerns controversial topics like civil liberties and anti-terrorist legislation, and it only strengthens the connection between just war theory and vital issues in contemporary social organization. Indeed, this reworking of just war theory strives to be a substantial, creative contribution to the tradition which goes well beyond the status quo. Some people, upon reading drafts of this work, asked me whether this actually is just war theory, since so many new understandings, connections and innovations are attempted. It *is* just war theory, and I like to think such questions show I'm on to something. You decide.

Notes

1. K. Holsti, *The State, War and the State of War* (Cambridge: Cambridge University Press, 1996).
2. M. Weber, *General Economic History* (London: Dover, 2003), 8–52.
3. Carl von Clausewitz, *On War*, trans. A. Rapoport (Harmondsworth, England: Penguin, 1995), 100–2.
4. M. Gelven, *War and Existence* (Philadelphia, PA: Penn State University Press, 1994), *passim*.

PART ONE

Just War Theory and International Law

CHAPTER 1
A Sweeping History of Just War Theory

"Some political theories die and go to heaven;
some, I hope, die and go to hell.
But some have a long life in this world ..."
Michael Walzer[1]

People have wrestled with the ethics of war and peace since the beginning of human history, not just in Western civilization but worldwide. Almost all major civilizations—from the ancient Egyptians to the Aztecs, from Babylonia to India, from China to ancient and contemporary Europe—have featured fairly fixed beliefs about acceptable reasons for going to war, and permissible means of fighting it.

Nearly all the major religious documents—from the Bible to the *Bhagavadgita*, from the *Tao-te-ching* to the *Koran*—refer to warfare and moralize about it.[2] The Old Testament, for instance, is filled with fierce battles. Yahweh and the prophets repeatedly permit, or even command, the Israelites to go to war against their enemies, such as the Canaanites. Sometimes the commands seem quite bloodthirsty, other times restraint in fighting is urged.[3] Jesus, by contrast, fills the New Testament with words and actions which seem at least anti-war and are, perhaps, at most pure pacifism. The Prince of Peace, as Christians know him, once famously commanded Peter to put away his sword.[4] Sun Tzu's *The Art of War*—from ancient Oriental civilization, yet often taught in today's Western business schools—details various kinds of battle, and the strategies required for victory. Yet it, too, includes a kind of ethic: of fighting only smartly and with honour, and not with rage, blunder and bloodlust.[5] So, in a way, the ethics of war is everywhere, and is as old as the hills.

One of just war theory's credits is that, over time, it has developed probably the most comprehensive consideration of the ethics of war and peace. So, even though just war theory first developed in the West—and, more narrowly, among Roman lawyers and then Catholic theologians—it genuinely deserves universal attention. The fact that just war theory has had such an impact on international law—which is truly global—only emphasizes how important it is for anyone wanting to think incisively about the ethics of war and peace. Just war theory, we saw in the Introduction, is a coherent set of concepts and values which enables moral judgment in wartime. Traditionally, it is split into two categories: *jus ad bellum* (i.e., when it is just to start war) and *jus in bello* (i.e., how it is just to fight war, after it has begun). International law, by contrast, refers generally to treaties freely agreed to by sovereign states, wherein they promise to behave in a way detailed by the treaty. Treaties are like international contracts between states. And so the concepts and values first originating in the moral philosophy of just war theory have, over the centuries, made their way into binding treaties regulating state conduct during war—treaties we collectively refer to as "the laws of armed conflict."[6]

The purpose of this opening chapter is to sketch out the history of just war theory itself: *who* contributes *what*, and then *when* and *why*. Above all: what's the context here? Which events and personalities are crucial? Which mistakes get made, and strengths endure? What are the trends and cycles, changes and debates? Where did we come from in this regard, and where are we heading? It must be stressed, however, that all which can be offered in one chapter is but a sweeping sketch. This book is not mainly a history book. It is a book about the ethics of war and peace *in our time*. So, while whole books could be written about each of the following paragraphs, it is not our goal to know every little detail and personality in the very long history of just war theory. The goal, rather, is to hit the high points and, above all, *to set the context for the concepts* which are going to be detailed in subsequent chapters.

The Greco-Romans

So where does just war theory specifically come from, and why should we care? Paul Christopher credits ancient Greek philosopher Aristotle (384–322 BC) with being the coiner of the term "just war."[7] This concept was in contrast to the older idea of a "holy war," as mandated by some Divinity and described in some of the religious texts mentioned above. Just war theory is, at heart, a secular concept (i.e., a way of thinking about war's rightness or wrongness without appealing to God or scripture). But we'll see that, historically, just war theory does come to be associated, for some time, with Christianity and, more narrowly, Catholicism.

Aristotle, and his teacher Plato (427–347 BC), reflected on war's justice, no doubt spurred on by all the wars fought between Greeks and Persians and, indeed, amongst the Greek city-states themselves. Plato, for instance, grew up during the destructive Peloponnesian War between Athens and Sparta and it profoundly affected his life and thinking. Aristotle, for his part, thought it morally justified to go to war to prevent one's community from being attacked and enslaved by another. Just war theorists today agree that self-defence is the most obvious just cause for war. More controversially, Aristotle thought it all right to go to war to gain an empire, provided: 1) this empire would benefit everybody, including the conquered; and 2) this empire would not become so large and rich that it would attract attackers and hence result in more wars. Most notoriously, and appallingly, Aristotle did allow warfare to gain slaves for one's community—providing that such slaves were "naturally servile" to begin with. Not a single just war theorist would today endorse these last two propositions but the empire issue retains real life. For example, does America now have an empire? Has it come by this empire justly? Have its many recent wars been those of defence or, rather, of expanding and fortifying its dominion?[8]

After the Greeks came the Romans, and they clearly did have an empire. The shattering success of Rome upon the battlefield provoked thought amongst such luminaries as the senators Cato and Cicero and emperors Julius Caesar and Marcus Aurelius. Cicero (106–43 BC) probably developed the deepest reflections on war amongst them, and probably deserves credit for co-founding just war theory with Augustine (still to come) and, perhaps to a lesser extent, Aristotle. James Turner Johnson's observation—that just war theory is, in its origins, *a synthesis of Greco-Roman and Christian values*—rings true.[9] Cicero endorsed wars of self-defence, and was not immune to the allure of empire. Crafty lawyer he was, though, in framing his support for imperial expansion with the rhetoric of defence: defence of Rome's *honour or glory* might call for wars of empire where defence of Rome's *safety* strictly might not. But Cicero rejected wars for gaining slave labour. He was also a stickler for procedure. And so, to Aristotle's primordial just cause requirement for a decent war, Cicero added the rules of proper authority and public declaration.

So often did the Romans find themselves in battle that they developed a formal procedure for going to war. Rome would first send a diplomatic party —ambassadors and their aides—to the target city or rival empire, announce the problem and demand rectification. The party would return to Rome and wait for a month. If nothing satisfying happened, the party would return to the enemy and threaten war. If they did not get an immediate, positive reply, the party would return to Rome and inform the Senate (seen as the proper authority for deciding war). If the Senate voted for war, the party would return to the enemy, read aloud the Senate's public declaration and then symbolically throw a sharp-pointed javelin into the enemy's soil. The party would then, obviously, quickly evacuate before the Roman army invaded and, more often than not, conquered. There are, in this procedure, some shades of the later rule of war only as a last resort: the military had to hold off until the political procedure had worked itself out to the end. Cicero also insisted on vague rules of right conduct in fighting, too. He commented repeatedly on the need for restraint in battle, and advocated loudly and effectively that soldiers surrendering to Rome deserved to be protected rather than slaughtered. Those who refused to surrender, however, deserved a different fate in Cicero's eyes.[10]

Early Christianity and Augustine

Church father Augustine (AD 354–430) is often credited with inventing just war theory all by himself. This is a huge exaggeration which downplays the Greco-Roman contribution, which we have just seen is substantial. Indeed, Augustine was not even the first Christian thinker to consider the justice of war: Tertullian (AD 160–230); Origen (AD 185–255); Lactantius (AD 260–340); and Augustine's mentor Ambrose (AD 340–397) all made contributions. Indeed, Ambrose added content to Cicero's vague *jus in bello* by stressing that soldiers should strive to display the classical virtues while fighting. These were courage, prudence, justice and moderation. More significantly, Ambrose added to the Greco-Roman rules of *jus ad bellum*—just cause, proper authority, public declaration, last resort—by saying that wars approved by God were also just. Augustine followed Ambrose in this regard, with the effect being a blurring of the line between *just* wars and *holy* wars which was to last about 1,000 years, and provide ostensible support for the pope-ordered Crusades—of Christianity against Islam—between approximately AD 1000 and 1300.[11]

Taking all this in, it is very hard to conclude that Augustine was the sole founder of just war theory. He was, however, a very high-profile and influential proponent of the theory, and Christianity's subsequent triumph in Western civilization led later thinkers to want to identify a Christian, rather than a Greco-Roman pagan, as the founder. (If we have to put names and faces on the foundation of just war theory, it would probably be the triumvirate of Aristotle, Cicero and Augustine. Traditions take some time to be created and congeal.) Augustine did add to the theory in an original way. He insisted on the rule of right intention, both in *jus ad bellum* and *jus in bello*. Augustine wrote during a time when Christianity had become—thanks to the emperor Constantine—the official, state-sanctioned religion of the Roman Empire. How could one, consistently, be both a Christian and a public official of Rome—especially when the Empire was coming under increasing armed attack from non-believing barbarians? Christianity seems, after all, to imply love and non-violence whereas the responsibilities of Roman officials regularly involved deploying armed force to hold the Empire together and keep the barbarians out. Augustine wrestled greatly with this dilemma, and concluded that a just ruler might permissibly use force to protect the innocent (i.e., ordinary civilians) from aggressive attack. *A Christian ruler has to show love for his own people.* But such a ruler must order war with only the greatest reluctance, and not with any pleasure or hatred for the enemy whatsoever. The right intention must be love for, and desire to protect, the endangered innocents. Soldiers executing this command of the ruler must likewise get no joy out of bloodlust and violence but, rather, should protect the innocents and fend off the guilty attackers with nothing but solemn duty as their focus. So, in addition to objective just causes, like defending one's community, there is the subjective requirement of being strictly motivated by love and duty alone. Augustine summarized his thoughts this way:

> The real evils in war are love of violence, revengeful cruelty, fierce and implacable enmity, wild resistance, and the lust of power, and such like; and it is generally to punish these things, when force is required to inflict the punishment, that, in obedience to God or some lawful authority, good men undertake wars.[12]

The Dark Ages and Holy Wars

The Roman Empire collapsed in Western Europe in the 400s AD, fragmenting in the face of repeated barbarian invasions. It had grown too large to govern efficiently, and too often its governors were corrupt and incompetent. It managed to endure in the Near East for over a thousand years more, but in the West the only institution to survive the collapse of Roman civilization was the Catholic Church. The western empire otherwise dissolved into a series of small ethnic groups, and tribe-like families, and many wars between them ensued. Not much information survives from this period, and so we call it the Dark Ages. What little does survive tells us, sporadically, of an anarchical and bloody existence, a dirty and decrepit life. Europe took major steps back during the Dark Ages, which lasted anywhere from 500–1000. At the same time, Islamic civilization in Persia and Africa, and Far Eastern civilizations in China and India, flourished.

During the Dark Ages' later years, starting around 800, attempts were made by ambitious local warlords to consolidate their control over larger pieces of territory. Alfred did this in Britain and Charlemagne on the Continent. While not immediately successful, these efforts pointed the way towards the future: local tribal heads gradually winning control over larger and larger pieces of territory, declaring themselves champions of the people in the process. They re-established law and order by force of arms, farm-by-farm and forest-by-forest. A handful of such warlords eventually became self-styled kings, monarchs of their realms. All the while, such warlords had to deal with the Church: its longevity; its land holdings; its moral authority over its flock. Most warlords were eager to win the Church's approval, for it was a powerful ally and could provide to their rule no better stamp of legitimacy. As a result, many European warlords heeded the call when the Church demanded a series of military crusades, between 1000–1300, against the encroachment of Islam into Europe. These Crusades were massive armed invasions of Muslim strongholds in Eastern Europe, the Middle East and North Africa.[13]

What exactly is the difference between just war and holy war, especially since so many early Christian thinkers conflated the two? A holy war (*bellum sanctum*) is a war approved of—either commanded or permitted—by God. The approval is thought to come from sacred scripture itself or from religious authorities, such as the pope. Pope Urban II, in 1095, inaugurated the First Crusade by declaring "*Deus Veult!*" (i.e., "God wills it!"). God was thought to "will" that Christians would re-take Jerusalem from Islamic control and prepare it for Christ's second coming. The Christian conquest of that city did indeed happen in 1099. The Muslims, under Saladdin, later took it back, and the Second and Third Crusades were motivated to recover it. The other main feature of a holy war (labelled a "*jihad*" in the Islamic tradition) is that soldiers fighting on behalf of the cause are seen, thereby, to be cleansing their sins and paving their entry into Paradise. Salvation of self, so to speak, through mutilation of others. A just war (*bellum justum*), by contrast, is not thought to be sacred, merely moral. There is no pretence of having divine approval, rather merely good reasons (like self-defence) for fighting a war. And while soldiers fighting just wars might be thanked or even praised (e.g., on Remembrance or Veteran's Day), there is no claim that their participation in the war has guaranteed them membership in Heaven. We see, then, that there need be *no necessary connection at all* between doctrines of just war and those of holy war. But Dark Age Christians, especially those involved in the Crusades, did forge such a connection—and so *jus ad bellum* became, frankly, polluted with some dark religious dimensions, like self-righteousness, inflexibility, demonization of others and fanaticism. It was to be a long time before such pollution was met with sufficient dilution, and today no just war theorist endorses the holy war concept as a good reason to go to war.[14]

While perhaps regressing on the *jus ad bellum* side, this era did manage big progress on the *jus in bello* front. Great specificity was added to Cicero's vague calls for moderation, Ambrose's insistence on fighting with virtue and Augustine's command for purity of intention. Two papal edicts—the "Peace of God" of 989 and the "Truce of God" of 1027—combined with the Second Lateran Council of 1139 and Gratian's *Decretum* of 1148 to form quite concrete and sensible rules of *jus in bello*. Non-combatants were specified— notably, women and children—and held to be ethically immune from attack or hostage-taking. A whole range of new weapons were prohibited, including cross-bows and anything—swords and arrows especially—dipped in poison or pestilence. Attacks on food sources, like crops, were completely ruled out, and churches officially declared "sanctuary" from military and indeed police activity. The sources of these rules were the Bible, Augustine's writings, experience with the new weapons, and even aristocratic sporting tournaments (featuring jousting) and their customs regarding fair play and chivalry.[15]

Aquinas and Legitimacy

By the time of Thomas Aquinas (1225–1274), we can properly speak of a reasonably settled and articulated "just war tradition," with many different people deploying the same concepts and values in aid of judging the same thing, in this case warfare—and often arriving at very similar conclusions.

We have at this time clearly separate and quite developed categories of *jus ad bellum* and *jus in bello*. Under the former, we have rules of just cause, right intention, public declaration by a proper authority and not exactly last resort but something like "give the enemy a chance to make amends before fighting." Under the latter, we now have non-combatant immunity, right intention, non-use of prohibited weapons, an obligation to accept offers of surrender without slaughter and something like "behave with virtue and chivalry on the battlefield." This constitutes, over 1500 years, huge theoretical progress from Aristotle's quick reflections on just cause. Aquinas was quite impressed with Aristotle's philosophy and, to the existing set of rules, the Italian theologian added proportionality to each category. This was good Aristotelian sense: war should be a proportionate response to the grievance (i.e., the problem should be so severe that only fighting seems the way to solve it) and the quantum of force deployed should be appropriate to the objective at hand on the battlefield. Aquinas also invented something called the Doctrine of Double Effect (DDE), which has important applications within *jus in bello*, and we will discuss them in subsequent chapters. Aquinas was also a transitional figure on two issues. The first is the acceptability of holy war as a just cause. Aquinas notably backed off here, saying that defensive wars to protect Christians from death (or severe persecution) at the hands of non-Christians *might* be permissible but aggressive wars designed to coerce non-believers into Christianity *definitely* are not. Jesus, after all, did not create Christians by cracking skulls. The spotty record of the Crusades also prompted Aquinas to pour cold water on the holy war concept. Unfortunately, the idea would still come and go, at least in the West, until Hugo Grotius' authoritative proclamations against holy wars in the early 1600s. Truly, even after that, holy-war-style rhetoric has been known to infect justifications of war to this very day.

Aquinas also marks a transition on the important issue of proper authority for declaring war. In Greece, the proper authority was the head of state, whether dictator or democratic assembly. In Rome it was the Senate and, during the late Empire, the Emperor. During the Dark Ages, it was the Pope. But in the run-up to Aquinas' life, there was a very fluid political situation in Europe. There was still the Pope and the Church, of course, but there was also the development of these tribal or national kings, like King John in England. Furthermore, some areas of Europe were essentially Greek-style city-states, like Venice. There were also very wealthy trading enterprises, with their own private militias or armed security corps—some so powerful they dwarfed those of towns and other political associations. Also sporting private militias were aristocrats out to challenge the king, on the belief that their families were just as entitled to the throne. Aquinas, perhaps surprisingly, did not side with the Church. Not so surprisingly, he condemned the private militias and armed trading companies. He favoured the non-proliferation of armies, so to speak. Common sense told him: the more armies we have got, the more likely they'll step on each other's toes and start fighting. Aquinas' middle-of-the-road solution was that only genuinely *political*—and not merely *mercantile*—associations could declare war, and the body which spoke for the political association was that: 1) capable of ordering that society; and 2) demonstrating clear intentions to rule for the common good of all (as opposed to the private greed of some, such as ambitious barons, dukes and earls). Essentially, then, Aquinas favoured more central authority, like a national king or prince, but still strongly advised such a ruler to heed the advice of the Church, with its centuries of experience in developing and applying just war theory. In this sense, Aquinas sided with the rise of the modern nation-state.[16]

Vitoria and The Spanish Conquest

It is important to note that, from the beginning, just war theory has been applied to real world conflicts and has served not just to *legitimize* but also to *criticize* the conduct of the powers that be. Augustine, it is true, was mainly looking for a legitimation of state violence: he wanted to square public Roman control with his private Christian beliefs. But later thinkers realized that when a state (or prince) fails to meet the standards of just war theory, then it (or he) must be morally criticized and urged to stop. For instance, in Spain in the early 1500s, numerous figures used just war theory to condemn Spain's aggressive invasion and colonization of parts of the New World. Spain was motivated neither by love nor by any kind of defence or protection, they said. The kingdom, delighted by Columbus' 1492 discoveries, became instead driven by greed and love of power and conquest, and the harsh treatment of the natives by the infamous conquistadors, in addition to being evil in itself, revealed this.

Key figures involved in the debate over the justice of the Spanish Conquest were: Bartoleme de las Casas (1474–1566); Sepulveda (1490–1574); Francisco de Vitoria (1492–1546); Francisco Suarez (1548–1617); and Alberico Gentili (1552–1608). Sepulveda and Gentili tried to use just war concepts to justify the conquest, with Sepulveda even resurrecting Aristotle's old canard about natural slavery. De las Casas, by contrast, offered a clear, eloquent and principled denial and critique. The entire faculty of the University of Salamanca, in 1520, bravely resolved in public that Spain's actions constituted an unjust war. It is important, indeed, to note that European colonialism and imperialism did not proceed with unanimous support. Vitoria's work has stood the test of time as the deepest theoretical contribution from this fertile period.[17]

Vitoria was the first to say clearly that even non-Christian communities have the rights implied by *jus ad bellum* (notably, a general right not to be attacked). He rejected the concept of holy wars and insisted on the secularism of just war theory. He helpfully suggested that all plausible just causes for going to war be subsumed under the one concept of "a wrong received." He thus banned both aggression and pre-emption (because the wrong had *to be received* before one could justly respond to it). On this latter point, he memorably commented: "It is quite unacceptable that a person should be killed for a sin he has yet to commit."[18] Vitoria did allow for armed humanitarian intervention as a kind of war of "other-defence." He actually justified the Spanish Conquest on this basis, at least in terms of just cause. He sharply criticized Spanish intentions of greed and power but did believe that the Conquest liberated the natives of the Americas from indigenous oppression and such brutal home-grown practices as human sacrifice and ritualized cannibalism. So self-defence and other-defence were, for Vitoria, the only just causes for going to war, and in either case it had to be defence from attack which already occurred and not from an imagined one merely suspected to come in the future.

One of the most important contributions made by Vitoria was his stress on the quality and objectivity of the evidence needed to support a decision to go to war. Vitoria strongly rejected the idea that the ultimate decision should rest with only one man—even the king—since any given man is subject to strong emotions and subjective biases. A just ruler must first invite counsel from groups of wise men, learned in just war theory *and who represent different opinions about the war action contemplated.* A hawkish ruler surrounding himself only with "yes men" is not being responsible and may find himself ordering, and then later accountable for, an ultimately unjustifiable war.[19]

Grotius and The Wars of Religion

Hugo Grotius (1583–1645) was similarly motivated by the colonial experience, in his case the Dutch, and particularly in the Caribbean Indies. His landmark work, *The Law of War and Peace*, was also driven by the terrible Wars of Religion—between Catholic and Protestant—then rocking Europe in the wake of the Protestant Reformation and the end of the Catholic Church's religious monopoly over Western Europe. The savagery of the fighting in both the New World and the Old concentrated Grotius' mind powerfully, and he vowed to do what he could to bring warfare within the confines of law once more. One of his biting remarks, in this regard, was that: "Throughout the Christian world I have seen a lawlessness in warfare that even the barbarian races would think shameful. On trifling pretexts, or none at all, men rush to arms and when once arms are taken up, all respect for law, whether human or divine, is lost as though by some edict a fury had been let loose to commit every crime."[20]

Grotius' work—not so much original as painstaking, comprehensive and plausible—is credited not only with being one of the landmark pieces of just war theory but also as the first product of the laws of armed conflict. Grotius thus straddles the gap between morality and law; he wrote that the very point

of law is to realize the ideals of morality. Not surprisingly, given the Wars of
Religion, Grotius was a relentless secularizer, echoing Vitoria's rejection of
holy wars and essentially sealing the debate on that issue for the remainder
of the just war tradition (though not, as we noted, in popular political culture). Religion is a matter of conscience and choice, or at least for each nation
to decide for itself, he wrote, and so it cannot figure into any just cause for
war. On just cause, Grotius essentially shared Vitoria's understanding of self-
and other-defence. Grotius did go further, however, in specifying that it was
allowable not merely to defend against aggression *in the process of happening* (whether against self or others) but also to punish *past* aggression which
still stood uncorrected. Grotius, as a lawyer, was big on there being concrete
penalties for violating principles, and so wars of punishment (as well as
defence) figured into his system. He actually justified some of the colonial
conquests as punishment for iniquitous (ungodly?!) practices on the part of
the natives. He also contributed the criterion of probability of success to *jus
ad bellum*: one should only go to war if one has a decent chance of winning.
It is, I suppose, to be lamented that the two just war giants from this period—
Vitoria and Grotius—both supported the *causes* behind European colonial
conquest, viewing them as justified forms of other-defence or humanitarian
intervention. That's true but both also criticized the intentions of the European imperialists and so, in the end, took a rather dim view of colonialism
or, at the least, viewed it as a mixed bag of crimes and benefits.[21]

We can see that, with Grotius, most of the general principles of modern
just war theory became set. Disagreements about what the theory exactly
implied in terms of each particular war, of course, remained—and just cause
remained especially contentious, and does so to this day. But the essentials
were all in place, and indeed a new focus for the theory developed: getting
nation-states to agree to the general moral principles in exact, formal, written, legal treaties. Just three years after Grotius' death, the Treaty of Westphalia (1648) brought the Thirty Years War (the bloodiest of the Wars of
Religion) to an end. Often seen as the first piece of modern international
law, Westphalia enshrined a form of tolerance over religion, with national
signatories pledging not to go to war with each over in an attempt at armed
conversion. A principle of non-intervention in "the internal affairs" of other
nations was generated, and just war theorists Samuel Pufendorf (1632–1704)
and Emmerich Vattel (1714–67) solidified this trend by rejecting humanitarian intervention as a just cause for war. This strong interpretation of state
sovereignty, and hostility to any foreign intervention in local affairs, was to
endure almost to the end of the 1990s. The prevailing interpretation of just
cause was thus: defence of one's nation from foreign attack; defence of
another nation (especially one's ally or friend) from foreign attack; and possibly (depending on the theorist) pre-emptive attack. Punishment was not
generally accepted, and humanitarian interventions were largely prohibited.
State sovereignty reigned supreme.[22]

Locke, Kant and The Revolutionary Era

Other prominent thinkers, such as John Locke (1632–1704) and Christian
Wolff (1679–1754), wrote in a just war vein in this era of Pufendorf and
Vattel. But they failed to add much of originality to the theory. Increasingly,
the just war tradition declined in prominence because it dealt with war
between states whereas the issue increasingly at hand was the right to make
a war of revolution *within* a state or empire. Here, of course, Locke had much
of import to say and his writings partly inspired the American Revolution
(1775–83) and, through it, the French Revolution (1789–1800).[23]

Now, the question of revolutionary war can logically be incorporated
within just war theory. It is, after all, a form of war—indeed, a kind of civil
war. As such, it would fall under the principles to be defended in Chapter 3.
These principles, we'll see, revolve around the legitimacy (or moral ade-
quacy) of the state in question. Locke remains the classical source for insisting that, to be legitimate, a government must respect the natural (or human)
rights of all its individual citizens to life, liberty and property (and—Thomas
Jefferson added—the pursuit of happiness). A government which fails in this
regard is illegitimate and, should it forcefully resist reform, it may be forcibly
resisted and overthrown in turn, paving the way for a rights-respecting regime
which the people support and recognize as their government. Locke's work
on violent revolution is perhaps the first clear linkage between *jus ad bellum*
and human rights, a linkage which was to be cemented following World War
II and which remains absolutely central today. But Locke did not think of
himself as a just war theorist, nor did the tradition embrace him in return.
This is unfortunate since Locke drew on Aquinas; indeed, venerable old Aristotle had much to say about revolutionary struggles. Perhaps Locke's staunch
Protestantism prevented a complete connection to what then remained very
much a Catholic or "scholastic" doctrine.[24]

This religious difference also prevented Immanuel Kant (1724–1804)
from making a connection with the just war tradition. Indeed, Kant explicitly
distanced himself from the tradition, even poked sarcastic fun at its classical
figures. However, as I have shown elsewhere, Kant's thoughts on war and
peace shared much of the moral logic of just war theory as it existed in his
day—with one big exception. This was the whole issue of *jus post bellum*
(or justice after war). More than any other thinker before him, Kant reflected
intensively on the justice of peace treaties, of forcing regime change, of post-
war reconstruction and of what might be needed for longer-term peace
between nations. In particular, Kant favoured widespread internal regime
change in the direction of rights realization, and thought some international
policies—like diplomatic engagement, cultural linkages and free trade—
would help bring this about. Pro-rights societies, he predicted, would eventually band together to form a prosperous, peaceful federation of free nations.
Their success, in turn, would spur other nations to change internally so as to

join the club, and a kind of peaceful "cosmopolitan federation" would grow and grow.[25]

In my view, we can all but credit Kant completely for inventing *jus post bellum*. It is true that Vitoria, for one, did insist that justice after war had to be part of just war theory—but he failed to add content to this observation. It is also true that just war theorists stretching all the way back to Aristotle intoned that peace must be the sought-after goal in war. But this assertion is banality itself: *every war ends in peace*, including an unjust one. This is to say that even an aggressor aims at, and looks forward to, the peace at the end of the conflict. The real question is: what kind of peace can justly be imposed via war? And on that difficult issue, there was fundamental silence, or else sweeping vagueness, until Kant came along. Indeed, to this very day a shockingly large number of just war theorists completely ignore *jus post bellum*. But they cannot do that and pretend they have a complete theory. We have Kant to thank for priming the pump of our thoughts on this issue, which is so vital to our own times. *Jus post bellum* will be discussed in Chapters 6 and 7.

The Coming of Codification

It really is remarkable that it was not until the mid-1900s that just war theorists equal to the stature of Grotius, Pufendorf and Vattel appeared. Many of the figures in the period 1750 to 1950, evidently believed that the existing synthesis could not be much improved upon. And those who did clearly improve upon the status quo—like Locke and Kant—were not recognized as card-carrying members of the tradition. There is another factor relevant in the explanation: after 1850, there is a veritable explosion in the number of international treaties and laws regulating armed conflict, in particular *jus in bello*. Grotius' dream of codification came true—two hundred years after his death. The period 1850–1914 was extremely fertile in this regard. I have no doubt that many of the diplomats, academics and lawyers who worked on such treaties and codes would have made first-rate just war theorists. But the opportunity was ripe for them to engage in legal construction instead of theory-building, and so pragmatically they chose the former. This may have come at the price of anonymity but the gain was the world's first formal codes enshrining just war principles within law.

The US Civil War was a major spark in this regard. The North or Union side, in 1863, issued very detailed instructions—on proper ways to fight—to its soldiers. These *jus in bello* rules were called the "Field Army Manual," or "Lieber's Code" after their author. European powers, for their part, signed the Declaration of St. Petersburg in 1868, which prohibited certain bullets and projectiles. The American Civil War also brought into stark relief moral issues of *jus ad bellum* (e.g., the justice of fighting a war to end slavery) as well as *jus post bellum* issues of proper post-war pacification and reconstruction of the vanquished enemy. In these manifold senses, this war remains a very relevant case for even the most contemporary just war theorist.

The culmination of this nineteenth century move towards codification (i.e., translating moral principles into specific legal codes) was the Hague Conventions, drafted and proclaimed in ten different treaties between 1899 and 1907. Incredibly detailed, particularly with *jus in bello* rules, they stand today as living and active pieces of international law which are a credit to their authors. They stand, in many ways, as the complete realization of Grotius' dream as far as he could have foreseen.[26]

World War I and Collapse

Grotius could not, of course, have foreseen the scale and depth of World War I (1914–18), which shocked the conscience of the world and provided an ugly birth to the ultra-violent twentieth century. The war—begun as a struggle of imperial rivalries between Germany, Austria-Hungary and Turkey on the one side and Britain, France and Russia on the other—degenerated into a long and tragic slaughterhouse of destruction. The human meat grinder which was this war ended its destruction only after America intervened in 1917 on the side of Britain and France. It is fair to say that the bleak experience of World War I made people very cynical about linking justice and warfare, and so once more just war theory fell into disuse. Indeed, even one of the popes declared just war theory out of date! There are three important exceptions to these observations. The first is that many people strongly criticized the 1919 Treaty of Versailles as an unjust peace treaty. (But no one went on to articulate a general theory about what a just peace treaty fully should be. They contented themselves with particular observations, like "Germany was treated too harshly," "Britain and France extended their empires out of greed," "America simply let all this happen," and so on.) The second exception was that, with the post-war formation of the League of Nations, there was an attempt to change *jus ad bellum* rules away from self-defence (or "unilateralism") towards collective security and mutual responsibility and protection in the face of aggression (or "multilateralism"). The final exception was that the chemical weapons deployment experienced in the trenches of Europe spurred the development and signing of a treaty, in 1925, banning the use of poisonous gas in wartime. But it must be admitted that these were all political and legal developments, and they went unaccompanied by any new major piece of just war theory at this time.[27]

Rebirth and World War II

The Kellogg-Briand Pact of 1928 was an ambitious piece of international law, designed to shrink radically the number of just causes for going to war, and to buttress the war-authorizing power of the League of Nations. We see, during this period, the first attempts at making the declaration of war an *international* responsibility and power. The rise of the fascist dictatorships in the 1930s effectively gutted both these institutions but it also resurrected interest in just war theory. Many Catholic scholars, and political leaders like Winston Churchill, explicitly used just war concepts to justify and generate public support for the war against Hitler's Nazis in Germany and Mussolini's fascists in Italy. Indeed, dissidents in Spain used just war theory to justify their civil war against Franco's fascists earlier in the 1930s. While not invoking just war theory explicitly, Franklin D. Roosevelt harkened all the way back to Aristotle when he explained that America had to enter the war in 1941 as a matter of self-defence following Japan's Pearl Harbor attacks.[28]

By 1941, the world no longer dismissed just war theory as sterile and of use only to European scholars of the history of Catholicism. Systematic works appeared, including English-language works by John Ryan and John Ford. Extensive effort was put into the justification of the war on the part of the Allies. But this rebirth was not merely one-sided, superficial Allied propaganda. It was the just war community, after all, who first raised the questions and criticisms which still haunt historians today: should the Allies, especially Britain, have engaged in deliberate terror bombing of Germany's residential areas—and emphatically the purposeful razing of Dresden to the ground in 1945? Should America ever have used the atomic bomb on Japan? There were no clear laws on these unprecedented issues—and so thoughtful people turned back to just war theorists for answers, or at least guidelines. It is fair to say most just war theorists were critical of these Allied actions, and this criticism perhaps reached a highpoint after the war when Elizabeth Anscombe wrote a much-read pamphlet, "War and Murder," criticizing Oxford University's decision to award an honorary doctorate to Harry S. Truman, the US president who had ordered the atomic bombing of Hiroshima and Nagasaki.[29]

World War II, and its immediate aftermath, provided great opportunities for just war theory, and the era bears its political marks in a number of ways. Grotius' emphasis on proper punishment found ready application in the Nuremberg and Tokyo war crimes tribunals, the first in modern history. The 1945 Charter of the United Nations (UN) rigorously addressed *jus ad bellum*, placing even more emphasis on collective security and international authorization than the now-defunct League of Nations did—but realistically allowing for armed self-defence as well. Echoes of the old votes of the University of Salamanca could be heard in the set-up of the UN's Trusteeship Council, an institutionalized process for aiding the gradual end to European colonialism, especially in Africa and Asia. But the clearest impact of just war theory resided in the 1948 Convention Banning Genocide, and the landmark 1949 Geneva Conventions, which are devoted to *jus in bello*, especially regarding the specification of "benevolent quarantine" for prisoners of war. These are two of the most important laws of armed conflict to this day.[30]

Of course, these international laws were not simply the effects of just war theory—indeed, the former impacted the latter just as much. The main impetus for these legal reforms was the Holocaust and its horrors, which also inspired the 1948 Universal Declaration of Human Rights.[31] This was a moment of great significance for just war theory, because now theorists saw that the new moral basis for the age was destined to be human rights, and so they got to work interpreting traditional just war theory in light of human rights. This took some doing, and it was not clearly done in a satisfying way until perhaps the 1970s. But the move was made and it probably saved just war theory from ethical oblivion. In other words, and at long last, the just war tradition essentially had to welcome John Locke in from the cold, and forcefully and fully deal with core issues of state legitimacy, human rights protection and above all the connection between the two. This linkage is one of the most vital, and still challenging, questions to this day—as aspects of this book will demonstrate.

Our Time

The onset of the nuclear age posed new problems for just war theory, and attention focused on the morality of atomic weapons and the ethics of nuclear deterrence (i.e., threatening to use such weapons so that the enemy will not use theirs first). This was especially the case in the 1950s and early 1960s, and then again during the 1980s when Ronald Reagan was US president. But America's experience during the Vietnam War, from 1955–75, sparked the biggest development in just war theory since at least World War II and perhaps even stretching all the way back to the Spanish Conquest. It is important to note that, historically, it tends to be the questionable wars—the Spanish Conquest, the Wars of Religion, Vietnam—which provoke the most soul-searching, and thus the biggest developmental spurts in just war theory. (Some might wish to include on that list America's 2003 invasion of Iraq.)

The centre of action, in just war theory, moved at this time firmly *out* of the Catholic Church and *into* the corridors of international law and power, as well as into the groves of academe and even the streets of non-violent protest. English-language works, especially by Americans, now became the "must-read" contributions to the theory—and it has stayed that way since, though of course one cannot discount the contributions of others, such as Australians, Canadians, Europeans and Israelis. (Israel's many post-1948 wars have sparked keen interest there in just war theory.) In the 1960s, the work of Ian Brownlie, Joseph McKenna, William O'Brien, Robert Osgood, Paul Ramsey and Robert Tucker stood out very prominently.[32]

In the 1970s, literally scores of important articles appeared, such as those published in the distinguished journal *Philosophy and Public Affairs* by R.B. Brandt, R.M. Hare, R.K. Fullinwinder, David Luban and Thomas Nagel. In terms of books, Sydney Bailey, Yehuda Melzer, J.N. Moore and Richard

Wasserstrom penned vital works.[33] But Michael Walzer's *Just and Unjust Wars* of 1977 remains the breakthrough work of that decade, directly inspired by Vietnam. It is not much of an exaggeration to say this work has been to current just war theory what Grotius' *The Law of War and Peace* was to prior centuries. As such, it will be referred to throughout this work; there's simply no avoiding it. Even when one disagrees with it, Walzer's book remains the fundamental contemporary reference, which everyone "in the business" must read and understand. It is in Walzer's book, above all, that the cementing of human rights theory within the core propositions of just war theory occurs and is offered satisfying treatment. On the application side, Walzer's book is devoted to showing that World War II embodies "just," whereas Vietnam embodies "unjust," wars.[34]

In terms of the laws of armed conflict, so many treaties were signed in the 1960s and 1970s that I simply direct the reader to Appendix A for topics, listings and locations. It was a tumultuous and therefore fertile time for just war theory. Just war theory grows in spurts, in reaction to war-ravaged events and—as noted—especially in response to wars about which people are sceptical and critical.

The 1980s, 1990s and forward have seen an explosion in the number of just war theorists, and important developments in the theory itself. In the 1980s, nuclear deterrence was front and centre, as Reagan's America stared down the USSR, and the Catholic Church got back in on the action, so to speak. In 1983, the US Catholic Bishops published a high profile reflection on nuclear ethics which was influential, eliciting responses from European bishops, and academics and think-tanks worldwide. Also important was the topic of training new soldiers in ethics and international law. The US military in particular—stung by episodes of misconduct during Vietnam—invested large resources in the education of its soldiers and officers in just war theory. Other militaries followed suit. Walzer was a primary reference, as were new works by Sidney Axinn, Anthony Hartle, James Turner Johnson, Douglas Lackey, John Langan, Robert Phillips, Jim Sterba and Jenny Teichman. Johnson deserves special mention as probably the most learned historian of the tradition. The morality of indirect (but still armed) American intervention in such Latin American countries as Nicaragua—highlighted by the Iran-Contra scandal—was also very topical in the 1980s, with proponents justifying the controversial moves as part of the larger chess game of defeating the USSR. Sometimes such figures justified the Cold War struggle between America and Russia in realist terms as a fight for survival between enemies; other times they made explicit appeals to morality, urging the need to destroy "the evil empire" and its godless, rights-violating system of police-state communism.[35]

In the 1990s, following the end of the Cold War and America's triumph in it, just war theorists returned to issues of collective security and the vigour of the United Nations, which the Cold War in many ways had sapped and frustrated. The 1991 Persian Gulf War generated a big just war literature—indeed, US President George Bush Sr. argued for the war using just war language[36]—as did the nasty civil wars and humanitarian crises ranging from Bosnia to Somalia, from Rwanda to Kosovo. We will detail each of these wars later in this text. The ethics of humanitarian intervention became the largest just war issue that decade, and it generated deep critical thought about whether the strong defence of Westphalian state sovereignty and non-intervention in local affairs—dating back to Grotius, Pufendorf and Vattel—was in fact a mistake. Perhaps, instead, renewed attention to the pro-humanitarian intervention doctrine of, say, Vitoria was more in order. The catastrophic consequences of the failure to intervene in Rwanda—800,000 people slaughtered, in an attempted genocide, in the spring of 1994[37]—put some clear pro-intervention flavour back into many just war works, and resulted in pro-intervention policies on the ground later in Bosnia and Kosovo.

Intervention was the big *jus ad bellum* issue of the 1990s; the big *jus in bello* issue was the set of sweeping sanctions slapped on Iraq following its defeat in the Persian Gulf War by America. Did the sanctions violate the principle of discrimination, wrongfully inflicting serious harm on millions of innocent civilians? We'll consider these issues in detail in Chapters 4 and 5. Prominent just war pieces were penned this decade by: Paul Christopher, Jean Bethke Elshtain, G.S. Davis, Michael Ignatieff and Richard Regan.[38] The major reform in the laws of armed conflict was the 1998 Treaty of Rome, which created the first permanent and international war crimes tribunal, set up to judge war crimes committed anytime, anywhere, by anybody. Grotius the punisher would have been pleased.[39]

This brings us to our present decade, and of course we're not far enough removed to make good judgments about which works will last and which issues will endure the most. Scores of smart people are actively creating important pieces of writing and others are crafting vital military and foreign policies on the ground. Clearly, though, the 9/11 terrorist attacks on the United States had a dramatic impact on the debate, and raised questions in particular about just wars against non-state actors. The subsequent 2003 invasion of Iraq created heated debate about the justice of pre-emptive war and/or preventive strikes. This is one issue around which there is very little consensus among just war theorists, stretching all the way back to its origins: may you justly strike another before he strikes you, if you sincerely believe he is just about to do so? Or is it, as Vitoria says, that you cannot punish someone for a sin they have yet to commit? These are big issues for Chapter 3.

An even deeper issue is whether, as some have argued, the laws of war and just war theory must be completely rethought in the Age of Terror. Why might this be? Well, the laws of armed conflict and just war theory have generally been constructed assuming that state governments, and their armed forces, are the main belligerents in the given conflict. But 9/11 revealed that non-state actors, like terrorist groups, can now pose state-scale levels of threat and destruction. Are new principles needed? Or do we have the tools already to evaluate the so-called "War on Terror"?[40]

The difficult, multi-faceted, and ongoing occupations of Iraq and Afghanistan raise profound issues of *jus post bellum*. Just war theorists are increasingly coming around to the importance of this topic, which Walzer himself has recently called one of the two most vital for the theory's future. The other is the *jus in bello* issue of soldiers striving to carve out a risk-free fighting environment for themselves via technology, perhaps off-loading their own risks upon powerless civilians. (Think of the long-range, high-altitude bombing of Kosovo and Serbia in 1999.)[41] I might add a third issue to Walzer's list of the most consequential current topics, and that concerns the ethics of detaining and torturing suspected terrorists to gain information thought needed to prevent future terrorist attacks. And let's add a fourth while we're at it: the justice of overthrowing governments and setting out, right from the start, to forcibly reconstruct their societies.

Conclusion

It might seem strange, in this sweeping but still substantial history of just war theory, that no mention has been made of realism or pacifism. This was deliberate, since the focus was on just war theory and, to a lesser extent, the laws of armed conflict. But of course the other two doctrines have their own robust histories, and at times these histories have had an impact on just war theory. This is true of realism in particular. Realism has been the main rival to just war theory, in terms of affecting the behaviour of those with the war power. Pacifism is principled, and it has had it own kind of influence through time, but pragmatically no nation-state or empire has ever based its foreign policy on pacifism. The only exceptions to this might be old, isolated religious communities and conquered nations engaging in non-violent (or, at least, non-warring) resistance.

Which has had more influence on foreign policy: realism or just war theory? The answer is that there is a kind of cycle, and at times realism is on the ascendant and at others just war theory is. Walzer says just war theory is ascendant in the post-Cold War era.[42] Perhaps this fact is connected with American hegemony during this era and America's self-image as an ethical force in world history, concerned with fighting only just wars. There is some irony in traditionally Catholic just war theory living and thriving perhaps most strongly in historically Protestant America. But perhaps that's not relevant. Perhaps it is more a fact, just like with Rome and Spain in their days, that the most powerful nation just naturally asks itself the most questions about the justice of its influence and its frequent resort to force. There is something substantial to Walzer's claim, no doubt. Recent armed conflicts have indeed been justified by vocal moral appeals to just war concepts like humanitarian intervention and self-defence. Other people have criticized the exact same wars using just war rules like right intention, proper authority, last resort and proportionality.

But perhaps the triumph of just war theory is already fading. The post-9/11 world does, after all, concern itself mightily with national security, and some have suggested the ongoing War on Terror is the next Cold War. And the Cold War (from approximately 1946–91) was obviously a time of realism triumphant, with the balance of nuclear terror and the cold-blooded chess game of geopolitical struggle between communism and capitalism. Only time will tell, of course. Other commentators view the recent wars not as isolated conflicts to be evaluated one-at-a-time with the tools of just war theory. They view them, rather, as parts of a larger, over-all strategy—an empire-building strategy—by the United States as it seeks (in arch-realist fashion) to protect itself, grab resources and to extend its domain, values, economy and influence as far and as deeply as it possibly can.[43]

More on the specific histories of realism and pacifism, and their competition with just war theory, will be found in Part Two. For the moment, now that we have completed our sketch of the history of just war theory—and laid down some context of people and places, of wars and nations—we must turn to the conceptual task of understanding the rules and values of present-day just war theory, and then applying them to recent cases of armed conflict.

Notes

1. M. Walzer, "The Triumph of Just War Theory," in his *Arguing About War* (New Haven, CT: Yale University Press, 2004), 3.
2. P. Christopher, *The Ethics of War and Peace* (Englewood Cliffs, NJ: Prentice Hall, 1994), 8–16; J. Kelsay, *Islam and War* (London: John Knox, 1993); S. Rosen, *Holy War: Violence and The Bhagavad Gita* (Bombay: Deepak, 2004).
3. See, e.g., *Deuteronomy* 20, *Joshua* or the *Chronicles*.
4. *Matthew* 26:52; *John* 18:10.
5. Sun Tzu, *The Art of War*, trans. S. Griffith (New York: Oxford University Press, 1963).
6. M. Reisman and C. Antoniou, eds. *The Laws of War* (New York: Vintage, 1994).
7. Christopher, *Ethics*, 10–11, citing Aristotle's *Politics* [1256b, 25]. See more specifically Aristotle, *Politics*, trans. by C. Lord (Chicago: University of Chicago Press, 1984), Book I, Chaps. 3–8 and R. Kraut, *Aristotle's Political Theory* (Oxford: Oxford University Press, 2002).
8. Christopher, *Ethics*, 7–13; N. Ferguson, *Colossus* (New York: Basic, 2004); M. Hardt and A. Negri, *Multitude: War and Democracy in the Age of Empire* (New York: Penguin, 2004); I. Eland, *The Empire Has No Clothes* (Oakland, CA: The Independent Institute, 2005).

9. James T. Johnson, *The Quest for Peace* (Princeton: Princeton University Press, 1987), 45.

10. Cicero, *De Re Publica*, 3, XXIII, trans. C. Keyes (New York: Putnam, 1928), 211–15; Cicero, *De Officiius*, trans. By W. Miller (Cambridge, MA: Harvard University Press, 1961); Christopher, *Ethics*, 13–16.

11. J. Eppstein, *The Catholic Tradition of the Law of Nations* (Washington, DC: CAIP, 1935); Christopher, *Ethics*, 17–29; J. Riley-Smith, ed. *The Oxford History of The Crusades* (Oxford: Oxford University Press, 1999).

12. H.A. Deane, *The Political and Social Ideas of St. Augustine* (New York: Columbia University Press, 1963); Christopher, *Ethics*, 30–48; quote from Augustine, *The City of God*, trans. R. Ryson (Cambridge: Cambridge University Press, 1998), 1:21. See also: Augustine, *The Political Writings,* ed. and trans. by H. Paolucci (Chicago: Regnery, 1962) and Augustine, *The Nicene and Post-Nicene Fathers*, ed. and trans. P. Schaff (Grand Rapids, MI: Eerdmans, 1969).

13. B. Rosenwein, *A Short History of the Middle Ages* (Peterborough, ON: Broadview, 2002); J. France, *Western Warfare in the Age of the Crusades, 1000–1300* (London: University College of London Press, 1999).

14. Riley-Smith, ed. *Oxford History*; James T. Johnson, *The Holy War Idea in Western and Islamic Traditions* (Philadelphia: Penn State University Press, 1997); J. Kelsay and James T. Johnson, *Just War and Jihad* (New York: Greenwood, 1991).

15. P. Temes, *The Just War* (New York: Ivan Dee, 2003); Christopher, *Ethics*, 49–52.

16. F. Russell, *The Just War in the Middle Ages* (Cambridge: Cambridge University Press, 1975); Aquinas, *Summa Theologiae* 2–2, Qs 40 and 64; J.D. Tooke, *The Just War in Aquinas and Grotius* (London: SPCK, 1975).

17. James T. Johnson, *Ideology, Reason and The Limitation of War* (Princeton: Princeton University Press, 1975); James T. Johnson, *The Just War Tradition and The Restraint of War* (Princeton: Princeton University Press, 1981); J.G. Sepulveda, *Democrates Alter*, trans. S. Poole in *Contemporary Civilization Reader* (New York: American Heritage, 6th ed., 1997), 39–51; B. de las Casa, *In Defence of the Indians*, trans. S. Poole (Chicago: Northern Illinois University Press, 1992).

18. F. de Vitoria, *Political Writings*, ed. A. Pagden and J. Lawrence (Cambridge: Cambridge University Press, 1991), 315–16.

19. Christopher, *Ethics*, 58–67.

20. H. Grotius, *The Law of War and Peace*, trans. L.R. Loomis (Roslyn, NY: WJ Black Inc., 1949), 10–11.

21. R. Tuck, *The Rights of War and Peace* (Oxford: Oxford University Press, 1999); Christopher, *Ethics*, 70–110.

22. D. Boucher, *Political Theories of International Relations* (Oxford: Oxford University Press, 1998).

23. Tuck, *Rights*, 166–96; J. Locke, *Two Treatises of Civil Government* (Cambridge: Cambridge University Press, 1988); B. Bailyn, *The Ideological Origins of the American Revolution* (Cambridge, MA: Harvard University Press, 1992); W.

Doyle, *The Oxford History of the French Revolution* (Oxford: Oxford University Press, 1990).

24. Tuck, *Rights*, 169–99.

25. B. Orend, *War and International Justice: A Kantian Perspective* (Waterloo, ON: Wilfrid Laurier University Press, 2000); I. Kant, *Political Writings*, trans. H. Nisbet and ed. H. Reiss (Cambridge: Cambridge University Press, 1995).

26. Reisman and Antoniou, eds. *Laws*.

27. J. Keegan, *The First World War* (New York: Vintage, 2000); M. Boemeke, ed. *The Treaty of Versailles* (Cambridge: Cambridge University Press, 1998); M. MacMillan, *Paris 1919* (Toronto: Random House, 2003); Reisman and Antoniou, eds. *Laws*.

28. Temes, *Just War*.

29. J. Keegan, *The Second World War* (New York: Vintage, 1990); J.K. Ryan, *Modern War and Basic Ethics* (Milwaukee, WN: Bruce, 1940); J. Ford, "The Morality of Obliteration Bombing," *Theological Studies* 5 (1944), 261–309; G.E.M. Anscombe, "War and Murder," in R. Wasserstrom, ed. *War and Morality* (Belmont, CA: Wadsworth, 1970), 41–53.

30. G. Best, *War and Law Since 1945* (Oxford: Clarendon, 1994).

31. M. Gilbert, *The Holocaust* (New York: Henry Holt, 1987); B. Orend, *Human Rights: Concept and Context* (Peterborough, ON: Broadview, 2002).

32. I. Brownlie, *International Law and The Use of Force by States* (Oxford: Clarendon, 1963); J. McKenna, "Ethics and War: A Catholic View," *American Political Science Review* 54 (1960), 647–58; W.V. O'Brien, *The Law of Limited Armed Conflict* (Washington, DC: Georgetown University Press, 1965); R. Osgood and R. Tucker, *Force, Order and Justice* (Baltimore: Johns Hopkins University Press, 1967); R. Tucker, *The Just War* (Baltimore: Johns Hopkins University Press, 1960); P. Ramsey, *The Just War* (New York: Scribners Sons, 1968); P. Ramsey, *War and The Christian Conscience* (Durham, NC: Duke University Press, 1961).

33. S. Bailey, *Prohibitions and Restraints in War* (Oxford: Oxford University Press, 1972); J.N. Moore, *Law and Civil War in the Modern World* (Baltimore: Johns Hopkins University Press, 1974); Y. Melzer, *Concepts of Just War* (Jerusalem: Hebrew University, 1975); R. Wasserstrom, ed. *War and Morality* (Belmont, CA: Wadsworth, 1970).

34. M. Walzer, *Just and Unjust Wars* (New York: Basic, 1977).

35. S. Axinn, *A Moral Military* (Philadelphia: Temple University Press, 1989); A. Hartle, *Moral Issues in Military Decision-Making* (Kansas City: University of Kansas Press, 1989); J.T. Johnson, *Can Modern War Be Just?* (New Haven, CT: Yale University Press, 1984); D. Lackey, *The Ethics of War and Peace* (Englewood Cliffs, NJ: Prentice Hall, 1989); J. Langan and W.V. O'Brien, eds. *The Nuclear Dilemma and The Just War Tradition* (Lexington, MA: Lexington, 1986); R. Phillips, *War and Justice* (Oklahoma City: University of Oklahoma Press, 1984); J. Sterba, *The Ethics of War and Nuclear Deterrence* (Belmont, CA: Wadsworth, 1985); J. Teichman, *Pacifism and The Just War* (Oxford:

Blackwell, 1986); M. Walker, *The Cold War: A History* (New York: Henry Holt, 1995).

36. J.B. Elshtain, ed. *But Was It Just? Reflections on The Morality of The Persian Gulf War* (New York: Doubleday, 1992), 12–13.

37. G. Prunier, *The Rwanda Crisis: History of a Genocide* (New York: Columbia University Press, 1995).

38. P. Christopher, *The Ethics of War and Peace* (Englewood Cliffs, NJ: Prentice Hall, 1994); J.B. Elshtain, ed. *Just War Theory* (Oxford: Blackwell, 1992); M. Ignatieff, *Blood and Belonging* (Toronto: Viking, 1994); M. Ignatieff, *The Warrior's Honor* (New York: Doubleday, 1997); M. Ignatieff, *Virtual War* (Toronto: Viking, 2000); R. Regan, *Just War: Principles and Cases* (Washington, DC: Catholic University Press of America, 1996).

39. W. Schabas, *An Introduction to the International Criminal Court* (Cambridge: Cambridge University Press, 2001).

40. J.B. Elshtain, *Just War Against Terror* (New York: Basic Books, 2003).

41. Walzer, "Triumph," 17–18.

42. *Ibid.*

43. Hardt and Negri, *Multitude.*

CHAPTER 2

Jus ad Bellum #1
Resisting Aggression

> "[N]o just war can be waged except for the purpose
> of punishment or repelling enemies."
> *Cicero*[1]

The core proposition of just war theory, uniting all its theorists, is this: *sometimes, it is at least morally permissible for a political community to go to war.* This is to say that there *can* be such a thing as a morally justified war; and World War II, on the part of the Allies, is often trotted out as the definitive modern example. Some even refer to this conflict as "The Good War."[2]

The goal of just war theory is to restrain both the incidence and destructiveness of warfare. Just war theory seeks to minimize *the reasons* for which it is permissible to fight, and seeks to restrain and limit *the means* with which communities may fight. Just war theory is *not* pro-war. It is, rather, a doctrine deeply aware of war's frightful dangers and brutal inhumanities. It seeks, accordingly, to reduce those dangers, and purge those inhumanities, by insisting that belligerents respect human rights as best they can during the grim circumstances of war.

While there are disagreements between just war theorists—no tradition or discipline generates unanimity—the clear majority endorse some version of the following principles. There is thought to be a fundamental division between the ethics of *resorting* to force—or in Latin "*jus ad bellum*" (literally "the justice *of* war") and the ethics of conduct *during* armed conflict (or "*jus in bello*," literally "justice *in* war"). Most just war theorists insist that *jus ad bellum* and *jus in bello* are, in a salient sense, separate. The notion is that a war can be begun for just reasons, yet prosecuted in an unjust fashion. (For instance, while World War II is called "The Good War" in terms of its cause, many still raise critical doubts about some Allied tactics, notably the use of atomic weapons.) Similarly, though perhaps much less commonly, a war begun for unjust reasons might (conceivably) still be fought with strict adherence to *jus in bello*. The categories are at least logically or conceptually distinct, and so we must consider them separately, each with their own rules and considerations. For example, the *jus ad bellum* criteria are thought to be the preserve and responsibility of political leaders whereas the *jus in bello*

criteria are thought to be the province and responsibility of military commanders, officers and soldiers. Ultimately in this book, I am going to argue
that there is a robust connection between *jus ad bellum* and *jus in bello*. This
defies tradition. Even so, I admit that one category can be *focused upon one*,
and then the other (without admitting they are literally separate). And so that
is what we shall do.

A state resorts to war justly only if it satisfies *each of six major rules*: just
cause, right intention, public declaration by proper authority, last resort,
probability of success and proportionality.

Just Cause

International law allows countries to defend themselves with force if they are
victimized by an armed attack; it also allows them to so defend other countries
should *they* be attacked. These entitlements commonly get referred to, respec-
tively, as "self-defence from aggression" and "other-defence from aggression"
(also called a "war of law enforcement"). These are the two most elemental
just causes for war in international law and just war theory. No other kinds
of warfare are allowed in international law unless explicitly authorized and
endorsed by the United Nations' Security Council (UNSC).

The UNSC is empowered by the UN Charter to try to keep war from
breaking out. It has 5 permanent members, who can veto any resolution.
These are: America, Britain, China, France, and Russia. It also features 10
non-permanent members, who hold rotating two year terms and can propose,
and vote on, resolutions—but can never veto them. This means that there are
15 UNSC members at any given time and a resolution on war and peace, to
pass, must enjoy majority support with no vetos.

Self-defence and other-defence are referred to as "inherent rights" (even,
in French, as natural rights) of states by Article 51 of the UN Charter. Note
that what is being defended against is aggression and *aggression is an armed
attack against another country who is a member of the UN*. A bit more on
the "armed attack" part: suppose that you are a small country, C, next to a
big neighbour, N. In response to domestic lobby groups, the government of
N decides to close its border to your forestry exports (trees, lumber, etc.).
You are devastated, because your forestry sector is your economy's biggest
and your economy is going to suffer severely (lost trade, layoffs, plant shut-
downs, a recession). This is pretty tough treatment by N against C: it is not
nice; it is completely undiplomatic; and it might even violate a trade treaty.
But international law, and just war theory, insist that, rough as it may be, it
is not treatment severe enough to merit warfare in response. It is only when
the tough treatment in question *is coupled with physical violence* that we can
begin to contemplate armed conflict. This makes clear sense: in interpersonal
life (e.g., we do not think getting fired is a sufficient reason to retaliate with
violence, even if the firing sharply harms our interests). The loss—the

danger—is merely economic. But most of us do think that, when someone physically attacks us (or those we love) with brute violence, we may employ physical force in response, seeking to resist the attacker, force him to stop and to protect ourselves or others from even deeper hurt. So for an international act to count as aggression, it must not merely be objectionable or even damaging to a country's interests. It must, at the same time, involve the infliction of serious, direct physical force. Almost always in international affairs, this involves the deployment of a country's armed forces—by land, sea or air—into the territory and/or against the people or government of another country. The classic example of international aggression is when one country uses its armed forces to launch an invasion into another country, with the objective being military, political and economic conquest, such as Nazi Germany did to Poland in 1939 or Iraq did to Kuwait in 1990.

International law only stipulates *that* aggression is wrong and punishable with war in response; it does not explain *why*. Similarly, international law only dictates that states *have* the right not to be subject to aggression; it fails to explain *why*. It is the job of just war theory to fill in these gaps. Let's start with the issue of state rights. Why do states—like the government of the US—have rights? Which rights do they have? What are the underlying principles here?[3]

STATE RIGHTS AND HUMAN RIGHTS

The main purpose of the state, in our era, is to do its part in realizing the human rights of its people. That is the state's reason-for-being, and if a state fails in that regard, its people have no reason to obey it and stick with the social contract. This is absolutely foundational: to believe otherwise is to reject any moral role for the state, and view it purely through the prism of power. Such a bleak view offers only fear as a reason to obey the state. This is not, however, a mature and fitting conception of political life for grown human beings: they have the right to participate in their own governance— since it so deeply affects their lives—and they need a moral reason to do so. There's no better one than that such participation will help them realize their own human rights, which is to say their own vital human needs. So state rights are *authorized and delimited by* the human rights of individuals, much as Locke had speculated.[4]

Human rights are core entitlements we all have to those things we *both* vitally need as human beings *and* which we can reasonably demand from other people and social institutions. Which things are these? As I have argued elsewhere,[5] the most important set of human rights objects are "the foundational five": physical security; material subsistence; personal freedom; elemental equality; and social recognition as a person and rightsholder. These are the things we all need to live minimally decent and tolerable lives in the modern world. They are, as James Nickel says, "what we want, no matter what we want." Whatever else we want out of life, we need the all-purpose means of security, subsistence, freedom, etc., which are required to pursue them in the first place. Try becoming a movie star without security; try becoming head of state without subsistence; try pursuing anything without the very freedom to do so. We each therefore have the most powerful reasons of self-interest to claim these foundational five objects as human rights. Such rights are, as John Rawls has said, the very basis for moral and political legitimacy in our time.[6]

What does it mean to realize human rights, thus defined? Human rights are realized or respected when everyone *actually possesses* the objects of their human rights. Your human right to physical security, is satisfied or ful-filled when you actually enjoy life in a safe, secure social setting. If state rights are dependent upon, and delimited by, individual human rights, what does all this imply for state rights? It implies that states themselves must have rights to those objects genuinely needed to enable them *to do their part* in realizing the human rights of their people. Which objects are these? Though there are others,[7] generally we speak of political sovereignty and territorial integrity.

Political sovereignty is the right of a people to govern itself. This is to say the right of a community to make its own choices about how life gets orga-nized in its land: the kinds of institutions it wants; the kind of laws it is willing to live by; the kind of culture, values and traditions it wishes to impart to the next generation; and so forth. Fundamentally, political sovereignty is rooted: 1) negatively, in our disdain for aggressive foreign domination; and 2) posi-tively, in the individual human rights to freedom and security possessed by everyone within that community.

It is a common human failing to want to tell other people what to do. It is a further failing *to force* other people to do what we want them to do, whether such "force" is through yelling, psychological manipulation or phys-ical violence. This is true between groups as well as persons. Usually, though, we think this wrong. Interpersonally, we call it coercion. Internationally, we call it aggression. In either case, it is a drive for dominance over others which fails to respect the right of others to live freely-chosen, and thus fully human, lives. *This core drive for dominance is, I believe, the basic cause of all unjust wars.* The right of political sovereignty is designed to resist foreign domi-nance, by stipulating that a people freely grouped together politically has the right to its own political life and hence the entitlement not to be forced to succumb to the rule of others whom it does not recognize as legitimate rulers or indeed as part of its community at all.

Territorial integrity depends upon political sovereignty; the latter is logically and morally prior to the former. A state needs territory because its people all have to live *somewhere*, and it needs resources because human rights do not come for free. For example, the human right to physical security implies the creation of law and order within a society, and that involves having a military and police force, and the construction and running of an effective judicial system—all of which absorb large resources. International law reflects these material needs by enshrining a state's right to territorial integrity, and by treating a state as the "owner" of all the natural resources within that territory and as the ultimate taxation authority within that land as well.

Political sovereignty and territorial integrity are tightly linked, and they are ultimately rooted in some of the deepest facets of human nature: 1) we strongly prefer to live in groups; 2) we prefer to govern ourselves; and 3) we need land and resources. To protect these traits and values, international law endorses territorial integrity and political sovereignty as bedrock principles.

Now, international law apparently extends these state rights to *all* member states of the UN, regardless of how unsavoury some of these regimes might be. The UN—even though it has the authority under its Charter to kick out terrible regimes—has decided that it is better for everyone to be "inside the tent," so to speak, with no state left outside, for fear it might get even worse. While there is some wisdom in this approach, it can also raise sharp moral questions, such as: why should we believe horrible states have rights? If a state has rights in order to protect and realize the human rights of its own people, and that state uses its power to violate the human rights of its own people, why should we respect its "sovereignty" and the "integrity" of its territory? The very grounding of its state claims has evaporated! Granted, there might be good *strategic* reasons to lay off such a state but it does not seem there's a *moral* case to view these states as having rights (which, after all, are moral entitlements). There has always been this tension in modern international law: do we recognize as legitimate a state or government merely because it has the most power in that society, or do we recognize it only if it *also* uses that power in a morally adequate way (at the least, by refraining from massively violating the human rights of its own people)?[8] The former way is the way of realism, and we shall discuss its nature and limitations in Chapter 8. Just war theory has always endorsed the latter, from at least the time of Aquinas. Only a morally fit—or, as I prefer to say, a minimally just—government has the right to go to war. *It is inescapable, as I have said, that all talk of justice regarding war must revolve ultimately around legitimate governance.*

MINIMAL JUSTICE AND STATE RIGHTS

Minimally just societies: 1) are generally recognized as such by their own people and the international community. The international community extends this recognition by allowing the society to enjoy membership in various international associations and events (e.g., the World Health Organization or The Olympics). Various countries also do things like send ambassadors to, and open embassies in, that society as well as enter into agreements with it (e.g., involving trade). The society is not shunned on a widespread basis nor is it the subject of pervasive official criticism or scepticism about its fitness to organize life in its community. The most obvious way for a people to show it recognizes its own government as legitimate would be through majority endorsement in periodic free and fair elections. It is not the only way— simply the most obvious and verifiable. Another way would be the prevalence of peace and stability in the country (i.e., the absence of civil war, revolutionary activity, sustained and large violent protests against the government and such). Crucially, though, this lack of internal conflict cannot be because of huge amounts of armed coercion on the part of the state against its people. There are, after all, ruthless police state dictatorships which impose social peace. So we must discern that the prevalence of social peace is not forced upon the people, rather, it is freely chosen by the people and hence indicative of their general acceptance of the political order.

Minimally just societies also: 2) avoid violating the rights of other countries. In particular, decent societies do not commit aggression against other states and nations. If they do so, they forfeit rights not to be resisted— with armed force if need be.

Finally, minimally just societies: 3) make every reasonable effort to satisfy the human rights of their own citizens. Why only "every reasonable effort" to satisfy and not, simply, "satisfies" these human rights? Well, we cannot require perfection, since even very good societies have some human rights problems. We can only require serious efforts and sincere intentions. There are two reasons why societies clearly fail to realize human rights: 1) they want to realize them but simply lack the resources needed; or 2) they do not want to realize them since they do not care about widespread human rights fulfilment. Only the second reason violates this category, since such regimes have wicked intentions and no desire to create minimally good lives for their people. Usually, such countries are governed by a malevolent minority, which hordes power and wealth, and either discriminates against and/or cares not a whit for, the well-being of the majority. The set of governments in the first group requires our assistance with human rights realization. The second set, though, does not deserve recognition as rights-bearing states with the authority to go to war.

It's fair to say that very many states around the world do satisfy these three criteria, and thus count as legitimate rights-bearing states. So international law and just war theory line up here. But some states do not, and will not. Here is where international law and just war theory must part ways a little bit. The laws of armed conflict recognize a country as a rights bearer if it is a member of the UN; nothing more being required. If you're a UN member state, and you're attacked with force, you have the legal right to go to war in response. Just war theory has traditionally insisted that states show some moral fitness before being authorized with the war power. Why? Well, why shower national governments with rights if these governments lack basic moral legitimacy? Indeed, it seems paradoxical to suggest an *immoral* form of governance has a *moral* right to arm and defend itself. Why privilege the governance of the nation-state (when other forms of governance are possible—cosmopolitan or regional or municipal) if the nation-state does not deserve it? *The only way it deserves it is by earning it through its respect for, and empowerment of, the human rights of its own citizens and those of others.* States which are like this truly do have moral value and are worth enabling and protecting.

Fundamentally, it is the difference between *legal* rights and *moral* rights. Legally, any UN member state has the right to go to war to resist aggression directed either against itself or another UN member. But morally, only those states which are minimally just have rights to sovereignty, territory and to resist aggression. So, most times just war theory and the laws of armed conflict run together and are mutually confirming: we'll see this throughout.[9] But other times they are not and I'm more concerned to defend and forward just war theory when that happens. Why? First, because just war theory explains its values whereas international law merely asserts them. Second, because international law (like all law) lags behind the times somewhat whereas our theories need not. Third, because international law is the product of state consensus, and sometimes consensus is wrong. Sometimes the laws of armed conflict enshrine a bad law, or fail to include a good law. Just war theory, better than any other, helps guide international law towards correction in this regard.

We'll say more about the role of human rights realization in the foundation for political legitimacy when we talk about the rule of proper authority. For now, we have what we need to progress on the just cause rule for going to war.

FORFEITURE AND THE MORAL CORE

Aggression is the focus in just cause, and aggression in the first instance is an armed attack which violates a state's rights and, in the most critical instance, is an armed attack which violates the human rights of people to live in security and freedom. It is a prominent feature of everything said so far that the commission of aggression causes a state to forfeit, or give up, its rights to territorial integrity and political sovereignty, rendering permissible an invasive military response on the part of the victim and/or any third-party "vindicators" or law enforcers. Let us add more rigour and depth here—it's harder, but it is worth it—and flesh all these thoughts out as our "Core Principle on Aggression" (CPA):

> the commission of aggression by any aggressor A, against any victim V, entitles V—and/or any third-party vindicator T, acting on behalf of V—to employ all necessary means to stop A, including lethal force, *provided* that such means do not themselves violate human rights.

This seems a complicated principle, but when it is broken down, we'll see that it is readily digestible and full of good sense. It stands at the foundation of everything which follows. Let us now understand the relevant agents A, V and T as states, and let us consider first the reasons why V possesses such an entitlement to go to war: reasonableness; fairness; responsibility; and implicit entitlement.

First, it would be *unreasonable* to deny V permission to take effective measures to protect its people from serious harm, or lethal attack, at the hands of A. Simply put, it is not reasonable, given the kinds of creatures we are, and the kind of world in which we live, to expect a state charged with the responsibility to protect its citizens to capitulate utterly—to just roll over—in the face of aggression. Indeed, one of the core functions of a government is precisely to protect its people from foreign invasion and the accompanying threats of slaughter or slavery.

The *fairness* argument stipulates that it would be not only unreasonable but unfair to deny V the permission to resist A with force, should A unjustly invade. Why? Because, in the absence of such measures, V will suffer substantial loss of life and liberty while A will actually *gain* whatever object it had in mind in attacking V. It seems clear that aggression, and rights-violation, ought not to be unfairly rewarded in this way, both in the particular case and for the sake of not eliciting more such behaviour in the future.

Not only would denying V permission to resist forcibly the aggression of A be both unreasonable and unfair, it would also ignore the fundamental issue of *who bears responsibility* for the choice situation. It is the aggressor A who is responsible for placing V in a situation where V must choose between its rights and those of the aggressor A. (And this point ties neatly into the reasonableness claim, since it is only reasonable to expect V, in such a situation, to choose its own rights.) The aggressor A, if it does not wish to subject itself to the consequences of the resort to defensive force by V, *can always cease and desist* from its aggression. Stop warring if you do not want to be warred upon. So if A does not cease and desist—if it keeps up its aggression—it is hardly in a position to cry foul should V decide to do the reasonable and fair thing and defend itself, and its citizens, with the needed force.

Finally, any victim V has the *implicit entitlement* to use whatever measures are necessary to realize the objects of its rights and those of its citizens. The relevant argument has the following form:

1 Minimally just states, as defined previously, have moral and legal rights to territorial integrity and political sovereignty.
2 These state rights entitle states *to employ reliable measures necessary to secure* the objects of these rights, and to protect them from severe, predictable threats, such as the violent aggression of others. (This follows as a matter of moral logic: if person P has the right R to object Q, and M is a means necessary to get and secure Q, then P must also have a

right to M. Otherwise, to what extent could we speak of P's original
right to Q?)

3 There is, presently, no reliable or effective international authority (or
global government) which can guarantee to states the possession of the
objects of their rights. States are, in the final analysis, on their own with
regard to protecting their rights and the objects thereof.

4 Currently, the most effective and reliable form of self-help with regard
to rights-protection—at least in the last resort against armed aggression
—is the use of defensive armed force.

5 Thus, faced with armed violation of their rights (i.e., with aggression),
states are entitled to employ armed force and war in order to *punish* the
rights-violator, *vindicate* their rights, and *re-secure* their objects and those
of their citizens' human rights. As Aristotle said, so long ago, the most
fundamental just cause for going to war is self-defence: resisting foreign
aggression against one's political community.

This brings us to the second core aspect of principle CPA: granted that V
possesses entitlement to respond to A's aggression with armed force, how is
V to do so *without itself violating rights*? There are two elements to note in
response: 1) state A, through the commission of aggression against V, forfeits
its state rights not to be attacked with lethal force in return; and 2) provided
that V adheres strictly to the norms of *jus in bello* during its just war against
A, it will succeed in offering the required "due care" owed to innocent civilians in both states, and thereby avoid violating their rights. It will therefore
fully satisfy CPA. Let us deal with each one of these elements in turn.

Why and how does A forfeit its right, as a state, not to be subject to armed
attack by committing aggression against V? A forfeits its rights because, as
we just saw, *the weight of reasons in the case indicates that no wrong is done
to A* in the event that victim V resists A's aggression with means of war. And
the weight of reasons in this case must draw on those just offered in defence
of V's entitlement to resort to force in the first place: it would be unreasonable, unfair, oblivious of responsibility, and at odds with implicit entitlement
to declare that V does wrong in resisting A's aggression with armed force.
And if V does no wrong in violently resisting A here, then A must fail to
have moral rights that such not be done. It must thus have forfeited its rights.

Since A forfeits its state rights by committing aggression, this permits *any*
third party T (or group of third-party states G) to intervene forcibly on behalf
of victim V. This legitimacy of other-defence is grounded in the normative
core of the victim's claim—namely, that the aggressor either stop or be
stopped, regardless of who is the agent. Provided that the demonstrable aim
is the protection of the victim and its citizens from rights-violation, armed
resistance is permitted to any state willing to take on its associated burdens.

So V's (or T's, or G's) resisting A's aggression against V with armed force will *not* violate A's *state* rights because, by committing aggression, A has forfeited its state rights. But what of the human rights of the individual persons in both A and V (or T and G)? Why and how will launching a just war at the state level not violate these *individual* rights? These rights will not be violated, I submit, provided that V (or T, or G) fully adheres to the other criteria of *jus ad bellum* and *jus in bello*, which will be discussed subsequently. *What this claim importantly asserts is that the principles of just war theory serve to fulfil the human rights of persons as best they can be fulfilled during warfare.*

To sum up so far: a state has a just cause for resorting to war if and only if: 1) it is the victim of aggression, or is coming to the aid of a victim of aggression; 2) it is a minimally just or legitimate state; and 3) its resort to armed force fulfils all aspects of the principle CPA. These three principles revolve, most centrally, around the general norm of protecting and defending minimally just communities and the lives and rights of their individual members. These are the very deepest ideas surrounding the core of just war theory in general, and those aspects of the international laws of armed conflict which have partially been derived from them.

Note how these principles—of reasonableness and fairness, of respect for life and rights, of responsibility for rights-violation—themselves seem implicated, at the most profound level, by the very meaning of a just society, and indeed by human civilization itself. The use of reason to inform action, and a value commitment to fair treatment are all major objectives in a mature and just society, as is the holding of everyone responsible for how they treat their fellows. Finally, respect for rights is truly one of the basic cements of civilization, and a decent and stable society must be committed to understanding, propounding and protecting such rights and, above all, to ensuring that rights-holders actually enjoy secure possession of the objects of their rights. On this intensive reading of the just cause rule, then, *aggression attacks the very moral spine of human civilization itself.* Indeed it does; it reverts us to the laws of the jungle, from which our ancestors struggled so mightily to escape. This is why, if need be, aggression can be resisted with something as strong and dangerous as warfare. Let's take it down from the clouds of abstraction now and look at a recent concrete case.

THE 1991 PERSIAN GULF WAR

In August 1990, Iraq invaded Kuwait. This was a classic instance of a large, militaristic country aggressively attacking a smaller neighbour. Why did Saddam Hussein, dictator of Iraq, order this armed invasion and takeover of Kuwait? He had several reasons, none of them justified but most of them revolving around the fact he had just finished a miserable, destructive conflict with Iran. From 1980–89, Iran and Iraq slugged it out in a very expensive and bloody war with roots stretching far back in the past. One million people lost their lives in the Iran-Iraq War, in which Saddam portrayed himself as the saviour of moderate Muslims from the fury of radical Islam, which had just come to power in a revolution in Iran in 1979. At the end of the war, Saddam was in a very difficult position. On the one hand, he was still in power and had prevented radical ayatollahs from taking over his country. On the other, the war pushed him into debt and he faced huge reconstruction costs. He asked both Kuwait and Saudi Arabia to forgive the debts he owed them, on grounds he "saved" them from being swept out of power by the ayatollahs. The two countries refused, and Saddam grew furious. His other big problem was that Iraq's military was restless—and huge. Having grown to over one million men during the long Iran-Iraq War, Iraq's military was disappointed that Saddam had called off the war against their despised enemy. Moreover, Iraq's military has long played important roles in various coups and revolutions within Iraq. Saddam feared armed revolt. So he hit upon a "solution": invade and conquer Kuwait. This would occupy the army, cancel part of Iraq's debt and give Iraq control over a lucrative asset it could use to help pay for reconstruction. And it might just scare Saudi Arabia into debt forgiveness as well. So the order was given and then executed in the hot days of August, 1990.

None of these reasons, of course, *justify* Iraq's invasion—they merely *explain* it. War for any kind of economic gain is strictly ruled out, as is the old politician's trick of using war abroad to try to solve (or, at least, distract attention from) problems at home. Saddam did try to argue that Kuwait had been driving down the world price of oil—and thus Iraq's own revenues—by supplying too much oil to the world market. But, again, even if that were true—and it is not clear it was—that's an economic issue and thus not one where military force is a proportionate response. (Remember our forestry example earlier.) Saddam then tried to suggest that—since the ancient Ottoman empire used to administer both Iraq and Kuwait together—Kuwait "belonged to" Iraq anyway, as its "Nineteenth province." Even if it were true it would be like now arguing that, since Canada used to be part of the British Empire, it should once again today be run from the Mother of All Parliaments in London. Such an argument ignores everything which has happened between then and now—notably, how a new political community came into existence and came therefore to deserve separate protection. Saddam, finally, tried to argue that Kuwait was stealing Iraq's oil by "slant-drilling" across the border into Iraq's wells. This was, however, a lie; and, even if it were true, it would still just be an economic issue wherein demanding compensation would be appropriate but not armed invasion. Saddam's base motives of plunder and pleasing his military became undeniably clear when he authorized them, in the fall of 1990, to pillage Kuwait: raping women at will; stealing private property on a whim; crushing any Kuwaiti resistance; and wreaking havoc constantly. Amnesty International's December 1990 special report, on the behaviour of Iraqi soldiers in Kuwait, makes for chilling—even revolting—reading in this regard.[10]

We know, from what we have already established, that this kind of freely-chosen, flagrant aggression causes a state to lose its usual right not to be subjected to armed attack, either by the victim community or others coming to its aid. Kuwait's puny armed forces quickly succumbed during the August 1990 invasion. In the fall of 1990, the international community—led by America—generated a huge military build-up in neighbouring Saudi Arabia (i.e., "Operation Desert Shield") and reflected on what to do.

Perhaps it might here be objected that the theory developed thus far establishes that states forfeit rights against attack only when they unjustly attack other states which do not deserve it (i.e., states which are minimally just). While Iraq's attack against Kuwait was unjust—because of the political and economic motives—was Kuwait itself a minimally just state deserving of protection? Well, Kuwait was widely recognized as the legitimate government of that territory; indeed, it had membership in the UN. Kuwait was also, at that time, not involved in violating the rights of other states; unlike Iraq, Kuwait was not using its army to invade, pillage and overthrow foreign governments. But was the Kuwaiti state seen as legitimate by its own people, and making every reasonable effort to satisfy the human rights of its own people? When regular elections are not held, it is hard to judge whether a people genuinely approves of its regime. Plus, the rights of women in most Muslim countries are often seen as not being as fully realized as they should. Does this mean the Kuwaiti regime was not legitimate? It certainly raises issues. But three points stand out: 1) there was uncoerced social peace in Kuwait prior to Iraq's invasion; 2) the Kuwait regime did not attack and brutalize its own people the way the invading Iraqis did in the fall of 1990 (thus the Kuwaiti government had a much better claim to rule that society than Iraq did); and 3) the Kuwaiti regime no longer existed when the West went to war in January, 1991, anyway. And most Western societies, including America, satisfy the criteria of minimal justice. The West went to war to defend *the Kuwaiti people* from Iraqi conquest and brutalization, not so much to restore the old Kuwaiti *regime*. The old regime was restored, it is true, in the spring of 1991 after the war was quickly won by America and its allies. This does not mean the war was unjust in its beginnings. The war may not have had all the desirable effects but the war was just (in its cause) as a war of other-defence against a country which committed aggression perhaps not the very second when it crossed Kuwait's borders but certainly when it unleashed its campaign of plunder and brutality against an unarmed Kuwaiti population.

Failure to resist such aggressive attacks rewards the aggressor and, as such, structures incentives in favour of more aggression in international society. It also penalizes the victim, by doing nothing to reverse the effects of the aggression. By attacking the Kuwaiti people, Saddam's Iraq committed aggression. When it did so, it forfeited its rights not to be attacked in response. There is very high consensus that this war was just in its cause, and indeed it was authorized by numerous UNSC resolutions and supported by a clear majority of just war theorists.[11]

COMPARATIVE JUSTICE OF CAUSE?

So the only just cause, for resorting to war, is in response to aggression. The response may be twofold: a war of self-defence on the part of the state victimized by aggression; and/or a war of other-defence, or "law enforcement," on the part of any other state coming to aid the victim. Walzer, for one, is adamant that there is no such thing as a war just on both sides. All things considered, he believes, the evidence can point in only one of two directions: *either* that, in a given war, one side is the unjust aggressor, the other the justified defender *or* that the war is unjust on both sides (a not infrequent occurrence in the real world). This "either/or" thinking sets Walzer apart from earlier just war thinkers, such as Vitoria, who suggested that it might be possible for all sides in a war to have some quantum of justice. Walzer disagrees with this graded or scalar approach, not only because the aggression/defence paradigm essentially forces him to—it seems silly to say a state is two-thirds of an aggressor—but also because he reasons that Vitoria's "comparative justice" conception confuses *jus ad bellum* with *jus in bello*. Vitoria included "comparative justice of cause" within his own account of *jus ad bellum* so as to mitigate the degree to which a state might pursue its otherwise just cause. Vitoria was afraid that a state with what we might call "100 per cent Justice" on its side would be especially ferocious in its conduct of war. It would have a Crusading mentality and obliterate the utterly unjust enemy. But Walzer contends, plausibly, that such mitigation can also be had from the distinct set of *jus in bello* rules. From the fact that just cause is defined by him in a binary way, *it does not follow* that a state satisfying its requirements is thereby justified in prosecuting its war effort however it likes. It must still confront and satisfy the rules of *jus in bello*, as contained for instance within the Hague and Geneva Conventions. More on the content of these rules will be found in Chapter 4.[12]

I too am sceptical of the older comparative conception, not only for the sound reasons Walzer gives, but also because it simply seems wrong in particular cases. What, for instance, was the comparative justice of Nazi Germany's cause in World War II? I would claim that it was nil—that the Allies had *complete* justice on their side in that struggle, and that this cause was resisting brutal, unbridled Nazi aggression. But from the fact that the Allies were completely justified in terms of their cause, it does *not* mean they could do whatever they wanted to win—it only means they had a clear just cause to start fighting. Now for a crucial point: what about those who might say the Nazis had some claim for "*Lebensraum*" (i.e., "living room," more space and territory for the large and ever-growing German people) and that

that was the small quantum of justice on their side? *But the fact that an actor in war claims his actions are just, does not make it so.* The actor, much like an accused person in court, must show how his *subjective* understanding of his actions actually corresponds to *objectively* plausible moral and legal principles, based on *inter-subjectively* available, shareable and discernible evidence. The point of just war theory, and the law of armed conflict, is precisely to serve as the objective principles in the process, and not to serve as the speaking points of rhetorical self-justification for any deluded dictator bent on aggression.

What is compelling in the thinking behind comparative justice is that the evidence in wartime can be difficult to interpret, and we can predict the players are all going to interpret it in a way maximally advantageous to their own interests. Some unscrupulous players will even lie, perhaps even fabricating phoney evidence. All this has been known to happen in wartime, and even to be committed by societies we're inclined to believe are decent. In World War I, Britain fabricated a fake "Zimmerman telegram" between Germany and Mexico wherein the Kaiser promised Texas to Mexico in exchange for Mexico's war partnership. Britain did this to spur American anger and entry into the war on Britain's side. And there is, of course, enormous controversy surrounding the evidence America enumerated in justification of its 2003 Iraq attack and subsequent regime removal. Iraq's weapons of mass destruction (WMD), Saddam's alleged connections to al-Qaeda, Bush Jr's pre-9/11 interest in Saddam's removal, possible CIA manipulation of data, Saddam's own lying about his residual strength: all these aspects figure in the debate about the justice of the start of that war. More on that war later; for now, we cite the old verity that "truth is the first casualty of war." War can make people desperate, and desperately self-justifying. I do not think this means the truth is impossible to find through the impenetrable "fog of war"—we now know the WMD claims were false[13]—but I do agree that it means we must subject war justifications to the most rigorous research scrutiny, and accordingly there is a duty for war-seeking governments to disclose publicly the evidence and sources behind arguments supporting something as deadly and far-reaching as war. Failure to provide such—especially when arrogantly citing a "national security" need to keep such information secret—renders the resort to war unjust. In war, both consequences and procedures are important, and the latter does not evaporate in the face of the former. One *can* be legitimately outraged in the face of aggression and take to the high road as a result, but one must *always* remain humble and truthful in the face of the evidence which proves such aggression. So I do not believe in comparative justice but I do believe in critical, ongoing examination of the evidence to determine who is the aggressor and who the defender—or whether, alternatively, it shows "a pox on both their houses" (i.e., injustice all around).

APPEASEMENT?

Victims of aggression are, in Michael Walzer's mind anyway, "always justified in fighting." In fact, in most cases, "fighting is the morally preferred response." Why is this so, especially when we realize that many—perhaps most—cases of aggression involve a (relatively) larger and more powerful state deploying its armed forces to coerce a less powerful state to make unjust concessions? Is not appeasement of the aggressor an *understandable* response from the victim, especially if that is its free collective choice? Is not neutrality, by third parties, a legitimate choice on their part, too? Walzer stresses that, ultimately, the decision to resist aggression, whether by the victim or by third party vindicators, can only be a free choice of the state in question. This follows from the right of political sovereignty. But he clearly articulates his preference in favour of resistance, especially by the victim. For resistance "confirms and enhances ... our common values [including] national pride, self-respect, freedom in policy-making" whereas appeasement "diminishes those values and leaves us all impoverished." Sometimes both appeasement and neutrality constitute "a failure to resist evil in the world." The unchallenged triumph of aggression is, Walzer asserts, "a greater evil" than war.[14]

By and large, I agree with this view on appeasement, yet sympathy arises in cases where small states are giving up simply to avoid the slaughter they would surely suffer if they fought back. Consider the difficulty of Edward Benes, the leader of Czechoslovakia in 1938–39, who woke one day to find the German army in his country and Hitler literally knocking on his door. When Benes met Hitler, the Nazi dictator gave him a stark choice: declare war and we'll slaughter you (we're already in control here militarily); or surrender and survive, but as part of the new Nazi empire. It is easy for us, with no stake in the decision, to say that Benes still should have fought, instead of giving up to save lives and to prevent his small country from being utterly demolished by its huge, well-armed neighbour.[15] Resistance, after all, can take several forms—whether a direct military response to the first act of aggression, or an indirect guerrilla campaign after the aggressor has been allowed a temporary win.

The decision not to resist directly probably will come at the cost of some national pride and, more seriously, moral integrity. Contrast Benes' choice with the Finns' own choice, scarcely a year later, to resist an invasion by Stalin's USSR. The Finns to this day look back upon their armed resistance with pride whereas the Czechs have more of a mixed attitude. But in both cases the short-term outcome was inevitable: victory and conquest by the overwhelming invading force. National pride and moral integrity are important yet they remain abstract, unquantifiable things. Benes obviously reflected on their cost but, on the other side of the ledger, were things that clearly *could* be counted: if the Czechs fought back, thousands of his people would die, infrastructure would be shattered, economic costs huge—and all merely to postpone the inevitable Nazi victory (at least at that time). I'm not saying the problem is insoluble, merely that it is difficult, and there are real costs no matter which option is chosen. While resistance is preferable because of the severe wrong of aggression, resistance can take several forms, and we have to respect people's free choices here—emphatically since it is their own lives and liberties on the line.

Right Intention

Having finished (for now) with the many complexities of just cause, we turn to the other five rules co-constitutive of *jus ad bellum*. Let us begin with Augustine's obsession with right intention. It is commonly thought, by just war theorists, that it is not enough to have an *objectively* just cause for going to war (like resisting aggression); you must also have the proper *subjective* intention, or state of mind, for your act to be moral. Why? Consider an analogy from personal life: say a child Billy steals a bicycle. Ethically, he must return it. But most of us think it is much better, morally, if Billy returns it because he is sincerely sorry (and not, say, because his parents order him or threaten him). His intentions and state of mind matter to our evaluation. Or suppose Sally drives through a red light, killing a pedestrian. We would evaluate that act very differently if we knew it was not an accident but, rather, brimming hatred and score-settling, that triggered the crash. Same physical act but different intention and thus a different moral evaluation: the latter is clearly worse than the former. Legally, for instance, the intention marks the difference between first-degree murder and mere manslaughter. A comprehensive system of morality seems not only to require the proper *external* behaviour but also *internal* reflection and the right attitude. It is more demanding to include right intention, true, but the whole point of morality is to demand a certain standard from people and the institutions they form.

Considering this rule's application to international affairs, Walzer observes soberly that "a pure good will [is] ... a political illusion." He also notes a vagueness in the just war tradition regarding whether this rule can be fulfilled only if there is *purity* of intention to secure the just cause, or whether it is possible to satisfy it, provided only that right intention is *present amongst the mix* of motives which usually animates state behaviour. Walzer himself opts for the latter course: he believes it is possible, and meaningful, to criticize some of the non-moral motives which states can have in going to war while still endorsing the moral motive. But that motive *must* be present: Walzer concurs that right orientation towards just cause is a necessary aspect of the justice of resorting to war. This is to say that it must be part of a state's subjective intention in pursuing war that it secure and fulfil the objective reason which gives it justification for fighting.[16]

A related question, which Walzer does not answer, is this: must the moral motivation merely be *present* in the mix of motives, or need it be *the main animating force* in the mix? Consider, for example, the mix of motives that the Allied coalition, led by the United States, might have had in 1991 for launching the first Persian Gulf War against Iraq: the repulsion of Iraq from Kuwait; the punishment of Iraqi aggression; the desire to secure the oil supply of the Persian Gulf region; President Bush Sr. wanting to demonstrate toughness in the run-up to the 1992 election; the desire by the United States to prove its superiority following the end of the Cold War with the Soviet Union; and the drive of the US military to test out its latest weaponry in real battlefield conditions, and perhaps to vanquish some ghosts left over from Vietnam. There are serious difficulties involved in discerning which motive dominates. Different parts of the American government, after all, might be seen as having had different intentions: which one would then count as the overall "dominant," or conclusive, one? Short-term aims might also have differed from medium- and long-term ones: which was the definitive motivation? This makes it more plausible, though less interesting, to conclude that the moral motive need *only be real and present* amongst the various non-moral motives for this criterion to be fulfilled.[17]

Perhaps the difficulty in discerning correct motivation is one reason why the right intention rule—unlike just cause—is nowhere to be found in the international law of armed conflict. This is interesting, and in my view an unfortunate omission, for several reasons. First, it is clearly part of common moral discourse surrounding war to speculate on, and judge, a state's resort to war based on its supposed motives. Both the first Iraq war (1991), and the second (2003), were labelled unjust by some people on grounds that America's motives supposedly revolved around oil, and/or imperialism, and/or chauvinism against Arabs and Muslims. Purists might object that an agent's intentions are a "mere" matter of ethics, whereas an agent's *conduct* is all that justice is, and can be, concerned with. But this fails to persuade. It is, for instance, part of justice systems the world over to include considerations of intention and motive when it comes to people on trial for such crimes as murder. Moreover, such trials also give indication as to how one might gain reliable knowledge of another's intent. *We know an agent's intent through his conduct.* Intentions can be, and ought to be, discerned through a reasoned examination of publicly accessible evidence, relying on behaviour, consideration of incentives and explicit avowals of intent. Intentions are neither infinitely redescribable nor irreducibly private and mysterious. They are connected to patterns of evidence, as well as constrained by norms of logical coherence, and so right intention is not an empty criterion for moral judgment during war. Though difficult, it is possible to tell whether a state is prosecuting a war out of ethnic hatred, for example, as opposed to vindicating its right of self-defence. Dark motivations produce distinctive and noticeable results, such as torture, massacres, mass rapes, and large-scale displacements. We have the civil wars, in the 1990s, in the former Yugoslavia to offer as historical evidence. We will take a closer look at Bosnia next chapter.

Perhaps a deeper critical question should be raised here: can collective agents, like states, have intentions at all? Implicit here is a systematic analogy between the behaviour of states and the behaviour of individual persons. But does it make sense to speak of state "rights" and "intentions"? To refer to "crimes" which states commit against each other, like aggression, which should be "punished"? Of states acting for the right reasons, out of the proper motives? This is "the domestic analogy."[18] This analogy, which also infuses international law, implies that one of the most *useful* ways to understand how states behave vis-à-vis each other is to liken such behaviour to the way in which individuals behave vis-à-vis each other. It is important to note that this analogy need *not* involve any kind of "statism": I have already said states are merely political associations, and their rights are derived from, and delimited by, the human rights of their individual members. The domestic analogy, rather, draws its vitality from the sheer difficulty of speaking about the behaviour of complex entities like states without employing simplifying assumptions—such as that they have a discernible identity, have intentions, face choices between alternatives, are thus responsible for their choices, and so on. It should also be emphasized that the domestic analogy is merely that: it is only generally persuasive and *neither* precludes the existence of important disanalogies *nor* commits us to a monolithic, naturalized and homogenous conception of the state. The main point here is interpretive: we have *always* employed the domestic analogy in our moral and legal discourse about the ethics of war and peace; it is inherent in the deepest structure of our talk about morality and war; and we all understand what is meant by it. It is an irreplaceable aid to understanding in this regard.

LINKING THE CATEGORIES AND CALLING YOUR SHOT

One interesting aspect of right intention is whether it should be part of the justice of the resort to war that a state commit itself, both publicly and in advance, to adhering to the other rules of war, contained in *jus in bello* (the justice of conduct in war) and *jus post bellum* (the justice of peace treaties ending war). The idea here, first proposed by Kant, is that a state should commit itself to certain rules of conduct, and appropriate war termination, *as part of its original decision to begin the war*. Why? Because if it cannot so commit, it ought never to start the process. Unless a state pledges to fight in accord with the Hague and Geneva Conventions, and to terminate its war according to proportionate principles, it should never involve itself in such morally serious business as warfare. This seems an important and forward-looking way in which one could, so to speak, run a bright red thread through each of the three just war categories, *tying them into a coherent whole*.[19] This addition is compelling not only because of the moral import of an agent's intent but, moreover, to ensure consistency of just behaviour throughout all three phases of a military engagement. Thus, in addition to having one's subjective intentions (in going to war) be consistent with one's objectively just cause, one must also clearly and publicly commit, in advance of the war starting, to adhering to the other rules of just war theory.[20]

In other words, I propose we understand the three just war categories as ultimately linked. We can separate them out for the purpose of focusing on different issues which different phases of war raise. But that just highlights things for the sake of analysis and perspective; it is not actually splitting the categories. I prefer to think of just war theory as forming one long procedure according to which each preceding step must be satisfied before setting on to the next one. This way of thinking stresses the value of each rule yet also properly emphasizes *just cause as the crucial opening note, which sets the tone for everything which follows.*

Another proposal I wish to make here is this: you have to call your shot, as in billiards. To tie it into the next rule: you have to declare publicly not merely your resorting to war but your *main reason* for resorting to war. This proposal is needed to block the "scatter-shot" approach to justifying war, where you throw out every possible argument in favour of war, hoping some will stick in terms of persuading the public or attracting evidence which will stand the test of time and scrutiny. This addition is needed for both historical and conceptual reasons.

In recent history, the "scatter shot" approach has been prominent, particularly in terms of America's 2003 Iraq attack and forcible regime change. Such was justified, we were told, because: 1) Saddam had WMDs, some of which could be deployed within forty-five minutes; 2) Saddam intended to give some of its WMDs to al-Qaeda, for use against America; 3) Saddam was actually involved with al-Qaeda in the 9/11 attacks; 4) Saddam needed to be overthrown as an act of humanitarian intervention on behalf of the Iraqi people; 5) Saddam posed a threat to regional security, especially regarding Israel and the Saudi oil fields; 6) Saddam kicked out the UN weapons inspectors in 1998 violating the Persian Gulf War treaty, which specified possible violent consequences for doing so; and 7) Saddam needed to be overthrown so as to create forcibly the first Arab democracy, which would serve as a Trojan Horse for better values throughout the Islamic world.[21]

Now, there's nothing wrong with having multiple reasons for going to war if these multiple reasons are all real and backed with evidence. What is wrong is mixing strong ones with weak ones so as to create a false impression of an "overwhelming pro-war case." Even if you do have multiple reasons, you have the right intention issue of whether you can plausibly intend them all. Human attention, and intention, is finite and needs to be focused. In my view, you need to focus on your main reason for going to war, have your intentions disciplined accordingly, and be prepared to be judged for how well you called your shot. (This focus will also increase your probability of success, since achievement requires concentration and commitment, as opposed to running off in all directions.) This leads into the conceptual reason here: the "scatter-shot approach" is objectionable because war is such a serious and destructive business. You must know what you're doing. And the "scatter-shot" approach, frankly, conveys the impression you do not. You're just letting it all hang out, hoping at least some of it will gather the support you need. But to unleash the terrible "black dogs of war," you need clear proof of a rock-solid reason for doing so, such as self-defence from actual aggression.

Public Declaration of War by a Proper Authority

War must be declared publicly by a proper authority. Why a *public* declaration? To inform the target, or enemy, country that they now face war and its sub-stantial hazards. This also gives the enemy one last chance, prior to hostilities commencing, to cease aggression and begin a process of atonement. Such entitlement to public notification is codified in the Hague Convention III, which mandates that signatory countries must not commence conflict without "… previous and explicit warning, in the form either of a reasoned declara-tion of war or of an ultimatum with conditional declaration of war."[22] Public declaration also alerts one's own citizens to the government's intentions and plans. If state prerogatives in times of war are to be kept reasonably in line with the human rights of their members—which ground such state rights in the first place—we cannot lose sight of this just war criterion. The people must, in some public procedure, meaningfully consent to the launching of a war on their behalf.[23] More on the fuller meaning of this consent dimen-sion later. For now, we continue to ask what "public" means. It means that the target country and one's own citizens can reasonably be expected to be informed of a declaration of war. Whether that be done through an official press conference, a formal speech, or a vote in an elected assembly is not that material. Delivering an official notice of hostilities, say to the enemy country's ambassador, is in my view nice (so to speak) but not required. What would fail to meet the meaning of a genuinely public dec-laration would be: burying a war declaration within another piece of leg-islation; or being insincerely cryptic in one's language surrounding the military steps one is about to take; or, more plausibly and expectedly, to refuse to admit that a war is on when a *de facto* unleashing of armed force is already on display. Recall, from the Introduction, that war is an actual, intentional and widespread armed conflict between political communities wherein the ultimate objective is to force the other side to accept one's will regarding governance.

The public declaration and domestic consent criteria need not preclude, or hamper the effectiveness of, rapid-fire responses to "blitzkrieg" attacks from dangerous aggressors. There are defensible procedures which can be put in place for just such reasons: for instance, empowering the executive branch of the national government to command the armed services to ensure rapid deployment, and then requiring legislative branch oversight and eventually approval (or not) of the executive's actions.[24]

DIVISION OF WAR POWER

Fundamental political issues arise when one considers which branch ought to be invested with the war power. The judicial branch is usually quite disempowered in this regard, with the executive and legislative branches enjoying—and often wrestling over—the vast majority of the war powers. America provides a compelling case study. On the face of it, Congress has the sole capacity to declare war. Yet the president also serves as Commander-in-Chief of the American forces. By convention, the president may deploy troops at will in all engagements short of war without Congressional approval. The precise definition of war can then become an important issue, as it did during Korea (1950–53) and Vietnam (1955–75). Executive orders to engage in "police actions" and "defensive operations" were issued, and some legislators argued angrily that war was being fought in violation of constitutional requirements for clear legislative endorsement. The War Powers Congressional Resolution of 1973 sought to clarify these issues, in particular by reasserting the authority of Congress.

In practice today, the president enjoys enormous short-term *de facto* control over the armed forces, thanks to his role as Commander-in-Chief which plugs him in directly to the military's chain of command. Congressional authorization of war thus suffers practical disadvantages, allowing the president at times to present Congress with a *fait accompli* for approval. More common in recent years—and emphatically since the 9/11 terrorist strikes—has been the president seeking, and getting, blanket authorization in advance of armed hostilities breaking out. There are some dangers with such a strategy. Yet Congress retains considerable medium- and long-term control over the armed forces, as it has within its powers sole final authority over military *expenditures*. The president may hold the whip of the war horse, so to speak, but ultimately Congress feeds it. This arrangement may represent a reasonable attempt to combine legitimate concerns—with enabling effective rapid responses that warfare often demands—with the ultimately deeper insistence that war must have public, constitutional authorization.[25]

Should the judiciary play a larger role in the war authorization process? There are good reasons to keep the status quo of judicial disenfranchisement throughout most countries. The judicial process is, and probably should be, methodical and slow, potentially delaying vitally needed military action. Second, its very disenfranchisement is a reason, of a kind, to prevent it having a say in authorizing war: it has no relevant experience or precedents to draw on. Finally, in almost all countries, the judiciary is the farthest removed from public authorization, *via* appointment rather than election to their office. Better to keep so momentous an issue as the war power closer to the public on behalf of whom it is exercised. The judiciary still has a vital role to play— in determining whether one of the other branches has exceeded its authority regarding war—but it should continue to have no substantive say in the authorization of war itself.

MINIMAL JUSTICE JUSTIFIED

Before leaving the domestic or national scene for consideration of the hot topic of international authorization of war, we need to reiterate and justify just war theory's standards on proper authority. These differ slightly, we have seen, from international law's. In legal terms, the proper authority for declaring war must be the constitutionally authorized body of a UN member state. We pointed out previously the limitations of having a purely legal standard without a background moral theory which explains why and how political communities, and the governments which organize them, can be legitimate and proper. This background moral theory is a conception of minimal justice, itself founded ultimately on the value of protecting and forwarding everyone's human rights. What justifies just war theory in anchoring its precepts in human rights? And here's where we really run up against it: are not these just Western values, ideological expressions of American imperialism— reflections of a Crusading mentality endemic to the Western mind? *The answer is no.* This accusation commits the "genetic fallacy," which is when one rejects an idea based on its origins instead of its merits, like when the Nazis resisted teaching relativity theory in German schools because it was devised by a Jew, Albert Einstein. The idea of human rights *did* originate in the West, but it *cannot* rationally be rejected on that basis alone. Indeed, the reason why it originated in the West was probably because the West needed it most: some of history's most gruesome human rights violations (like The Holocaust) occurred in the heart of Western Europe.

As for the merits, the concept of human rights has plenty going for it. It is genuinely *universal* in that everyone gets to claim human rights, and genuinely *beneficial* in that the things claimed—like the foundational five of security, subsistence, liberty, equality and recognition—serve both objective human need and subjective human want. Whatever else you want, you *must* want the life and liberty needed to pursue them. Life requires subsistence and security; security requires recognition from others and freedom from their domination; and liberty implies personal choice and the absence of brutal discrimination (i.e., equality). Everyone—not just Westerners—has over-riding reason to believe in human rights and to work towards their realization. Human rights, perhaps alone amongst political concepts, genuinely acknowledges the worth of each individual human life and the importance of that life's value being protected against all the other people, forces and institutions who might otherwise plot to use that life as a mere prop in their own projects.[26]

This might be one reason why human rights attract so much cross-cultural consensus—in moral commitment and in international, regional and domestic human rights documents, protections and procedures. For example—and note the overlap—becoming a member of the UN commits a state, under the Charter, to realizing human rights.[27] Of course, human rights still get violated, but that *does not* count against their universality because the universality is normative, not descriptive. It is about what we *should* believe and how we *should* act, and this *cannot* be dislodged or undermined by the behaviour of rights-violators. They do not get to define justice, any more than thieves get to define property rights, or rapists bodily integrity. Indeed, is it not odd (and noticeable) how often the accusation of "Western moral imperialism" is made by those who wish to violate human rights? Think of various outspoken governments in East Asia or the Islamic world: they stand to lose enormously by the spread of human rights, so they have a huge incentive to resort to cultural chauvinism to stem the tide. But bad faith does not a good argument make.

Human rights, as a theory on how society should be shaped, is: 1) thinner; 2) more accessible; and 3) more widely beneficial than rival doctrines on political legitimacy. It is thinner because it focuses *only* on the most elemental aspects of good social interaction, leaving everything above the baseline open to different commitments and to cultural and even personal preferences. It is not a comprehensive world view the way communism was, or religion can be. This makes it more reasonable and accessible, as does the fact that the concept of human rights is pitched at every individual regardless of ethnicity, nation, religion, age, gender or language. The fact that human rights stand to benefit everyone also recommends the doctrine highly against those promising to benefit only, or disproportionately, the rich, or the workers, or the believers, or white people, or Americans, or adult males, and so on.

A longer-term reason justifying these thoughts on legitimacy concerns the link between the satisfaction of human rights domestically with peaceful behaviour internationally. Kant believed, and the recent researches of Michael Doyle support the notion, that rights-respecting societies do not go to war against each other.[28] There is, apparently, much empirical evidence substantiating this claim, otherwise known as the "democratic peace thesis." In any event, it makes clear conceptual sense: if a government does not care about the rights of its own people, how is it going to start caring about the rights of a foreign state and its citizens? If we look at history, we see that the embodiments of international aggression have, indeed, made horrible domestic regimes: Nazi Germany, Stalin's Russia, Hussein's Iraq. There is a clear connection here, and it probably runs quite simply like this: a rights violator is a rights violator. A group engaging in domestic rights-violation will not hesitate, if it can and if it wants, to violate rights internationally. That is why—and this is the profound conclusion—*we all have reason to be seriously concerned about rights-violating regimes wherever they are*. In fact, minimally just states have one further right as a consequence of these connections, and that is to do what they can, over the long term and in concert with others where needed, so that all states become human rights-respecting.

Finally, consider a straightforward macro-comparison, regarding quality of life, between those societies which generally respect human rights and those which do not. Where would you rather live: in Australia, Canada, Japan and Sweden or in Sudan, North Korea, Iran and Cuba? Human rights respect does *not* make for a perfectly just society, but history clearly suggests it makes for a better, more enjoyable life for the average person.[29]

All these powerful reasons—of self-interest, of autonomy, of accessibility and universality, of strong consensus, of good consequences and connection to international peace—do not amount to "proof" of the "objective truth" of human rights. But such a proof is never forthcoming in moral and political life: sceptics holding such impossibly high standards can wait for Godot as long as they like. The rest of us realize that we have got to get on with the business of life and social organization, and here it is *the weight of reasons* which must be decisive, based on the *judgment* of sincere, sensible and experienced persons. In the final analysis, you must have a theory of legitimate governance to talk comprehensively about the ethics of war and peace. It is my judgment that an appealing and sound theory of governance must incorporate human rights. Ultimately, this is where the entire theory contained in this book rests: on the appeal of the idea of a minimally just, human rights-respecting society for everyone. Only states which are minimally just are entitled to rights, including the various war powers and authorities mentioned throughout this book.

INTERNATIONAL AUTHORIZATION?

We know, from our just cause discussions, that Article 51 of the UN Charter famously proclaims that, should an armed attack occur against a member state of the UN, both the victim and any vindicators have "inherent rights" (or "natural rights") to self-defence and other-defence. So most international law experts agree that a United Nations Security Council (UNSC) vote is *not* needed to ground wars of self-defence or other-defence against obvious acts of cross-border aggression. That's clear. But what about wars where such is *not* the case: the aggression is *not* clear-cut; or the violence stays *within* borders and does not cross them (i.e., civil wars or humanitarian catastrophes); or indeed no aggression has *even occurred yet* (as in anticipatory attacks or "pre-emptive strikes")? Many international lawyers argue that, with these latter cases, UNSC authorization is absolutely necessary because: 1) they are not covered by the "inherent right" reference to self- and other-defence in the face of armed attack; 2) they are clearly more controversial than straightforward defence against an act of aggression which has already happened; and 3) the background ideals of the Charter include substantial UN and UNSC responsibilities for war and peace. (Indeed, the very first article of the UN Charter declares that one of the UN's core purposes is to "maintain international peace and security," and Articles 23–54 detail exhaustive procedures and powers for the UNSC to deploy in pursuit of this ideal.) So, a pro-UNSC vote for action in any of these controversial cases is a must.[30]

This was the position of most of the world in the run-up to America's 2003 Iraq attack. America was engaging in a pre-emptive strike (i.e., aggression had not yet happened), moreover one aiming to forcibly change the regime of a UN member. Thus, it needed a UNSC vote. It did not get one, and so the war was illegal and unjust. The official American line was different. While the UNSC did not vote explicitly in favour of "war" or an "American attack," it *did* demand Saddam resume UN weapons inspections or else face "serious consequences." Bush Jr. asserted that the war power was contained within the phrase "serious consequences" and so argued that UNSC authorization was in fact given. In any event, the Americans continued, the terms of the 1991 Persian Gulf War treaty (which was ratified by the UNSC in 1991) pledged Iraq to complete compliance with post-war measures, and also threatened a possible return to hostilities should complete compliance not be forthcoming. Since Saddam booted out the UN weapons inspectors in 1998, he was in violation of that UNSC resolution, which contained this explicit warning of, and authorization for, armed force. Failing all that, America said, the Iraq attack was needed to defend America from future acts of terrorism, and self-defence is indeed recognized by the Charter as an "inherent right."[31]

So who was right? It is not so clear if by "right" you mean "has the best interpretation of international law." Believe it or not, both sides have serious and strong legal arguments; and it is not obviously the case that one side is more powerful; and there's no overriding global legal authority to render a decision. Indeed I venture to say this is one of the reasons why international law is not completely satisfying in connection with *jus ad bellum*. Not only does it not directly deal with the hardest cases—like pre-emptive attacks, terrorist strikes, humanitarian crises and civil wars—the principles which it enumerates are not clear. Indeed, they are predictably vague because international law is the product of state consensus and it is very hard to get that on such controversial issues. The vagueness, in turn, allows for indeterminacy and for opposing sides to present strong arguments with little prospect of resolution. Thus, just war theory is stronger and more insightful on *jus ad bellum* than are the laws of armed conflict. (But note that the reverse is probably true in connection with *jus in bello*, where the detail of international law achieves incredible sophistication. See Chapter 4.) But if by "right" you mean who is morally correct, then please consult the next chapter for an investigation into the justice of the Iraq attack, where I think answers can be had.

Should we buy into UN claims about its sweeping authority in connection with international peace and security, which get asserted throughout the Charter and other documents in a very robust way? I personally believe that it is a very *desirable* thing to get UN authorization to go to war but I hesitate to say it is strictly *morally necessary*. On the one hand, requiring international authorization would represent one more barrier to overcome in any pro-war move, and so would make the resort to war more difficult. Isn't that a good thing? I guess so, but against that very point is that requiring international authorization might consume precious hours, days and weeks, with the result being that the aggressor gets entrenched and becomes more difficult to resist. We can easily imagine cases where the international community does not know enough, or care enough, about a local or regional war to get involved: so why give it authority in that regard? Let's leave it to the people with their fundamental interests and rights actually at stake.

There's also the very fitness and legitimacy of the UN and the UNSC themselves to consider. At any given time, only fifteen members are on the UNSC and, of those, only five hold vetos and permanent seats. These five form the world's most exclusive club, and they are all rich, northern, nuclear powers, and all but one is Western. What gives such an exclusive club the right to legislate on war and peace for the world—especially in regions they know quite little about? Second, it is important not to succumb to naïve and romantic ideas about what the UN *is*, based on visions of what it *might ideally become*. The UN is not a world government; it is merely a voluntary association of states. It has, over the years, faced searing questions about its competence, efficiency, treatment and oversight of staff, and even over its integrity. (The UN has recently been embroiled in a huge corruption scandal alleging thefts and kickbacks in its administration of the Oil-for-Food program in Iraq in the late 1990s.) And the UNSC record authorizing wars and peacekeeping missions is spotty at best. While the UN has had real success— over Suez, over East Timor—it has had many controversies and failures, such as Cyprus and Congo. UN peacekeepers were so ineffective in Bosnia they were actually taken hostage by the Serbs and, most notoriously, the UNSC failed to intervene at all in the near-genocidal civil war in Rwanda in the summer of 1994. *This*, we might ask, is the institution to which international lawyers would have us hand over ultimate authority on war and peace issues?

There is also the most important fact that, in spite of globalization, the state remains the crucial scene of political action in our lives. Recall that the UN is a voluntary association of states, and thus is ultimately their creature. The UN Charter itself enshrines state rights to political sovereignty and territorial integrity. And states remain, in terms of causal impact, the best poised to do serious harm to, or serious good for, their citizens. No wonder in recent history so many national groups have sought their own independent state, and why so much attention is paid to the legitimacy or moral quality of state structures. We still experience political life first and foremost as members of nation-states—Americans, Brazilians, Canadians, etc.—and only secondarily (or even less) as citizens of the globe. We strongly prefer to live in groups; and while this fact never justifies shoddy treatment of other groups, it is a reality which must be accommodated by any theory of international justice.[32]

My overall view on international authorization of war is this: it is certainly not required in straightforward cases of defence (whether of self or others) from actual aggression: no UNSC fiat could overturn those pre-existing rights of people. In more contested cases—humanitarian intervention and especially anticipatory attack involving regime change—the desirability of international authorization increases very considerably but might not even then, pending the details, strictly be required. I do not wish to be completely dismissive: at the very least, the UNSC always provides an ongoing forum for countries to discuss and debate these issues and to present their cases for going to war on a formal basis, and that is always going to be worth something indeed.

Last Resort

Winston Churchill once said, memorably, that it was far better to "jaw jaw" than to "war war" (i.e., to try to talk a problem over through diplomacy before fighting). Walzer concurs, observing that: "It is obvious that measures short of war are preferable to war itself." He continues: "One always wants to see diplomacy tried before the resort to war, so that we are sure that war is the last resort." In spite of this endorsement of the traditional last resort criterion, which is codified in Articles 2(4) and 33–40 of the UN Charter,[33] Walzer is quick with some helpful caveats. First, he points out that, strictly speaking, there is no such thing as a *last* resort. No matter how fearful the situation, there is always something else which can be tried—yet another round of diplomatic negotiations, for instance—prior to the resort to war. So it would be absurd, in this literal sense, to say that states may turn to war only as a last resort.[34] A second caveat concerns the fact that negotiations, threats and economic sanctions are frequently offered as morally better means of international problem-solving than the use of force. At face value, this claim is indisputable: if a reasonable resolution to the crisis in question can be had through a credible and permissible threat, or through a negotiating session, or perhaps through sanctions, then surely that is preferable to running the sizeable risks, and certain destructions, of war. Upon closer inspection, however, much depends on the nature of the particular act of aggression and the nature of the aggressive regime itself. Sometimes threats, diplomacy and sanctions will not work. The incidents leading up to the 1991 Persian Gulf War are instructive: Saddam Hussein, in the face of all three, refused to be budged from his ill-gotten Kuwaiti gains.[35] Care must be taken that appeals to last resort do not end up rewarding aggression, by giving the aggressor extra time to entrench himself inside the victim. Finally, Albert Pierce and

Lori Damrosch have pointed out that the levelling of systematic economic
sanctions on an aggressor often violates the *jus in bello* principle of non-
combatant immunity, since it is most often innocent civilians (often the poorest and most vulnerable) who bear the brunt of sweeping economic embargoes levelled on their country. In the absence of force directed against them,
outlaw regimes always seem to find a way, within their own borders, to take
care of themselves. The Hussein regime in Iraq, once more, offers lessons—
surviving twelve years in the teeth of sweeping sanctions, which were then
given up after the March 2003 US-led strike, that forcibly removed the
regime from power. How much innocent civilian deprivation had to be
endured while waiting for the sanctions to do their job—which they never
did? I direct the reader to the relevant literature on the effects of the Iraqi
sanctions in the 1990s.[36]

It seems much more plausible to contend *not* that war be the literal last
resort—after all other imaginable means have been totally exhausted—but,
rather, that states *ought not to be hasty in their resort to force*. There ought
to be a strong presumption against the resort to force. Article 2(4) of the UN
Charter is clear evidence of our deep commitment to such a presumption. It
reads that all UN Members "shall refrain ... from the threat or use of force
against ... any state."[37] But beyond this general principle, much depends on
the concrete details of the actual situation in question. It is critically important, for example, when the aggressor is mounting a swift and brutal invasion,
to respond effectively before all is lost. It is also relevant to consider the
nature of the territory of the victim of aggression; if it is a tiny country, like
Israel, the need for a speedy and effective response against aggression will
likely be much greater than that required by a country the size and strength
of the United States. Any response from the international community is likewise relevant. But attention must always be focused on the nature and severity of the aggressor and its actions, for frequently the international
community is sluggish in mounting an effective response to aggression. The
key question this criterion demands to be always asked, and then answered
in the affirmative, is this: is the proposed use of force *reasonable*, given the
situation and the nature of the aggression?

Probability of Success

Probability of success is another *jus ad bellum* rule for which only general
principles can be convincingly conveyed. Its prudential flavour explains this:
probability of success is always a matter of circumstance, of taking reasonable options within the constraints and opportunities presented by the world.
The traditional aim of this criterion—which, like right intention, is actually
not contained within international law—is to bar lethal violence which is
known in advance to be futile. As such, the principle is laudable and necessary for any comprehensive just war theory. Great care, however, needs to be

exercised that this criterion, like last resort, does not amount to rewarding aggression, and especially that by larger and more powerful nations. This is so because smaller and weaker nations will face a comparatively greater task when it comes to fulfilling this criterion (which I think explains its absence from international law). And the calculation of expected probability of success for resorting to war is difficult. The vicissitudes of war are, as we know from history, sometimes among the most difficult phenomena to predict. Even when the odds seemed incredibly long, remarkable successes have sometimes, somehow, been achieved. Such are the stuff of military legend, like the ancient Greeks fending off the onslaught of Persians or perhaps even the American revolutionaries overthrowing the rule of the mighty lion of the British Empire. The lack of predictability, though, does not always turn out for the better. A notorious example is that the armies of Europe expected, in September 1914, to be home to celebrate Christmas.[38] Walzer also suggests that there are considerations of self-respect here, according to which victims of aggression ought to be permitted at least some resistance, should they decide on it, as an expression of their strong objection to the aggression and as an affirmation of their rights. It thus seems reasonable to judge that, given an act of aggression and given that the other *jus ad bellum* criteria are met, there is a presumption in favour of permitting some kind of armed response, even when the odds of military success (however defined) seem long. At the same time, this rule is not dormant: it remains important that communities contemplating war in response to aggression still consider whether such an extreme measure has any reasonable probability of success. That is the least, we might say, that they owe themselves.

Proportionality

Proportionality, codified at Articles 22–3 of the Hague Convention III, is one of the most contentious and challenging *jus ad bellum* criteria, ranking close to just cause itself. It mandates that a state considering a just war must weigh the expected *universal* (not just selfish national) benefits of doing so against the expected *universal* costs. Only if the projected benefits, in terms of securing the just cause, are at least equal to, and preferably greater than, such costs as casualties may the war action proceed. Walzer wrestles at length with the considerable difficulties presented by this otherwise sensible rule. On the one hand, the unchecked triumph of aggression is for him "a greater evil" than war. He also comments that "prudence can be, and has to be, accommodated within the argument for justice." On the other hand, Walzer comments on "the terrible presumption" behind the cost-benefit comparisons implicit in appeals to proportionality. He declares that "we have no way that even mimics mathematics" of making such proportionality judgments. He asks rhetorically: "How do we measure the value of a country's independence against the value of defeating an aggressive regime?"[39] In other words, how can we pretend to measure, on the same scale of value, the benefits of defeating aggression against the body count needed to achieve it? For example, it sounds ridiculous—literally, groundless—to say things like: "My country's freedom from aggression is worth $300 million dollars and 245,000 casualties." The numbers appear completely arbitrary, and the comparison between an abstract, like independence, and a concrete, like cash and casualties, seems as ill-conceived as one between apples and exchange rates—they are simply different things.

The challenges of proportional "calculation" explode, in both number and complexity, as soon as one puts further thought to the question. What things actually count as costs and benefits in wartime? Only elements we can *quantify*, like the body count and economic expenditures? But usually we also want to appeal to *qualitative* elements, like the value of sovereignty and not enduring life as slaves to a foreign invader. Is there a distinction between explicit and implicit costs, such as costs of mobilization on the one hand and, on the other, what else besides war might we have done with our time and treasure? Is there a difference between short-term and long-term benefits? Is it only the costs and benefits of prudence that matter, or do those of morality count as well? How to weigh the "universal" costs and benefits against each other when, usually during war, those who pay the costs *are not the same group* as those who enjoy the benefits, as when soldiers pay the present price for the future independence of their fellow countrymen? The manifest, and manifold, difficulties involved in proportionality calculations cause vexation for just war theorists, and rightly so. The calculations needed are simply too complex and wide-ranging. It is wildly improbable that we could ever devise a completely satisfying set of cost-benefit formulae with regard to wartime action. Far better, I believe, to stick to a firm set of clear and universal rules to guide conduct, which is what the rest of just war theory strives to offer.

Walzer's final judgment on this issue, which seems sound, is that there is *some* truth in the proportionality maxim. But he insists that "it is a gross truth," an unrefined and imprecise truth, which can only point to obvious considerations of prudence and utility *as limiting conditions* on the pursuit of rights-respecting justice in wartime. Proportionality, at best, provides some checks and balances, *some outside constraints*, on the drive to secure a just cause. In other words—and with some irony—we know much better what disproportionality is than proportionality. We can usually recognize the former but frankly have trouble precisely defining the latter. We know when a war is a disproportionate (i.e., exaggerated, harmful and inappropriate) response to a problem, just like we know that, within the context of a marriage, threatening divorce over a disagreement over what to have for dinner is disproportionate. Proportionality has, so to speak, negative content: it does not really positively add anything except to remind us that the problem in question has to be so severe (like unjust armed invasion) that war is, in fact, an appropriate response—and to suggest that the good to be gained from the war must be better than the substantial costs and evils we know war always brings in train.

Providing some war examples, Walzer says that, even though justice may have permitted otherwise, it was appropriate on grounds of proportionality that the United States did not go to war against the Soviet Union after the latter invaded Hungary in 1956, or Czechoslovakia in 1968. The real threat of a broad-based nuclear exchange between the superpowers was simply greater, and more universally fearful, than allowing Soviet expansion at the particular expense of the independence of these nations.[40] Slightly different, more obvious, examples—deeper in history—include some of the old European wars sparked by marriage (or failure to marry) or failure to agree on who would succeed to the throne, or simply by some personal slight delivered to one monarch by another. None of these reasons balance with something as deadly as war as a "solution." To go even farther back, if the Trojan War really was fought over Helen—"the woman whose face launched a thousand ships"—then we can certainly ask questions of justice whether ordering all that fighting and killing was truly proportionate to the problem.

Summary

This is a contemporary updating of the classical account of *jus ad bellum*. Any state, seeking to go to war against any other state, must show that its resort to armed force fulfils *each* of the six rules explained above: just cause; right intention; public declaration by a proper authority; last resort; probability of success; and proportionality. Failure to fulfil *even one* rule renders the resort to force unjust, and thus subject to criticism, resistance and punishment. This allows us to appreciate just how *demanding and stringent* is just war theory. The laws of armed conflict make much the same claims, except that they: 1) do not endorse the rules of right intention and probability of success; 2) are more vague; and 3) are based on a looser conception of political legitimacy. Just war theory is thus *even more demanding than international law*, which is predictable since, quite often, morality sets itself a higher standard than law.

Since *jus ad bellum* is the province of those exercising the war power—often, but not always, heads of state or the executive branch of government—it is their responsibility to ensure that its standards are fulfilled. By the same token, it is they who must answer for any *jus ad bellum* violations, for instance in war crimes trials after the war is over. As an illustration, consider that the Nazi high command, or what was left of it, was charged—among other things—with "crimes against peace" by the prosecutors during the Nuremberg war crimes trials after World War II. This is to say that they were accused—and many eventually convicted—of violating *jus ad bellum* (i.e., of committing aggression, of having waged an unjust war).[41]

The ultimate concepts and values underlying contemporary just war theory are the idea of a minimally just and therefore legitimate political community and the human rights of its individual citizens. It is for the sake of defending a minimally just state, and the human rights of its citizens, that we can morally contemplate the use of measures as forceful and destructive as those of war. We have this moral permission as a result of what aggression means—how it attacks the most basic values and possibilities of human civilization—and of the need to respond to it with effective resistance.

Case Study: World War II

Almost all just war theorists agree that World War II, on the part of the Allies, is the definitive modern example of a morally justified war, at least in connection with *jus ad bellum*. Let us briefly delve into this case, to see how the facts operate against the standards. For the sake of greater clarity and specificity, I shall focus mostly on the United States as the relevant actor. Of course, given the deep complexities of these real-world cases, attention cannot be paid to every element: the aim, in this section, is simply to give one application, of the six *jus ad bellum rules*, to a real and important historical case.[42]

JUST CAUSE. Did the Allies, and particularly the US, have just cause in resorting to war between 1939 and 1941? It is clear that, in the European theatre, Nazi Germany was the embodiment of precisely that kind of ultra-aggressive, totalitarian, outlaw state which just war theory holds up as the kind of threat against which the resort to armed self- and other-defence seems most plausibly grounded. Imperial Japan was likewise an ultra-aggressive totalitarian regime. Both of these powers were blatant aggressors: Nazi Germany in Czechoslovakia in 1938, in Poland in 1939, and then in 1940 through the Low Countries into France; and Imperial Japan first in Korea in 1910 and then in China in the mid-1930s and then into the surrounding areas of the "East Asian Co-Prosperity Sphere." There was no just cause whatsoever grounding the actions of these regimes: they were animated solely by desires for more territory, resources, power, glory—and even darker motives, related to their beliefs in their own ethnic superiority and their "racial destiny" to rule. Germany and Japan posed severe threats to those countries they invaded and, once they conquered them, subjected them to brutalizing rights-violative measures which still rank amongst the foulest in history. The commission of aggression caused both of these regimes to forfeit their state rights to non-interference and not to be attacked in return. So the Allies, as a matter of self- and other-defence, general rights-vindication and punishment for rights-violation, did no wrong—violated no rights—in responding with war. So the resort to war in 1939 by England and its Commonwealth, for instance, and in 1941 by the United States, was justifiable on this basis.

Indeed, in the case of the United States, resort to war was made (explicitly) only after the Pearl Harbor aggression by Japan, and Germany's accompanying declaration of war on America. The moral requirement to defeat such regimes stands out as one of history's most compelling causes for resorting to force.

RIGHT INTENTION. The Allies, in particular the United States, seemed to undertake World War II with the right intention, namely, the defence of their own nation and those of others, the defeat and punishment of aggression, and the repeal of its gains. Did the Allies display a reasonable commitment, prior to launching into war, to upholding the norms of *jus in bello* during its course and *jus post bellum* following its end? This is less clear, given the immense destruction that was eventually carried out during the war, and indeed is one of the reasons why I argued above that such ought to be newly incorporated into the right intention criterion. In fairness, the post-war actions and activities of the Allies—meaningful reconstruction of the defeated enemies, the Nuremberg and Far East War Crimes tribunals, and the formation of the UN—might, in retrospect, reveal some of the laudableness of their pro-rights intentions. In light of this conflicting data, perhaps all that can be said firmly, with regard to this criterion, is that the Allies really did seem to undertake the war with at least the proper *jus ad bellum* orientation of rights vindication.

PUBLIC DECLARATION OF WAR BY A PROPER AUTHORITY. Let us here take the case of the United States. America in 1941 was a minimally just society: widely recognized by the international community, with widespread and stable, uncoerced social peace domestically; it was not violating the rights of other societies; and it was seriously committed to the human rights and decent treatment of its citizens. America's explicit entry into the war, in 1941, was indeed declared through the appropriate constitutional channels, with both the executive and the legislative branches concurring. The declaration, on both Japan and Germany, was also publicly declared.

LAST RESORT. It seems that the Allies did not hastily rush into war in the 1939–41 period. England and France, the major Allied powers in Western Europe, made a serious diplomatic effort to placate Hitler with the Munich accords in 1938. (Indeed, many people subsequently condemned these accords for appeasing an aggressor.) Hitler disregarded any such aspirations for peace; in fact, he used the Munich process as a bad-faith cloak with which he could legitimize his past actions and disguise his future ambitions. He then launched his ultra-aggressive attempt to conquer Europe on behalf of the Aryan race. Similarly, the Soviet Union signed the Molotov-Ribbentrop pact of mutual non-aggression with Germany in 1939. The Soviet Union clearly wanted to avoid war. However, that pact was sundered when Hitler, having conquered continental Western Europe, proceeded to turn his sights eastward in 1940–41. Indeed, it seems clear that, as of 1939–40 in Western Europe, and as of 1940–41 in Eastern Europe, there was no other feasible alternative to halting the aggression of Hitler than through the use of armed force. As such, the resort to war on the part of the Allies was not unreasonably quick.

It also seems that the United States' resort to war against Japan was not precipitate. After all, Japan had been committing aggression throughout East Asia, particularly in northern China and Korea, for many years prior to the outbreak of World War II. Secondly, Japan itself launched the armed attack on Pearl Harbor in 1941. Once Japan launched such a large-scale bombing raid, its intentions were clear and manifest: it wanted to fight the United States for supremacy in the Pacific. America was not hasty in resorting to force in light of that attack.

PROBABILITY OF SUCCESS. This criterion is less clearly fulfilled in the case of Allied countries like Poland and France, and perhaps even England, but it seems that the United States clearly fulfilled it. Even though it was to fight enemies on opposite sides of the world at the same time, the United States could reasonably have foreseen, in 1941, that its manpower, industrial sophistication and productive capacity, to say nothing of its military might, were second to none. It had every reason to believe, at the time, that it could eventually outproduce, outfight and overwhelm both of its enemies. And this would have been a strong argument even if those enemies were at the peak of their fighting capacity, which they were not: their earlier campaigns had drained huge military resources. With regard to Hitler, he was just beginning to be sucked into the endless morass of the campaign in Russia and was inordinately distracted, on the domestic front, by setting into motion the madness of the Holocaust. It was very predictable, in 1941, to see that Hitler, faced with the might of the Soviet Union on one front, and the nexus between England, her Commonwealth (notably Canada and Australia) and the United States on the other, was outmatched. He was sandwiched between huge powers. At the very least, it seems that the United States entered the European war with a considerable probability of success.

PROPORTIONALITY. It is very important to consider the extent of Allied, and especially American, fulfilment of this category solely in terms of *the time of the decision to resort to war*. It is reasonable to contend that no one could have foreseen, in 1939–41, the full and total extent of the immense costs and casualties of World War II, much of which were tallied up in the final few months of the war in 1945. At the time, say, of the American entry, it was reasonable to suggest that the defeat of these two ultra-aggressive regimes was worth the projected prudential and moral costs of doing so.

In terms of Japan, it could have been foreseen that this would be a difficult and costly war, given the ferocity and resources of the enemy and the logistics involved in organizing fighting across the immense Pacific. But America had local allies in the Australians and the British based in Hong Kong. It could count on sympathy and support from civilian populations in China and Indonesia, which were under the Japanese boot. The nub of the matter was this: what choice did America have, given the Pearl Harbor strike? Japan wanted and started that war, so it was indeed appropriate to respond with armed defence.

In Europe, given that Hitler was going to be so clearly outgunned on both fronts, it would have been reasonable to contend, at the time, that the *military* casualties in Europe would be absorbable, and that damage to the United States itself would probably be negligible. One thing that would have weighed on the conscience at the time, however, was the quite foreseeable fact that, given Europe's population density, there would be considerable *civilian* casualties from stepping up the war effort, and moving onto the continent itself to roll Hitler back within his own borders. As we have seen, there is no uncontroversial calculus for balancing foreseen but unintended civilian deaths and the great importance of defeating regimes like Nazi Germany. But Walzer, for one, clearly believes proportionality was met, and he justifies himself thus:

> Nazism was an ultimate threat to everything decent in our lives, an ideology and a practice of political domination so murderous, so degrading even to those who might survive, that the consequences of its final victory in World War II were literally beyond calculation, immeasurably awful. We see it (and I do not use the term lightly) as evil objectified in the world, and in a form so potent and apparent that there never could have been anything to do but fight against it.[43]

Notes

1. Cicero, *De Re Publica*, (III, 23), trans. R. Regan at p. 16 of his *Just War: Principles and Cases* (Washington, DC: Georgetown University Press, 1996).
2. M. Walzer, "World War II: Why Was This War Different?" *Philosophy and Public Affairs* (1971/72), 3–21.
3. For the laws of armed conflict themselves, see Appendix A. Consult also W. Reisman and C. Antoniou, eds. *The Laws of War* (New York: Vintage, 1994); A. Roberts and R. Guelff, eds. *Documents on the Laws of War* (Oxford: Oxford University Press, 1999) and G. Best, *War and Law since 1945* (Oxford: Clarendon, 1994).
4. J. Locke, *Two Treatises on Civil Government* (Cambridge: Cambridge University Press, 1988); J. Narveson, *Respecting Persons in Theory and Practice* (Lanham, MD: Rowman and Littlefield, 2002).
5. B. Orend, *Human Rights: Concept and Context* (Peterborough, ON: Broadview Press, 2002).
6. Orend, *Human Rights, passim*; J. Nickel, *Making Sense of Human Rights* (Berkeley, CA: University of California Press, 1987); J. Rawls, *The Law of Peoples* (Cambridge, MA: Harvard University Press, 1999).

7. B. Orend, *War and International Justice: A Kantian Perspective* (Waterloo, ON: Wilfrid Laurier University Press, 2000), 89–126.

8. I. Brownlie, ed. *Basic Documents in International Law*, 4th ed. (Oxford: Oxford University Press, 1995); T. Nardin, *Law, Morality and The Relations of States* (Princeton: Princeton University Press, 1983); T. Pogge, *Realizing Rawls* (Ithaca, NY: Cornell University Press, 1989).

9. Regan, *Principles*; T. Nardin, ed. *The Ethics of War and Peace: Religious and Secular Perspectives* (Princeton: Princeton University Press, 1996); M. Walzer, *Just and Unjust Wars*, 2nd ed. (New York: Basic Books, 1991).

10. T. Abdullah, *A Short History of Iraq* (Toronto: Pearson, 2003); L. Freedman and E. Karsh, eds. *The Gulf Conflict, 1990–91* (Princeton: Princeton University Press, 1993); W. Danspeckgruber and C. Tripp, eds. *The Iraqi Aggression Against Kuwait* (Boulder: Westview, 1996).

11. D. Decosse ed. *But Was It Just? Reflections on the Morality of the Persian Gulf War* (New York: Doubleday, 1992); James T. Johnson and G. Weigel, eds. *Just War and Gulf War* (Washington, DC: University Press of America, 1991); A. Beyer and B. Green, eds. *Lines in the Sand: Justice and The Gulf War* (Louisville: John Knox, 1992).

12. Walzer, *Wars*, 63–72; F. de Vitoria, *Political Writings*, ed. A. Pagden and J. Lawrence (Cambridge: Cambridge University Press, 1991).

13. B. Woodward, *Plan of Attack* (New York: Simon and Schuster, 2004); US Congress, *The 9/11 Commission Report* (Washington, DC: United States Congress, 2004).

14. Walzer, *Wars*, 51, 67–72, and 233–38.

15. It must be noted that Benes' decision was controversial amongst his own people. For more, see E. Benes, *My War Memoirs* (London: Greenwood, 1971).

16. Walzer, *Wars*, xix.

17. Walzer, *Wars*, xix-xx.

18. Walzer, *Wars*, 58; H. Suganami, *The Domestic Analogy and World Order Proposals* (Cambridge: Cambridge University Press, 1989).

19. Thanks to Thomas Pogge for the image.

20. For more on this proposed addition to right intention, and the original Kant scholarship, see Orend, *Kantian Perspective*.

21. Woodward, *Plan*; W. Murray and R. Scales, *The Iraq War* (Cambridge, MA: Harvard University Press, 2003).

22. Reisman and Antoniou, eds., *Laws*, 40.

23. Walzer, *Wars*, 34–40 and 138–43.

24. This is not to say that only Western-style constitutional democracies can fulfil this rule: clearly different regime types can and should publicly declare war. But that fact will not stop me from discussing issues of special importance to Western societies, such as the division of war powers.

25. L. Fisher, *Presidential War Power* (Lawrence, KS: University of Kansas Press, 1995); and Regan, *Principles*, 20–47.

26. H.L.A. Hart, "Are There Any Natural Rights?" *Philosophical Review* (1955), 175–92; A. Gewirth, *Human Rights* (University of Chicago Press, 1982); H. Shue, *Basic Rights* (Princeton, NJ: Princeton University Press, 2nd ed., 1996); O. O'Neill, *Constructions of Reason* (Cambridge: Cambridge University Press, 1989).

27. Brownlie, *Law*, 255–387.

28. M. Doyle, "Kant, Liberal Legacies and Foreign Affairs," *Philosophy and Public Affairs* (1984), 204–35 and 323–53; and M. Brown, et al, eds. *Debating the Democratic Peace* (Cambridge, MA: MIT Press, 1996).

29. I detail the pros and cons of justifying human rights versus their critics in Orend, *Human Rights*, 67–100 and 155–90.

30. Reisman and Antoniou, eds. *Laws*, 3–35; Regan, *Principles*, 20–47 and 213–31.

31. Woodward, *Plan*.

32. M. Walzer, *Thick and Thin* (New Haven: Yale University Press, 1995).

33. Reisman and Antoniou, eds., *Laws*, 3–9.

34. Walzer, *Wars*, 84, xiv.

35. Walzer, *Wars*, xiii-xiv.

36. Walzer, *Wars*, xxv-xxxii; A. Pierce, "Just War Principles and Economic Sanctions," *Ethics and International Affairs* (1996), 99–113; L.F. Damrosch, "The Collective Enforcement of International Norms Through Economic Sanctions," *Ethics and International Affairs* (1994), 60–80; G. Simons, *The Scourging of Iraq* (New York: Macmillan, 2nd ed., 1996); R. Clark, *The Impact of Sanctions on Iraq* (London: World View Forum, 1996) and A. Arnove and A. Abunimah, eds. *Iraq Under Siege* (London: South End Press, 2000).

37. Regan, *Cases*, 214; and Reisman and Antoniou, eds., *Laws*, 5–9.

38. Walzer, *Wars*, 67–74.

39. Walzer, *Wars*, xv-xxi.

40. Walzer, *Wars*, xv-xxi.

41. J. Persico, *Nuremberg: Infamy on Trial* (New York: Penguin, 1995).

42. A.J.P. Taylor, *The Origins of the Second World War* (New York: Atheneum, 1962); J. Keegan, *The Second World War* (New York: Vintage, 1990).

43. Walzer, *Wars*, 253.

CHAPTER 3

Jus ad Bellum #2
Non-Classical Wars

> "[T]he injustice of the opposing side ...
> lays on the wise man the duty of waging wars."
> *Augustine*[1]

The classical account of *jus ad bellum*, developed last chapter, cannot be considered complete. For it deals solely with standard inter-state conflicts, like World War II or the Persian Gulf War, leaving out such important intra-state conflicts as civil wars. Furthermore, what happens when the aggressor is not another state, nor even a rival internal group striving to establish its own state but is, rather, something like a terrorist group? Finally, how is the so-called "aggression paradigm" consistent with such things as anticipatory attack and humanitarian intervention? To respond meaningfully to such important issues, we must amend the standard account of *jus ad bellum*. But we must stress, crucially, that *all the forthcoming amendments have to do with the just cause requirement*. All the other rules for a justified resort to force—right intention, proportionality, etc.—still hold straightforwardly for the four revisions which follow. The amendments are all in terms of *carefully expanding the just cause* for resorting to armed force beyond the classical scope of responding to interstate aggression. I should add that, in this chapter, we are squarely within just war theory; international law is profoundly unclear about these cases beyond a general norm to get prior United Nations Security Council (UNSC) endorsement.[2]

Non-State Threats, 9/11 and the Iraq Insurgency

Because of September 11, 2001, the world is wary of attacks by so-called non-state actors, particularly terrorist groups. What is terrorism? Terrorism is a tactic; it is not itself an actual, full-blown "ism" (i.e., a coherent, developed political ideology with a systematic view of how social institutions should be structured). There were radicals in the 1800s who referred to terrorism as a full-blown "ism"—some writing passionate, bizarre manifestos about random violence and the subversion of order—but they were mistaken. Terrorism *is a tactic used in the service of some other "ism."* In the case of the nineteenth century radicals it was anarchism (i.e., the idea of society without a coercive governing structure—like the state).[3] Terrorism, defined, is the use of random violence—especially killing force—against civilians with the intent of spreading fear throughout a population, hoping that this fear will advance a political objective. Crucial to terrorism is not just the deed itself but also what some have called "the propaganda of the deed." Since terrorists want to spread fear, it is vital that their deed not only be terrible but be so terrible that it gets covered by media, and word and image about the threat become disseminated throughout the population. The 9/11 attacks, e.g., were clearly motivated not just by the desire to kill civilians but also by the drive to maximize the propaganda value of the high-profile attacks.[4]

Though we might imagine cases where terrorism gets used by other "isms,"[5] most often it occurs historically in three contexts. The first is as a tool of authoritarian regimes to crush their own populations into submission: the dictatorship under Robespierre, during the French Revolution, established the "Reign of Terror" (which I believe is the root source of the word "terrorism" in Western vocabularies). The Reign of Terror, 1793–94, was when "Enemies of the Revolution" were rounded up and, in a very deliberate, public, propagandistic way, given their own special "close shave" by Mme. La Guillotine. At the Terror's peak, Robespierre had 40,000 people guillotined in just one month.[6] The second context is when terrorism gets used as a tool of extremist outsiders against representative regimes. In this context—which is obviously where the 9/11 attacks fit—terrorism is a violent attempt to circumvent such democratic processes as rational persuasion, coalition- and consensus-building, the rule of law, and the will of the majority expressed in free elections. The terrorist seeks to short-circuit all these things and simply inflict his will on a population, probably because he knows his extreme beliefs would have no chance of achieving mainstream success. He cannot persuade people, so he seeks to coerce them. The terrorist, in this sense, is actually much like a tyrant—but without the power and control the tyrant already has. The terrorist is a tyrant-in-waiting, and he dreams of becoming someone like Robespierre, who is able to radically refashion all of society from the top-down through what he views as the cleansing power of violence. The personnel of al-Qaeda fit this mould precisely.[7]

The third common context of terrorism is as a tool in guerrilla warfare. Guerrilla warfare refers to the use, by at least one side, of irregular military tactics against the standard tactics, and regular forces, of the other side. Often, guerrilla warfare is resorted to by weaker forces against more powerful ones: the weaker side knows it will be crushed by the stronger should it engage the stronger in open, classical combat. Instead, the weaker side uses irregular tactics like surprise attacks, traps and ambushes, quick strikes followed by rapid disengagement and disappearance, assassinations, clandestine and camouflage operations, sabotage and even terrorism. Consider the ongoing insurgency in Iraq. The insurgents realize that directly engaging US forces in open warfare—in a so-called "set-piece battle," for instance—would result quickly in their own annihilation. So they refuse to engage, instead: planting landmines in the road to blow up US soldiers as they drive by; launching ambush-style missile attacks on US helicopters when they are in the middle of loading and are thus "sitting ducks"; hiding amongst civilians and then blowing themselves up when US soldiers come close by on daily patrol; and so on. Now, such actions don't count as terrorism, because they target military forces. How can terrorism come into play in a guerrilla war? Well, the guerrillas might view it in their interests to spread terror throughout the civilian population—even if it is their own. Why? Consider again Iraq. The Americans, and American-supported Iraq government, are in control (or, at least, they have more control than the insurgents want). The insurgents oppose all this. Using terrorism, they think, will challenge that control—making the authorities look ineffectual and incapable of ruling. So the insurgents randomly blow up civilians, striking especially during religious observances when people's guards are down. The people, scared and exhausted by the violence, will then push for political change, and the insurgent forces will step in to fill the gap left by the vacating Americans. That is their theory, anyway. And it shows the extreme extent to which these ruthless insurgents are willing to go: gladly killing their fellow citizens to advance their own partisan objectives of winning power for themselves.[8]

Whether terrorism as a tactic is consistent with any "ism" or "ocracy" is a difficult and delicate debate. Fortunately, I don't have to resolve it here. From just war theory's point of view, *terrorism is always an impermissible tactic*, since it involves the deliberate killing of innocent civilians—which right-thinking people view as murder. We'll talk more next chapter about just war theory's ban on deliberately killing innocents—what does it mean, what justifies it, what consequences does it have, and so on. For now, we merely diagnose terrorism for what it is and note how, clearly, it can pose a dangerous non-state threat to the existence and peace of legitimate states (especially in the second context).[9]

Terrorists are not the only non-state threats which states confront. Mercenaries, which used to be major threats in this regard, continue in some parts of the world to be of real concern. Mercenaries are soldiers who do not have a political objective, only a financial one: they offer their killing services to the highest bidder, and have no political objective of their own. Finally, in some parts of the world, Mafia-style criminal gangs, and/or drug cartels, can pose enough of a threat that the state(s) in that region respond with force that is warlike in scale and seriousness. Consider Colombia, in South America. For a long time, the government and the cocaine cartels have fought something very much like a war. But the cartels don't have a political or state-related objective: they only want to be left alone to profit from the drug trade. The government, however, is unwilling to let them, since cocaine is everywhere illegal. What has made their conflict warlike has been the scale and ferocity of the fighting, along with a combination of the weakness of the Colombian state and the strength and wealth of the cartels.[10]

Usually, non-state threats are best dealt with using measures *short* of war. Which ones are these? All the tools of domestic law enforcement: surveillance; information-gathering; investigation; "making a case"; infiltration; strong border controls; drug and crime "stings" and "busts"; a robust and effective police force; an efficient and non-corrupt legal system; and a sustained political commitment to weed out the threat. Sometimes, however, these measures might not be enough, and the more extreme measures of warfighting can be contemplated. This might happen when the state itself is weak, perhaps because it is generally under-resourced owing to the poverty of its people, or else owing to systematic corruption or inefficiencies in its own structure. Both are true of Colombia. The other possibility is that the non-state threat is abnormally well-endowed, and represents a genuine state-scale security threat, as in the case of the Colombian cocaine cartels and the terrorist group al-Qaeda, which is flush with the wealth of ex-Saudi billionaire Osama bin Laden. Al-Qaeda also received expert military training back in the 1980s, when America was keen to supply and educate the USSR's enemies during Russia's aggressive war against Afghanistan.[11]

There is very little amendment to the just cause rule which is required to deal with these threats. Why? Because there is nothing, in just war theory or international law, which says that aggression can only be committed by states. Aggression, recall, is the use of armed force in violation of a legitimate state's right to either territorial integrity or political sovereignty. And states have these rights insofar as they help realize the human rights of their people. Ultimately, then, *aggression is the violent violation of human rights*. So either states or non-state actors can commit aggression, which we have seen is what roots a morally justified resort to war.

Consider the 9/11 attacks, which were clear instances of aggression. They involved the use of armed force, first to hijack the planes and then to use the planes themselves as high-powered missiles. They violated America's right to territorial integrity, in so far as they were lethal attacks on American soil, having penetrated American airspace. And they violated America's right of political sovereignty, by attempting to force serious foreign policy changes upon a freely-choosing population. America, moreover, was in 2001 a legitimate state: by being widely recognized by the international community; by enjoying widespread, uncoerced social peace; by making serious efforts at the realization of its citizens' human rights; and by not—at that time— violating the rights of other states and peoples. So 9/11 was an act of aggression, very reminiscent of Pearl Harbor, just as it was obviously designed to be ("propaganda of the deed" and all). And aggression, we explained last chapter, justifies a defensive war in response.

The only "wiggle room" here, for any supporters of that attack, would be to argue that America violated the last condition of minimal justice by somehow violating the rights of foreign political communities and their citizens at that time. I suppose they would focus on Iraq, Saudi Arabia and the Palestinians. But you cannot just throw out accusations; you have to make a sustained and reasonable argument *and* have it backed by publicly accessible evidence.

America had a presence in Iraq in 2001, no doubt. In fact, it enforced no-fly-zones (NFZ) in both the south and north of that country. It also supplied aid to humanitarian camps contained within the NFZ. But it was entitled to do so by the terms of the treaty ending the Persian Gulf War in 1991, to which Iraq agreed. More controversially, America still maintained sanctions on Iraq in 2001. While these hurt Iraq, they were being maintained to ensure full compliance with the 1991 treaty terms, and the Americans felt the treaty provisions regarding full disclosure of Iraq's program for developing weapons of mass destruction (WMD) were not being met. Legally, the Americans had the right to do this: it is clearly there in the 1991 treaty which Iraq signed. As for the privations which the sanctions created in Iraq, detailed comment will be made next chapter. For now, we note that Saddam's regime also contributed substantially to the sanctions-related deprivations suffered by the Iraqi people in the 1990s. In fact, it benefited from them: the sanctions actually made Iraqis more dependent on Saddam's regime and, if he truly wanted the sanctions to stop, all he had to do was fully comply with UN and US demands. So to blame Iraqi civilian suffering—an admitted reality—solely or even mainly upon the US is not clear-cut. It is certainly nowhere so clear-cut as to justify mass murder in retaliation.[12]

How exactly did America's presence in Saudi Arabia violate that community's rights? America's military was there at the request of the Saudi Arabian government, and indeed had been so since the days of Desert Shield (against Iraq) in 1990. If the terrorists were then to argue that the Saudi government was and remains illegitimate, they'd have to tell us why. It is not a democracy, true, but: 1) we left open last chapter the possibility that non-democratic states might still be legitimate; 2) the Saudi government, in spite of its imperfections, is still widely recognized internationally; and 3) besides, if al-Qaeda had its druthers, it would not institute a democracy in Saudi Arabia anyway—it would institute an Islamic theocracy (i.e., a union of "church" and state, based on a strict, fundamentalist reading of the *Koran*). Would such a regime be consistent with human rights? It is hard to make that case, for such would probably deny freedom of belief and association to non-believers as well as radically curtail female access to such human rights as participation in governance, recognition as equals, elementary education, property ownership, and so forth. The "offensiveness" of America's military presence in Saudi Arabia, to al-Qaeda, is based on non-believers "defiling" the Islamic holy land with their very presence, as well as the more narrow, strategic reason that America's presence there simply makes it harder for al-Qaeda to overthrow the Saudi regime and institute an Islamic theocracy there. But the latter is a self-interested strategic reason, not a sincere, objective moral one. Even the former is not a moral one, it is a religious one.

(Islamic extremists—like al-Qaeda and the Taliban, the radical ex-ruling party of Afghanistan—don't hate the West for its own sake. To them, we're just infidels who refuse to believe the truth of the *Koran*. We're write-offs, so to speak, destined for Hell. What makes these extremists truly hate the West, especially America, is that America stands in the way of their ultimate goal: the overthrow of governments in traditional Arab lands, and their replacement with strict Islamic theocracies *à la* the Taliban or even Iran. They especially wish to do this in Saudi Arabia, since that is Islam's holy land. But America supports numerous Arab governments—Egypt, Kuwait, Pakistan, Saudi Arabia—and thus frustrates their goal. America also supports Israel, which the Islamic radicals view as being on traditional Arab land, too. So the extremists decided to commit large-scale terrorism against America, hoping such would create enough pain and fear among the American people that *they* would force the US government to withdraw from the Middle East.)[13]

This leaves America's "offensive" support for Israel, and the association in many Arab minds between that and the persecution of the Palestinians. The Israeli-Palestinian problem is difficult, and cannot easily be swept aside—or solved for that matter. There seem to be serious issues of disenfranchisement and aspirations for statehood. But, in the first instance, it is Israel which has front-line responsibility, not America. Secondly, it is not as though Israelis have no claim to the disputed territory, either—which they, unlike their neighbours, have actually turned into a democracy with sincere commitments to human rights (at least for citizens).[14] To count as a systematic violation of human rights sufficient to justify armed attacks in response, it must be a directly, clearly culpable action, not indirect support for another country which has some controversial policies. And it must deal not merely with what your group wants, or schemes to get, but with the substance of vital human need which human rights denotes. All too often people inflate their mere preferences into the status of human rights claims because they know the language of human rights commands attention. But, as I have said, *just because you claim it, doesn't make it so.* You need a sober, non-religious argument—accessible to any reasonable person—which draws on real evidence and fits the definition of what a human right actually is. Without such an argument, proving America's mass human rights-violations (and not merely its preponderance of power and its policies which you don't like), you cannot question America's status as a legitimate state. And if you cannot question that, you cannot justly attack America out of the blue.

STATE SPONSORSHIP OF TERRORISM

A connected issue, of vital importance, concerns whether the non-state actor's aggression was itself "sponsored" by a state actor. If so, war is justified *not only* against the non-state threat but the state sponsor as well. Aggression is, in this regard, a symmetrical relation: if Q commits aggression against R, and Q had substantial support from P in doing so, then P also aggressed against R. Consider again the 9/11 attacks. It immediately came to light, following the strikes, that al-Qaeda was receiving substantial and knowing support from the government of Afghanistan, known as the Taliban. The Taliban embodied strict Islamist principles, and found common cause with al-Qaeda's terrorist objectives, in particular the desire to spread Islamic theocracies throughout traditional Arab lands. So the Taliban allowed al-Qaeda refuge within Afghanistan, knowing full well al-Qaeda was running terrorist training camps with the objective of committing terrorism around the world. In doing so, the Taliban made itself a legitimate target in the "war on terror" following the 9/11 attacks. Since al-Qaeda committed aggression, and the Taliban's Afghanistan made it possible for them to do so, it was a material part of their aggression (i.e., a co-conspirator, a material accomplice). The term most often applied to states that sponsor terrorism is that they are "rogue" or "outlaw" states (i.e., states disobedient of international law and moral custom in such a flagrant way that they become dangerous). America, along with 28 other countries, invaded Afghanistan in November 2001 and, within two months, routed the Taliban from power. Since early 2002, Afghanistan has been in a state of uneasy post-conflict resolution, to which we shall return in Chapters 6 and 7.[15]

Care must be taken to show, however, that any suspected sponsorship is actually there. We can imagine cases, especially in the developing world, where states simply lack the resources to know everything that is going on within their territory. Some states might unwittingly be host to terrorists—as indeed America itself was, during the few weeks before 9/11. The implied duty for states here is one of good citizenship in the international community: actively co-operating in the identification of, and hunt for, terrorists; helping other states to weed out any of their terrorists; and being open and self-critical to the possibility that perhaps terrorists are located on one's own soil. Such are much-needed attitudes in furthering the legitimate aims of the war on terror. It is only when there is an adamant refusal to do so, coupled with concrete evidence of a material link between that state and a terrorist group, that the state itself may be subjected to criticism and opposition, in extreme cases leading to armed resistance. "Material links" include: financing; the provision of weapons, intelligence and/or training; the knowing provision of safe harbour, residence or citizenship; and any blending between the state's own resources and personnel with that of the terrorist association.

Anticipatory Attack and Preventive War

This is a thorny issue much on people's minds since America's decision, in March 2003, to launch an ostensibly self-defensive attack on Saddam

Hussein's regime in Iraq. To get theoretical grounding, let's consider Walzer's thoughts on this topic.

Walzer wants to walk a fine line between two extremes: denying that anticipatory attack by one state on another—or on a non-state actor—is ever justified; and supporting the doctrine of preventive war. A preventive war, as he defines it, is a war prosecuted in the *present* for the sake of maintaining the *future* balance of power, itself thought necessary for long-term peace and security. Such wars used to be very frequent in Europe, especially in the eighteenth century. The grounds most frequently offered for preventive war are utilitarian (i.e., we must war *now* to avoid *future* costs and/or gain *future* benefits). European powers used to do this to prevent any one power from getting too big and threatening. War was, so to speak, a way of taking powers down a peg or two, so they wouldn't cause "an even bigger war" down the road. Walzer believes, soberly, that the calculations required to morally ground preventive war are simply too fantastic to be plausible. *We just don't know that much about how the long-term future will unfold.* Furthermore, the danger to which preventive war is intended to respond is too distant and speculative. It simply doesn't seem to justify the *certain* deaths in the present to go to war based on *speculation* of what another country might be like in, say, 35 years. If any kind of advance action is to be grounded at all, the danger aimed at must be *imminent*, not distant; it must be a threat which is *concrete*, not merely abstract.[16]

"Anticipatory attack" denotes an armed attack wherein you strike first but do so *not* out of aims for a distant, future balance of power but, rather, out of immediate aims to pre-empt an attack you know is coming in the very near future. This is "pre-emptive," as opposed to "preventive," war. (I prefer the term "anticipatory attack" to avoid any confusion between the two, and also because the "pre-emptive" vs. "preventive" distinction is too refined to be helpful.) A sufficient threat for justifying an anticipatory attack, Walzer suggests, is composed of three needed elements. The first is "a manifest intent to injure," revealed *either* through a bitter history of conflict between the communities in question, like the Arab-Israeli struggle, *or* through recent and explicit threats. Walzer suggests that the recipient of a justified anticipatory attack can only be "a determined enemy," one demonstrably committed to doing severe harm to one's political community. The second element of sufficient threat is "a degree of active preparation that makes the intent a positive danger." Mere malign intent, even given a conflict-ridden history and/or recent hostile declarations, is *not enough* to ground anticipatory strikes. *There must also be a measurable military preparation* on the part of the proposed recipient of the attack, such as its build-up of offensive forces along the border. Finally, the situation must be one "in which waiting, or doing anything other than fighting, greatly magnifies the risk [of being attacked]." Only under all three conditions is an anticipatory attack justified.

In general, Walzer suggests, "states may use military force in the face of threats of war, whenever the failure to do so would seriously risk their territorial integrity or political independence." Indeed, he goes so far as to contend that, should State X be faced with these three conditions involving Bellicose State (or Non-State) Actor Y, then Y *has already committed aggression* against X, and thus X at least has just cause to launch an attack. We now see how, for Walzer, the actual deployment of force is not a strictly necessary condition for aggression to have occurred. It is no less a violation of state rights to pose "a serious risk" to the political sovereignty and territorial integrity of a legitimate state than it is to launch an armed invasion against it. Though there are obvious and substantial concerns to be raised here with regard to loosening the concept of aggression, Walzer himself stresses that anticipatory attack can only be truly *exceptional*, and a very burdensome *weight of justification* is borne by the attacker to prove, with evidence, that the three general criteria really do hold in its case.[17]

The key here, in my view, is that defence—as in defence from aggression —can be construed either descriptively or normatively. Descriptive defence means you must wait to be, empirically, the *second* one to use force—that your use of force comes *after* that of the aggressor's. He takes his shot, and then you're entitled to take yours in reply—like the textbook cases of self-defence. Normative defence, by contrast, means that there *might* be circumstances where, empirically, one's use of force can come first against an aggressor. A just war is one which is *normatively* defensive—it defends people from aggression and seeks, in response, to resist and repeal it—whereas the tactics which may be employed, within the context of such a just war, may be either empirically defensive or offensive.

Aggression, after all, is universally defined by just war theorists and international law as the violation of state rights to territory and sovereignty. This violation occurs when a state, or non-state actor, obviously presents itself as a *severe* threat to another state and its people. And a state, or non-state actor, can present itself as such a threat in at least one of two ways: 1) by actually attacking a state without just cause; or 2) by posing a *credible, grave and imminent threat*, based on compelling evidence, of launching such an aggressive attack. So a just war of self- or other-defence need not be wholly reactive: there is a bit of room here, I believe, for anticipatory attack as well.

The key notion, with regard to anticipatory attack, is that forcing states to wait for the actual attack, despite its evident and imminent coming, is *not* a reasonable insistence. This is especially the case if there are compelling, public grounds for believing that the coming attack is going to be of considerable force and destruction. A state would be derelict in its duty to protect its members if it did not reserve the right to make well-grounded anticipatory attacks in this regard. It is no less a violation of fundamental rights to deliberately pose a credible and imminent severe threat (i.e., a clear and present danger—to another person or state). Such interferes with the lives and liberties of states and peoples as readily as does an explicit and actual invasion because it leaves them just waiting for the oncoming attack. The coercive threat functions, and is *intended* to function, in the same manner as an actual attack: to bring about the unjust capitulation of the other country or person. From a just war point of view, the resort to arms by the victim is hence equally justified in either event.

Think of a personal case where an attacker breaks into your home with a gun and declares repeatedly his intention to kill and rob you. He then releases the safety switch on his gun, leaving him free to fire. It is not unjust in such a case, if one has a gun oneself, to fire at that point: the attacker has violated your space, declared terrible intentions, shows himself capable of realizing them and then he takes the final step of just leaving you waiting for the hammer to fall. Given the potentially final consequences of waiting for that hammer, it seems quite reasonable for you to defend yourself. And *it is clearly still defence, even though you're the one firing first.* An even better analogy, representing the state more accurately, would be if a policeman happened upon the scene. Every police force I have heard of allows the policeman to fire at this point, and probably sooner—at the point when the attacker raises his gun towards you—in defence of your life. The cop, or you, fires first but the moral damage and physical danger has first been done by the attacker, rendering him open to being resisted. You're not creating the menacing conditions after all: he is. You are defending yourself from what you have every reason to believe is a credible, grave and imminent threat to your life and rights.

Jeff MacMahan makes an important point here when he says that, even when we go to war in response to an attack which has already occurred, a prime objective in doing so is to prevent even further damage inflicted by the attacker. This suggests that the difference between reactive and anticipatory defence is not so rigid and black-and-white. When we see aggression, we move: 1) to punish it; 2) to resist it in the moment; and 3) to prevent further harm in the future. We can, moreover, plausibly say that all three are done in defence: defence *of values* and defence *of lives.*[18]

The just war tradition is, admittedly, seriously split on this issue. We know, from Chapter 1, that Vitoria disagrees with both Walzer and myself here: the Spaniard insists you must wait for the actual attack before you may go to war to fend the attacker off and punish him. International law, for its part, seems to concur with Vitoria, at least in the absence of special permission from the UNSC. Most pre-9/11 writers and international lawyers would be in this camp, other than Walzer of course. Many of the medieval writers, however, argued strongly in favour of the idea—inspired by Augustine—that "protection of the innocent" was a prime purpose of the state, and a just cause for war. And they concluded, upon reflection, that there could be *rare occasion* when a first military strike could be consistent with this principle. If you wait to receive the first strike, some of your civilians will die and you'll have failed in your duty to protect them. Post 9/11, and in the era of WMD, this view is gathering renewed attention.[19]

The American government, in its 2002 *National Security Strategy*, makes the case that—in light of modern terrorism and its objectives of spectacular, hard-to-predict instances of mass civilian slaughter—a responsible government must reserve the right to strike first *if* it will most likely prevent such instances from occurring. "The greater the threat," the document reads, "the greater the risk of inaction—and the more compelling case for taking anticipatory action to defend ourselves, even if uncertainty remains as to the time and place of the enemy's attack. To forestall or prevent such hostile acts by our adversaries, the United States will, if necessary, act pre-emptively."[20]

It is vital to understand that these considerations do *not* lighten the load of a government making use of first strike. For such a government must then publicly justify its first strike in light of Walzer's three grounds for anticipatory attack *and* show, fundamentally, how such action is consistent with its function and duty of protecting its people.[21] All this amendment to just war theory does is refuse to rule out such strikes as a matter of conceptual stipulation or verbal fiat. It leaves it open to reasonable argument, and appeal to public evidence, whether such attacks might be morally justified in particular instances. Just war rules need to offer firm and clear guidance, yes, but to remain relevant over time some aspect of flexibility and openness to considering new situations is an absolute must.

AMERICA'S 2003 IRAQ ATTACK

Now let's examine an actual case of anticipatory attack: America and Britain's strike into Iraq in the spring of 2003.[22] There were many arguments trotted out in support of a pre-emptive strike on Iraq, prior to its launching on March 19, 2003. But the one most relevant, for our concern in this section, was that the regime in Iraq posed a clear and present danger to the United States. Why did the Bush Jr. Administration believe this? Because it thought Iraq *either* harboured al-Qaeda terrorists, who carried off the 9/11 attacks, *or* at the least because it possessed WMD, which it was willing to give to such terrorists (whom we know from 9/11 would not hesitate to use them). The moral structure of this argument is similar to that offered above, but it adds a further player that we must note with clarity, and some emphasis, in light of recent events. This player is that of the roaming terrorist organization, which moves from state to state, or which operates on a clandestine basis in a variety of states. The principle here seems to be that it is justified to perform a pre-emptive attack on a bellicose state *either* because: 1) its own actions fulfil Walzer's three criteria as outlined above; *or* 2) it harbours a terrorist organization which fulfils the three criteria; *or* 3) the mixture between the actions of the state offering sanctuary to the organization and the actions of the organization itself fulfil the three criteria. In the case of the 2003 attack, the final category seems to have been the one foremost in mind of the American war-planners and executors.

There *was* a history of recent armed hostility both between Iraq and the United States and between al-Qaeda and the United States. Iraq and America (as well as the UK and others) clashed in the 1991 Persian Gulf War, and exchanged sporadic fire in connection with the NFZ enforced over Iraq between 1991 and 2003. Al-Qaeda attacked America in 2001, and America replied by invading Afghanistan a few weeks later and, according to some commentators, driving some al-Qaeda members out of that country and into Iraq. Throughout the 1990s, in fact, America had engaged, and been targeted by, Islamic terrorist organizations on a number of occasions and throughout a variety of Middle Eastern, African and American locales. So, supporters of the 2003 pre-emptive strike could argue plausibly that the "bitter and determined enemy" condition of Walzer's was here obviously fulfilled, both with reference to Iraq and al-Qaeda. I agree. We know, however, that that is *not enough*, that there must be *both* indication of a political willingness of the bitter enemy to attack, *and* clear military indications that the bitter enemy is imminently about to attack, before an anticipatory strike can be justified in terms of just cause.

Here is where the existence of WMD clouds the picture. Essentially, the United States government argued that the military build-up condition was satisfied, in the spring of 2003, simply because Iraq had WMD. (Or so they thought.) In an era when weapons which can kill tens of thousands can be deployed within under an hour, how meaningful is it to have the military "build-up" criterion? Doesn't just having them count as satisfying that condition? The most plausible answer, I believe, must be *no*, otherwise we'd have to define all the major military powers as severely dangerous, as ticking time bombs. What has to change is how we conceive of the military build-up, or offensive capacity, condition when it comes to WMD. The key here is *not* the raw fact of possessing these weapons, but the recent history regarding their use. It is relevant, for example, to consider the fact that the Hussein regime in Iraq deployed chemical weapons at least twice in recent history: once against Iran in the middle 1980s, the other in 1988 against the Kurdish minority group within Iraq itself. Contrast that with the recent behaviour of other powers who admittedly *have* such weapons, yet who have *not* used them. In the latter case it seems most plausible to infer, from their behaviour, that such powers have such weapons for defensive and deterrent purposes, and are making a reasonably responsible use of them. The Hussein regime did not, and thus could be counted as a serious danger. This judgment is only underlined by considering that the Hussein regime had a record of recent international aggression—in 1990 into Kuwait—and also deliberately shot missiles into Israel's civilian population centres during the Persian Gulf War which followed. What this reasoning establishes is that the military build-up condition is to be understood as outlined above when it comes to conventional forces (i.e., as a literal build-up, usually along the border). But, when it comes to WMD, *mere possession* of such weapons *can* count as a severely threatening military capacity *only when coupled with* recent history of: 1) using them; or 2) of having committed international aggression; or 3) of having deliberately targeted civilians during wartime.

We have now established our rule regarding WMD, but a large problem for America's pro-attack case is whether Iraq actually had them. We know, post-attack, that the UK and USA have yet to find any and, indeed, have given up looking. That is a stinging fact which reflects poorly on the war. There are also indications that the "evidence" in favour of Iraqi WMD possession was highly "massaged," raising sharp questions about the professionalism of the intelligence services ostensibly serving their head of state to the best of their ability. Indeed, in December 2005, President Bush Jr. himself admitted in a public address that: "It is true that much of the intelligence turned out to be wrong."[23] Yet it is not all so badly lopsided. Iraq did, after all, actually have and use WMD in the 1980s—so why wouldn't they still have a few tucked away somewhere? The answer might be that the UN weapons inspection process—authorized by the peace treaty of the 1991 Persian Gulf War, and continuing throughout the 1990s—actually succeeded in identifying and stripping Iraq of its WMD. There was obviously severe scepticism, by American intelligence, that the UN could have achieved such success. But *that is allowing one's expectations to shape one's perception of the evidence, instead of the other way around.* A further complication is that, apparently, Saddam was still on the record asserting Iraqi WMD possession. Why would he lie if this wasn't true? One possible answer is that he still wanted to seem tough and dangerous in a very rough part of the world. Should we really be surprised to learn a man like Saddam might lie, or spread disinformation exaggerating his military strength? I don't think so: his miscalculation was in failing to realize how risky such posturing might turn out to be.

In any event, the main question is: what was it reasonable for Bush Jr., of the USA, and Tony Blair, of the UK, to believe in the spring of 2003—and did they make serious efforts to inform these beliefs to the best of their ability? On the one hand, their intelligence services were advising them of Iraqi WMD possession. On the other, many participants within the decision-making process behind that war noted a marked rush to judgment—with pre-formed expectations slanting perceptions of evidence. Usually, that is not what we mean when we talk about making an effort to inform your beliefs. Considering the stakes—not only war but an anticipatory attack involving violent regime change—I think here we must hold the actors to the very highest standards when it comes to clear evidence, reasonableness of belief, and effort at critically cross-checking beliefs and their sources. The decision to go to war is a decision in favour of deliberate mass killing after all, and an attempt to change the course of history for millions of people. Ethically, it is far too serious to be based on pre-formed expectations, impetuous judgment and perhaps over-excited emotions—emotions like antagonism against Saddam and fear of future terrorist strikes. The standard with anticipatory attack is *higher, not lower* than that for a classical, reactive response to a prior act of aggression. The case, for this to be justified at all, must simply be *impeccable*.

This leaves the final issue of the bitter enemy displaying a political willingness to deploy an offensive military capacity on an imminent basis. Many more questions can be raised here. Iraq seemed fairly docile following its humiliation in "Gulf War One," coupled with the strict post-war sanctions and NFZ. America and Britain argued that Iraq's refusal to submit itself to further UN weapons inspections not only violated the peace treaty of that first war, it was evidence of Iraq's new-found determination either to hide its existing WMD and/or to construct new ones. Even if true, does this count as a growing political willingness to *deploy* WMD *imminently*? Here is where the reference to al-Qaeda came in: even if the Hussein regime was not itself willing to deploy such weapons, it was willing to supply them to the al-Qaeda terrorists who had fled Afghanistan following America's destruction of the Taliban government. Since we know, from 9/11, that al-Qaeda would eagerly be willing to use such weapons, what we have is essentially a conspiracy, by both a belligerent state and a belligerent terrorist organization, to imminently attack America, and with WMD no less.

The *structure* of this argument seems right, according to the criteria defended above. The real issue here, of course, is whether these normative criteria *were actually fulfilled* when the strike was launched in March 2003. In other words, the principles seem right but was the evidence wrong—or, even worse, manipulated and exaggerated? We have just considered the question of Iraqi WMD possession. Now let's turn to the supposed "substantial connection" between al-Qaeda and the Hussein regime. The Bush Jr. Administration said it had evidence of a handful of sporadic meetings between low-level al-Qaeda and low-level Hussein regime officials. OK, but is such clear evidence of conspiracy? You'd think there'd be regular, high-level meetings. Some of these low-level people might have had personal, not political, reasons for meeting each other. Or, if they were political, they might have dealt with a range of issues—including a coup attempt against Saddam—which had nothing to do with America. Many Middle East experts have noted that al-Qaeda and Saddam would make for genuinely bizarre co-conspirators, since al-Qaeda are religious fanatics and Saddam's regime was a secular dictatorship in the style of Stalin. Indeed, Iraq fought a long war, in the 1980s, against Iran *to resist* any export of Iran's Islamic extremism. Saddam seemed to *purge, rather than protect*, any fundamentalists on his soil. Truly, given the aims of al-Qaeda to install Islamic governments throughout the Middle East—including Iraq—why on earth would Saddam give them

WMD? They'd be much more likely to use such weapons *against his regime* than on the USA. It just doesn't add up.

Mere acknowledgement that here were two dangerous organizations, in the same general region of the world, both with reason to loathe and perhaps attack America, does *not* add up to a strong and plausible connection of a conspiracy between them to do so in the very near future. Indeed, the US Congressional Commission on the 9/11 attacks, in June 2004, said it had no evidence of any connection between Saddam and al-Qaeda.[24]

(Note that here the supporters of America's Iraq attack might switch tracks regarding which terrorist organization is most relevant here, moving away from al-Qaeda and underlining firmer, demonstrated connections between the Hussein regime in Iraq and suicide bombers in Palestine against Israel.[25] The grounding of America's attack would then move from anticipatory *self*-defence to anticipatory *other*-defence. This might be a stronger move, but it doesn't deal with the issue which the Bush Jr. White House put so much emphasis on, which was pre-emptive self-defence for America. Recall our discussion last chapter of the importance of calling your shot correctly in wartime, and not simply throwing out all possible reasons in favour of attack.)

To summarize: while the condition of the bitter, determined enemy *was* clearly satisfied in connection with the Spring 2003 attack, it is quite doubtful whether the other two conditions were satisfied (i.e., whether the enemy was both capable and imminently willing to launch an attack). Al-Qaeda seemed imminently willing, whereas Iraq—perhaps as a result of its own disinformation—seemed imminently capable. Put the two together and you have got your case. *But it is precisely that putting together which is in deep and profound question*, alongside the reasonableness of the belief that Iraq was actually capable in the first place. Until more information surfaces to the contrary, it seems that far too many questions and ambiguities remain to declare this cause of war justified. I believe, as I have mentioned, that the grounds for an anticipatory attack—even in the post-9/11 world—have to be *crystal clear*, in order that the permission not become so flexible as to allow for anything to get through. In my judgment, then, the 2003 Iraq attack was much better justified *not* as an anticipatory attack of pre-emptive self-defence but, rather, as an act of humanitarian intervention (of which we will say more below). As anticipation, the argument on the whole *fails*, satisfying only one of the three needed conditions.

All these questions and difficulties might seem to stretch beyond this particular case, and into the very principle of anticipatory attack. But I don't necessarily see why. It is, admittedly, *much more difficult* to ground a pre-emptive strike than it is to ground an empirically defensive manœuvre. The bar is set much higher, and rightfully so, in order to reign in warfare and to limit the grounds for launching it. But the abstract analogies above suggest that it is not impossible; and even in relatively clearer instances of justified wars, there are always deep questions to raise about any interpretation of the empirical evidence cited and what it most plausibly shows. Think, for instance, of the right intention condition, or the probability of success condition. An empirically defensive justified war does not escape from these difficulties any more than an empirically offensive justified war does. The devil truly is in the details, and knowing what they show. But in either case it does *not* follow, from the fact that the details can be difficult to make out, that the principles which authorize force themselves get called into question. That is a separate matter which has to be dealt with at the level of principle alone.

Civil Wars

There are two main moral questions when it comes to civil war. The first is whether it can ever be just to fight one; the second is whether it can ever be just to intervene in somebody else's. The answers to both questions, however, revolve around the same issue: that of the minimally just and hence legitimate state.

MINIMALLY JUST POLITICAL COMMUNITIES

The issue of a minimally just political community, introduced last chapter, is of central importance to just war theory. The reason why we should limit ourselves to talking about "minimally just" political communities is twofold. The first aspect is modesty: there is no perfectly or "maximally" just political community in existence. Some are better than others, of course, and some pass the threshold of minimal justice while others fail it. But no existing political community embodies the ideal; all are, in some ways, flawed or suboptimal. As Kant once insightfully intoned, "out of the crooked timber of humanity, no straight thing was ever made."[26] The second relevant aspect to the "minimal justice" construction is that the political community in question must at least have that degree of moral value, otherwise it has no ethical reason to exist. From the fact that we humans live in groups, and have formed nation-states, it does not follow that we have to respect all such groupings and state structures. For such might be brutally exploitative, slavery-condoning, tyrannical, or warmongering. *The groupings we freely create, and the state structures we condone, have value only if they are minimally just.* I have already suggested in the last chapter that a minimally just state: 1) is recognized as legitimate by its own people and most of the international community; 2) avoids violating the rights of other legitimate states; and 3) makes every reasonable effort at satisfying the human rights of its own citizens.

The most basic purpose of a national government is defence: defending its citizens from outside aggression by another state (or non-state actor), and also defending its citizens from predatory criminals residing within its borders. If a state is fundamentally incapable of being reasonably successful in this regard (i.e., of providing its citizens with security) then the social contract dissolves. There is no reason for the people to obey such a state and participate in it. Such a state must be radically transformed into a new one, or several, which can offer reasonable success in this regard, otherwise its people cannot count on living a life at all, much less a happy and enjoyable one. There simply must be a baseline of physical security, and freedom from severe and systemic violence, if there is to be a political community at all.

This quick reminder of the basics of the minimally just or legitimate state is essential to an understanding of the ethics of civil war (as indeed we have seen it is for war in general). For many, perhaps most, political communities today are, in fact, *composites* of many sub-groups and communities. Sometimes, group rivalry within the one state becomes so intense that fighting breaks out, either to control the one government shared in common, or else to secede and form a new state, out from under control of the old one. When, if ever, is it just to fight a civil war? One case would be when the central government fails any of the criteria of minimal justice. Any such government has no moral reason to exist, and so to resist its tyranny with force of arms is permissible.

BLUE VS. GREY

One case of a justified civil war was the North's war against the South in America from 1861 to 1865.[27] But the North represented the Union—the central government. So how does this case fit? For here it was the secessionist South which represented injustice. It did so because the South was the aggressor in the war, deliberately starting hostilities by bombing the federal Fort Sumter in South Carolina. Moreover, the South explicitly fought to form and preserve a mode of government which condoned slavery. Slavery is a massive social injustice, a hideous and widespread violation of human rights—depriving slaves of freedom, basic equality, social recognition as persons and, quite often, their very physical security. As such, the Confederate government of the South, led by Jefferson Davis, failed the criteria of minimal justice and had no moral value which could root a permissible defence against aggression. There has to be something there which has moral value for it to be permissible to go to war to gain and/or defend it. (This is the key question in a civil war: *who has minimal justice on their side?*) Is the central government minimally just (like the Union in the US Civil War) in contrast to the seceding state which either is, or aims to become, unjust (like the South)? Or is the central government an oppressive tyranny, or a severe discriminator which respects the rights of one privileged group while violating those of another? In the latter two cases, the seceding group would have justice on its side *provided that*, should it win, it clearly commits to establishing a legitimate state. Unfortunately, new states have sometimes been known to engage in discriminatory human rights violations against hated minority groups within their new borders—especially if such minorities were part of the majority in the old state they formerly shared. Of course, if new states do this, they themselves fail the criteria of minimal justice, and their secessionist struggle is revealed to have been dark and tyrannical, not bright and liberating. In sum, the civil war, to be just, must be done *either* in defence of an existing minimally just state, *or* with the aim of escaping an illegitimate political structure and creating a new, legitimate one. This all supports the · accuracy of our core conception of war as, ultimately, a massively violent struggle over the governance of a territory.[28]

WALKING AWAY?

Now, what if both sides have minimal justice on their side, which is to say we simply have two communities, formerly united, which now wish to separate? We cannot pronounce this unjust. Preserving union, just for the sake of union, is not sufficiently serious to justify warfare. Borders, while possessing real value, are not sacrosanct and eternal. Communities, like people, do change and so political associations can change too, provided they each remain minimally just in their essential structurings. The compelling analogy here is to a "no-fault divorce" between a couple. Here we have no injustice—"no fault"—on the part of both sides; we simply have a case of both sides having changed, wanting something different for the future, and hence wanting to dissolve the current set of rules. This is totally fine but note that, like divorce, the separation agreement must be comprehensive and fair. These agreements, predictably, are complex—involving splitting of territory and assets (as well as debts), custody and support issues relating to any "dependents," and perhaps even support or "alimony" payments as well. When we think of splitting a country, new borders and territory are vital issues, as is access to water and farmable land. Dividing the assets and liabilities of the old central government must be done fairly, and especially important for security and the avoidance of war is the dissolution of the old armed forces and the sound distribution of military assets.

Particularly sensitive is the treatment of "dependents." Take the case of Canada, which has contemplated these issues from time to time as Quebec separatism flares and then fades. If Quebec, which has a French-speaking majority, separates from Canada, what happens to the English-speaking minority concentrated in Montreal, and the Native or Aboriginal communities concentrated in the north of that province? The peaceful and just answer is that a negotiated settlement has to be arrived at, which might involve anything from Quebec giving land back to Canada to house these minorities or else Quebec keeping all its land but coming to arrangements with these groups to protect their human rights in an independent Quebec. The reason why this is such a sensitive issue is that, in European history anyway, the failure to resolve minority rights issues peacefully has sparked many a dreadful armed conflict.

There might also be issues of "international alimony" arising in such a split, say where one side agrees to let the other have a chunk of territory in exchange for a cash payment. Or perhaps a valuable resource deposit resides in the territory of one side—perhaps to keep it, that side must promise and deliver an ongoing share of the profits to its ex-partner. Or perhaps one side, after secession, will be so poor that it cannot afford to ensure minimal justice for its citizens, which after all takes resources. In such an instance, a transfer payment would have to be required, until the poor side develops more and its economy gains the needed traction to generate rights-respecting resources.[29] These are all politically explosive issues, and fighting has often broken out in connection with them. *But it doesn't have to*—the recent split, in the early 1990s, between the Czech Republic and Slovakia (formerly Czechoslovakia) shows that new communities can be formed in ways which are peaceful and minimally just. Both sides, if you ask them, are quite proud, and justifiably so, of their "Velvet Divorce."[30]

PICKING SIDES AND INTERVENING

We now turn to the issue of justifying armed intervention in some *other* country's civil war. This seems justifiable only when there is an obvious injustice on one side of the civil war, and you are intervening on the side of justice. There must be substantial injustice at stake—no country, for example, would have been justified in sending their army to bust up "The Velvet Divorce," or to slant the terms of that break-up to favour their own country. That would itself be aggression. But if there is substantial injustice at play in a civil war—either on the central government side or on the secessionist/reformer side—then armed intervention on behalf of the just side is permissible, assuming that side has requested outside assistance. If it has, you are entitled to intervene. Moreover, you are entitled to try and win the war for your side. Walzer's notion—that you are only entitled to "counterbalance" or "neutralize" the unjust side's influence, and then "let local forces prevail"—is to me not operational.[31] It is not operational in the sense that *the only objective which is coherent and action-guiding on the ground in war is seeking victory.* Think of the general's point of view on the field of battle: how do you know when your forces have merely "offset" or "neutralized" the unjust side, versus when they have defeated them? Are you only supposed to knock out two-thirds of a division? Take only four-fifths of a valley, or city? Walzer's aim of counterbalance is simply too abstract actually to be acted upon. *We are entitled to try to win the just wars we fight*, not merely to enhance our odds or to neutralize certain countervailing forces. And winning a war means forcing the enemy to both surrender and accept decent terms of peace.

Intervening in a civil war will always remain controversial. There is a lingering, intuitive suspicion that "this is their struggle, let them fight it out and resolve it themselves." This attitude might be compelling when both sides in the war are unjust, or if both sides are just and are simply having difficulty negotiating a separation. But I don't share this hands-off attitude when one side is just, the other clearly unjust. In such a case, it is more important for justice to be served than it is for "local forces" to be balanced. What matters most in political life is justice, not washing one's hands of what is going on next door. More on this when we shortly discuss humanitarian intervention.

THE VIETNAM WAR

It is hard not to feel for the people of Vietnam, one of the most war-ravaged pieces of territory in the twentieth century. Formerly a French colony, Vietnam was conquered by Japan and occupied throughout World War II. France, during the peace settlement of that war, reclaimed Vietnam. But a focused, armed group of Vietnamese—who also happened to be communist—resisted this return to French control. They came to be called the Viet Minh, or Viet Cong, and they wanted an independent Vietnam. When they saw that they would not get their way, they started to fight. We can call what followed something like the French-Vietnam war, from 1945–54. It was an anti-colonial struggle, and it eventually split Vietnam between North and South, with the communists prevailing in the North and the French and their Vietnamese sympathizers in the South. The Vietnam War was thus a civil war—a brutally long one, with different phases—and one featuring extensive foreign intervention on both sides.[32]

In 1954, the Geneva Settlement was supposed to have ended the issue. It called for Vietnam to be temporarily split into North and South, with free elections to be held in 1956, and then for the temporary split to be dissolved, and re-unification begun, based on the election results. France would quit the country entirely, and there would be a new, unified and independent Vietnam. On the basis of this deal, relative peace was obtained for nearly two years.

What reignited war was the fact that the government of South Vietnam, led by Diem, betrayed its pledge to participate in the 1956 elections. In response, insurgents from the South, who identified with the North, tried to forcibly overthrow Diem: if Vietnam would not be unified by ballot, it would be so by bullet. What is interesting, though, is that France decided to leave anyway at this point, and the Diem regime begged for, and received, extensive American support to fill the gap: cash, weapons, military training, technology and eventually US troops themselves.

The Americans got involved, under presidents Eisenhower and Kennedy, because of the Cold War with communism. China had experienced a communist revolution in 1949, and American decision-makers in the 1950s were terrified of a so-called "domino effect" of communism toppling government after government throughout Southeast Asia, as it had several years prior in Eastern Europe. They decided to draw a line at Vietnam, and when the

French got out the Americans felt they had to go in. So began the American-Vietnam War, which probably lasted from 1956–73, though some would debate the starting point and argue for anywhere from 1956 to the Tonkin Gulf Resolution, of the US Congress, in 1964. This Resolution was in response to the North Vietnamese attacking US ships in the Gulf of Tonkin. The battle lines were by now firmly drawn: on the one side, southern insurgents, North Vietnam and to an extent communist China; on the other, the southern establishment (Diem and later others) and the United States.

Critics of the Vietnam War, like Walzer, argue that it was unjust for a number of reasons, but mainly two. First, America entered the war not out of any sincere concern for the Vietnamese people but rather for reasons of *realpolitik*. Its motivation for fighting had nothing to do with resisting aggression; rather, it had everything to do with this cynical Cold War chess game of preventing communism from expanding beyond the Soviet Union, Eastern Europe and China. In just war terms, America failed right intention. Secondly, it has been established that it is unjust to intervene in somebody else's civil war *unless* you are intervening on behalf of the just side, and at its request. Well, the Diem government certainly did request American help, but many questions can be raised about whether it was a minimally just regime. First, it betrayed its pledge to the North, and the international community, to participate in the 1956 elections. The elections were meant to decide the future of the country: to fail to participate was bitter bad faith—violating a pledge and preventing voters from exercising political sovereignty. Second, Diem's regime had clear streaks of corruption, discrimination and authoritarianism, showing lack of respect for human rights, especially those of non-Catholics. Part of this oppression might be explained by the pressure of the civil war, but most experts sensed a real disconnect between Diem and the South Vietnamese people, and they weren't surprised when he was assassinated in 1963, just days before JFK. After Diem, South Vietnam lurched unstably from regime to regime, and people like Walzer argue that this political instability showed that the people of South Vietnam simply didn't endorse American-supported governments. As Walzer puts it: "(T)he continuing dependence of the new regime on the US [was] damning evidence against it ... a government that receives economic and technical aid, military supply, strategic and tactical advice, and is still unable to reduce its subjects to obedience, is clearly an illegitimate government."[33] And armed intervention on behalf of an illegitimate government is not just.

The counter-argument, made by supporters of the war, is that America was indeed responding to an act of aggression: the South may have backed out of the election, but it was the Southern insurgents who first attacked the Southern government with the object of armed conquest in the name of communism. Secondly, there was clear evidence that the North, and China, were involved in creating the political instability in the South. Thus, you cannot use that instability as evidence of the illegitimacy of the Southern regimes:

it doesn't reflect the choices of the Southern people so much as pressure from outsiders. Indeed, the Americans could say they were merely "counter-invading" after the prior invasions of the North and China. Finally, the Diem regime might have been bad, but communism was a terrible form of government, which we all know now was complicit in massive human rights violations. Some of the most terrible mass slaughters of the twentieth century were perpetrated by communist regimes, like Stalin's purges in the 1930s, China's Cultural Revolution in the 1960s and Cambodia's Khmer Rouge "Killing Fields" in the 1970s. Communists believe that only the mass (of workers) has worth, and that individuals themselves have no human rights.[34] What could be more just than trying to save the South Vietnamese from that?

Coming at a final judgment on Vietnam is very difficult, since there are these seriously competing considerations. Civil wars usually are more complicated to figure out than classical inter-state struggles. The cause of resisting communism was compelling, and the North and China were on the scene as early as the Americans were. On the other hand, the election betrayal was major, and Diem's legitimacy was deeply questionable. There is the almost inscrutable issue of popular support—with whom did the people of South Vietnam identify? There is some indication it was with the North. Indeed, Diem arguably betrayed the election pledge *precisely because* he feared a Northern victory. Furthermore, America absolutely pummelled the Viet Cong communists in the late 1960s with massive—probably disproportionate—bombing raids, and over a half-million active US troops in the thin sliver that is Vietnam. It seems to me that the only way the Viet Cong could have survived such an incredible onslaught, from a superpower, was precisely because, as Walzer says, they came to enjoy the support of most of the Vietnamese people. This public support allowed the Viet Cong to engage in the covert attacks and guerrilla tactics that so frustrated conventional US forces: they would strike, and then melt back into villages, farms and cities, where they were provided cover. Another relevant piece of information is this: after the US withdrew in 1973, it took the Viet Cong only one year to control all of Vietnam, and the communists remain firmly in control over thirty years later. Such quick and enduring success seems possible only with considerable public support. One might say the alternative explanation is the sheer force the North Vietnamese, backed by China, brought to bear. It is a difficult call. My own call is that it was probably more the indigenous support factor, which itself was fuelled more by furious anti-colonial sentiment than by any genuine pro-communist feeling. Don't forget that Vietnam had been a colony at that time for more than one hundred years.

This is not to say the current Vietnamese government is legitimate, for the people might not have known what they were getting into and may feel betrayed by the police state communism put into place in the unified Vietnam. Countries, like people, can make bad choices under pressure. But so long as those choices aren't so bad as to justify humanitarian intervention

—to be discussed below—it seems they are free to make them outside of foreign intervention.

In sum, I'm saying that *the Vietnam War was unjust on both sides*: on the American side, owing to South Vietnamese popular support for the non-colonial side and, on the communist side, for aiming at the institution of communism in South Vietnam. The tragedy was that the non-colonial side *was also* the communist side, and so popular support—in a very pressured situation—had a severe downside. The people could not, at the time, get their non-colonial regime without it being communist. Is this like selling yourself into slavery? Perhaps quite so and, odd as it seems, that remains your own choice.

One quote from the Vietnam War which sheds light here is the infamous quip of an ordinary US soldier: "We had to destroy the village in order to save it." This line is often quoted as a kind of dark joke, or else to ridicule the pretensions and naivety of American imperialism. Instead, the quote captures precisely the cruel dilemma of that war: America went into Vietnam to save it from the imposition of communism, ostensibly a just cause. It turns out, however, that the communists had widespread public support—probably not so much because they were communists but because they were Vietnamese and the people were sick of foreign forces—French, Japanese, Americans—ruling them. Plus, the Diem alternative to communism had its own legitimacy issues. So the people sympathized with the communists—who were, admittedly, extremely aggressive and themselves foreign-supplied—and resisted. The ultimate result: destroyed villages all over. To call that kind of destruction just, you need crystal clear justification, not strength on some issues and weakness on others, as in this situation. *When there is no clear justified side, just war theory insists you pronounce the war questionable on both fronts.*

Armed Humanitarian Intervention

The fourth, and final, revision to the classical account of *jus ad bellum* concerns humanitarian intervention, such as occurred in Kosovo in 1999. This is a hotly disputed topic, and the body of international law is nowhere near as settled as it is when it comes to individual and collective self-defence. In general, there is a very strong presumption in international law—going back to Grotius, Pufendorf and Vattel—against any outside interference with the domestic situation of any country, especially interference backed up with the force of arms. But it should be noted that a considerable number of such interventions have nevertheless been authorized by the UNSC, such as in Somalia in 1992–94 and, in a more complex fashion, in the former Yugoslavia in 1992–95. Recall that most international lawyers believe UNSC authorization is absolutely necessary prior to humanitarian intervention.[35]

Humanitarian intervention seems, at first, to pose a special problem for the prevailing aggression-based paradigm, since it involves armed intrusion in a country which has *not* committed aggression against another state. Moreover, such intervention is animated by moral and political ideals which may seem to lack universal endorsement, and thus raise the ugly spectre of violent paternalism on the global stage: "Treat your people the way we think you should, or else feel our wrath."

The only kind of armed humanitarian intervention which Walzer accepts is intervention designed to rescue citizens of a state from "acts that shock the moral conscience of mankind." He is willing to endorse armed humanitarian intervention *only* in cases where the state in question is using military force to engage in wicked and widespread human rights violations. This is the key: I propose we think of such a state as an *"internal aggressor,"* since here too we have the use of rights-violating military force on display. We have a failure to meet the conditions of minimal justice, which in turn renders that state illegitimate and, as it were, attack-able. The International Commission on Intervention and State Sovereignty (ICISS), in its influential 2001 report, comments similarly that protection of a population is a key implication of, and responsibility within, the right to sovereignty. If a state cannot provide such— or, worse, if it itself becomes the threat—then *it is actually consistent with the concept of sovereignty* for others to go in, in order to protect that population.[36]

Walzer is keen, I think correctly, to stress the degree to which the armed human rights violations in question must be "massive" and "terrible," such as incidents of "massacre and enslavement," to ground armed intervention by a foreign power. As examples of justified interventions, Walzer cites Vietnam in Cambodia in the mid-1970s and the North Atlantic Treaty Organization (NATO) in the former Yugoslavia throughout the 1990s.[37] In the Cambodia case, for instance, the unbelievably brutal and bloody Khmer Rouge regime put into operation its "Killing Fields," murdering one million fellow Cambodians deemed to be enemies of the regime, which was attempting to forge an entirely new, severely socialist "utopia."[38] The unified government of Vietnam invaded and overthrew the regime, stopping the "Fields" and all the dislocation and refugees they were producing. In the case of the former Yugoslavia, the countries of NATO—led by America—bombed Serbia in 1995 to make it stop its involvement in massacres of Muslims in such cities as Sarajevo. The bombing is widely credited with forcing Serbia to sign the Dayton Accords, which ended the Bosnian civil war that developed out of Yugoslavia's collapse. (See below for the case study.) When the Serbian regime went back to its old brutal tricks—massacring and forcibly displacing tens of thousands of Muslims (and perhaps many more) in 1999 in Kosovo— NATO again attacked, this time much more aggressively, resulting in a change of regime in Serbia.[39]

Let's comment more on the extent of government brutality which needs to be actual before we can consider armed humanitarian intervention. Faced with what we might call "run-of-the-mill" government insensitivity to some human rights claims (say, non-discrimination), citizens need to take it upon themselves to begin the kind of political activism and struggle needed to win such freedoms and benefits. Self-help is the order of the day; that is part of what we mean by political sovereignty and self-determination. Thus, it is *only* those truly terrible human rights violations which, in Walzer's words, "make talk of community or self-determination … seem cynical and irrelevant" which justify armed humanitarian intervention by a foreign power. In these extreme cases, it is precisely the incapacity for self-determination that draws foreigners in, and rightly so. *The domestic citizenry is not only desperate but doomed without international armed rescue.* Interestingly, Walzer believes that such humanitarian intervention is morally *obligatory*, whereas intervention in a secessionist struggle, or in a civil war, is merely *permissible*. I concur. This sense of obligation in the face of humanitarian catastrophe is clearly displayed when Walzer swears that: "People who initiate massacres lose their right to participate in the normal … processes of domestic self-government. Their military defeat is morally necessary."[40]

Walzer is especially critical of those who, when confronted with such a grave and genuine humanitarian emergency, reason as follows: yes, there is a fire burning and firefighters are probably needed to put it out; but it is not *our* building, so there is no claim on our resources, much less our firefighters. Walzer's effective rejoinder: "[T]he price of sitting and watching is a kind of moral corruption that … [we] must always resist." What about those who argue against intervention not so much out of a misplaced respect for whose turf it is but, rather, out of fears of intervening in a conflict they know little about and of running the risk of making things worse? Walzer answers compellingly: "Of course, every fire has a complicated social, political and economic background. It would be nice to understand it all. But once the burning begins something less than full understanding is necessary: a will to put out the fire—to find fire-fighters, close by if possible, and give them the support they need." Fires like the ethnic cleansing and Muslim massacres in Bosnia in the mid-1990s, or the mass expulsion of Kosovars from Serbia in the late 1990s, require us to "see the fires for what they are: deliberately set, the work of arsonists, aimed to kill, terribly dangerous."[41]

What about those who urge non-intervention, even in such obvious humanitarian catastrophes, on grounds that such might be a slippery slope to imperial aggrandizement—to great powers meddling in vulnerable communities? Walzer's reply is that such is always a risk, but not one so real it justifies wilful non-intervention in a clear humanitarian emergency. The moral balance, between *certain* massacre and *possible* imperialism, is obviously on the side of preventing, or stopping, the massacre. Consider, as Walzer says, that in recent history those countries which have cried out for armed humanitarian intervention—Somalia, Bosnia, Rwanda, Kosovo—haven't exactly been prime pieces of global real estate. The temptation to take another's territory has simply not been there. The deeper answer is that the risks of imperial tinkering are more distant and abstract than the closer and more palpable risks of watching people get murdered when one could have done something about it. The risk far greater than great power meddling or aggrandizement is the moral indifference that leads to non-intervention, even in spite of overwhelming evidence of a grievous and preventable humanitarian tragedy. Rwanda, of course, serves as the most searing and terrible example of this in recent history. In the spring of 1994, almost 800,000 people—again, 800,000 people, in just one season—were slaughtered in an act of near-genocide, and the international community failed to respond effectively. Indeed, it hardly responded at all. Typically, everyone pointed the finger of responsibility and blame at everyone else. Most agree that it was a heinous and deeply shameful event. Some wondered aloud whether, in light of Rwanda, we had actually learned the clearest lessons of The Holocaust.

Perhaps a little bit more on Rwanda, in central Africa, would be insightful. Rwanda, during its colonial days under the rule of Belgium, was dominated by a minority group, the Tutsis. The majority group, the Hutus, resented being dominated and, when independence from Belgium came in 1959, the Hutus turned the tables and took control. Relations between the groups were always tense, and at times broke out into armed conflict between the Hutu-dominated Rwandan Army and the Tutsi-dominated rebel force, the Rwandan Patriotic Front (RPF). In 1993, after several years of fighting, a peace accord and power-sharing arrangement were achieved. Before they could be implemented, Hutu extremists formed private militias to carry out an audacious and murderous plan: not only to destroy the peace accords but to eliminate the Tutsis and even any moderate Hutus who supported peace with the Tutsis. They truly had genocide on their minds: to destroy the Tutsi people. The Hutu extremists seized power in a coup in early 1994, killing the moderate Hutu leadership. While the UN did have a peacekeeping force already in Rwanda, as soon as some of its (Belgian) members were killed in the coup's early days, the UNSC ordered a complete withdrawal—in spite of the pleas of the peacekeeping unit's own commanding officer, Romeo Dallaire. He knew what was going to happen and presented the UN with evidence of a genocidal plot. But all Western troops left the country, taking their own nationals with them. They even closed their embassies. The Hutu extremists had free reign to execute their horrible plan and, by April, had killed about 800,000 people, both Tutsi and Hutu. Most were butchered brutally with machetes or shot at point-blank range with small guns. Fully one-third of all Tutsis on earth were murdered. France, alone amongst Western countries, re-intervened late in June and helped re-establish some sanity (though some say France allowed the perpetrators to leave the country as well). Then—then!—the UNSC voted to return "peacekeeping" forces back to Rwanda.[42]

So concerned has Walzer become over this threat of non-intervention—or even of withdrawing in the face of mass slaughter—that he has actually changed his views about what justice requires of an intervener in an humanitarian emergency. Whereas he used to believe that the goal of a justified intervener was "the in-and-out rule," he now believes more extensive obligations may be involved, and it is important to hear him out. The "in-and-out rule," designed precisely to mitigate the likelihood of great power meddling, called for interveners to focus on "rescue, not rule": to get in, rescue the people who need it, and get out as soon as the rescue has been secured. The goal was to make intervention *as little like* intervention as possible, thereby maximizing space for local self-determination. Now, however, Walzer believes that recent international experience demonstrates that interveners need to make a deeper commitment than simply "in-and-out," and they need to make it explicit even before they go in. On the limits of this deeper commitment, Walzer is vague, if not silent.[43] But its content, I believe, clearly involves some kind of post-intervention assistance in reconstructing the society that required rescue. The question ties into deep perplexities of post-war, or post-conflict, settlement and rehabilitation: issues that are only starting to get the depth of attention and inquiry they deserve. We will return to these vital issues in later chapters. This is all to say, importantly, that those who intervene face an additional burden when it comes to just cause: they must commit themselves, in meaningful fashion, to reasonable aid and assistance in the post-conflict situation. The ICISS puts it thus in its report: "… to provide, particularly after a military intervention, full assistance with recovery, reconstruction and reconciliation, addressing the causes of the harm the intervention was designed to halt or avert."[44]

Note that post-conflict aid and reconstruction is premised on *actually being able* to aid and reconstruct, and this usually means being in a strong position at the end of the intervention. This is a vital point, in light of contemporary experience with humanitarian intervention: *if you go in, you must go in with the goal of winning*. We saw, in America's 1992–93 intervention in Somalia, that a very mild and limited intervention—aimed at separating belligerents and alleviating starvation—was perhaps doomed to fail from the start because the goal was not the military defeat of the culpable side, merely the separation of forces and the interdiction and arrest of one of that side's leaders. As soon as serious resistance was met, the US turned tail and ran.[45] The result? Somalia was no better off than before America intervened. So what did those US troops die for? Even worse, the Somalia failure was almost certainly the real reason why America did not intervene in Rwanda a year later, to the loss and misery of staggering numbers of people. America feared another failure in Africa and thus didn't even risk it the second time around. Inserting a small armed force to try to keep the peace between rival factions *does* have a time and place—notably when the belligerents *agree* to be so separated—but that time and place is *not* during a humanitarian intervention. The side slaughtering the other needs to be *defeated* militarily. The size and strength of the intervening force should be adjusted accordingly, and the terms of engagement (i.e., instructions to soldiers) must be clear, and allow fighting forces to do what they do best and are actually trained to do: pursue victory and force the other side either to surrender or be destroyed. As the ICISS puts it here, effective intervention demands "… clear objectives, clear and unambiguous mandates at all times; and resources to match."[46]

There are some anti-imperialist thinkers who want to say that the interveners must also be freely invited into the country on behalf of the group they are intending to aid. I think this is mistaken, and naïve. Naïve, because it fails to grasp the brutalities under which the victims may be suffering: they may not have meaningful chances to articulate a clear communal petition to the international community while they are running, and fighting, for their lives. Mistaken, because their failure to make a formal request might prevent someone from going in, with the result being a terrible massacre and perhaps even worse. The anti-imperialist position is like saying a cop shouldn't intervene in a gang's brutal street attack on an innocent bystander until she formally requests his help. *From the dreadful deeds alone*, we can infer that the victims of massacre do indeed consent to any intervention on their behalf, at least in the absence of any explicit non-consent. No formal requirement of request seems reasonable here, given the gravity of the threat.

Finally, what of those who object to armed intervention, even in humanitarian catastrophes, on grounds that it is unclear who exactly should bear the duty of intervention? Walzer's reply: the duty to intervene forcibly in cases of humanitarian emergency is admittedly imperfect—it picks out no one specific country. The duty is, rather, borne at large by the international community. This does not, however, imply that only global agencies like the UN have the moral legitimacy to authorize and execute armed rescues in states which remain externally non-aggressive. Walzer submits, and I concur, that *any* state willing to take on the burdens of armed rescue is permitted to do so, provided of course that all the criteria for a just intervention, as here laid out, have been fulfilled. The imperfection of the duty to intervene has caused much of the controversy surrounding armed rescue, since a main temptation in favour of sitting on the sidelines has been a belief—sometimes sincere, sometimes otherwise—that another country, or regional grouping, is better placed to intervene. Walzer has recently grown more accommodating to the idea of experimenting with a global security force, for instance under UNSC auspices, that might one day have responsibility for such actions. Indeed, NATO has recently created a rapid reaction brigade to act in similar fashion within its jurisdiction, which is to say North America and now most of Europe including Turkey. Until we have rapid reaction forces in regions around the world, or else under UNSC control, there seems little prospect for changing from what we already have: an imperfect situation wherein *we must rely on our own moral responsiveness to move in*, where needed, to rescue people from being massacred, enslaved or displaced by their own government. And it is indefensible to suggest that failure to have intervened in one spot (for example in Tibet, or Rwanda) implies that for the sake of some twisted concern for consistency we should fail to intervene everywhere else. The more appropriate response is to regret and condemn our past mistakes— our previous acts of weakness of will—and move ahead to rescue those who need it on a more reliable basis.[47]

BACK TO IRAQ

Now, what of the prior declaration that the strongest justification for America's 2003 war of regime change on Iraq was as an act of armed humanitarian intervention? The war was, after all, labelled "Operation Iraqi Freedom," freedom from the rights-violating brutalities of Saddam's unjust dictatorship. In light of the failure to locate Iraqi WMD, President Bush Jr. himself, in December 2005, boldly re-asserted this justification for the war, claiming: "[W]e are in Iraq today because our goal has always been more than the removal of a brutal dictator. It is to leave a free and democratic Iraq in his place."[48]

I do believe that this *was* the strongest reason available to America but that *doesn't* mean I believe the war was justified. Why? First, there is the requirement to call your shot, defended last chapter. Even if the most traction came from arguing humanitarian intervention, we all know this was *not* the main reason advanced in the run-up to the war in early 2003. The focus was on pre-emptive self-defence for America; and we effectively called that into question above. The fact that America's real reason in going to war was pre-emptive self-defence, I speculate, probably fuelled things like the Abu-Ghraib prison tortures: the wrong reason attracted the wrong intention, and the perception of self-defence (as opposed to other-rescue) motivated and sharpened the treatment of those prisoners in violation of the principle of benevolent quarantine enshrined in *jus in bello* and the Geneva Conventions.[49] *Had the real reason and motive behind the war been the rescue of the Iraqi people, such actions would probably not have occurred.* It was the obsession with pre-emptive self-defence, and getting information about any forthcoming terrorist strikes, which produced them.

Second, even if I *were* to agree that the war was an act of armed humanitarian rescue, all that does is satisfy the just cause criterion. But many criticisms can be made of the other *jus ad bellum* criteria—which *all* must be fulfilled—in this case. Questions can notably be raised regarding whether this war was a last resort, whether proper authorization occurred, whether it was a reasonable and proportionate response to the problem of Saddam's tyranny and, above all, whether the war was animated by the right intentions and had decent probability of success in achieving its aim. In terms of right intention, many have raised the issue of a Bush family animus against Saddam, and Iraq's role as a key world oil and gas supplier. Others have said, much like Walzer's criticism of American intentions during Vietnam, that the war was animated not so much by genuine concern for Iraqi well-being as it was by

Iraq's potential strategic role serving as a Trojan Horse for more acceptable values against the new enemy in the New Cold War: militant Islam. In terms of probability of success, the war did admittedly overthrow Saddam. But whether, as a result, it has improved conditions of peace, security and rights realization for ordinary Iraqis is, so far, not entirely evident.

It might even be wondered whether this was a fitting case of armed humanitarian intervention after all. Saddam was a rights-violating tyrant, to be sure, but his regime was still recognized as the government of Iraq by most of the international community. So did his reign truly "shock the conscience of mankind," as Walzer insists we ask? Further, it is not clear that Saddam was violating the rights of other countries during the run-up to the invasion (though admittedly he had certainly done so in the past). The real problem with his regime, in 2003, concerned domestic human rights satisfaction. Here, serious violations must be noticed—no press or political freedoms, discrimination against non-Sunnis and even rapes, kidnappings and killings of political opponents. This might add up to a case that the Iraqi people were, in fact, "enslaved" by Saddam's regime. I admit it very well might; I'm no apologist for Saddam's Stalinesque hold on Iraq and the utter ruin which his long dictatorship brought to that society. At the same time, it does not seem as though Iraq in 2003 was comparable to the huge-scale massacres of Rwanda in 1994, or Khmer Rouge Cambodia in the 1970s—cases which stand out clearly as humanitarian emergencies needing quick and decisive stopping. It is a judgment call, I concede: my only purpose in raising this point is to stress that it *is* a judgment call, and not a crystal-clear observation with which any reasonable observer must agree. Usually, with armed humanitarian intervention, I think, we want to achieve that degree of overwhelming consensus before we authorize force. Obviously, there was no such consensus with Iraq.

I'm on the record, in this book, as declaring that regimes which fail the conditions of minimal justice are not legitimate and thus have no state rights, including the right not to be attacked and overthrown. It seems as though Saddam's regime violated the condition of making every reasonable effort at domestic human rights satisfaction: who doesn't pass that test if he is allowed to pass? So I admit that Saddam's regime had no right not to be attacked. But one can have the right to do something which it is still not wise, or prudent, or smart to do. My overall judgment is that it is deeply questionable whether America's going to war in 2003 was the best way not merely to remove Saddam but also to create pro-rights realization for the Iraqi people. I think the grim post-war situation so far has revealed this. So, last resort and proportionality questions haunt this war, as does the matter of probability of success.

Summary

In this chapter we finished our look at *jus ad bellum* by examining cases not covered by the classical account, such as civil and guerrilla wars, terrorism, anticipatory attacks and humanitarian rescue. In each case, we detailed reasons for carefully expanding the standard just cause rule to allow for responsible military action. These reasons were, however, kept fundamentally consistent with the essence of just cause, which permits armed force only as resistance to aggression. We suggested, for example, that a regime can commit "internal" aggression against its own people as readily as "external" aggression against foreigners. Non-state actors, like terrorists, can commit aggression, too. It might even, rarely, be consistent with the need to defend people from aggression to make the first strike. Justified military action can be taken in each of the non-standard cases, provided it meets the demanding criteria defended in this chapter, as well as the remaining *jus ad bellum* principles, such as right intention, proper authority, proportionality, and so on.

Case Study: Bosnia

To cap off this chapter, let's consider the West's, and particularly America's, intervention in the Bosnian civil war of 1992–95.[50] This intervention was both intervention in somebody else's civil war, as well as an act of humanitarian rescue. Let's mirror last chapter's case study by putting this complex, non-standard armed intervention to the test, not only in terms of just cause but of the full complement of *jus ad bellum* principles.

Bosnia was part of Yugoslavia. Conflict broke out in the region after the Cold War ended and communism collapsed in Eastern Europe, in 1989–91. As communists fell, new politicians struggled to influence the development of the post-communist era. Some of these leaders found that appealing to traditional ethnic, religious and nationalist loyalties and identities made them powerful. Amongst the strongest of these new leaders was a Serb named Slobodon Milosevic. Serbs traditionally were the dominant group in Yugoslavia, and they made moves to keep it that way in 1989–91. But the forces of nationalism, ethnicity and religion drove the other groups in Yugoslavia, such as the Croats and Slovenes, to want their own separate states. So they broke away from Yugoslavia in 1991, and there were some battles between the new Croatia and Serb-dominated Yugoslavia. Then trouble erupted in Bosnia, a province right in the heart of the old Yugoslavia. Bosnia was somewhat unique in that it contained a mixture of three large ethnic groups: Croats, Serbs and Muslims. Originally, it looked as though Bosnia might just split into three parts, with the Croat part joining the new Croatia, the Serb part remaining with Serb-dominated Yugoslavia and a Muslim-dominated part to retain the name "Bosnia." But the deal fell through, partly because of international pressure to stay together, but mainly because the Serbs backed out of the deal. The Serbian army (i.e., the old Yugoslav army) then moved into Bosnia to prevent the separation of Bosnian Croats and Bosnian Muslims. The Bosnian civil war was then on, between Croats (backed by Croatia), Serbs (backed by Serbia) and Muslims (on their own).

Terrible battles ensued and a process of "ethnic cleansing" took place, according to which groups dominant in one area would, through armed coercion, drive minority groups out of that area—leaving them to go "where they belonged" and leaving behind only members of the dominant group. The result? The part of Bosnia beside Croatia became almost exclusively Croat and the part beside Serbia became almost exclusively Serbian. The Muslims were driven into a handful of cities, notably Tuzla, Srebrenica and Sarajevo. The Serb army was very successful during this 1992–94 period, capturing 70 per cent of Bosnia. Milosevic, now president of Serbia proper, said he wanted to keep the new war gains as part of a "Greater Serbia" and he enjoyed very close ties with Bosnian Serb leaders, such as Radovan Karadzic.

JUST CAUSE. The United Nations (UN) had tried early on to intervene in this process, to no positive effect. In 1991, it slapped an arms embargo on all of former Yugoslavia. Still the war raged. In 1992 UN peacekeepers arrived in Bosnia. They were, however, small in number and poorly armed. So poorly armed, in fact, that they were actually taken hostage by the Serb army several times, to be used as bargaining chips with the UN and sometimes as shields against enemy armed forces. Peace negotiations had begun as early as 1991, but the war was not to end until 1995.

America, frustrated at the UN's impotence—due in some measure to the influence of Russia, a traditional Serb ally—activated the old structure of NATO. America knew that would give them more control. America's just cause in going to war against Serbia and the Bosnian Serbians revolved around two concepts: the minimally just state and humanitarian intervention. In terms of the first, it was clear that Serbia did not have justice on its side. It was the one who sent in the army, first sparking the war. Moreover, Serbia's actions during the war showed that it would not impose a just peace. Serbia, under Milosevic, had quickly grown into an ultra-nationalist, authoritarian regime. Like other such regimes in history, it wanted to aggressively increase its territory—into a "Greater Serbia"—and it also acted to purge its own territory of those not part of the ideal ethnic mould. Hence the ethnic cleansing, some of which produced mass graves of Muslim men—the first mass war graves in Europe since The Holocaust. (Admittedly, the other sides engaged in some ethnic cleansing practices as well.) In terms of the second cause, the Serbs showed repeated, and marked, violent aggression against the Bosnian Muslims in particular. Several times in the war, the Serb army deliberately shelled the Muslim-dominated cities, resulting in tens of thousands of civilian casualties. There were also the mass graves noted above, as well as Serb army rape campaigns against Bosnian Muslim women, and torture and starvation of Bosnian Muslim male prisoners of war (POWs), held in Serb concentration camps.

After a particularly bloody Serb shelling of Sarajevo in 1995, NATO under US command intensively bombed both Bosnian Serbia and Serbia itself. For two weeks, the bombs fell, forcing the Serbs to sign The Dayton Accords, which ended the war. These Accords forced the Serbs to give back land they had conquered, agree to some war crimes trials, and submit to constitutional restructuring—but only in the Serb part of Bosnia, not Serbia itself. (The latter would happen 4–5 years later when Milosevic returned to his ethnic cleansing ways in the Kosovo province of Serbia—this time against ethnic Albanians—forcing NATO into action again, and this time resulting in his overthrow. He was on trial for war crimes, at The Hague in Holland, until his sudden death in March 2006.)

RIGHT INTENTION. Recall that purity of motive is not required here, only that the moral motive actually be present. Whatever else America wanted in intervening, rescuing the Bosnian Muslims from slaughter was clearly on the agenda. Did America want to rub it in the face of Russia, Serbia's traditional ally? Did it want a successful intervention after the failures of Somalia and Rwanda? All these things might be true, but they don't imply failure to meet the condition. America's actions post-war also show that it had no ambitions for controlling Bosnia or Serbia—only preventing slaughter and trying to make institutional changes more conducive to peace.[51]

PUBLIC DECLARATION BY PROPER AUTHORITY. America, a minimally just and legitimate state, publicly declared all its plans and intentions (e.g., to switch from the UN to NATO). The Dayton Accords were likewise fully public, and highly profiled. All America's acts were performed through its own appropriate domestic channels as well. But was America the proper authority? The answer seems to be yes—but only by default. The UN did get involved first, but its intervention was ineffective. The Europeans couldn't get their act together sufficiently to perform on their own, in spite of the fact that it was their own backyard. America was willing to act—at least eventually, when all the evidence of Serb misbehaviour and atrocity piled up to the point where it demanded recognition. America then used the NATO infrastructure, which represented a union between North America and Europe working on a common problem, and other countries such as Canada and Britain joined the force. NATO and America may not have been the obvious choice but became the only one after the UN failed and Europe didn't materialize. We must recall Walzer's principle that, when it comes to humanitarian rescue, *any* state (or collection of such) may act, given the prime importance of saving people from slaughter.

LAST RESORT. If anything, America waited too long to act. The events in Bosnia burned warm and hot for nearly four years before decisive action was taken. So this criterion was met—and may show that, for humanitarian interventions any way, certain requirements *of speed and responsiveness* are implied before all is lost. But, as traditionally stated, this rule was obviously satisfied: multiple negotiations were held; arms embargoes were tried; UN peacekeepers were tried; multiple threats and warnings were issued; and, finally, when the Sarajevo shelling showed the Serbs hadn't changed at all, it was war.

PROBABILITY OF SUCCESS. Serbia might have been a regional power in the Balkans, but it was no match for the United States and NATO. Indeed, it only took two weeks of bombing to bring about surrender. America at the start could have counted on victory, especially since it had learned from Somalia that it had to intervene to win, not just to separate the factions as the UN had failingly attempted. I suppose longer term questions of "success" might be raised, since Milosevic was left in power and another war against his side was necessary four years later regarding Kosovo. That is true, and it highlights the importance of how we should define "success." I think we should leave long-term success for consideration when we reflect on *jus post bellum*, justice after war. When it comes to aiming at success at the start of the war, we need only hold actors to reasonable foresight of the war and its immediate aftermath. In this sense, America could have readily foreseen a successful stop to the slaughter and cleansing, and being able to force a Serb surrender and signature on a reasonable peace agreement in The Dayton Accords.

PROPORTIONALITY. When we see what Milosevic was up to, we can agree with decision-makers at the time that it was proportional to use force. He and his Bosnian Serb cronies were up to aggression, ethnic cleansing, and growing and expanding an ultra-nationalist, authoritarian regime. After they conquered Bosnia, what would be next? The Serbian forces, moreover, conducted themselves with appalling violence—deliberately shelling civilians, starving POWs, and raping women in a systematic way to instil fear and to "reward" themselves. Such a force, morally, had to be stopped. And when it couldn't be stopped with all the other things they tried, it really does seem as if force was the only effective option left. And it turned out better, in the short- and medium term, than what NATO dared hope for—only two weeks worth of bombing, with minimal civilian casualties.

Notes

1. Augustine, *The City of God*, trans. D. Knowles (Harmondsworth: Penguin, 1972), 862.
2. See Appendix A for international law sources.
3. M. Bakunin, *Statism and Anarchy* (Cambridge: Cambridge University Press, 1990).
4. Jim Sterba, ed. *Terrorism and International Justice* (Oxford: Oxford University Press, 2003); Der Spiegel Magazine, *Inside 9/11* (New York: St. Martin's Press, 2002).

5. Some believe, e.g., that the deliberate Allied bombing in 1945 of residential centres in Germany and the atomic bombings of Japan count as acts of terrorism. That would be *democracy's use of terrorism* to serve its ends. While that's very controversial, if you look at the definition it is not totally empty, either. I suppose the issue is whether the intent was to terrorize or, rather, gain revenge. More during the next chapter.

6. Mind you, in the end things turned out badly for Robespierre, getting the guillotine himself. W. Laqueur, *The Age of Terrorism* (Boston: Little Brown, 1987); W. Laqueur, *New Terrorism* (New York: Oxford University Press, 1999).

7. J. Corbin, *Al-Qaeda* (New York: Nation Books, 2002); P. Berman, *Terror and Liberalism* (New York: W.W. Norton, 2003). Thanks to Judy Wubnig for discussions on this.

8. Thanks to an anonymous reviewer, and John Burbidge, for pushing me on this. See also R. Pape's *Dying to Win: The Strategic Logic of Suicide Terrorism* (New York: Random House, 2005). To be crystal clear: as I'll suggest below, terrorism is *always impermissible* but that *doesn't* mean guerrilla warfare is always impermissible. It just rules out one tool that guerrillas have been known to use. We can imagine scenarios where a powerful and unjust aggressor conquers a country and the most effective (indeed, perhaps the only realistic) means of resistance left to the justified victim community is irregular tactics. Such tactics are fine, provided they remain *aimed at the unjust occupier's military forces and not at civilians.*

9. J.B. Eshtain, *Just War Against Terror* (New York: Basic Books, 2003); R. Falk, *The Great Terror War* (New York: Olive Branch Press, 2002).

10. See <www.economist.com/countries/Colombia>.

11. R. Gunaratna, *Inside al-Qaeda* (New York: Berkely Group, 2003).

12. T. Abdullah, *A Short History of Iraq* (Toronto: Pearson, 2003).

13. Gunaratna, *Inside*; Corbin, *Al-Qaeda*.

14. Journalists of Reuters, *The Israeli-Palestinian Conflict* (New York: Reuters, 2002).

15. A. Rashid, *Taliban* (New Haven, CT: Yale University Press, 2001) and M.T. Klare, *Rogue States and Nuclear Outlaws* (New York: Hill and Wang, 1996).

16. M. Walzer, *Just and Unjust Wars* (New York: Basic, 2nd ed., 1991), 74–80. This should especially be noted by those hawkish US commentators already talking up the threat of China to American security—based on speculation of what China might become in 20–50 years.

17. Walzer, *Wars*, 74–85.

18. J. MacMahan, "Preventive War," a chapter in a forthcoming collection on just war theory to be edited by David Rodin and published by Oxford University Press. Thanks to the Press for the advance reading.

19. M. Ignatieff, *The Lesser Evil: Political Ethics in an Age of Terror* (Princeton: Princeton University Press, 2004).

20. *The National Security Strategy of the United States of America.* September 2002, available at <www.whitehouse.gov/nsc/nss.pdf>, p. 15.

21. So I agree with Ignatieff (Note 19) that the post-9/11 era is one where anticipatory attacks might be more permissible but I disagree with him when he says Walzer's criteria are out of date. I always hesitate to agree when people talk about the "dawn of a new age," etc., and the need for completely different principles. Such declarations are too often proven hasty and false. These principles have stood the test of time and can be incorporated into the new risk context.

22. Information for this section comes from W. Murray and R. Scales, Jr. *The Iraq War* (Cambridge, MA: Harvard University Press, 2003); S. Ritter, *War on Iraq* (New York: Profile, 2002); B. Woodward, *Plan of Attack* (New York: Random House, 2004).

23. President George W. Bush, *Public Address*, December 14, 2005. See <www.whitehouse.gov>.

24. *The Congressional Commission Report on the Attacks of 9/11*. (Washington, DC: US Congress, 2004).

25. There was clearer evidence that the Hussein regime provided training camps for members of terrorist groups (such as Hamas) seeking to strike against Israel, and even made a bounty/bereavement payment to families of successful Palestinian suicide bombers.

26. I. Kant, *Perpetual Peace and Other Essays*, trans. T. Humphrey (Indianapolis, IN: Hackett, 1983), 31–2; I. Berlin, *The Crooked Timber of Humanity* (Princeton, NJ: Princeton University Press, 2nd ed., 1998).

27. J. McPherson, *Battle Cry of Freedom* (Oxford: Oxford University Press, 1988).

28. A. Buchanan, *The Morality of Political Divorce* (Boulder, CO: Westview Press, 1991); S. Macedo and A. Buchanan, eds. *Secession and Self-Determination* (New York: New York University Press, 2003).

29. B. Orend, *Michael Walzer on War and Justice* (Montreal, PQ: McGill-Queen's University Press, 2000), 153–79; M. Walzer, *Thick and Thin* (Notre Dame, IN: Notre Dame University Press, 1994); the special 2000 issue on secession in the *Canadian Journal of Law and Jurisprudence*.

30. R. Sheperd, *Czechoslovakia: The Velvet Divorce and Beyond* (New York: St. Martin's, 2000).

31. Walzer, *Wars*, 96–100.

32. Material for this section comes from: S. Karnow, *Vietnam: A History* (New York: Penguin, 1997); G. Herring, *America's Longest War* (New York: McGraw Hill, 4th ed., 2001); R. Regan, *Just War* (Washington, DC: Georgetown University Press, 1996), 136–50.

33. Walzer, *Wars*, 99.

34. B. Orend, *Human Rights: Concept and Context* (Peterborough, ON: Broadview Press, 2002), 162–72; S. Courtois, et al, *The Black Book of Communism* (Cambridge, MA: Harvard University Press, 1999); F. Firet, *The Passing of an Illusion* (Chicago: University of Chicago Press, 1999).

35. See Regan, *Just War*, 179–211 for more on Somalia and Bosnia from a just war perspective. For a detailed look at the international law regarding armed

intervention, see S. Chesterman, *Just War or Just Peace? Humanitarian Intervention and International Law* (Oxford: Oxford University Press, 2001). On the politics of humanitarian intervention, see: N. Wheeler, *Saving Strangers* (Oxford: Oxford University Press, 2003); N. Mills, ed. *The New Killing Fields* (New York: Basic Books, 2002); M. Finnemore, *The Purpose of Intervention* (Ithaca, NY: Cornell University Press, 2003); J. Holzgrefe and R. Keohane, eds. *Humanitarian Intervention* (Cambridge: Cambridge University Press, 2003); S. Hoffmann, ed. *The Ethics and Politics of Humanitarian Intervention* (Notre Dame: Notre Dame University Press, 1997).

36. The International Commission on Intervention and State Sovereignty, *Report: The Responsibility To Protect* (Ottawa: International Development Research Centre, 2001).

37. Walzer, *Wars*, 103–8.

38. B. Kiernan, *The Pol Pot Regime* (New Haven, CT: Yale University Press, 1998).

39. W. Clark, *Waging Modern War: Bosnia, Kosovo and The Future of Combat* (New York: Public Affairs, 2002); T. Judah, *Kosovo: War and Revenge* (New Haven, CT: Yale University Press, 2002).

40. Walzer, *Wars*, 103–8.

41. M. Walzer, "Kosovo," *Dissent* (Summer 1999), 5–7; B. Orend, "Crisis in Kosovo: A Just Use of Force?" *Politics* 19 (1999), 125–30.

42. G. Prunier, *Rwanda: History of a Genocide* (New York: Columbia University Press, 1995); M. Barnett, *Eyewitness to a Genocide: The UN and Rwanda* (Ithaca, NY: Cornell University Press, 2003); L. Melvern, *A People Betrayed: The Role of The West in Rwanda's Genocide* (New York: Zed, 2000); R. Dallaire, *Shake Hands with the Devil* (New York: Random House, 2004).

43. M. Walzer, "Preface to the Third Edition," in his *Just and Unjust Wars* (New York: Basic Books, 3rd edition, 2000), xv.

44. ICISS, *Report*, xi.

45. Regan, *Just War*, 179–211.

46. ICISS, *Report*, 57–68.

47. Walzer, "Preface," xiii–xvi.

48. President George W. Bush, *Public Address*, December 14, 2005. See <www.whitehouse.gov>.

49. Walzer, *Wars*, 127–224.

50. Information for this case study comes from: D. Rieff, *Slaughterhouse: Bosnia and The Failure of The West* (New York: Simon and Schuster, 1995); Human Rights Watch, *Slaughter Among Neighbours* (New Haven, CT: Yale University Press, 1995); R. Holbrooke, *To End a War* (New York: Modern Library, 1999); Clark, *Waging Modern War, passim*; Regan, *Just War*, 192–212.

51. Both Bosnia and Serbia are still undergoing complex institutional changes; it is by no means a resoundingly successful "done deal." Serious challenges remain. For the latest, see <www.bosniapost.com> and <www.serbiapost.com>.

CHAPTER 4

Jus in Bello #1
Just Conduct in War

> "The greatest difficulty in the right of nations
> has to do precisely with right during war;
> it is difficult even to form a concept of this
> or to think of law in this lawless state
> without contradicting oneself."
>
> *Kant*[1]

"*Jus in bello*" is the Latin term just war theorists use to refer to justice *in* war—to right conduct in the midst of battle, after the war has started. Most just war theorists insist that *jus in bello* is an ethical category separate, in some sense, from *jus ad bellum*. Why? We have not finished our task of evaluating warfare once we have determined whether a community has resorted to war justly, using the principles developed in the last two chapters. For even if a state has resorted to war justly, it may be prosecuting that war in an unjustified manner. It may be deploying perverse means in pursuit of its otherwise justified end. Just war theory insists on a *fundamental moral consistency between means and ends* with regard to wartime behaviour.

Concern with consistency, however, is not the only, or even the main, reason behind our endorsement of separate rules regulating wartime conduct. Such rules are also required to limit warfare, to prevent it from spilling over into an ever-escalating, and increasingly destructive, experiment in total warfare. If just wars are limited wars, designed to secure their just causes with only proportionate force, the need for rules on wartime restraint is clear.

All that being said, and sincerely endorsed, I wish to reiterate my conviction that the so-called "separation" between *jus ad bellum* and *jus in bello* is mainly for focusing attention on different issues. It does not denote a complete split between the two, as if they had nothing to do with each other. Indeed, I assert that the three just war categories *must* morally be linked, with *jus ad bellum* setting the tone for all that follows. There is nothing worse, conceptually, than to adopt the "check list" approach to just war theory, as if all the rules and criteria were simply separate "boxes" to be checked off during the war, like ticking off the items on your grocery list as you buy them. The rules and criteria all presuppose shared values, such as: rejecting aggression; restraining warfare; and protecting the state rights of legitimate communities and the human rights of their individual residents. We'll see that we literally cannot make moral sense of some *jus in bello* rules—notably, proportionality—and probably the entire *jus post bellum* category without considering the just cause of the war to begin with.

The best metaphor—regarding just war theory as not segregated but, rather, as united into one long procedure with different phases—is probably something like surgery. You have got, quite literally, an opening phase, an operational phase and a closing phase. Different phases raise different questions and concerns, and there needs to be well-founded and well-understood rules governing each. But everything is connected and substantially affected by what happened prior, and the ruling concern which started the whole process was why surgery was necessary in the first place.

As for the sewing up and the post-surgery rehabilitation, we have the future *jus post bellum* chapters. For now, we inaugurate the operational phase. We have diagnosed the need for surgery, have made our cut and gone in. We're in the thick of it: now what do we do? This is the topic of *jus in bello*.

We can distinguish profitably between external and internal *jus in bello* rules. The external rules concern how a state, in the midst of war, should conduct itself regarding the enemy state and its civilians (and/or the enemy non-state actor). The internal rules, by contrast, concern how a state, in the midst of war, should treat its own citizens, be they soldiers or civilians.

Before examining and explaining these rules, it is worth stressing how responsibility for fulfilling *jus in bello* differs from the responsibility inhering in *jus ad bellum*. Responsibility for the justice of resorting to war, we saw, rests on those key members of the governing party most centrally involved in the decision to go to war, particularly the head of state or any body authorized to declare war. Responsibility for the conduct of war, by contrast, rests on the state's armed forces. In particular, responsibility for right conduct rests with those commanders, officers and soldiers who command and control the lethal force set in motion by the political hierarchy. In general, anyone involved in formulating and executing military strategy during wartime bears responsibility for any violation of *jus in bello* standards. In most cases, such violation will constitute a war crime. Detailed discussion of war crimes trials will be reserved for Chapter 6.

The External Rules

DISCRIMINATION AND NON-COMBATANT IMMUNITY

The requirement of discrimination and non-combatant immunity is the most important *jus in bello* rule. It is also the most frequently, and stridently, codified rule within the international laws of armed conflict.[2] The substance of the rule is this: soldiers charged with the deployment of armed force may not do so indiscriminately; rather, they must exert every reasonable effort to discriminate between legitimate and illegitimate targets. How are soldiers to know which is which? *A legitimate target in wartime is anyone or anything engaged in harming.* All non-harming persons, or institutions, are thus ethically and legally immune from direct and intentional attack by soldiers and their weapons systems. Since the soldiers of the enemy nation, for instance, are clearly engaged in harming, they may be directly targeted, as may their equipment, their supply routes and even some of their civilian suppliers. Civilians not engaged in the military effort of their nation may not be targeted with lethal force. In general, as Michael Walzer asserts: "A legitimate act of war is one that does not violate the rights of the people against whom it is directed."[3] In response, we might ask: how is it that armed force directed against soldiers does not violate their rights, whereas that directed against civilians violates theirs? In the chaos of wartime, what exactly marks the difference?

One of the murkiest areas of Walzer's just war theory concerns the moral status of ordinary soldiers. His references to them exhibit, on the one hand, a humane sympathy for their "shared servitude" as "the pawns of war." On the other, his references occasionally display something like a glib callousness, as when he concurs with Napoleon's (in)famous remark that "soldiers are made to be killed."[4] How can soldiers be made to be killed when, as human beings, they enjoy human rights, to security amongst other things? The answer must be that soldiers do something which causes them to forfeit their rights, much as an outlaw country forfeits its state rights to non-interference when it commits aggression. One could be forgiven for inferring, from this principle, that *only soldiers of an aggressor nation* forfeit their rights, since they are the only ones engaged in the kind of rights-violating harm which grounds a violent, punitive response. Interestingly, and perhaps problematically, Walzer denies this. He believes that *all* soldiers forfeit their right not to be targeted with lethal force, whether they be of just or unjust nations, whether they be tools of aggression or instruments of defence.[5]

The Moral Equality of Soldiers?

Walzer's concept here, which is widely accepted, is of "the moral equality of soldiers." The first "war right" of all soldiers is to kill enemy soldiers: this is indeed part of international law. We do not, and should not, make soldiers pay the price for the injustice of the wars they may be ordered—perhaps even conscripted—to fight. That is the logically and morally separate issue of *jus ad bellum*, for which we have already elaborated a theory of justice, focusing on the responsibilities of political leaders. But lawyers like the chief British prosecutor during the Nuremberg trials, and philosophers like Thomas Pogge, ask: why shouldn't we hold soldiers responsible for the justice of the wars they fight? If we held soldiers responsible in this regard, wouldn't that constitute *an additional bar against aggressive war*? Wouldn't that account for the fact that, even though the war was set in motion by others, soldiers remain its essential executors? Wouldn't such a move impose and highlight an important responsibility for soldiers, namely, to refuse to participate in the prosecution of aggressive war?[6]

Walzer experiences difficulty answering this argument fully. As an opening gambit, he contends that soldiers "are most likely to believe that their wars are just." But this alone cannot justify their actions, since their beliefs may not be well-grounded, especially considering the incentive they.have to believe such justification in the first place. Walzer also says that soldiers rarely fail to fight, owing to "(t)heir routine habits of law-abidingness, their fear, their patriotism [and] their moral investment in the state."[7] But the fact that soldiers rarely fail to fight does not demonstrate that they are always justified in fighting, especially if the cause is unjust. Walzer next suggests that knowledge about the justice of the wars soldiers fight is "hard to come by." This is a truly surprising claim from a just war theorist who has tried to make such knowledge more accessible and comprehensible. Perhaps, then, this is a reference to the soldier's historical lack of education, as well as to government tendencies towards secrecy. Fair enough, but ignorance at best constitutes an excuse, and not a justification, for willfully fighting in an unjust war: it seems a stretch to assert that such ignorance can morally ground a "war right" to deliberately kill enemy soldiers. Walzer's subsequent move appeals to the authority of Vitoria, who suggested that if soldiers were allowed to pick and choose the wars they were willing to fight, the result would be "grave peril" for their country.[8] (This argument has recently been endorsed by the Israeli government, which has found itself in Israeli courts being sued by a handful of its own soldiers, who do not want to fight in the ongoing struggle with the Palestinians. Israel has a system of compulsory military service for all citizens.) But this empirical generalization is specu-lative: why wouldn't the result actually be the preferred one, namely, that states would be seriously hampered *only* in their efforts to prosecute an aggressive war, which they could not justify to their soldiery?

Walzer then claims it is a plain fact of sociology that we do not blame soldiers for killing other soldiers in the midst of war. We blame soldiers *only* when they deliberately kill either civilians or surrendered enemy soldiers kept by them as disarmed prisoners of war (POWs). We extend to all soldiers, in the midst of battle, the right to deploy armed force on behalf of their own country. This *is* a true legal contention—equal belligerent rights seem estab-lished by international law[9]—and while it is not an implausible moral one, the latter is not quite so obvious as Walzer suggests. Do we really believe that those soldiers who fought for Hitler, for example, were utterly blameless for their bit part in the execution of his mad aggression? No doubt, we tend to exonerate conscripts like the Hitler Youth in the closing days of the war, presuming they were far too young, gullible and propagandized to have made a morally responsible choice. But what about those mature German soldiers

—many with prior war experience—who invaded Poland, or France, at the war's outset? It is not so clear to me that we do not blame them for fighting on behalf of their country. Indeed, today, ex-soldiers, living abroad, who played very small roles in Hitler's army can, if found out, be stripped of their citizenship and deported back to Germany—even in spite of their very advanced age.

Walzer stresses more generally the pervasive socialization of soldiers of *any* nation, their relative youth, their frequent conscription, and their usual background as members of underprivileged classes as grounds for not holding soldiers responsible for the wars they fight. While soldiers "are not ... entirely without volition," he says, "(t)heir will is independent and effective only within a limited sphere." This sphere contains only those tactics and manœuvres soldiers are engaged in, like training, loading their weapons, engaging in particular live-fire skirmishes, handling prisoners, and so on. It would thus constitute unfair "class legislation" for us to hold soldiers like these responsible for the justice of the wars they fight. We should focus on those most to blame, the elite and powerful leaders who set the war in motion.[10] But from the fact that political leaders are, I admit, *mostly* to blame for the crime of aggression, does it follow that they are *solely* to blame, as Walzer here insists? In my view, the more compelling alternative would be to suggest that, for the many reasons Walzer mentions, there should be *a presumption against* holding soldiers responsible for the crime of violating *jus ad bellum*. But this presumption does *not* preclude us from concluding, in particular cases based on public evidence: that some soldiers of a particular aggressor state either *did* know, or *really should have* known, about the injustice of the war they were fighting; that they could have refused to participate in it; and thus that they may be held responsible, albeit with much lesser penalties than the elites. Such soldiers would be like minor accomplices to a major crime. This is one way in which I do not believe in the absolute separateness of *jus ad bellum* and *jus in bello*.

Soldiers who fight for an aggressor do not have strict moral equality with those who fight for a victim or defender. The former are not mainly to blame for the aggression but they still *are* to blame, in a smaller but material sense. Soldiers are not automatons. Their merely professional function does not dislodge the ordinary human duty not to inflict severe, unjustifiable harm on others. Soldiers must inform their beliefs regarding the justice of the wars they are ordered to fight. Exceptional ones, upon seeing injustice, will refuse service, or else surrender to the other (just) side at the first non-life-threatening opportunity. Ordinary soldiers, when confronted with the fact that the war they fight is unjust, will probably still go along with the crowd of their buddies and fight—the pressures to do so are very strong. For them, we reserve the moral right to criticize and castigate them at war's end. Perhaps we will finally excuse them, on the basis of these pressures, but perhaps also, in some well-documented cases, we will have to prosecute them as minor accomplices to the one large "crime against peace" which is aggression.[11]

Engaging in Harm

Even if we agree with my proposal that some soldiers may be held responsible for *jus ad bellum* violations, can we still concur with the idea that all soldiers *generally* remain legitimate targets during wartime? After several false starts, Walzer offers us a compelling reason to do so: soldiers, whether just or unjust, are "engaged in harm." Soldiers bear arms effectively, are trained to kill for political reasons, and are "dangerous men": they pose serious threats to the lives and interests of those they are deployed against, whether for a just cause or no. Walzer suggests that an armed man trying to kill me "alienates himself from me ... and from our common humanity" and in so doing he forfeits his right to life. This establishes, I believe, a strong *prima facie* (i.e., "first glance") case that soldiers are justified in targeting other soldiers with lethal force. Soldiers, whether for just or unjust reasons, remain among the most serious and standard external threats to life and vital interests. Only public, compelling and accessible knowledge about the injustice of the cause of his own country can undermine a soldier's entitlement, in the face of such an opposing threat, to respond in kind.[12]

The converse of this general principle, of course, is that those who are not "engaged in harm" cannot be legitimate targets during wartime. *This is the clearest sense of who is "innocent" in wartime: all those not engaged in creating harm.* The first application of this converse rule regarding harm has to do with soldiers themselves: when soldiers no longer pose serious external threats—notably by laying down their weapons and surrendering—they may no longer be targeted with force and should, in fact, be extended what international law calls "benevolent quarantine" for the duration of the war.[13]

Benevolent Quarantine and Torturing Terrorists

"Benevolent quarantine" means that captured enemy soldiers can be stripped of their weapons, incarcerated with their fellows, and questioned verbally for information. But they cannot, for example, be tortured during questioning. Nor can they be beaten, starved or somehow medically experimented on. They cannot be used as shields between oneself and the opposing side; in fact the understanding is that captured enemy soldiers are to be incarcerated far away from the front lines. Very basic medical and hygienic treatment is supposed to be offered—things like Aspirin, soap, water and toothbrushes— and, while making captives engage in work projects is permitted, the Geneva Conventions actually require that, in that event, captives be paid a modest salary. I have never heard of that actually happening—the incredible detail of the Geneva Conventions means they do not always get realized—but it is fairly common for combatants to disarm, house and feed their captives, keeping them out of harm's way and ensuring their basic needs are met until the war ends. When it is all over, they are then usually freed in exchange for POWs on the other side.[14]

Controversies here focus around when, or if, aggressive questioning becomes a form of torture, and also around when non-state actors, like terrorists, are taken prisoner. The latter issue concerns whether non-state captives deserve the same quality of treatment as state captives. There's a sense that a soldier fighting for his community deserves better than a terrorist fighting for his pet cause. I think this distinction can be difficult to sustain and that, generally, non-state actors brought into capture by soldiers should be accorded the same rights as captured enemy soldiers. If soldiers fighting for an *unjust* cause deserve this treatment, then surely so do terrorists—whose method, if not the cause, is likewise unjust. In other words, if it is wrong to torture Nazi soldiers—whose cause was heinous and irredeemable—then it is wrong to torture radical Islamic terrorists (much less mere suspects). This topic has recently been highlighted regarding America's round-up of alleged terrorists, some of whom were held for intensive questioning in Guantanamo Bay, Cuba over a long period of time.[15]

The incidents in Abu Ghraib prison, in Iraq, also come to mind. In the late spring of 2004, the world saw some shocking photos of American troop conduct in that jail. Iraqi prisoners—captured during the war and the subsequent insurgency—were subjected to questionable treatment. Some of it—like deliberate, prolonged sleep deprivation, and using dogs to attack or threaten already prone and naked people—clearly violated the Geneva Conventions. Others might have been visually disturbing but do not obviously count as human rights violations, such as forcing the prisoners to wear dog collars, or having American women ridicule their private parts, or putting female panties on their faces temporarily. Combine it all, though, and you have a violation of both the letter and the spirit of the principle of benevolent quarantine. Some of the US soldiers involved have since been charged, tried and sentenced (which I would argue shows official American acceptance of the idea that non-state captives deserve the same treatment as state captives).

There is, at writing, an ongoing investigation as to whether any authorization of this treatment came from higher up the US chain of command. It does seem unlikely, after all, that some "mere" reservists would repeatedly conduct such flagrant prisoner abuse on their own, and apparently there was a vaguely-defined policy of "softening up" prisoners for subsequent anti-terrorist questioning by the CIA. Perhaps the very vagueness of such a policy was itself a moral error, even if direct orders did not explicitly authorize prisoner abuse.[16]

I suppose we might condone efforts at psychological pressure—mocking, aggressive cross-examination, ridiculing, criticizing, etc.—when the goal is getting information which might save innocent lives. Questioning is, after all, permitted under the Geneva Conventions. But the infliction of physical harm cannot be, even if it supposedly serves the questioning process and is glamourized by such TV shows as "24." Why? Because it is impossible to square the infliction of physical *harm* with the concept of *benevolent* quarantine. Benevolent quarantine may not mean actually being nice to your prisoners but it certainly cannot, logically, include things the Geneva Conventions define as torture: prolonged sleep deprivation; starvation; slapping, punching, biting or strangling; the breaking or severing of limbs or digits; urging or allowing an animal to attack; any kind of drowning-based, or electrocution-based, session; sexual assault or rape; poisoning or medical experimentation; shooting; and so on. These things are simply prohibited. Not even war—not even a *just* war—can justify the deliberate infliction of such things upon other human beings, even if such people are suspected, or even guilty, of terrible things themselves. In domestic society, we do not permit prison guards to torture anyone—even those convicted of the very worst crimes. So why should we allow it in international society? The thing to do with terrorist suspects is to question them within the rules, and then prosecute them for war crimes and, upon conviction, send them to jail—not to strip them, beat them and sick dogs after them. Dare I say, such activities are not only unjust but against the very self-perception of being "civilized" on the part of the forces and countries engaged in these activities. To speak more frankly, that's just not the American way. The forces of civilization must remain civilized even as they confront ruthless barbarism.[17]

As important as it is to prevent future terrorist attacks and to protect innocent lives torture is universally agreed to be one of the very worst things a person can do. Torture is everywhere banned in the laws of war and human rights law.[18] The methods cause revulsion and disgust—as we saw in the worldwide reaction to the Abu Ghraib photos. Torture also hardens the heart and corrupts the character of the torturer. It inflicts absolutely devastating pain upon the tortured—who must endure not only the raw pain of the act(s) but also the experience and knowledge of being utterly enslaved to the whims of another. Torture inflicts severe pain, combines slavery with violence, disregards human autonomy and even renders the torturer worse off. It is, as a method, intrinsically corrupt and even evil. Moreover, torture is extremely questionable as an information-gathering device because evidence shows that people will say *anything*—even deny things they know are true, and assert things they know are false—just to get the torture to stop. Torture is not the answer to terrorism; it is a surrender to a world of brutality and barbarism—a world where the terrorist already resides. I'm not saying torture and terrorism are morally equivalent—presumably torture is more discriminating and localized than terrorism. What I am saying is that, as methods, they are both wrong—*always*—and ultimately indefensible regardless of the cause they supposedly serve.[19]

Civilian Immunity

The second application of the harm principle deals with civilians. Even though some civilians may inwardly approve, or even have voted in favour of, an unjust war effort, they nevertheless remain externally non-threatening. They do not bear arms effectively, nor have they been trained to kill, nor have they been deployed against the lives and vital interests of the opposing side. Civilians, whatever their *internal* attitude, are not in any *external* sense dangerous people. So they may not be made the direct and intentional objects of military attack.[20] Although I endorse this conclusion, it remains controversial with others.

Some people—including Osama bin Laden[21]—argue that the fact that civilians' taxes fund the military renders null and void any pretence of their being "innocent." Civilians are *causally involved* in financing the harm soldiers do. Others view nationality as shared destiny, or suggest that modern warfare is totalizing anyway and so wonder what the point of discrimination really is in our age. If you're at all in the enemy country, you're fair game.[22] These are not trivial arguments but they fail to persuade. It is hard to see, for example, how infants and young children could be anything other than innocent during wartime. Only the most dogmatic believer in collective responsibility could deny this, and then at the cost of his credibility. Just because a baby—through no fault of her own—happens to live in the enemy country, she's fair game? Even though she's not even old enough to be morally responsible for anything? It makes no sense, and amounts to stupidity for the sake of simplicity.

And the relationship between paying one's taxes and the execution of military acts remains, on an individual level anyway: 1) *coerced*, since taxes are everywhere mandatory; and 2) *extremely indirect*, with manifold agents, transfers and responsibilities intervening in-between. The degree to which the state is centrally involved in this coercion and transfer process—of taxes-to-warfare—renders *it* clearly the vastly larger, indeed the only, concrete permissible target. The state—its agents and appendages—is the main organizer and focal point of warfare. It always has been and always will be. It is thus *the* legitimate target and no attempt to "fuzzify" the difference between a government and its people can overcome this. Belligerents target civilians in warfare *not* because they think the people deserve it but, rather, because they think this will give them leverage against the state, which remains the armed, potent threat—the true adversary and target. It is sort of like kidnapping a rich man's family to force *him* to pay you blackmail: give in, or your favourite innocents get it! Just war theory and international law command, by contrast, that you may only attack the true adversary in warfare (i.e., that entity directly engaged in physical harm).

There is, moreover, little evidence that modern warfare is intrinsically totalizing: the 1991 Persian Gulf War, for instance, or the 2001–03 takedowns of the regimes in Afghanistan and Iraq, did not escalate into indiscriminate slaughters. Indeed, what seems more the recipe for ever-increasing slaughter is the idea that civilians may be targeted as readily as soldiers. No doubt there are some questions about the exact specification of "innocents" in wartime but I follow just war theory and international law in believing that it remains a crucial just war category, needed *not only to restrain violence* but also to express our strong, almost foundational, moral commitment to *punish only those who deserve it*. In the midst of "the fog of war," one of the most concrete and verifiable ways to cash out this concept is to define it in terms of external engagement in serious harm. In the midst of war, we cannot peer into the hearts of every civilian; we can only look sweepingly at external behaviour. When we do so, we notice a large and obvious difference between those engaged in harm (i.e., those in the war machine) and those not. Since harm is an important concept for justice and morality, it makes sense to say that it establishes a dividing line between those who may, and those others who may not, be targeted with force.[23]

Difficulties arise, of course, when we consider those people who seem, simultaneously, to be *both* civilians *and* engaged in harming, such as civilian suppliers of military hardware. What is the status of such people? Walzer suggests that "the relevant distinction is ... between those who make what the soldiers need to fight and those who make what they need to live like all the rest of us." So targeting farms, schools and hospitals is illegitimate, whereas targeting munitions factories is legitimate. Walzer stresses, however, that civilians engaged in the military supply effort are legitimate targets *only when they are engaged in that effort*, so to target them while at home in residential areas would be illegitimate: "Rights to life are forfeit only when particular men and women are actually engaged in war-making or national defence." Consider Thomas Nagel's further explanation that "hostile treatment of any person must be justified in terms of something *about that person* [his italics] which makes the treatment appropriate." We distinguish combatants from non-combatants "on the basis of their immediate threat or harmfulness." And our response to such threats and harms must be governed by relations of directness and relevance. It is only military—and military-related—targets which pose a *direct* and *relevant* threat of serious harm; thus, it is only they which may be resisted with lethal force.[24]

Walzer's overall judgment on targeting—which is very helpful, and essentially condenses international law—is this: soldiers may target other soldiers, their equipment, their barracks and training areas, their supply and communications lines and the industrial sites which produce their supply. Presumably, core political and bureaucratic institutions are also legitimate objects of attack, in particular things like the Defence Ministry. Illegitimate targets include residential areas, schools, hospitals, farms, churches, cultural institutions and non-military industrial sites. *In general, anyone or anything not demonstrably engaged in military supply or military activity is immune from direct attack*. Walzer is especially critical of targeting basic infrastructure, particularly food, water, medical and power supplies. He criticizes American conduct during the 1991 Persian Gulf War on this basis, since very heavy damage was inflicted on Iraq's water treatment system, and presumably would also frown upon NATO's targeting the Serbian electric power grid during its 1999 armed intervention on behalf of the ethnic Albanian Kosovars. The aim there had very little to do with bona fide military tactics; it was a raw demonstration of sheer power designed to "shock and awe" the enemy into submission with an overwhelming display of capability. And that it did: the Serbs could not turn on a toaster, watch TV, heat their homes, run their businesses, etc., unless NATO said so. You can see how this would give the Serbs rather strong incentive to please NATO.[25] While it is true that soldiers cannot fight well without food, water, medicine and electricity, those are things they—and everyone else in their society, including innocents—require *as human beings* and not more narrowly as externally threatening instruments of war. Thus, the moral need for a direct and relevant response only to the source of serious harm renders these things ethically immune from attack.

The Doctrine of Double Effect

Another serious perplexity about wartime targeting concerns the close real-world proximity of illegitimate civilian targets to legitimate military and political ones: munitions factories, after all, are often side-by-side with non-military factories, and at times just around the corner from schools and residential areas. This raises the complex issue of the Doctrine of Double Effect (DDE).[26] The core moral problem is this: even if soldiers intentionally aim *only* at legitimate targets, they can often *foresee* that taking out some of these targets will still involve *collateral* civilian casualties. And if civilians do nothing to lose their human rights, doesn't it follow that such acts will be unjust, since civilians will predictably suffer some harm or even death?

The DDE stipulates that an agent A may perform an action X, even though A foresees that X will result in *both* good (G) and bad (B) effects, *provided all* of the following criteria are met: 1) X is an otherwise morally permissible action; 2) A only intends G and not B; 3) B is not a means to G; and 4) the goodness of G is worth, or is proportionately greater than, the badness of B. The DDE, at first, can seem overly technical, and thus for some people "fishy." But it is an idea rendered complex by the complexity of the situation it deals with. Since it is a common wartime situation, however, we cannot avoid it. Let's break it down. It is a doctrine of "double effect" since it deals with actions which are going to have two effects, one good and one bad. It seeks to respond to the question: "Can one ever perform such an action?" It answers "yes," provided the criteria just listed are *all* satisfied; if even one criterion fails to be satisfied, the doctrine forbids the performance of the action. Assume now, using these criteria, that A is an army and X is an otherwise permissible act of war, like taking aim with a weapon at a military target. The good effect G would be destroying the target, the bad effect B any collateral civilian casualties. The DDE stipulates that A may still do X, provided that A only intends to destroy the military target and not to kill civilians; that A is not using the civilian casualties as means to the end of destroying the military target; and that the importance of hitting the target is worth the collateral dead.

The first objection commonly raised against the DDE concerns its controversial distinction between *intending* Z's death (or harm) and *merely foreseeing* that one's actions will result in Z's death (or harm). Some have argued that the DDE is so elastic as to justify anything: all an agent has to do, to employ its protective moral cloak, is to assert: "Well, I did not intend *that*; my aim, rather, was this…" It is clear, however, that agents are not free to claim whatever good intention they want in order to justify their actions, however heinous. Intentions must meet minimal criteria of *logical coherence* and, moreover, must be *connected to patterns of action* which are publicly accessible. The criminal justice system of most countries is based on these ideas: for such serious crimes as murder, the case must be made by the prosecution that the accused had *mens rea*, or the intent to kill. This is done by offering publicly-accessible evidence which is tied to the accused's actions, behaviour and assertions leading up to the time of the murder. Also needed is a consideration of whether the accused had both incentive and motive to commit the crime. Juries, as reasonable and experienced persons, are then invited to infer the accused's state of mind. The plausibility of this procedure undermines the popular academic claim that the DDE can be used to justify *any* heinous action, whether in war or peace. Walzer agrees, suggesting that *we know the intentions of agents through their actions*: "(T)he surest sign of good intentions in war is restraint in its conduct." In other words, when armies fight in strict adherence to *jus in bello*—taking aim only at legitimate targets, using only proportionate force, not employing intrinsically heinous means—they cannot meaningfully be said to intend the deaths of civilians killed collaterally. Their actions, focusing on military targets and taking due care that civilians not be killed, reveals their intentions.[27]

What exactly constitutes "due care" by armies that civilians not be killed during the prosecution of otherwise legitimate military campaigns? For Walzer, it involves soldiers accepting more risks *to themselves* to ensure that they hit only the proper targets: "We draw a circle of rights around civilians, and soldiers are supposed to accept (some) risks in order to save civilian lives." Walzer suggests we locate the limits of additional risk-taking—that soldiers can and should shoulder on behalf of those civilians they endanger— at that point where "any further risk-taking would almost certainly doom the military venture or make it so costly that it could not be repeated."[28] This principle might entail, for instance, that soldiers use only certain kinds of weapons and avoid others. America has recently pioneered the use of so-called "smart bombs" that use satellite technology to improve drastically the "hit rate" on desired targets. America also employs laser- and satellite-guided cruise missiles, which can be exceptionally precise (and are exceptionally expensive). Compare these advances with the older method of simply flying over a target, dumping one's bomb load, and beating a hasty retreat before getting shot down.

The due care principle might also mean moving in more closely on the military target to increase the likelihood of hitting it, and avoiding collateral civilian damage. America encountered criticism, in this regard, during the armed intervention in Serbia over Kosovo in 1999. Some, such as Michael Ignatieff, contended that the extensive bombing was not really that "smart," and that too much of it came from too high a distance. In other words, the participating American pilots were *willing to kill but not willing to risk dying*—and in opposition to the due care principle they actually went out of their way to increase the distance between themselves and their targets. This is permissible activity, in my view, only if one's bombing payload is not conventional explosives—with their disturbingly high rate of collateral damage—but, rather, reliable smart technology. If one's payload is otherwise, Ignatieff's criticism is both sound and scathing: it is a violation of the warrior ethos itself.[29]

Although this might sound silly at first, the due care principle might also, under certain conditions, require some kind of advance warning to nearby civilians. Consider, for example, that the Israeli military occasionally does this. Say it decides to destroy a building which it believes serves as a haven for pro-Palestinian terrorists. If this building is in a residential area, the Israeli military has sometimes been known to announce publicly its intent to destroy this target, declaring that civilians left in the area at the declared time will not be its responsibility. This warning might, admittedly, allow terrorists to escape with valuable equipment, but the Israelis still believe it important to destroy military-use targets while showing clear respect for civilians.[30]

What the due care principle implies, above all else, is this: *offensive tactics and manœuvres must be carefully planned, in advance, with a keen eye towards minimizing civilian casualties.* This demands competent and well-trained officers and soldiers, as well as the need to gather and analyze quality intelligence on the precise nature of suspected targets. While Kant thought spying morally decrepit since it involves deception, I argue that: a) with advances in technology, intelligence gathering need not involve deception; and b) in any event, intelligence gathering can serve the vital ethical need of being more precise in targeting, knowing what to hit and what is out of bounds.[31]

So Walzer, in the end, maintains that civilians are *not* entitled to some implausible kind of fail-safe, or absolute, immunity from attack; rather, they are owed neither more nor less than this "due care" from belligerent armies. Providing due care is, in fact, equivalent to "recognizing their rights as best we can within the context of war." These exact conclusions are also contained in the laws of armed conflict.[32]

We have seen explanations of the first two, of the four, criteria of the DDE. What about the third, regarding the prohibition on the use of the bad effects (like civilian casualties) to produce the good ones (like eliminating the military target)? An example of such a violation would be deliberately bombing the residential area around a munitions factory on grounds you're probably killing the workers in that factory, hence using civilian targeting to effectively eliminate a military target. It seems possible to discern whether a belligerent, such as country C, is employing civilian casualties as a means both to its immediate end of hitting the legitimate target and to its final end of victory over rival country D. If there are systemic patterns—as opposed to unavoidable, isolated cases—of civilian bombardment by C on the civilians of D, it is compelling to conclude that C is directly targeting the civilian population of D. Conversely, if the systemic pattern of C's war-fighting indicates its targeting of D's military capabilities, with only incidental and occasional civilian casualties resulting, then it is reasonable to infer that C is not trying to use civilian casualties as a pressure tactic to force D to retreat and admit defeat.

The truly difficult aspect of the DDE, in my view, is the final criterion: contending that the goodness of hitting the legitimate military target is "worth," or proportional to, the badness of the collateral civilian casualties. A pacifist, for example, will always deny this. Is the need to hit a source of military harm *sufficient* to justify killing people whom just war theory admits have done nothing to deserve death? Does the source of harm have to pass some threshold of threat before one can speak of the need for its destruction outweighing civilian claims? If so, how to locate that threshold? More sharply, can one refer to the ultimate "worth" of hitting the military target to justify collateral civilian casualties *without* referring to the substantive justice of one's involvement in the war to begin with? Personally, I fail to grasp how it can be morally justified to foreseeably kill innocent civilians in order to hit a target which only serves the final end of an aggressive war. The *only* justification sufficient, in my mind, for the collateral civilian casualties would be that the target is materially connected to victory in an otherwise *just* war. This suggests, importantly, that aggressors not only violate *jus ad bellum*, but *in so doing* face grave difficulties meeting the requirements of *jus in bello* as well. To be as clear as possible: to satisfy the *jus in bello* requirement of discrimination, a country when fighting must satisfy all elements of the DDE. But it seems that only a country fighting a just war can fulfil the proportionality requirement in the DDE. Thus, an aggressor nation fighting an unjust war, *for that very reason*, also violates the rules of right conduct. Here too we see that the traditional insistence on the separateness of *jus ad bellum* and *jus in bello* is not sustainable. Kant was more correct when he remarked on the need for a consistent normative thread that runs through all conduct during the three phases of war: beginning, middle and end.[33]

PROPORTIONALITY

The *jus in bello* version of proportionality mandates that soldiers deploy only proportionate force against legitimate targets. The rule is not about the war as a whole; it is about tactics within the war. Make sure, the rule commands, that the destruction needed to fulfil the goal is proportional to the good of achieving it. The crude version of this rule is: do not squash a squirrel with a tank, or swat a fly with a cannon. *Use force appropriate to the target.* Walzer is as uncertain about this requirement as he was about its *jus ad bellum* cousin, and there is reason to follow him in this regard. He notes that while the rule is rightly designed to prohibit "excessive harm" and "purposeless or wanton violence" during war, "there is [nevertheless] no ready way to establish an independent or stable view of the values" against which we can definitively measure the costs and benefits of a tactic. One case where he talks about, and endorses, a form of proportionality involves the Persian Gulf War. During the War's final days in early 1991, there was a headlong retreat of Iraqi troops from Kuwait along a road, subsequently dubbed "The Highway of Death." So congested did that highway become that, when American forces descended upon it, it was a bloodbath whose aftermath was much photographed and publicized. Although the Iraqi soldiers did not surrender, and thus remained legitimate targets, Walzer suggests that the killing was "too easy." The battle degenerated into a "turkey shoot," and thus the force deployed was disproportionate. Perhaps another example, from the other side of the same war, would be Saddam Hussein's very damaging use of oil spills and oil fires as putative means of defence against a feared amphibious invasion of Kuwait by the Allies.[34] As with the *jus ad bellum* case, we note that it is much easier to diagnose a *disproportionate* use of force than a merely proportionate one. The common sense of the abstract need for balance and moderation is clearly there, but it remains very difficult to define precisely, especially under battlefield conditions. Here, too, it may turn out that proportionality is more of a limiting factor, a negative condition, so to speak—setting outside constraints on force—than it is a positive condition which adds new content to the just war equation.

PROHIBITED WEAPONS

Walzer insists that the "chief concern" in wartime is the question of *who* may be targeted with lethal force. Thus, separating out civilian from military targets is all important. The question of *what means* may be employed in the targeting is, in his view, "circumstantial." He suggests that the elaborate legal rules—contained in the Hague and Geneva Conventions—defining what means may, and what others may not, be employed during war is beside the point. These rules—such as those prohibiting the use of chemical weapons on the battlefield—may be desirable, he says, but are not morally obligatory. After all, if solders may be killed, how can it matter by what means they are killed? While that is a persuasive way of putting the matter, Walzer should not be flippant about setting these rules aside, or assigning them second-place status in *jus in bello*, behind discrimination and the DDE. For the robust and elaborate set of legal rules banning the use of certain weapons in wartime seems to indicate a high level of international consensus. There is a vast number of relevant conventions and legal treaties on this issue, aside from the canonical Hague and Geneva Conventions, such as those banning the use of chemical (1925 and second protocol 1996), biological (1972) and "excessively injurious weapons" (1980). Also relevant are the conventions against genocide (1948) and against methods of warfare which alter the natural environment (1977). Prohibiting weapons also puts an added restriction upon belligerents and, as such, is consistent with the deepest aim of *jus in bello*, namely, to limit war's destruction. It is simply not enough, in my view, to let weapons development proliferate, as if to say: "Develop and deploy whatever weapon you want, just do not aim it at the suburbs." So I think international law corrects a weakness in Walzer by adding this further rule regarding weapons prohibition.[35]

The legal conventions regarding *jus in bello* are much more detailed, specific and thickly textured than those mentioning *jus ad bellum*. It is interesting to reflect on the disparity. I suggest it has to do with two factors. First, usually those with the war power—like the executive branch—also negotiate international treaties, and they want maximum latitude in connection with reasons for going to war. Second, *jus in bello* seems to have developed first,[36] coming out of ancient and medieval conventions regarding chivalrous ways of battling, rules for knights' fighting tournaments, and so on. Indeed, even the Old Testament talks about not laying waste to fruit trees when attacking enemy cities.[37] So *jus in bello* has had more development than *jus ad bellum*, and so we should expect more detail. Just to sample the flavour of a *jus in bello* rule in international law, consider the following snippet on "booby traps" from the convention banning excessively injurious weapons:

1 Without prejudice to the rules of international law applicable in armed conflict relating to treachery and perfidy, it is prohibited in all circumstances to use:
   (a) Any booby trap in the form of an apparently harmless portable object which is specifically designed and constructed to contain explosive material and to detonate when it is disturbed or approached, or
   (b) Booby-traps which are in any way attached to or associated with:
      (i)   Internationally recognized protective emblems, signs or signals;
      (ii) Sick, wounded or dead persons;
      (iii) Burial or cremation sites or graves;
      (iv) Medical facilities, medical equipment, medical supplies or medical transportation;
      (v)   Children's toys or other portable objects or products specially designed for the feeding, health, hygiene, clothing or education of children;

(vi)   Food or drink;

(vii)   Kitchen utensils or appliances except in military establishments, military locations or military supply depots;

(viii) Objects clearly of a religious nature;

(ix)   Historic monuments, works of art or places of worship which constitute the cultural or spiritual heritage of peoples;

(x)   Animals or carcasses.

2 It is prohibited in all circumstances to use any booby trap which is designed to cause superfluous injury or unnecessary suffering.[38]

In addition to these remarkably detailed legal conventions, one might suggest that there is a widely shared moral convention which stipulates that even though soldiers may be targeted with lethal force, some kinds of lethal force—such as burning them to death with flame-throwers, or asphyxiating them with nerve gas—inflict so much suffering, and involve such cruelty, that they are properly condemned. Moreover, the reasoning which distinguishes between legitimate and illegitimate weapons is very similar to the reasoning which generates the combatant/non-combatant distinction. For example, there is a legal ban on using bullets which contain glass shards. These shards are essentially impossible to detect. If the soldier survives the shot, and the bullet is removed by surgery, odds are that some glass shards will still remain in his body. These shards can produce massive internal injuries long after the soldier has ceased being "a dangerous man" to the other side. Parallel reasoning was behind the 1999 passing into law of the International Treaty Banning Land Mines: land mines, too frequently, remain weapons of destruction long after the conflict is over. Finally, restrictions on weapons can play a causal role in reducing destruction and suffering in wartime, something which *jus in bello* as a whole is designed to secure.

Walzer does not even explicitly object to particular weapons on grounds that they are more likely than not to have serious spillover effects on civilians, and thus run afoul of discrimination. Biological weapons would fall under this category, as would many land mines. Such a stance is consistent with the fact that one does not hear from him any criticism of America's extensive use of napalm and Agent Orange in Vietnam, which inflicted long-term damage to Vietnamese agriculture. The aim, at the time, was to defoliate all the jungle vegetation which was providing such effective cover for the Viet Cong. The consequences include abnormally low soil fertility for staple crops like rice and continue to the present. Walzer is curiously unreflective about these considerations, and I cannot agree in this regard: in addition to the general *jus in bello* principles, all belligerents must adhere to the applicable international laws regarding weaponry.[39]

Walzer recovers his reflectiveness about weaponry only when he considers nuclear arms, which for a number of reasons have not been declared illegal by ratified international treaty. The main reason, of course, is that the major powers are all nuclear powers, and they would never agree to such a treaty, as it would eliminate a major military advantage they all share. "Nuclear weapons explode the theory of just war," Walzer famously declares.[40] This is a graphic and gripping, but unfortunate, formulation since it seems to endorse the popular academic view that just war theory is out of date in the post-Hiroshima world. But Walzer cannot believe this, for he believes that the atomic bombing of Japan was unjust. Thus, what his dramatic declaration must really mean is that nuclear weapons can never be employed justly. Why not? First, and most crucially for Walzer, they are radically *indiscriminate* weapons. Perhaps only a handful of the most volatile biological weapons are more uncontrollable in their effects. Second, nuclear weapons are unimaginably destructive, not just in terms of short-term obliteration but also long-term radiation poisoning and climate change, so that their use will always run afoul of *proportionality*. Finally, there is the hint in Walzer that, owing to these two factors combined, deliberate use of nuclear weapons—and emphatically an all-out nuclear war—is an act evil in itself.[41]

Some people, perhaps first starting with Henry Kissinger, believe it might be possible to use nuclear weapons in a discriminate way. Their notion is to use very low-yield nuclear bombs directly on a battlefield against the enemy. I suppose in theory that might be possible but then: 1) there's still the question of proportionality; and 2) what would be the real difference between such bombs and conventional explosives? Perhaps it would just be the expense and strategy of five low-yield nukes versus 50 very high-yield conventional bombs. But I suspect the real strategy behind having nukes in the first place is the massive intimidation factor, in which case the low-yield nukes are useless. Low-yield nukes might be more discriminating—though it would be comforting to hear nuclear scientists say this rather than foreign policy strategists—but then their deterrent and intimidation factors would be undercut. The most useful aspect of nuclear weapons is precisely the deterrent and intimidation properties brought about by their highly destructive yield. Yet it is that exact yield which is morally objectionable, owing to the incredible destruction and lack of discrimination. In other words, if nukes can be made discriminate they will not be much different from conventional missiles—they might save a few bucks on transportation. The really useful nukes, so to speak and by contrast, are precisely the ones it is never morally permissible to use—wildly powerful and indiscriminately destructive.[42]

What about building, testing and threatening to use such nukes but never actually using them (except twice on Japan)? Generally, moral thinkers agree that it is wrong to *threaten* to do something which it is *actually* wrong to do (e.g., threaten to murder someone), and so there are deep moral questions to be raised even about this. (Our legal systems reflect this: it is a separate crime merely to utter a death threat.) On the other hand, some politicians and historians credit America's nuclear deterrence with having stopped Soviet expansion and with having won the Cold War. These latter are sweeping claims, and probably untrue. Communism still expanded massively in the 1945–85 era after all, so what exactly did American nuclear deterrence stop? Thus, I think that, from a just war point of view, nuclear weapons are going to be dimly viewed no matter how they are interpreted. Nuclear deterrence does, though, raise issues of realism and emergency which we'll return to in later chapters. In particular, someone might admit that there are these serious moral problems with having, and certainly with using, such weapons but, given that "the genie is out of the bottle," isn't it alright to seek such weapons more for self-protection than anything else? The morality of having/using such weapons occurs in a context, not a vacuum, and given that the context is one in which others already have/use them, isn't it consistent with the state's duty to protect to try to avail itself of these weapons—at least so it cannot be bullied by those with the intimidating nuclear deterrent? This problem—a real one—is in my view best dealt with in our forthcoming discussions of emergencies and particularly realism, and the question of the degree to which just war theory must make accommodations in this direction. The short answer now, which we'll explain more then, is that it might under very rare conditions be *excusable* to build or even perhaps to use nuclear weapons but that it will never be *morally justified* to do so.

No Means "Mala in Se"

There is a traditional ban on "means *mala in se*," or "methods evil in themselves." The imprecise yet interesting idea here is that some weapons and means of war are forbidden not so much because of the badness of the consequences they inflict but, more importantly, because they themselves are intrinsically awful. Using rape as a tool of warfare—e.g. to drive a population off a territory, or to reward one's troops after battle—is a clear example. Rape is ruled out not so much because of all the pain it produces, or because it is aimed at civilians, but because the act itself is rights-violating, a disgusting disregard for the humanity of the woman raped: a coercive violation of her bodily integrity and her entitlement to choose her own sex partner(s).[43] Methods like campaigns of genocide, ethnic cleansing and torture probably also fall under this category. We do not have to do a cost-benefit analysis to determine whether such are impermissible in warfare: we already judge such acts to be heinous crimes because of their very nature. We have an almost visceral rejection of them. Indeed, the international community passed a convention in 1948 banning genocide, and recently resorted to armed force over Kosovo in Serbia to punish its practice, though it failed to do so earlier in Rwanda.[44]

Reprisals

Reprisals are not permitted in the laws of armed conflict: there is a prohibition on them. At the same time, they have happened in history, are rather frequently threatened during wartime, and just war luminaries such as Walzer allow for reprisals in their theories. Let's examine the controversy. The reprisal doctrine permits a deliberate violation of *jus in bello* rules *but only* in response to a *prior* violation by the opposing side. To his credit, Walzer refuses to condone any violation of the rule of discrimination as part of reprisal: "we must condemn all reprisals against innocent people." What of proportionality and no means "*mala in se*"? While he does not say so, one supposes Walzer cannot allow a violation of the latter rule for mere reprisal purposes. His single example of a justified reprisal focuses on proportionality and prohibited weapons. He claims that Winston Churchill was "entirely justified when he warned the German government early in World War II that the use of [poison] gas by its army would bring an immediate Allied reprisal." Such threats by heads of state have apparently become rather commonplace, since American President George Bush Sr. warned Iraq in 1991 that, should it deploy chemical weapons on the battlefield, America would reserve the right to deploy other weapons of mass destruction, up to and including nuclear armaments. It is important to note here that, presumably, Walzer means that not only the threat but also the threatened action are grounded by his doctrine of reprisal.[45]

Walzer justifies his permission for retaliations on the need to enforce the rules of the war convention during battle: "(I)t is the explicit purpose of reprisals … to stop the wrongdoing *here* [his italics] with this final act" of *jus in bello* violation. Reprisals are designed to make the enemy stop its own *jus in bello* transgressions: state S violates proportionality, say, and state T responds in kind so as to punish S and hopefully prevent future violations.[46] Can we come up with relevant modern examples? Perhaps America's 1986 bombing of Libya, as retaliation for the latter's involvement in previous terrorist strikes, or America's 1998 bombing of suspected terrorist sites in Sudan and Afghanistan as reprisals for presumed involvement in American embassy bombings throughout Africa in the 1990s.

Walzer's reprisal doctrine is worrisome. It ignores the serious likelihood that reprisals, far from chastening the organization which originally violated *jus in bello*, will actually spur further violations. Libya, after all, sponsored the Lockerbie jet bombing in 1988—*after* the American strike—and we know that the US cruise missile attacks on al-Qaeda training sites in 1998 did not deter 9/11, 2001. To put it in just war terms, reprisals have dubious probability of success. In fact, the doctrine of reprisal seems a recipe for escalation, at its extreme risking the onset of total war, a phenomenon just war theory utterly rejects.

Walzer might contend that a certain kind of reprisal may well succeed in stopping escalation. Of course it *may*, but what kind of reprisal is that likely to be? Realistically, it seems, only a very severe, disproportionate one. And while Walzer extends his reprisal permissions solely in terms of relaxing proportionality (and not, thankfully, in terms of relaxing discrimination), we can still ask: how much is too much relaxation? Or is there ever too much relaxation when it comes to reprisals? Might Walzer, for example, condone the Gulf War "turkey shoot" incident on the Highway of Death if it were in reprisal, say for Iraq setting Kuwait's oil wells on fire? Or if state T were to lose one brigade of its soldiers to nerve gas unleashed unbidden by state S, does that mean for Walzer that, to ensure an effective enforcement of the rules, T should now gas two, three, four brigades of S's soldiers in response? Or perhaps deploy a tactical nuclear device against S's battlefield positions? For me, these are rhetorical questions requiring a negative answer.

Reprisal is a very tempting option in warfare, especially when one notes that, given its nature, the aggressor nation will most likely be the one which first violates *jus in bello*. And while relaxing proportionality against legitimate targets may feel like a fitting response to prior violations of a principle as important as discrimination—for instance, gassing enemy soldiers who engaged in civilian massacre—it is unlikely to achieve its more reasoned goal of deterring future violations. As deterrence, reprisal is dubious. As retribution, reprisal may seem elemental, yet it is unlikely to achieve more than a modest, temporary satisfaction of popular outrage. It would thus seem far better to adhere to the following policy on reprisals, adopted from a familiar phrase: *winning well is the best revenge*. This is to say that the aim should be to win the war without violating *jus in bello* at all. But what if, Walzer would ask, one cannot put the two together: what if winning cannot be had, in the real world, by fighting well and by resisting the sinful pleasures of revenge? What if, ultimately, violating *jus in bello* seems the only way to stave off devastating loss?

Walzer notes that, when it comes to war, "we want to have it both ways: moral decency in battle and victory in war; constitutionalism in hell and ourselves outside."[47] We are therefore confronted with a grave dilemma when it looks as though we can win the war *only by setting aside* the rules of right conduct. Walzer, to his credit, refuses to indulge the fantasy that such situations cannot actually happen. His way out of this dark dilemma, however, is one of the most difficult and controversial aspects of his just war theory. It is his doctrine of supreme emergency and it permits not merely violation of proportionality against enemy soldiers but even violation of discrimination against enemy civilians. It is something like the ultimate, no-holds-barred reprisal against the ultimate threat. How does Walzer pose, and then respond to, this grave problem? This is such a difficult question that it deserves a separate chapter: the next one.

RULES FOR THE RICH?

Before switching from external to internal *jus in bello*, we must confront a criticism of external *jus in bello*. There are some people who argue that only rich and powerful nations can afford to satisfy these rules. These rules are thus unfairly stacked in their favour. Poorer countries, lacking things like smart bombs, are thus doubly condemned: condemned to lose and condemned as war criminals for using the more "dirty," older and indiscriminate weapons and tactics which are within their means. I agree with these people that the rules must be fair but disagree with the rest of this complaint. It boils down to the analogous claim that poor people cannot be ethical. This elitist claim, with a history going back to Plato and Aristotle, is not true. Perhaps poor people cannot give as much money to charity as rich people but they are just as capable of being honest, kind, decent, hard-working, courageous, moderate and just. And poor people, in domestic society, are perfectly capable of obeying laws against murder, rape and assault. Similarly, poor nations can fight in accord with these *jus in bello* rules. It is not too much to ask them to refrain from bombing or terrorizing civilians, torturing prisoners, dropping down nukes, engaging in reprisals, and so on. They might resent the wealth and weaponry of rich nations, but these emotions do not give them a "poor man's right" to fight dirty. We know from history, after all, that wealth and advanced weaponry are no guarantee of decent behaviour on the battlefield. Indeed, aggression is usually committed by powerful nations against the weak. Fundamentally, whether rich or poor, a nation makes a decision to fight decently or dirtily: you can fight within your means decently or fight within your means dirtily. In other words, it is not a question of means but rather of moral choice. Fighting decently is no guarantee of victory, I concede. But there's never any guarantee that doing the right thing is always going to serve one's interests or make one happy. Think of personal cases where you do your duty (e.g., avoid stealing) even though it prevents you from doing something which would make you happier (e.g., getting a new car without having to pay for it). Poverty, or relative underdevelopment, is no justification for committing war crimes. This complaint is a pathetic plea to excuse terrible actions when none are justly warranted.

Transition from External to Internal *Jus in Bello*

We have established that, externally or vis-à-vis the enemy, a society in the midst of war must adhere to the following rules: 1) discrimination and noncombatant immunity; 2) benevolent quarantine for POWs; 3) due care for civilians; 4) the DDE; 5) proportionality; 6) no means *mala in se*; 7) no reprisals; and 8) adhere to all the international treaties regarding *jus in bello*, many of which concern weaponry. But what of the internal issue? How should a government, in the midst of war, conduct itself vis-à-vis *its own citizens*? This is not a question commonly asked, much less answered by, conventional just war theorists. But we wish to go beyond convention and be as comprehensive and up-to-date as we can. Manifestly, these are issues of justice in wartime, and thus fall under the logical scope of just war theory. So consider the principles which follow.

The Internal Rules

ADHERE TO THE EXTERNAL RULES

This principle, simply put, is this: follow the external rules, both in terms of *jus ad bellum* and *jus in bello*. How is this an "internal" rule? It is internal owing to the force and grounding of its sense and meaning, as well as to the tight conceptual and moral linkages drawn between the internal and external rules. That branch of government constitutionally entitled to the war power should commit to following all the external rules *not only* for the sake of being dutybound to the enemy country or to the international community either politically or legally, *but also* for the sake of owing it to one's own people. This is to say that it is a fundamental obligation of every government not to engage in aggressive war or to commit war crimes. This was already established above, but what this section highlights is that this duty is owed to several entities: it stretches out to the international community and especially to any enemy countries, but also pulls inward to one's own populace. One is, after all, declaring war *in their name*, launching war to protect *them* and to vindicate *their* fundamental rights, whether as individual persons or national communities. *They* are not entitled to engage in aggression or war crimes, and since their individual human rights ultimately ground all the war entitlements under investigation here, one is not entitled to engage in aggressive war or war crimes on their behalf. One needs to make a firm, sincere public commitment—whether by public declaration, statute or constitutional entrenchment in those provisions outlining the war power—to adhere to each and every one of the external rules. One owes it to one's own people to wage war only in conformity with *jus ad bellum*, and then to fight that war without resorting to war crimes.

RESPECTING DOMESTIC HUMAN RIGHTS

The second, and perhaps most vital, internal rule is to respect the human rights of one's citizens—be they soldier or civilian—as best one can during wartime. For this norm is codified in the Second Amendment to the Geneva Convention.[48] Let us discuss some of the most fundamental issues, as well as stress their vital importance. This is not an idle thought experiment; human rights protection comes at a price. It takes real resources and commitment to make rights real. During a serious war, there will be strong incentive for even legitimate governments to use as many resources as possible—including some previously devoted to domestic rights satisfaction—in order to fight the war as best they can. In fact, this consideration of rights protection on the domestic front is an *especially important aspect* of just war thinking, since some of the most gruesome human rights violations in wartime (e.g., The Holocaust and the Rwandan genocide) have occurred *within, and not between*, national borders. Belligerent governments are not entitled to use the cloak of war with foreign powers in order to commit massive human rights violations domestically, usually vis-à-vis some disfavoured racial, ethnic, linguistic and/or religious minority. More recently, in connection with the aftermath of 9/11, legitimate governments around the world have drafted controversial sets of anti-terrorist, or emergency-regime, legislation which legal scholars amongst others have questioned, especially regarding whether such extraordinary powers are genuinely needed to fight the war on terrorism or whether, in fact, they count as excessive abrogations or curtailments of civilian rights. Relatedly, in December 2005, President George Bush Jr. admitted he had—in the name of national security—authorized US government spying on American citizens on US soil, and did so without a court warrant.[49]

Truly, there are eerie similarities between our present period, which is the early phase of the war on terror, and the 1945–55 period, the early phase of the Cold War. In both instances, there is deep concern over a ferocious enemy with a profoundly opposing system of beliefs. In the Cold War, it was the communists, especially as located in Russia and China; today it is the radical Islamic terrorists and their "rogue state" sponsors. In both cases, obsession with weapons of mass destruction (WMD) pervades strategic planning. Furthermore, in both time frames we see an expectation of ultra-patriotism, and something of a pervasive culture of not criticizing too forcefully government policy. Finally, there is shared between the eras strong legislation curtailing aspects of traditional civil liberties. Compare and contrast, for example, the American Patriot Act of today with the US House of Representatives Un-American Activities Committee of yesteryear, as led by Joe McCarthy. McCarthy went on a witch hunt for communists "hiding" in American society, bullying many into naming the names of those with radical political views. Similarly—and actually more forcefully—US law enforcement now has considerable powers to arrest, question and even detain indefinitely those merely suspected of having radical connections or beliefs.[50]

Rights on the Civilian Side

Much of the literature on this complex issue focuses on what a regime, which finds itself embroiled in an emergency, may or may not do regarding the suspension or abrogation of human rights on the domestic front.[51] The so-called "Paris Minimum Standards" and the 1977 Second Amendment to the Geneva Convention were both designed with this explicitly in mind, and they enshrine a list of human rights which are to be regarded as "non-derogable"—which is to say untouchable or absolute—even in such a public emergency as war.[52] These rights include: life; not to be tortured; not to be enslaved; not to be taken hostage; "minimal judicial guarantees"; non-discrimination; not to be subject to medical experiment; not to be subject to retroactive laws; recognition as a legal person; freedom of thought, conscience and religion; a fair trial; a subsistence level of food and water; and special protections for children.

While that is a very laudable list, there seems to be movement within the international human rights community *away from* the very concept of derogability. Derogability, after all, suggests that, under usual circumstances, there is a set of human rights which governments are to respect as a condition of legitimacy. However, when push comes to shove (e.g., during an emergency like wartime) the state can cut back on some human rights, but must still preserve a small core, the so-called "non-derogables," such as those listed above. The preference nowadays, and certainly my own, is that human rights must be thought of as forming *an interlocking whole*, for instance, that entire set of entitlements demanded when we focus on the one concept of guaranteeing to every human being a minimally good life. Since human rights form an interlocking whole, there is no question of picking some for privileged protection, while the others may fall away when pressure is put on public resources. It is all or nothing, and I believe this is demanded by the quest for consistency in human rights theory: to what extent can we refer to the ones which may be "pruned away" as genuinely human rights at all? Better not to refer to them in that way, owing to the primary value and importance we wish to attach to human rights as, in John Rawls' words, constituting the very foundation of political and legal morality in our era.[53]

Failing to endorse derogability does not mean that one must, fancifully, commit a government shouldered with the real burdens of fighting a just and difficult war to an extravagant agenda regarding human rights fulfilment. *It means, rather, that one has to be both strict and frugal when one is deciding what truly counts as a human right in the first place.* There has been a noticeable trend of "human rights inflation" over time, according to which ever more, and ever more luxurious, items have been claimed as a matter of human right. But human rights are precious things, and they are cheapened when people try to elevate any old claim or preference they have into the status of a struggle over human rights. As I have written elsewhere,[54] as human beings we are only entitled as a matter of human right to claim those objects we genuinely need to live a minimally good life in the modern world. A minimally good life is one where we are both assured, as Jim Nickel says, of *having* a life (i.e., the minimal subsistence and physical security conditions we require to exist in society) and of *leading* that life as well (i.e., the freedom, recognition and non-discrimination we each require to pursue our own life plans).[55] Moreover, all such claims must be such as to put only reasonable, bearable burdens upon the shoulders of others and social institutions. I have already argued that this means that we all have claims to only five foundational human rights objects: personal security; material subsistence; personal liberty; elemental equality; and social recognition.

All this by way of considering, in a deeper sense, what rights standards ought to be adhered to by governments hard-pressed in wartime. The general answer is that governments must be committed to respecting each and every *bona fide* human rights claim made by civilian or soldier. The human rights outlined above form a package. *They are a whole, not a hierarchy.* It is *not* true that as human beings we need security more than we need subsistence, or subsistence more than we need freedom. *We need them all* if we are to lead minimally good lives, as creatures who both have a life and can lead it as well. Thus, for example, to prune away the freedoms (or civil liberties) on the grounds that such pruning is needed to provide for greater security is in principle fallacious and misguided: it does not give up what is less important in exchange for what is more; it gives up something *just as important* as the other and actually attacks people's ability to lead minimally good lives in any event. To take it to the extreme, why should citizens care if they still have their lives if such lives are not minimally good anyway—if they feel their lives are not worth living?

We should reject the thinking that turns rights into mere social privileges, granted by generous governments. Human rights are not mere privileges, they are *entitlements* which governments *owe* to their people. Nor are human rights mere social utilities; in fact human rights were explicitly designed to guarantee a minimally good life *to everyone* in the face of utility calculations and pressures to make social trade-offs which favour the majority. Human rights form a coherent, non-hierarchical whole where each of them is needed as a component of what it means to live a minimally good or decent life in the modern world. Without their satisfaction, no one has reason to sign on to the social contract constitutive of political order in the first place.

Curtailing Human Rights?

History contains a litany of massive overkill when it comes to government suspension of civil liberties in wartime. While the one end of the spectrum deals with such terrible events as The Holocaust, the more moderate end of the spectrum deals with events like the forced internment of North Americans of Far Eastern descent in World War II. Legitimate governments, like other governments, enjoy power and have internal bureaucratic impulses towards the expansion of that power. It is very natural for them to take advantage of the wartime atmosphere to pursue that agenda, when resistance will be distracted or minimal. But governments have as their ultimate point and purpose the fulfilment of the human rights of all their citizens, and thus cannot consistently engage in an attack on, or derogation of, those same human rights, even if during wartime. In my view, most (but perhaps not all) emergency-regime legislation is probably *not* morally justified, but rather constitutes an unjustified invasion of civil liberties and human rights by governments which are either panicked by a severe, yet temporary, external crisis and/or which have their own internal impulses towards increase of power at the expense of those very entitlements whose realization actually constitutes their reason-for-being. Suspension of such things as freedom of peaceful assembly, free speech and freedom of the press, we know, are things which cannot contribute in any meaningful way to augmenting the resources one has to fight a war. They merely make criticism of government, and protests against its war policy, more difficult. Suspension of *some* aspects of freedom of movement might, by contrast, be more defensible in wartime. While people might still otherwise be free to move around the country or to leave it altogether, it makes for clear sense to prevent them from wandering into battle zones. In this event, the heaviest burden rests with any government proposing any such restriction—it must have a clear and manifest connection to the legitimate operation of an otherwise justified war.

Suspension of the right to vote is an especially fearsome thing. While it might be argued that running an election in the midst of war has *bona fide* costs—running into many millions, which might be otherwise spent on the war effort—the risks in favour of tyranny, or at least an unjustified extension and growth of government power at the expense of civil liberties, are simply too extreme. There are relevant historical cases here. Take a big country like America, where running elections is indeed a huge and costly enterprise. Both Abraham Lincoln and Franklin Roosevelt won presidential elections which were held under deeply dramatic, very pressured wartime conditions. Surely, then, elections can be run elsewhere, in smaller countries with fewer voters facing less severe challenges. Or there might be reasonable, middle-of-the-road solutions, such as the requirement laid out in Canada's Charter of Rights and Freedoms which allows, in time of warfare, for Parliament to continue sitting beyond the normal maximum of five years provided no more than one third of the current elected members opposes such a move.

The story is similar when it comes to the suspension of due process rights, which are amongst the most frequently targeted by a government in the midst of war. It might be argued that running a proper police and court system is quite expensive, and such resources could be used instead to fight the war. In the current war on terror, moreover, it is argued that, owing to the suddenness with which the enemy can exert incredibly deadly force, the slowness of police and court procedures actually puts public safety in jeopardy. To a point, these are true claims. Yet entitling a government to run roughshod over due process rights is extremely dangerous, in some cases looking much like the regular practice of a rights-violating and thus illegitimate regime. There might be room for plausible middle-of-the-road compromises here, which retain much of the substance of the right without sacrificing its principle. For instance, powers of seizure, arrest and detention might be augmented, enabling for timely and efficient capture of suspects, but then the court system and due process remain fully intact so that those genuinely innocent will be fully empowered to be released and exonerated in due course as well. Suspects are quickly off the street and in custody, yet still fully entitled to due process. It fits in with this line of thinking to note that the US Supreme Court decided, in June 2004, that terrorist suspects detained in Guantanamo Bay, Cuba, can avail themselves of US court procedures to determine whether their detention is appropriate under American law.

Here you have the mix of rapid detention alongside material aspects of due process.[56]

Conscription

In terms of the just war literature, by far and away the most written-about aspect of domestic rights fulfilment during wartime is the issue of conscription. A just, rights-respecting society ought, on the basis of the human right to freedom of conscience, to abide by the good-faith claims of conscientious objectors, and/or pacifists, to be exempt from military service. A just state in the midst of a serious and justified war may, however, reasonably ask for some assistance from conscientious objectors, such as clerical or administrative work, in return for respecting their personal beliefs that they ought not to kill (much less be forced to kill) for political reasons. So, a state ought to meet its military needs through voluntary enlistment, where possible. There are many incentives which armed forces can, and do, employ to keep enlistments at the desired levels: subsidized post-secondary education, housing and food, alongside guaranteed job slots, are some of the most popular. As most military experts agree, very rarely is there a credible military, as opposed to political, case for universal conscription: there are diminishing marginal returns and huge inefficiencies when it comes to dealing with such an enormous body of conscripts. The whole trend in the military arts is away from huge, labour-intensive fighting forces in favour of more nimble, less-manned and more technology-laden solutions, in any event.[57]

The Judiciary

Here is an ideal role for the judiciary to play in connection with wartime ethics. While it was argued, in Chapter 2, that the judiciary is correctly disenfranchised with regard to the proper authority to declare war, the judiciary *ought to be empowered* when it comes to determining any proposed infringement or suspension of any civil liberty or human right during wartime. We just noted how the US Supreme Court recently asserted itself in this regard, in connection with the Guantanamo detainees. The judiciary is one of the bulwarks regarding human rights satisfaction in most legitimate societies, and so it should here play a manifest and integral role. Its expertise in diagnosing, in detailed instances, when a civil liberty or constitutionally guaranteed right has been infringed *must* here be drawn upon. There is no reason why the standard slowness of the judicial process should be an objection to this proposal. During wartime, or leading up to wartime, government lawyers could for instance propose desired curtailments directly to higher levels of the judiciary in special sessions. Opponents of any such curtailments, such as bar societies, civil liberties lawyers, civil society or non-governmental organizations, could be welcomed into such hearings as friends of the court, entitled to give counter-arguments and counter-proposals. But the judiciary's decision ought to be recognized as decisive, and in my view must give the heaviest priority to ensuring human rights satisfaction and ensuring that those very rights-respecting principles which make governments legitimate are not taken away in haste or insidiously eroded under the auspices of security.

In sum, we can predict how, in crisis, even legitimate governments will naturally incline towards utility-based thinking which plays to popular opinion—"national security," "the public or greater good," "what's good for the country," etc. But the whole point of rights—or, at least, human rights—is not merely to benefit the masses and to protect the well-being of the majority but, moreover, to benefit everyone and be mindful of every individual human being's need for protection. There is no defensible hierarchy according to which one can sacrifice one human right for the sake of another—they all go together and form a package. There is also historical evidence showing the tendency to overkill regarding civil liberties suspension, and so we should wonder not only about the morality but also about the strategic usefulness of any proposed wartime clipping of vital entitlements. Some *small* ones, admittedly, might be permissible, provided there's a *substantial* connection to a *just* war effort, *and* assuming the judiciary—the institutional bulwark of rights claims—concurs.

Rights on the Soldier Side

What human rights can soldiers claim vis-à-vis their own governments in the midst of war? It is often thought that any such claims must be minimal, if they exist at all. Soldiers are, after all, the very agents of war, and wars cannot effectively be fought if soldiers are busy clogging up the court system with human rights litigation against their own government. While this is true as far as it goes, it is manifestly untrue that soldiers fail to have human rights. As human beings, they are entitled to the foundational five objects of security, subsistence, liberty, equality and recognition. The question, we have seen, has less to do with their forfeiture of any of these claims and more to do with the precise meaning of them in a wartime, soldierly context. Let's run through our list of "the foundational five" and consider the human rights issues more fully.

The right to personal security, which is older and better phrased than the now-loaded "right to life," means something quite different in a soldierly context than it does in a peacetime civilian context. It does *not* mean that soldiers have a right not to be killed, or not to be put in circumstances where it is foreseeable that some of them might be killed. That is a promise which simply cannot be squared with the very practice of being a soldier. What it does mean is that—given that being a soldier is an inherently dangerous profession undertaken in defence of someone else's life and liberty—soldiers have the right: to sound and serious military training; to be free from severe and dangerous inaugural or "hazing" rituals; and to good, functional equipment and weapons which enable them to perform their job. A government which fails to provide these to its soldier class violates their human right to physical security: it fails to deliver the goods needed to realize the principle in the relevant context.

As part of this entitlement, soldiers also have the right to have had their commanding officers competently trained, so that they do not order strikes or actions which are so poorly planned as to constitute a negligent failure to provide that minimal level of personal security which even a soldier has the right to expect. Of course, military mistakes do get made, and sometimes they cost lives. War is a very dangerous business, and people are going to die. That is not at issue. What *is* at issue is a failure of officer training, and/ or sloppy command-and-control design over military orders, so grievous that what results, predictably, is a senseless slaughter of one's own troops. Historical instances of deploying troops as mere "cannon-fodder," for instance, plausibly count as internal human rights violations in my view. World War I was rife, disastrously, with such cases. By becoming soldiers, these men and women do *not* "contract out" of all their human rights. In the absence of human rights-violating or criminal behaviour on their part, soldiers as human beings retain all their human rights, whether their enlistment was voluntary or through conscription. What changes upon enlistment is that the specification of what their human rights entitle them to, in their context, is different in many respects from analogous civilian claims. So soldiers have the right to good training, sound equipment and to decently-planned strikes, not only in terms of military effectiveness but also in terms of their adherence to *jus in bello* norms. Soldiers have the right not to be ordered to commit war crimes. Finally, soldiers have, as part of their personal security entitlement, a subsidiary claim to a due process of military justice wherein any alleged violation of protocol on their part can be tried and considered fairly. Though war be hell, we try (often failingly) to make it a rule-bound hell; and though a soldier's life be hard, he too is owed a predictable form of rule-bound discipline as an extension of his right to personal security.

Subsistence is straightforward compared with security. A soldier has claims on his government to means of material subsistence or at least an income sufficient to purchase such means. Most states (even ostensibly impoverished ones) have little difficulty in providing subsistence to their soldiers, often offering a mixture of salary with subsidized food, housing and health care services. Though a soldier's life will never be the road to riches, it does seem that governments may have some work to do assisting soldiers, to a greater degree than presently, with subsistence *after* their enlistment ends. While this may not involve the generosity of the G.I. Bill—which provided extensive education and housing benefits to American veterans of World War II—it should involve things like: career counselling and placement services; marketable job training; considerations of subsidized housing; and participation in a decent pension scheme to provide for subsistence in retirement. These subsistence claims should flow to the immediate family (i.e., spouse/partner and dependents) of a soldier as well, especially when he is away on a tour of duty or killed/missing in action. Why should soldiers be provided such things as a matter of human right? The short answer is because they lead such difficult lives in defence of our own. They do much more, and risk much more, than the average citizen in defence of our common security from aggression, and so they can plausibly make a slightly larger claim on public resources for their subsistence needs. Not at the expense of the subsistence needs of others, of course; a just government must do everything reasonable to meet *everyone's* subsistence needs. By and large, this is readily achievable and affordable in most societies, since the majority of people can provide subsistence for themselves, not needing direct assistance but, rather, only respect for their rights in their property. Taxation, authorized through representative means, thus allows for the small minority who genuinely cannot provide it for themselves to be provided with subsistence assistance from the state.[58]

Freedom for soldiers is more problematic. The limitations flow here more plausibly and readily than with any other human rights object. Command and control, and obedience to hierarchy, are of the very essence of military life, and are drilled into a soldier's head from day one of enlistment. Cohesion is, indeed, necessary to achieve an effective fighting force. Soldiers may not have much freedom of movement, but as citizens they must retain the right to freedom to vote and to run for public office. I also believe that the conjunction of personal security and freedom gives soldiers the right to refuse to be subjected to medical or biological treatments or agents (for instance, "immunizing" agents) which have risks they are not willing to take. This was an issue in the 1991 Persian Gulf War for both American and Canadian soldiers, who were essentially forced to receive an injection which would supposedly protect them in case Saddam Hussein used chemical weapons. This injection may, however, have itself caused longer-term health problems for these soldiers. I think soldiers should have a right of refusal here, based on their bodily integrity. Of course, the armed services may, in return, justly refuse that soldier the opportunity to fight or circulate alongside his comrades.

What about the larger issue, mentioned earlier, of whether soldiers should be allowed to pick and choose which wars they wish to fight in? Vitoria argued, that extending any such right would result in "grave peril" for a political community. If by this he meant that it would make it harder for a state to defend itself effectively from aggression, I disagree. Soldiers, generally, are spoiling for a fight. Usually ultra-patriotic, they are often eager to use their training in a real context. If it really were a justified war, I very much doubt that the state in question would find a problem regarding a slippery slope of defections leading to helplessness in the face of aggression. In fact, I would argue that enshrining this entitlement would *only* make it more difficult for a regime to mount an aggressive war, something it is *not* entitled to do in any event. If, by his warning, Vitoria was hinting that a military force might become harder to control by civilian authorities, then I admit that could be a serious concern. Societies must always be vigilant to keep the military under representative civilian control, and perhaps empowering soldiers to pick and choose which wars to fight might enable them to thumb their nose at civilian authorities, perhaps holding out for more pay, or even making a play for political power. Provided, however, that this is a mature and stable representative regime in view here, this seems empirically unlikely, since the deep political culture of such a society will make soldiers personally committed to civilian control. There remain the reasons mentioned above in favour of having enough soldiers more than willing to fight most fights. In my view, this case is *less* about potential military blackmail of civilian control and *more* about religious or conscientious pacifists objecting to conscription. The number of soldiers who will refuse to fight in any particular war will, predictably, be few and far between—all the pressures point the other way. Yet there might remain some who do. They should, like the civilian conscientious objector, be given administrative support or training roles in exchange for respecting their freedom of conscience that this was the wrong war to fight.

Equality might be hard to see in the midst of so hierarchical a place as the armed services, but its substance is actually comparatively easy: all soldiers are equally entitled to all these claims. In terms of recognition, the armed services can be impersonal. But what is meant by this value, in this context, is that soldiers still be acknowledged by the military command and state hierarchy as *persons* entitled to these rights while working towards the common moral purpose of defence and security, and not merely as useful *cogs* in a well-oiled killing machine. Here too arises the issue of entitlements which endure after enlistment ends. Soldiers often experience readjustment problems, whether with marital breakdown, post-traumatic stress disorder, or with controlling the violence they have been conditioned to deploy. Their human right to social recognition as soldiers demands something deeper than the civilian equivalent, which centres around recognition as a rights-bearing person before the law. Soldiers, in exchange for the deeper sacrifices they make on behalf of secure citizenship, are owed more efforts by governments on this front than they have recently been given. Medals and official days of honour and gratitude *are* forms of superior recognition, yet they are applied superficially to the surface of what the substance of this right entails, which is the provision of resources needed to live a life of minimal value in the modern world.

Summary

In the midst of war, a state should adhere to two sets of rules: one external, the other internal. The external rules are the familiar *jus in bello* rules, and they regulate one's conduct with the enemy. They include: discrimination and non-combatant immunity; benevolent quarantine for POWs; due care for civilians; the DDE; proportionality; no means *mala in se*; no reprisals; and obey all international laws on weapons prohibition. The internal rules, just as important but not stressed nearly enough, concern one's conduct with one's own citizens, be they civilian or soldier. Ultimately, these rules boil down to the need to realize their human rights as best as can reasonably be expected during wartime.

Notes

1. I. Kant, *The Metaphysics of Morals*, trans. and ed. M. Gregor (Cambridge: Cambridge University Press, 1995), 117.
2. W. Reisman and C. Antoniou, eds. *The Laws of War* (New York: Vintage, 1994). For more sources on the laws of war, see Appendix A.
3. M. Walzer, *Just and Unjust Wars* (New York: Basic Books, 3rd ed., 2000), 42–3, 135.
4. Walzer, *Wars*, 37, 40, 136; J. Dubik, "Human Rights, Command Responsibility and Walzer's Just War Theory," *Philosophy and Public Affairs* (1982), 354–71.
5. Walzer, *Wars*, 135.
6. Walzer notes the British prosecutor's arguments in his *Wars*, 38. For the trials, see Chapter 6.
7. Walzer, *Wars*, 127, 39.
8. Walzer, *Wars*, 39.
9. Walzer, *Wars*, 128; Reisman and Antoniou, eds. *Laws*, 41–57.
10. Walzer, *Wars*, 40, 138.
11. J. MacMahan, "Preventive War," a chapter in a forthcoming collection on just war theory to be edited by David Rodin and published by Oxford University Press. Thanks to the Press for the advance reading.
12. Walzer, *Wars*, 142.
13. Walzer, *Wars*, 142, 46.
14. Reisman and Antoniou, eds. *Laws*, 35–230.
15. E. Saar, *Inside the Wire* (New York: Penguin, 2005); M. Ratner and E. Ray, *Guantanamo: What The World Should Know* (New York: Chelsea Green, 2004).
16. S. Hersh, *Chain of Command: The Road from 9/11 to Abu Ghraib* (New York: Harper Collins, 2004); M. Danner, *Torture and Truth: America, Abu Ghraib and The War on Terror* (New York: New York Review of Books, 2004). In late 2005, allegations surfaced about the CIA running secret prisons in various locations, off American soil, for the sole purpose of aggressive anti-terrorist detainment and questioning.
17. A. Dershowitz, *Why Terrorism Works* (New Haven, CT: Yale University Press, 2003).
18. Reisman and Antoniou, eds., *Laws*, 153–393; I. Brownlie, ed. *Basic Documents in International Law* (Oxford: Oxford University Press, 4th ed., 1995), 255–388.
19. B. Innes, *The History of Torture* (New York: St. Martin's, 1998); J. Glover, *Humanity* (New Haven, CT: Yale University Press, 2001).

20. Walzer, *Wars*, 146–51.
21. R. Gunaratna, *Inside Al-Qaeda* (New York: Berkley Group, 2003).
22. M. Gelven, *War and Existence* (Philadelphia: Penn State University Press, 1994).
23. R.K. Fullinwinder, "War and Innocence," *Philosophy and Public Affairs* (1976), 90–7.
24. Walzer, *Wars*, 146, 219; T. Nagel, "War and Massacre," *Philosophy and Public Affairs* (1971/72), 123.
25. Walzer, *Wars*, xx.
26. P.Woodward, ed. *The Doctrine of Double Effect* (Notre Dame: University of Notre Dame Press, 2001).
27. Walzer, *Wars*, 106.
28. Walzer, *Wars*, 151, 157.
29. M. Ignatieff, *Virtual War: Kosovo and Beyond* (Toronto: Viking, 2000).
30. Journalists of Reuters, *The Israeli-Palestinian Conflict* (New York: Reuters Books, 2002).
31. T. Erskine, "Moral Agents and Intelligence," *Intelligence and National Security* (Spring 2004), 38–54.
32. Walzer, *Wars*, 152 and 156, in the note; Reisman and Antoniou, eds. *Laws*, 80–4.
33. B. Orend, *War and International Justice: A Kantian Perspective* (Waterloo, ON: Wilfrid Laurier University Press, 2000).
34. Walzer, *Wars*, 129; xxi.
35. Walzer, *Wars*, 42 and 215; Reisman and Antoniou, eds. *Laws*, 35–132.
36. James T. Johnson, *Ideology, Reason and The Limitation of War* (Princeton, NJ: Princeton University Press, 1975).
37. *Deuteronomy* 20:19.
38. Convention II, Article 6, of the Convention on Prohibitions or Restrictions on the Use of Certain Conventional Weapons which may be Deemed to be Excessively Injurious or to have Indiscriminate Effects. This Convention was ratified in 1980. See Reisman and Antoniou, eds. *Laws*, 53.
39. R. Regan, *Just War: Principles and Cases* (Washington, DC: Catholic University of America Press, 1996), 87–99, 136–50.
40. Walzer, *Wars*, 282. While there have been two UN General Assembly resolutions, in 1961 and 1972, banning the use of nuclear weapons (see Reisman and Antoniou, eds. *Laws*, 66–7), and a 2004 one calling for the ultimate dismantling of them all, these do not carry the binding force of a ratified international treaty.
41. Walzer, *Wars*, 263–83.
42. Regan, *Just War*, 100–22; H. Kissinger, *Diplomacy* (New York: Harper Collins, 1995).
43. Walzer, *Wars*, 129–37; C. MacKinnon, "Crimes of War, Crimes of Peace," in S. Shute and S. Hurley, eds. *On Human Rights* (New York: Basic, 1993), 83–110.
44. Reisman and Antoniou, eds. *Laws*, 84–94; Walzer, *Wars*, 257, 323.
45. Walzer, *Wars*, 207–22; Regan, *Cases*, 172–8.
46. Walzer, *Wars*, 207.

47. Walzer, *Wars*, 47.

48. Reisman and Antoniou, eds. *Laws*, 84–7.

49. President George Bush Jr., *Public Remarks*, Dec.16, 2005. See <www.whitehouse.gov>.

50. R.J. Daniels, et al, eds. *The Security of Freedom* (Toronto: University of Toronto Press, 2001); D. Cole, et al, eds. *Terrorism and The Constitution* (New York: The Free Press, 2nd ed., 2002); R. Leone and G. Anrig, eds. *The War on Our Freedoms* (New York: Public Affairs, 2003); M. Walker, *The Cold War: A History* (New York: Henry Holt, 1995).

51. On "emergency regimes" and rights-protection on the domestic front, see: J. Nickel, *Making Sense of Human Rights* (Berkeley: University of California Press, 1987), 131–46; A. Rosas, "Emergency Regimes: A Comparison," in D. Gomien, ed. *Broadening the Frontiers of Human Rights* (Oslo, Norway: Scandinavian University Press, 1992), 162–200; The International Commission of Jurists, *States of Emergency: Their Impact on Human Rights* (New York: ICJ, 1983); J. Fitzpatrick, "Protection against Abuse of the Concept of Emergency," in L. Henkin and J.L. Hargrove, eds. *Human Rights: An Agenda for the Next Century* (Washington, DC: The American Society for International Law, 1994), 203–28; and J.F. Hartman, "Derogation from Human Rights Treaties in Public Emergencies," *Harvard International Law Review* (1981), 1–52.

52. Lists of so-called "non-derogable" human rights also exist in both the International Covenant on Civil and Political Rights and the European Convention on Human Rights. But the Second Amendment and the Paris Standards are the most comprehensive, and hence discussed here. See: J. Oraa, *Human Rights in States of Emergency in International Law* (Oxford: Oxford University Press, 1997); S. Chowdhury, *Rule of Law in a State of Emergency* (London: Palgrave, 1997) and J. Fitzpatrick, *Human Rights in Crisis* (Philadelphia, PA: University of Pennsylvania Press, 1994).

53. J. Rawls, *The Law of Peoples* (Cambridge, MA: Harvard University Press, 2000).

54. B. Orend, *Human Rights: Concept and Context* (Peterborough, ON: Broadview Press, 2002).

55. Nickel, *Making Sense*, 42–71.

56. R. Dworkin, "What the Court Really Said," *New York Review of Books* (August 12, 2004), 26–9. (Not that there aren't other issues of due process to raise in connection with the Guantanamo detainees, notably their access to lawyers and freedom from torture.)

57. Walzer, *Wars*, 34–40, 138–43; W. Clark, *Waging Modern War* (New York: Public Affairs Group, 2002).

58. For more on the overall affordability of human rights, including those to subsistence, see Orend, *Human Rights*, 129–54.

CHAPTER 5

Jus in Bello #2
Supreme Emergencies

> "[W]e have a right, indeed are bound in duty,
> to abrogate for a space some of the conventions of the very
> laws we seek to consolidate and reaffirm."
> *Winston Churchill*[1]

The supreme emergency exemption is a doctrine which pushes to the very limits the relationship between *jus ad bellum* and *jus in bello*. Though it is *nowhere* written into international law, the supreme emergency exemption nevertheless has high profile support, including such luminaries as Churchill, John Rawls and Michael Walzer. But it is Walzer who is fundamentally responsible for this exemption within just war theory—Churchill merely inspires it, and Rawls merely apes it.

As Walzer defines it, the supreme emergency exemption allows a country victimized by aggression to set aside the rules of *jus in bello* and fight however it wants, *provided*: 1) there is public proof the aggressor is just about to defeat the victim militarily; *and* 2) there is similar proof that once it does so, the aggressor will not simply crush the political sovereignty of the victim community but, moreover, institute a brutal policy of widespread massacre and enslavement against its individual members. Walzer's favourite, and only, example of such an aggressor is Nazi Germany.[2] More on the example shortly. Let's push our definitions, and sense of the stakes, toward greater clarity.

We saw last chapter that (external) *jus in bello* contains a number of general moral rules within which the stunning number of legal conventions and prohibitions can be located. These abstract rules include: 1) non-combatant immunity from direct and intentional attack; 2) benevolent quarantine for captured soldiers; 3) due care to civilians; 4) use of proportionate means only against legitimate military targets; 5) no reprisals; 6) no prohibited weapons; and 7) no use of means "*mala in se*," or "evil in themselves," such as forcing captured soldiers to fight against their own side. Walzer is saying here that, under supreme emergency conditions, the country with *jus ad bellum* on its side (i.e., the victim of aggression) may set aside all *jus in bello* rules and fight *however it wants to*—without restraint—to stave off the threat posed by the aggressor. In particular, the victim country may wilfully violate non-combatant immunity, and do such things as deliberately attack

enemy civilians with lethal force. Traditionally, we have seen that such trans-
gression has counted as the clearest violation of *jus in bello* rules, and has been
seen as one of the very worst war crimes. Indeed Hugo Grotius once said
that non-combatant immunity is a rule so powerful that it "cannot be
changed, even by God."[3] So, what we have in the supreme emergency exemption is probably the most controversial, and consequential, amendment to just
war theory ever proposed. The stakes regarding its acceptance into just war
theory are enormous and disturbingly relevant to an era not unacquainted
with genocide and weapons of mass destruction (WMD).

Which Cases Count?

Churchill, Walzer and Rawls concur that Britain experienced a supreme
emergency in the early 1940s. By 1940, Nazi Germany stood triumphant in
Western and Central Europe as well as Scandinavia, following its shattering
success during the Blitzkrieg. Neither the USA nor the USSR were, at this
point, in the war to drain the pressure off Britain. Hitler indeed had plans to
invade the UK, and was "softening up the target" with *Luftwaffe* bombing
raids, especially on Coventry and London itself. These Nazi bombing raids
were indiscriminate and terrorist. Churchill, who coined the phrase "supreme
emergency" in this regard, argued that as Prime Minister he had to authorize
exceptional measures under such ultra-menacing conditions. He suggested
that the British were "fighting to re-establish the reign of law and to protect
the liberties of small countries. Our defeat would mean an age of barbaric
violence and would be fatal, not only to ourselves, but to the independent
life of every small country in Europe." "It would not be right," Churchill
declared, "that the aggressive power should gain one set of advantages by
tearing up all laws, and another set by sheltering behind the innate respect
for law of its opponent. Humanity, rather than legality, must be our guide."
And so Churchill authorized the Royal Air Force to begin bombing raids on
German cities, knowing full well—even intending—that German civilians
would be killed. This was partly in retaliation, or reprisal, for Hitler's own
original bombings of London and Coventry, but was also designed to deter
any conquest of Britain. It was thought that the German people, delirious
with the Blitzkrieg's success, had to be made to feel the sting of war—needed
some wind taken out of their sails—lest their approval drive Hitler's armed
ambitions even further. Air power was the only tool at Churchill's disposal
in this regard, and he employed it to the full during this period, which culminated in the Battle of Britain—when so few did so much for the safety of
so many. The fact that Hitler then gave up his UK invasion plans and turned
his murderous attention towards the Russian border was cited by Churchill
as evidence his supreme emergency strategy worked.[4]

Walzer and Rawls agree with all of this, yet are even more permissive
than Churchill himself regarding the time during which Britain experienced

a supreme emergency. After all, Britain "stood alone" against the Nazis in the West until America entered the theatre in substance, in 1942. Even then the Allies didn't experience much success until the campaigns in North Africa and Italy in 1943. In the East, the Soviets didn't get involved until 1942, and initially suffered terrible setbacks. Both American theorists are inclined to think Britain's supreme emergency lasted from 1940 until well into 1943, and thus all RAF bombing of German residential centres during this time was permissible. Walzer puts the core moral issue in the stark terms we need to reflect on: "(C)an one do *anything* [his italics], violating the rights of the innocent, in order to defeat Nazism?" He answers yes, and justifies himself in a phrase already quoted but worth repeating: "Nazism was an ultimate threat to everything decent in our lives, an ideology and a practice of domination so murderous, so degrading even to those who might survive, that the consequences of its final victory were literally beyond calculation, immeasurably awful. We see it—and I don't use the phrase lightly—as evil objectified in the world."[5]

When supreme emergency conditions evaporate, however, the justification for deliberate civilian targeting dissolves. So Walzer and Rawls argue that continued Allied bombing of German cities—and emphatically the fire-bombing and razing of Dresden in 1945—was unjust. Indeed, Churchill himself grew to regret the later bombings, admitting they were motivated more by bloodlust, the passions of war-fighting and, above all, by a desire for revenge for the London and Coventry bombings, than by any plausible moral or even strategic concern.[6]

Rawls, in his writings on supreme emergency,[7] is mostly concerned with using the doctrine as a tool for criticizing America's use of the atomic bomb on Japan in 1945. He suggests that perhaps the only thing which could justify the use of nuclear weapons—which of course are wildly destructive and unusually indiscriminate—is the experience of a supreme emergency. But America in August 1945 was not in a supreme emergency at all; on the contrary, it had just triumphed in Europe and had Japan by the throat. In fact, America was one of the most powerful and privileged societies on earth at that time. So the moral case for its using WMD was nil. In Rawls' view, US President Harry Truman's decision to do so anyway was a cynical piece of *realpolitik*, designed to show Japan and the world just how powerful America had become. The bombing was not done to stave off devastating loss; it was done to secure whatever terms of Japan's surrender America wanted—at minimal cost to the US—as well as to impress potential future rivals like the Soviets and Chinese with American capability. How stunning, then, was Truman's notorious comment that he never hesitated at all to order the bombing, that he never lost a moment's sleep over it. Walzer reflects insightfully on Truman's problematic cost-benefit approach: "Commonly, what we are calculating is *our* benefit (which we exaggerate) and *their* cost (which we minimize or disregard entirely)."[8] [his italics]

Truman's reply would be that the atomic bombings, in spite of their destructiveness, actually saved lives. How so? The Japanese, in July and August 1945, were irrationally refusing to surrender when they were clearly beaten and after their other former allies, Italy and Germany, had already given up. Moreover, in the previous battle of Okinawa—the first piece of Japanese territory on which US and Japanese forces clashed—the Japanese showed themselves capable of some of the most ferocious and bloody resistance in military history. So US decision-makers were in a dilemma: the Japanese were beaten yet refused to admit it, and apparently the only way to force surrender was an invasion of Japan itself. But Okinawa foretold that such an invasion would be an absolute slaughter for both US forces and Japanese soldiers and civilians: one million dead was the minimum predicted casualty total. By contrast, the Hiroshima and Nagasaki bombings killed about one-quarter that number—and they forced the Japanese to surrender without a blood-soaked invasion. So the bombings, while dramatic and using unprecedented technology, actually served both sound military and even moral objectives of forcing the surrender of an unjust aggressor while minimizing casualties.[9]

Walzer and Rawls refuse to be swayed by this reasoning. The figure of one million dead, and so many more injured, seems completely speculative and thus probably inflated. It is always convenient when we construct counterfactual numbers and arguments—and they end up "revealing" that our choices were right, leaving our opponents no way of either confirming or refuting the "evidence." Moreover, even if the numbers *were* true, Walzer and Rawls insist that they miss the point. The point is not to minimize the casualties while pursuing policies designed to advance majority interests regardless of whether there is rights violation or not. The point is to minimize casualties while pursuing policies, and using means of war, *which do not violate human rights.* And they believe the atomic bombings violated human rights because the explosions violated the core principles of discrimination and non-combatant immunity. It was foreseen, and intended, that innocent civilians would die *en masse* in both cities as a result of the bombings: that was supposed to happen to provide the leverage on the Japanese government to surrender and avoid suffering even more threatened bombings in the future. That was indeed what happened—but even if that was a happy consequence (i.e., the final surrender of an unjust, aggressive Japanese regime) it doesn't provide after-the-fact justification for the rights violation used to generate it.

What is also interesting in Rawls' reflections is that they are not merely backward-looking, designed to render correct judgment regarding historical cases. They are also forward-looking, in that they provide conditions for future use of controversial wartime measures. It is a clear inference from Rawls' reflections that a country suffering from a supreme emergency might be justified in using nuclear weapons, and perhaps other WMD, to prevail against an aggressor.

Which leads me to speculate whether we might imagine possible future instances. Consider the case of Israel. Israel, of course, occupies a quite precarious position in the Middle East: very small geographically, surrounded by hostile (or, at best, cool) neighbours, essentially the only democracy amidst a sea of authoritarian regimes, each of which it has encountered in war in the past 60 years. The concentration of population in its few major cities also makes Israel quite an easy target, compared to most others, for utterly devastating widespread destruction. The continuing controversy over the Palestinians, moreover, fuels an almost constant security crisis in Israel, and remains a *cause célèbre* amongst Arabs, fuelling rage and terrorism. What if a dystopian future unfolded, according to which Israel found itself in a condition of supreme emergency at the hands of its neighbours and/or domestically-located terrorists? If so, what may Israel permissibly do at that moment, especially in connection with its nuclear arsenal? Could it contemplate nuking Tehran, Riyadh, or Damascus? More bitingly, what about its own West Bank, or Gaza Strip, holdings? This horrible hypothetical underlines the continuing relevance of the proposed supreme emergency exemption—it is not just an outdated device for contemplating "Churchill versus the Nazis." In fact, in the era of terrorism and WMD, it is every bit as relevant as when Hitler darkened the world.

Some academics and politicians have actually argued that America, post-9/11, is in a condition of supreme emergency (or something very close to it). US Secretary of Defense Donald Rumsfeld has repeatedly made this assertion, as has former NYC mayor Rudy Guiliani; even President George Bush Jr. has appeared to assert this, what with his references to the "axis of evil" and his frequent claim that nothing less than civilization itself is at stake in the current conflict. All three men have drawn direct analogies between the ongoing war on terror and the war against fascism on Nazi Germany and Imperial Japan in World War II. Guiliani most directly—and I suppose not surprisingly, given his experience that day of 9/11—has drawn an absolute analogy between the war on terror and the situation of Churchill's Britain during the Nazi Blitz. These men have all argued that we need completely new rules to regulate wartime since it is a completely new era, owing to the potential blending between terrorists and WMD. Just war theory—quaint, decent, state-centric—must go the way of the dodo bird in the harsh, post 9/11 world.[10] But I doubt it.

Historically, we have heard the death of just war theory—and even international law—pronounced many a time before, and never has it turned out to be the case. The moral truth has a reassuring stability and resilience to it, and can survive trendy proclamations of its imminent demise and the dawn of a new era of brutality, wherein we can and should fight however we want, as bare-knuckled and bloody as we want.

We should be very hesitant to agree that America is in a supreme emergency, and we should consider sceptically the motives and incentives of those who do so. Why might they want to hype the notion that America suffers from supreme emergency? Well, perhaps that makes it easier for them to start and justify controversial wars, as in Iraq. Perhaps it makes it easier for them to target suspected terrorists with killing or capture, alongside any civilians they believe are supporting the terrorists. It makes all those collateral civilian casualties in the Middle East readily justifiable. The mega-crisis atmosphere also makes the extra-judicial detention and even torture of terrorist suspects much easier, and creates an environment wherein the people rally around the government in patriotic panic, and the government enacts forceful legislation which may violate classical civil liberties. Recall what was said last chapter about the similarities between the early Cold War period and our era, the early phase of the war on terror: the ferocious, demonized enemy; the starkly competing ideologies; the obsessive fear about WMD; the civil liberties issues; and the culture of self-restraint, patriotism and reluctance to criticize the establishment.

Declaring a supreme emergency in America, post 9/11, is an invitation to: 1) irrationality (since it is not true and stimulates panic); 2) moral violation or even atrocity (on far-away battlefields and prisons); 3) internal political repression; 4) external strategic mistakes (Abu Ghraib, and probably Iraq in general); and 5) experiencing profound regret later, when the country comes to realize that, in knee-jerk reaction to the shock of 9/11, it accidentally authorized a whole slew of controversies which it should have resisted. I have heard it said that America today is both the most powerful and the most scared country on earth—an incredibly dangerous combination. And dangerous not just for those on the receiving end of American wrath but even, in the senses just described, for the American people, too.

When we look at the three criteria for a supreme emergency, we see that America meets only one: it was genuinely victimized by aggression on 9/11. But there is little to show that America's military defeat, then or now, was close or imminent, much less that America will soon suffer widespread massacre or enslavement. Indeed, America has gone on the military offensive since 9/11, quite decisively taking down two regimes in countries on the other side of the world. America faces security threats of varying severity, yes, but not plausibly a supreme emergency. It is difficult to imagine any state actor, or combination of such, putting America in such a position, much less a non-state actor.[11] The only way would be in connection with WMD: if a group could somehow detonate enough WMD to truly devastate America—a very big, massively populated, resourceful and diverse country—then that would fulfil the three supreme emergency requirements of: 1) victimization by aggression; 2) military collapse; and 3) imminent threat of widespread massacre and/or enslavement. This indeed gives America, and other legitimate countries, strong reason to be very vigilant regarding the spread and control of WMD.

(After all, it is often said that terrorists don't want such weapons for deterrent purposes, since they aren't states with territorial interests to protect.

Terrorists want WMD for either blackmail or actual use, and in that sense can, in some circumstances, be even more dangerous than enemy states, even though they have fewer resources. This is true, and it underlines the seriousness of contemporary terrorist threats and ambitions as well as being resolute and determined in confronting them.)

But this possible use of WMD does not, as yet, give Western nations reason to deliberately attack civilians in the ongoing war on terror. The 9/11 attacks *were* outrageous and shocking acts of aggression, and they justified the return strike on the Taliban in Afghanistan, since that regime was sponsoring al-Qaeda in the way defined in Chapter 2. But the attacks manifestly did *not* put America into a condition of supreme emergency, with all the permissiveness and laxity in targeting which Walzer has it imply. When it comes to genuine victims of supreme emergency, we are much more likely to find them *at the other end of the power spectrum*—the small, weak and vulnerable communities which are decidedly unlike the one and only "hyperpower" which the United States has become.

Consider, for instance, communities targeted with, or victimized by, genocide, such as Turkish Armenians in the 1910s, European Jews in the early 1940s, Rwandan Tutsis in the mid-1990s and perhaps Albanian Kosovars in the late 1990s. More recently, in 2004–5, there have been rumblings that the large-scale killings and displacements in the Darfur region of Sudan amount to an attempted genocide of black Christian Sudanese at the hands of Arab Muslim Sudanese. If any community experiences a genuine supreme emergency, it is those confronted with genocide, which means trying to kill or enslave an entire people. Examples more distantly rooted in history might include Native Americans at the hands of the Spanish conquistadors, or Black Africans on the eve of the armed slave trade.[12] Reference to all these instances of genocide is made to underline the reality and urgency of the supreme emergency debate—to illustrate that it is not just about the Nazis, or science fiction scenarios sketching out nuclear wars between Russia and America. Supreme emergencies—thank goodness—are not regular occurrences, even in war. But they seem actually to have happened several times in history and, if the record of warfare teaches us anything, we should not be surprised at the depth and breadth of violent atrocity of which humanity is capable. As responsible thinkers, we must confront this proposed exemption and consider its nature.

Options Regarding Supreme Emergency

There seem to be five major—insightful, influential and logical—options for considering how to conceive of the supreme emergency doctrine. Let's examine each of them in turn.

Before we do, we should note how the Doctrine of Double Effect (DDE) —very often called upon by just war theory to solve difficult wartime dilemmas—is *not* a viable option when dealing with supreme emergencies. Why?

Because, as we saw last chapter, the DDE (among other things) only lets one perform actions which are otherwise permissible, and in which the unintended bad effects are *not* the means to producing the intended good ones. But in supreme emergencies, the actions contemplated are *not* otherwise permissible (e.g., deliberately killing civilians), and the bad effects *are* the means to producing the good (e.g., hoping, as Churchill did, that the civilian casualties will, somehow, quell the aggressor's appetite and force it to back off).[13]

OPTION #1: NO SUCH THING

This first perspective, or option, asserts that there really is no such thing as a supreme emergency, and that Walzer's proposal is thus a bastardization or corruption of just war theory. The objection here is rooted both conceptually and historically. In the conceptual sense, the supreme emergency conditions might seem too abstract and subject to interpretive disagreement to be useful and immune from gratuitous, self-serving abuse. Consider the vagueness of Walzer's conditions. First, they require that there be a clear victim, and perpetrator, of "aggression." We are all now quite familiar with disputes regarding what exactly counts as "aggression" and "defence" from it—witness the whole debate on anticipatory attack. Second, Walzer says there must be "public proof" of imminent military defeat *and* subsequent massacre or enslavement. Such "proof," though, can be hard indeed to come by. They famously say, after all, that truth is the first casualty of war. Discerning the future tides of war-fighting, and the intent of one's opponent, can be very difficult, especially amidst the heat of battle. We know generally that, in war, people overestimate the risks they face. Everything seems like a super-heated crisis. We have also recently witnessed, in connection with America's 2003 Iraq attack, the apparent failure of even the best-funded intelligence agencies to come up with plausible and well-grounded conclusions, in this case regarding a connection between Iraq and al-Qaeda as well as Iraq's possession of WMD before the attack. Third, there is the issue of what counts as an imminent "military defeat." Is it simply a big, crushing loss in a high-profile battle? Is it loss of one's political capital to the enemy? Or is it, as I would suggest, something more like the total collapse of an effective armed forces capability, literally rendering you defenceless? Next, there is vagueness regarding what "close and imminent" means. Are we talking weeks, days, or hours? Are we agreeing, with Oliver Wendell Holmes, that the threat of supreme emergency must (merely) be "a clear and present danger"? Or are we saying something more stringent, as I would be inclined to believe, such as: you have imminency only when you'll lose and then be massacred unless you switch to exceptional measures. Finally, the criteria require that, after the military defeat, you know you will be subjected to "widespread massacre and/or enslavement." Massacre and enslavement seem fairly straightforward in meaning, but "widespread" is not. How much is widespread: five per cent, ten per cent, fifty per cent or more of your population? Or a distinctive sub-set of your population—such as a visible or especially powerful minority group—even if, overall, it doesn't add up to many numbers or a large percentage?

This first, sceptical perspective might also wonder whether the one example that these theorists all seem to agree on—namely Britain in 1940—actually was a supreme emergency. After all, while Nazi *invasion* seemed imminent, Britain's *military collapse* was not, or at least it is not a clear causal connection to go *from* suffering invasion *to* suffering total military collapse. We also cannot forget Churchill's political self-interest in exaggerating the threat that Britain faced: doing so would drive the British people to greater efforts, and it would also serve as a strong rhetorical and moral tug on the United States to finally get involved in the war on the Allied side. Moreover, Walzer and Rawls surely err when they talk of Britain "standing alone" against the Nazis at this time. For Britain had all of its colonies and ex-colonies fighting alongside it from the first days in 1939. They included Australia, Canada, India, New Zealand and the Caribbean island nations. This is to say that Britain had far greater resources to draw on than any of the Continental countries that fell to the Nazis during the Blitzkrieg, including France. In fact, Britain probably had more resources to draw on than all those countries put together, and had the advantage of geography to boot: an island has a natural ring of defensive water all around. To what extent, then, did it actually face a supreme emergency as Walzer defines it? Drawing on these considerations of conceptual vagueness and questionable historical application, the sceptical perspective might well conclude that the supreme emergency exemption is a big, bad, dangerous *moral loop-hole* in just war theory, and we're better off without it. Perhaps this is why it appears nowhere in the international laws of armed conflict. The rules are the rules, and we shouldn't allow for exceptions to them, or ways for belligerents to get around them.

While I do think that this perspective adds some very healthy precautionary scepticism regarding the supreme emergency exemption, in the end I believe it fails to persuade. While far too many just war theorists accept the exemption uncritically, and apparently on little more than Walzer's authority, it really does seem as though supreme emergencies can be real. Witness the examples of genocide offered last section. Also, from the fact that supreme emergencies can be hard to define conceptually, it does not follow that we should get rid of, or dismiss, the very idea itself. There is, after all, a whole roster of vitally important ideas in moral and political philosophy (e.g., freedom, equality, human rights, justice, democracy) that we should have to throw out as well if that were the case. The conceptual difficulty just means that our jobs aren't easy. The same holds for the objection regarding liability of the concept to self-serving abuse. We know full well that, subjectively, *all* belligerents in *every* war will try to claim for their side *any* concept which justifies their actions. There is an old saying: "Even the Devil can quote

Scripture." Just because people or countries *claim* that their actions are justified does *not* make it so. The task for them, as we have strongly asserted, is to show that their subjective beliefs correspond to objectively defensible standards and to intersubjectively plausible evidence. This is an absolutely vital point, not just for supreme emergency but for all of just war theory and international law, and it seems it cannot be made forcefully enough, or repeated often enough.

OPTION #2: CHURCHILL'S CONSEQUENTIALISM

This second perspective states that, when in supreme emergency, only *jus ad bellum* matters, therefore the rules of *jus in bello* may be set aside. Churchill clearly believed this, and Walzer partially believes it. (More on Walzer's nuanced view to follow below.) Other exemplars of this view may be Generals Grant and Sherman during the US Civil War. Both believed that the South was the aggressor, and that its social system of slavery was so unjust that it could not, under any conditions, be allowed to win. Thus, they both took a very permissive view regarding what the North was entitled to do to bring about victory. Note, for instance, Sherman's notorious "scorched earth" policy against the state of Georgia wherein, after his divisions conquered territory, they set it ablaze so as to ruin it for any Southerners who might re-group to plan future military action.[14]

The strength of this view is that it offers a morally coherent response to the supreme emergency dilemma. And depending on your views regarding the essence of ethics, it may offer you complete satisfaction on this issue. Upon reflection, though, I think this perspective has four fatal flaws to it.

The first flaw is precisely that it violates the human rights of enemy civilians, understood by international law and just war theory to be non-combatants. As such, this view violates our core commitment not to punish the innocent. As Thomas Nagel eloquently puts it: "hostile treatment of any person must be justified in terms of something *about that person* [his italics] which makes the treatment appropriate." We distinguish combatants from non-combatants "on the basis of their immediate threat or harmfulness." And our response to such threats and harms must be governed by relations of directness and relevance.[15] But it is not the enemy civilians who are threatening us, it is their military machine, and so it is impermissible to strike out deliberately at the civilians, because even in a supreme emergency it is not they who are the direct and active agents of the brutal force.

Churchill's consequentialism is also problematic because it seems to endorse the proposition that "the ends justify the means." We all know the flaws in this proposition, notably the one that it violates the principle never to treat persons as mere subjects to be sacrificed against their will, or for the sake of some glorified social project. Individuals all have autonomy unless they themselves forfeit it, and this nicely ties in with the previous claim about the human rights of enemy civilians, and how they do nothing to forfeit them. Believing and acting on this proposition—that the ends justify the means—can also be morally corrupting in the following sense: isn't civilian murder the very thing feared at the hands of the aggressor? If so, what entitles you to commit the very same action?

Thirdly, why have *jus in bello* at all if *jus ad bellum* is what ultimately matters? Now some people, apparently Grant and Sherman, seem to believe this: "war is hell," whether just or unjust, so at least let's make sure that the just side wins. Let's give the just side wide, or even complete, sway regarding its selection of tactics and targets. This attitude, however, ignores the compelling reason we have in favour of maintaining *jus in bello* rules: they prevent escalation into indiscriminate slaughter and total, no-holds-barred warfare. And if just war theory stands for anything, it is that total warfare must be avoided. The very essence of just war theory, we now know, is to insist on *restraints* in the reasons for fighting, and in the means used in fighting.

Finally, Churchill's consequentialism is at odds with our moral convictions in an analogous inter-personal case of supreme emergency. Suppose that aggressor person A murderously attacks victim B, and B drags in innocent bystander C, to serve as a shield between him and A. How should we evaluate B's actions during his own personal supreme emergency? I suggest that none of us, upon reflection, would argue that B's actions are morally justified. Indeed, the immediate reaction, normally, is that B is behaving like a selfish and despicable coward, endangering an innocent person's life instead of confronting his own danger like a man. Upon consideration, though, it is compelling to understand that this immediate response may be too judgmental, since it is offered by those of us who reflect in comfort upon a fellow person's desperate choices amidst terrifying danger. (We like to comfort ourselves by supposing we would make better choices under such conditions. But until we experience similar extraordinary pressure and fear, we might want to climb down from our tower of condemnation.) It seems equally erroneous, however, to pretend there is nothing wrong with B doing whatever he wants—including sacrificing C—to save his own life. Yet that is precisely what Churchill's consequentialism would here imply. Clearly, B has no right to violate C's rights in this case: C has done nothing wrong, nothing that would render her rights forfeit. She is an innocent bystander that B decides to use as a mere tool in service of his own end of survival. B utterly disregards C's humanity in this instance; he treats her as a prop, not a person. In my view, he is almost as culpable for her death as A, should she succumb from her injuries sustained while serving as a shield between the two.

The most complete and accurate judgment of this interpersonal analogy seems to be this: B has no right to drag C into the situation, and if he does so he commits a severe moral wrongdoing. However, we might be willing to excuse B's actions, on grounds that the terrible duress and mortal fear operative on him, in the situation, drove him to make the terrible choice he did. Like any animal filled with mortal terror, he desperately reached out for any means necessary to stave off death. This doesn't make his choice *right* or morally justifiable; it merely makes it *understandable* and, depending on the exact circumstances, *excusable* from criticism or punishment. It will be excusable if we determine that the pressure, in the case, was so extreme that B acted more out of animal instinct than out of a morally culpable decision-making capacity. We would say, under such conditions, that *he was forced to do something terribly wrong*. This case, and this distinction between having moral justification for doing X, and being excused for doing X, are vital in my mind to a proper understanding of a supreme emergency.

OPTION #3: STRICT RESPECT FOR *JUS IN BELLO*

This third perspective says that, even in supreme emergency conditions, one must still scrupulously respect the rules of *jus in bello*. Colloquially, this is the view that "let justice be done, though the heavens fall." Kant and Socrates are probably exemplars of this view, as is a different part of Walzer, and the international laws of armed conflict themselves. Nowhere, in any piece of international law, does it say that military necessity is a valid reason for setting aside the rules of armed conflict. In fact, in several places it is stated quite clearly that, since the rules have been framed *in the first place* with military necessity already in mind, no appeal to necessity can override the need to respect the rules.[16]

This view has seductive strengths from the moral point of view. Notably, it avoids each of the four problems detailed with Churchill's consequential-ism. Unlike that perspective, this one respects the human rights of enemy civilians, does not endorse the proposition that "the ends justify the means," maintains *jus in bello* as a meaningful category, and can be brought into accord with our considered judgment in the interpersonal analogy. It is also a consistent and coherent response to the supreme emergency dilemma and, if one has certain moral leanings, it may offer total satisfaction in this regard. Think of Socrates' powerful pronouncement that it is always better to suffer injustice than to inflict it oneself. Yet this view, in spite of its moral force, also has flaws.

The first flaw with this view is that it seems quite unrealistic. Strict respect for *jus in bello*, in this case, might result *not just* in victory for the aggressor, *but also* the kind of horrible slaughter or slavery previously detailed. Realis-tically, who is going to follow the advice of this option? Respecting *jus in bello* is, to an extent, agreeing to fight with one arm tied behind one's back. Now, this might be fine so long as one can still win, or at least if one loses, it is simply a "run-of-the-mill" military defeat involving things like territorial concessions. But that is *not* what we're talking about with supreme emer-gency: we are talking about not just defeat but slaughter, slavery and total catastrophe. In the face of such a threat, who in their right mind is still going to fight with one arm tied behind their back?

John Fiala says that Kant will still agree to fight with one arm tied, but only because he has a philosophy of history—i.e., a system of beliefs about how history will unfold—which guarantees the eventual, complete victory of liberal democracy. In other words, one day the planet will be covered with nothing but legitimate, rights-respecting regimes. So Kant can relax about the occasional supreme emergency, and insist on respect for *jus in bello*, since in the end rights-respecting democracies are destined to triumph, and brutal, rights-violating aggressors will disappear from the face of the Earth.[17] While that is an accurate description of Kant's philosophy of history—about which more in the next two chapters—I don't believe that that is *why* Kant still insists on respecting *jus in bello*. For Kant, elsewhere, says there is no guarantee that doing the right thing will improve the world, or even serve your self-interest. Doing one's duty might not make one happy—but it remains one's duty. Perhaps this is just an instance of this conviction. Here in supreme emergency we perhaps discern the full strength and import of Kant's commitment to morality: you are to adhere to moral demands even if it costs you your life. Morality is thus revealed to be the single most important thing in life for Kant: the act which shows humanity at its very best. Something of the same can be said of Socrates, with his own example of sticking to his principles even though it led to him being forced by the Athenian court to drink poison and die.[18] Critics of Kant and Socrates (and we can hear them baying at this point) alternatively suggest that first you have to survive, and then you can be moral. Existence precedes ethics, so to speak.

The second weakness with this option is that, as Walzer notes, it is fundamentally irresponsible on the part of the victim country's government, which has an obligation to protect its country's citizens from massacre and enslavement. There's a vital moral duty which the government owes its own people to do what it can to stave off the horrifying suffering and death which are part-and-parcel of the supreme emergency condition. Walzer says that if the state has any moral value at all, it is precisely to defend those whom it represents. Failure to provide such defence—much less deliberate standing-down in the face of holocaust—is an abdication of office and it dissolves the social contract which formerly united rulers and ruled, the people and their state. In other words, it is one thing to sacrifice *oneself* for one's own principles, like Socrates; it is quite another to sacrifice *others*. The state's duty to protect implies that it cannot deliberately sacrifice its own citizens when effective resistance might still be available.[19]

OPTION #4: WALZER'S PARADOXICAL DIRTY HANDS

As previously mentioned, part of Walzer endorses Churchill's consequentialism, while another part of him supports Kant's strict respect for the rules.

Walzer thinks that being politically realistic in supreme emergencies drives one towards the former, while being morally sensitive inclines one towards the latter. We have, on the one hand, his before-quoted remark that one can, in fact, do anything to defeat Nazis. Similar to it is his recommendation, during a supreme emergency, to "wager this determinate crime (the killing of innocent people) against that immeasurable evil (a Nazi triumph)." On the other, Walzer also tells us that civilians are not in any material sense "dangerous men." Thus, "they have done nothing, and are doing nothing, that entails the loss of their rights." So they may not be made the direct and intentional objects of military attack. He declares, moreover, that "the destruction of the innocent, whatever its purposes, is a kind of blasphemy against our deepest moral commitments."[20] He then asks: "How can we, with our principles and prohibitions, stand by and watch the destruction of the moral world in which those principles and prohibitions have their hold? How can we, the opponents of murder, fail to resist the practice of mass murder— even if resistance requires us, as the phrase goes, to get our hands dirty (that is, to become murderers ourselves)?"[21]

Walzer accordingly describes his position on supreme emergency as paradoxical. The victim community may set aside *jus in bello* rules, so as to protect its people and defend itself from slaughter, *yet* doing so is still morally wrong, in that it will involve the murder of enemy civilians. Walzer says that when "the very existence of a community may be at stake," "the restraint on utilitarian [or consequentialist] calculation must be lifted. Even if we are inclined to lift it, however, we cannot forget that the rights violated for the sake of victory are genuine rights, deeply founded and in principle inviolable."[22] The deliberate killing of innocents, though murder, can nevertheless be justified in a supreme emergency: it is simultaneously right and wrong. At the same time and with respect to the same action, we say "yes and no." Bomb the residential areas deliberately—murder those civilians—but do so only because you are "a nation fighting a just war [which] is desperate and survival itself is at risk." "(I)n supreme emergencies," Walzer concludes, "our judgments are doubled, reflecting the dualist character of the theory of war and the deeper complexities of our moral realism; we say yes *and* no, right *and* wrong [his italics]. That dualism makes us uneasy; the world is not a fully comprehensible, let alone a morally satisfactory place."[23]

Walzer's position underlines the sheer difficulty of the supreme emergency dilemma, whereas the other positions might seem simplistic and one-sided by contrast. His reconstruction of contemporary just war theory possesses great authority, and is aimed in this specific regard at balancing the insights of the two extreme positions of respecting the rules scrupulously, on the one hand, and discarding them completely, on the other. Yet we might wonder about the coherence of his doctrine, as well as its action-guiding properties. The upshot of just war theory, after all, is precisely to devise coherent rules that statesmen and soldiers can refer to as they make choices under pressured wartime conditions. This has been a major objective throughout this book. With Churchill's consequentialism, the nature of the advice is—in spite of its substantive problems—quite clear: disregard *jus in bello*, and do whatever you can to stave off supreme emergency. Kant's doctrine, despite its limitations, likewise provides coherent guidance: you must still adhere to *jus in bello* even in the teeth of a supreme emergency. Where, we might ask, is the coherent advice in Walzer's position of paradox? He seems, after all, to stress that the various options in a supreme emergency are *both* right and wrong. Consider the most relevant quote here: "A morally strong leader is someone who understands why it is wrong to kill the innocent and refuses to do so, refuses again and again, until the heavens are about to fall. And then he becomes a *moral criminal* [my italics] ... who knows that he can't do what he has to do—and finally does."[24] It is in reflection on this curious pronouncement that we see Walzer's position is, ultimately, not so evenly balanced between the two options as his self-reference to paradox would have us believe.

In the final analysis, Walzer leans a little bit towards Churchill's consequentialism, and this allows him at least to offer coherent advice, but it comes at the cost of some of the moral controversy attaching to that attitude. Walzer's advice to statesmen and soldiers in a supreme emergency is this: you must set aside *jus in bello* and do what you can to stop the supreme emergency, even though this will involve horrible wrongdoing. You actually have a duty to do this—to get your hands dirty, to shoulder personally the burden of this crime—because the function of your office is to defend your people. This is coherent advice, but still somewhat paradoxical: you have an important moral duty to violate another important moral duty; you have the right to do something that is not right. Even though Walzer urges this "dirty hands policy" upon statesmen and soldiers, he says they should not face war crimes trials after the war ends. They should, at most, be criticized and shamed after the war. Walzer here cites approvingly the British policy to withhold highest honours to RAF Commander Arthur Harris, who was humiliated by being the only senior UK military official denied such honours after World War II.[25]

OPTION #5: MORAL TRAGEDY, PRUDENTIAL STRATEGY

The point of this section—the fifth perspective—is to present an alternative way of thinking about supreme emergency which, on balance, is superior to all the previously-discussed rivals.[26] I stress that what follows applies *only* to the *external* issue of how to treat one's enemies. In my view, the *internal* issue of domestic human rights satisfaction remains as discussed last chapter. The entry point of this option reminds us that we can look at a person, or action, from at least two different perspectives. Consider, for example, Kant's thoughts on the nature of a human being. Famously, Kant argued that humanity is a composite of "animal instinctuality" and "free rationality." Considering the human being as *phenomenon*, we see a quite limited, corporeal animal entity, subject to all the physical laws of nature, hard-wired to seek its own survival and satisfaction. Considering the human being as *noumenon*, we see not so much finite body as expansive mind, we discern moral freedom instead of physical necessity, and we witness commitment to reason and justice even at the cost of our own happiness, and perhaps sometimes even of life itself. It is the exact same object—the human person—yet seen as possessing radically different properties depending on the perspective chosen. While Kant clearly sided with the noumenal self, he knew the phenomenal self to be in some sense inescapable, and in fact viewed much of life as a struggle between the two for primacy.[27] I propose that much can be gained from viewing the supreme emergency condition analogously under two different perspectives: the moral and the prudential. Morally, a supreme emergency is a terrible tragedy. Prudentially, it is a struggle for survival.

From the moral point of view, a supreme emergency is a moral tragedy. A moral tragedy occurs when, *all things considered*, each viable option you face involves a severe moral violation. It is a moral blind alley: there is no way to turn and still be morally justified. Colloquially, in a supreme emergency, "you're damned if you do, and damned if you don't." You're damned if you do, so to speak, because if you "do," you violate *jus in bello* and commit widespread civilian murder. You're damned if you don't, on the other hand, because if you "don't," you fail to protect your own civilians from widespread murder. On this understanding, there is no supreme emergency exemption, where such is conceived as a *moral* exemption, permission or loophole. *The whole thing is a wretched moral tragedy and, no matter what you do, you're wrong.* This option differs from Walzer's in two important respects. First, it captures and highlights not merely the difficulty of the dilemma but its full-blown tragedy. I think reflection upon war's tragedy is something which just war theory can benefit from, and which has hitherto been ignored.[28] Not everything in war can be morally justified—in supreme emergency we hit a wall where we see that, morally, we run out of permissible options. Yet still we must choose and act—the world forces this upon us. Second, this option retains no aspect of paradox, as Walzer's still does. Walzer suggests that, in a supreme emergency, you have the right to do wrong, and/or a duty to violate duty, whereas no such confounding claims are here made, resulting I believe in a more coherent understanding. You don't have the right to do wrong, nor a duty to violate duty: if you do wrong, you do wrong, even under the pressure of supreme emergency conditions.

From the prudential point of view, a supreme emergency is a desperate, Hobbesian struggle for survival, and as a matter of fact any country subjected to it *will do* whatever it can to prevail. The animal instincts are going to kick in, just as in our interpersonal analogy involving A, B, and C. Yet these instincts can still be channelled by rules of rational choice—you want your self-saving actions to work, after all. Which rules would here help? First, make sure resort to supreme emergency measures are, in fact, *a last resort*. Wartime can create an overheated crisis atmosphere, in which people discern "emergencies" which aren't, in fact, there. There are a great many options, permissible according to standard just war theory, to be tried prior to actions which violate the rules. As the war goes badly, perhaps things like conscription or assassination should be tried. Perhaps, as the Russians have sometimes done historically, the thing to do is pull back from one's borders, moving one's people and maybe strategically despoiling some territory, so as to put distance between oneself and the aggressor. We have to make sure supreme emergency measures aren't taken hastily, out of a failure of imagination surrounding standard tactics.

A second rule of prudence is *to publicly declare* what one intends to do. This ties into last resort: it gives the aggressor pause, articulating the extreme measures to be taken if he, in fact, persists to push one into a condition of supreme emergency.

The public declaration should also serve as an *appeal to the international community*. The international community clearly has a moral duty of humanitarian intervention to aid a country in supreme emergency and do everything reasonable to stop the aggressor. The victim has every self-interest in appealing for such intervention, just as individuals in personal supreme emergencies should yell "help!" "police!" or "fire!" to bring in outside support. At the same time, the reaction of the international community has, sadly, been known to be inefficacious, half-hearted or absent altogether—we think here of Rwanda[29]—and so, pending the imminency of the supreme emergency, the victim must always act of its own accord and not pin inflated hopes on the historically fickle replies of the international community.

Fourth, one must, to the extent possible, keep one's mind clear of other temptations, such as the passions of revenge and bloodlust or just an inclination to destroy, to take others down with you, so to speak. This is to say that even here there should be *a right intention*—not one of moral purity, but rather one of prudential effectiveness, namely, that the purpose of one's actions is one's survival.

Any supreme emergency measures, above all, must have a *reasonable probability of success*. This fifth rule is absolutely vital: are the extreme measures contemplated actually going to make a difference? This is particularly important in connection with civilian targeting: if it is the aggressor's military machine which is pushing one into supreme emergency, *how is killing his civilians actually going to help*? To be blunt—if it came down to this—why not employ a tactical WMD against the aggressor's front line, instead of unleashing civilian slaughter?[30] Churchill argued that his policy of civilian bombing worked, because Hitler gave up his UK invasion plans. True, but the bombing didn't actually beat Hitler—what did was standard tactics, aimed at his military machine and industrial supply, for several sustained years after that. In my view, the probability of success regarding deliberate civilian targeting is probably very limited, and more utility can likely be had by violating other *jus in bello* rules while still aiming at legitimate military targets, notably the ban on prohibited weapons. We should note that probability of success is relevant on several levels: not just, will our first strike stave off supreme emergency? But how is the aggressor likely to respond to that first strike? And can we withstand his response and formulate a forceful second strike? And so on.[31] This is, of course, very difficult to do under the crush of these conditions, yet some consideration simply must be given to it, since the ultimate goal remains one's survival.

Having this twofold perspective on supreme emergency is very advantageous. It raises the important issue of moral tragedy, and it contains more detailed, practical rules of thumb for soldiers and statesmen than any of the other four approaches. It thus provides concrete, considered advice. I suppose the final question is this: which perspective is more important, the moral or the prudential?[32] I view this as a loaded and misleading question. Both perspectives are vital to a complete analysis: victims of supreme emergency are going to fight to survive, and they need rules of thumb to help them achieve that goal. At the same time, supreme emergency measures—while (hopefully) prudentially useful—remain morally wrong insofar as they involve *jus in bello* violations. I view the scenario as directly analogous to the interpersonal case: the victim was forced to do wrong. The measures remain wrong even though aimed against a terrible aggressor. Owing to the severe duress of the supreme emergency condition, the victim resorted to immoral measures to stave off disaster and death. Owing to this duress, we can excuse the victim's actions, but never justify them. And I think the excuse from punishment should be extended to everyone involved in the extreme measures. Picking out one official, like "Bomber Harris," for public shaming seems both *pro forma* and unfair. *Pro forma*, because it is purely symbolic, and unfair because in Harris' case many others—including Churchill himself—were involved in the bombing, but only he was singled out.

I do believe that the victim country, supposing its supreme emergency measures to succeed, owes its citizens and the international community a full public accounting, after the war, for what it did and why it did it. But that is all—no war crimes trials, no shaming, no symbolic hand-wringing. It was forced to do terrible things in order to survive. Indeed, depending on the circumstances, the international community might also have some explaining of its own to do, regarding why it failed to intervene effectively and to stop the situation from becoming so desperate and bleak in the first place.

Summary

This chapter considered the case of supreme emergencies, which are nowhere defined, or permitted to be cited, in international law. Discussion of them has continued, however, owing to historical and recent events, speculation on dark scenarios and the authority of figures like Rawls and Walzer. We considered five options for thinking about ethics with such emergencies. We rejected four of the most common and settled on the fifth option, which suggested that violating *jus in bello* in crisis remains morally wrong but might nevertheless be excused on grounds of duress and tragedy. There are still prudential (and familiar) rules of thumb which should be followed, and of course a genuine supreme emergency is perhaps the clearest instance demanding armed humanitarian intervention from the international community. So here, too, we see that deep, sustained reflection on one concept of just war theory (i.e., supreme emergency within *jus in bello*) necessarily raises material connections to the other categories, especially *jus ad bellum*. Ultimately, it all relates—and the tone of the relation is first established by issues of just cause and political legitimacy.

Notes

1. W. Churchill quoted in M. Walzer, *Just and Unjust Wars* (New York: Basic Books, 3rd ed., 2000), 245. For primary sources: W. Churchill, *The Gathering Storm* (London: Macmillan, 1961), 488–90; W. Churchill, *The Hinge of Fate* (New York: Bantam, 1962), 770 f.
2. Walzer, *Wars*, 251–68.
3. Grotius quoted in P. Christopher, *The Ethics of War and Peace* (Englewood Cliffs, NJ: Prentice Hall, 1994), 109.
4. Churchill, *Storm*, 488; Churchill, *Hinge*, 770.
5. Walzer, *Wars*, 253.
6. Churchill, *Storm*, 490–2; Churchill, *Hinge*, 770.
7. J. Rawls, *The Law of Peoples* (Cambridge, MA: Harvard University Press, 1999), 98–105; J. Rawls in *Dissent*'s Summer 1995 symposium on the bombing of Hiroshima.
8. M. Walzer, *Arguing About War* (New Haven: Yale University Press, 2004), 39.
9. J. Costello, *The Pacific War* (New York: Harper, 1982).
10. D. Kellogg, "Reaping the Whirlwind: Terrorism, Supreme Emergency and the Abandonment of *Jus in Bello* Restrictions on Attacking Enemy Civilians," Unpublished paper, 2002, University of Maine; R. Scarborough, *Rumsfeld's War* (New York: Regnery, 2004); R. Guiliani, *Leadership* (New York: Miramax, 2002), 3–28, 341–80; B. Adler, ed. *The Quotable Guiliani* (New York: Pocket, 2003), 23–54; the post-9/11 speeches of President George Bush Jr., all available in complete text at <www.americanrhetoric.com>.
11. In terms of state actors, we could I suppose imagine a grisly scenario involving war between the USA and, say, Russia and/or China. The latter two probably do have enough WMD to put America into supreme emergency.
12. Thanks to Neta Crawford for these examples. On the history of genocide, see F. Chalk and K. Jonassohn, eds. *The History and Sociology of Genocide* (New

Haven, CT: Yale University Press, 1990); and S. Totten, et al, eds. *Century of Genocide* (New York: Garland, 1997).

13. For more on the DDE, see Walzer, *Wars*, 151–60 and our discussion last chapter. Thanks to Alex Moseley for discussions on this.

14. Walzer, *Wars*, 29–34. This is the option Walzer describes as "the sliding scale."

15. T. Nagel, "War and Massacre," *Philosophy and Public Affairs* (1973), 133–41.

16. W. Reisman and C. Antoniou, eds. *The Laws of War: A Comprehensive Collection of Primary Documents Governing Armed Conflict* (New York: Vintage, 1994); A. Roberts and R. Guelff, eds. *Documents on The Laws of War* (Oxford: Oxford University Press, 1999).

17. J. Fiala, "Terrorism and the Philosophy of History: Liberalism, Realism and the Supreme Emergency Exemption," *Essays in Philosophy* (Vol. 3, 2002), 1–15; M. Doyle, *Ways of War and Peace* (New York: Norton, 1997); M. Doyle, "Kant, Liberal Legacies and Foreign Affairs," *Philosophy and Public Affairs* (1983), Vol. 12, pp. 205–54 and 323–53; M. Brown, ed. *Debating the Democratic Peace* (Cambridge, MA: MIT Press, 1996).

18. B. Orend, *War and International Justice: A Kantian Perspective* (Waterloo, ON: Wilfrid Laurier University Press, 2000).

19. Walzer, *Wars*, 251–68.

20. The quotes, in order, from: Walzer, *Wars*, 231, 259, 146–51, 262–8.

21. Walzer, *Arguing*, 37.

22. Walzer, *Wars*, 195, 228.

23. Walzer, *Wars*, 325–8 and 251–68.

24. Walzer, *Arguing*, 45.

25. Walzer, *Wars*, 251–68; M. Walzer, "Political Action: The Problem of Dirty Hands," *Philosophy and Public Affairs* (1972/3), 160–80.

26. I wish especially to thank Patrick Hayden, Danny Statman and Toni Erskine for stimulating and sharpening my thoughts regarding what follows.

27. Orend, *Kantian Perspective*, 10–36.

28. Another concept which just war theory might gain by adding would be mercy.

29. G. Prunier, *The Rwanda Crisis: History of a Genocide* (New York: Columbia University Press, 1995); R. Dallaire, *Shake Hands with the Devil: Humanity's Failure in Rwanda* (New York: Random House, 2003).

30. In other words, and as an accommodation to realism, I do admit there might be extreme, very rare conditions when WMD use—perhaps including nukes—might at least be excusable (but probably never justifiable). More on realism in Chapter 8.

31. Thanks to Neta Crawford for emphasizing this.

32. Toni Erskine has urged this question, and choice, upon me. But I don't think I have to choose, for reasons explained.

CHAPTER 6

Jus post Bellum #1
Justice after War

> "The object in war is a better state of peace."
> *B.H. Liddell Hart*[1]

This is one of the hottest topics in just war theory: how should wars end? It might seem surprising, but only very recently has the issue of justice after war—or *"jus post bellum"*—come into the prominence it deserves. All too often, still today, just war theorists stick with the first two categories—of *jus ad bellum* and *jus in bello*—and pretend that is all they have to talk about. International law, sadly, has joined just war theory regarding its relative silence on proper war termination.[2] This is a decrepit state of affairs that must be remedied, both for conceptual and concrete historical reasons:

1 Conceptually, war has three phases: beginning, middle and end. So if we want a complete just war theory—or comprehensive international law— we simply *must* discuss justice during the termination phase of war. After all, there is no guarantee that if you fought justly, for the sake of a just cause, that you will automatically impose a just set of peace terms upon your vanquished enemy. Mistakes are possible, and made frequently, during each of the three phases. It is, indeed, difficult to fight a truly just war.
2 Failure to include *jus post bellum* in your just war theory leaves you open to a sharp, potentially devastating objection from both realists and pacifists, namely, that just war theory fails to consider war in a deep enough, systematic enough kind of way. It simply considers war on a case-by-case basis, dusting off its precious old rules for yet another ethical application. Pacifists, for example, have long objected that just war theory, with its hitherto narrow focus, is fundamentally passive and complaisant about war—that it does not ultimately care why war breaks out and does not seek to improve things after war's end so as to make the international system more peaceful over the longer term. I believe this objection *succeeds* against just war theorists who have no account of *jus post bellum*; if we are not to meet their sorry fate, we must include such an account to surmount this challenge.

3 More concretely, recent armed conflicts—in Bosnia and Kosovo, in central Africa, in Afghanistan and twice in Iraq—demonstrate the difficulty and illustrate the importance and controversy surrounding a just peace settlement. The major issues of contemporary international affairs simply demand we look at *jus post bellum*. We know that when wars are wrapped up badly, they sow the seeds for future bloodshed. Some people, for example, think that America's failure to remove Saddam Hussein from power after they first defeated him in 1991 prolonged a serious struggle and eventually necessitated the second war, for regime change, in 2003. *Would the second war have happened at all had the first been ended differently* (i.e., more properly and thoroughly, with a longer-range vision in mind)? Many historians ask the exact same question of the two World Wars and the recent, related Serb wars, first in Bosnia and then over Kosovo.

4 Failure to construct principles of *jus post bellum* is to allow unconstrained war termination. And to allow unconstrained war termination is to allow the winner to enjoy the spoils of war. This is dangerously permissive, since winners have been known to exact peace terms which are draconian and vengeful. The Treaty of Versailles, terminating World War I in 1918–19, is often mentioned in this connection. It is commonly suggested that the sizeable territorial concessions and steep compensations payments forced upon Germany created hatred and economic distress, opening a space for Hitler to exploit, saying in effect: "Let's vent our rage by recapturing our lost lands and let's rebuild our economy by refusing to pay compensation, and by ramping up war-related manufacturing."[3]

5 Failure to regulate war termination probably prolongs fighting on the ground. Since they have few assurances or firm expectations regarding the nature of the settlement, belligerents will be sorely tempted to keep using force to jockey for position. Since international law imposes very few clear constraints upon the winners of war, losers can conclude it is reasonable for them to refuse to surrender and, instead, to continue to fight. Perhaps, they think, "we might get lucky and the military tide will turn. Better that than just throw ourselves at the mercy of our enemy." Many observers felt this reality plagued the Bosnian civil war, which we saw in Chapter 3 had many failed negotiations and a three-year "slow burn" of continuous violence as the negotiations took place.[4]

Peace treaties should still, of course, remain tightly tailored to the historical realities of the particular conflict in question. There are all kinds of nitty-gritty detail integral to each peace treaty. But admitting this is *not* to concede that the search for general guidelines or universal standards is futile or naïve. There is no inconsistency or mystery in holding particular actors, in complex local conflicts, up to more general, even universal, standards of conduct. Judges and juries do that on a daily basis, evaluating the factual complexities of a given case in light of general moral and legal principles. We should do the same regarding war termination. The goal of this chapter, accordingly, is to construct a general set of plausible principles to guide communities seeking to resolve their armed conflicts fairly and decently.[5]

The Ends of a Just War

The first step is to answer the question: what may a participant rightly aim at with regard to a just war? What are the goals to be achieved by the settlement of the conflict? We need some starting assumptions to focus our thoughts on these issues. First, this chapter will mainly consider classical cases of inter-state armed conflict to provide a quicker, cleaner route to the general set of post-war principles sought. But I do believe that these principles, owing to their generality and moral strength, clearly apply as well to non-classical wars, such as those we discussed in Chapter 3. The point here is to fashion an overall blueprint which can be amended, as details demand, in particular and unconventional cases.

The next assumption is that the following set of post-war principles is offered as guidance to those participants who want to end their wars in a fair, justified way. Not all participants do, of course, and to that extent they act unjustly during the termination phase. Violations of *jus post bellum* are just as serious as those of *jus ad bellum* and *jus in bello*. As in *jus ad bellum*, responsibility for fulfilling *jus post bellum* is primarily political as opposed to military, although some cases may blur that line, for instance if there is a need to impose short-term, direct military occupation over a shattered society. A related assumption is that there is no such thing as "victor's justice." The raw fact of military victory in war does not, *of itself*, confer moral rights upon the victor, nor ethical duties upon the vanquished. It is only when the victorious regime has fought a just and lawful war, as defined by international law and just war theory, that we can speak meaningfully of rights and duties, of both victor and vanquished, at the conclusion of armed conflict.

This is to say, importantly, that when or *if an aggressor wins a war, the peace terms will necessarily be unjust.* The injustice of cause *infects* the conclusion of the war, as readily as it infected the conduct (as I argued in Chapter 4 in connection with proportionality). Unlike other just war theorists, I believe that the three just war categories are not separate but, rather, connected. And *jus ad bellum* sets the tone and context for the other two categories, and to that extent is probably the most important. This is *not* to say that meeting *jus ad bellum* will automatically result in your meeting *jus in bello* and *jus post bellum*. But it *is* to say, conversely, that failure to meet *jus ad bellum* results in automatic failure to meet *jus in bello* and *jus post bellum*. *Once you're an aggressor in war, everything is lost to you, morally.*

Now, we might still say that some terms which a victorious aggressor imposes are better or worse than others. A winning aggressor might—though it is unlikely—have milder peace terms than we might expect. But we cannot call these terms *just*, since they remain the product of a war which, overall, was unjust. So, for the rest of this chapter, I shall assume that the winning side fought the war with *jus ad bellum* on its side. It is in this sense that I develop an "ideal" conception of post-war justice, to arrive at some rules and values against which we can measure and evaluate the non-ideal cases with which the world confronts us.

With these assumptions declared, let us return to our opening question: what are the ends or goals of a just war? Some say that the just goal of a just war is the proverbial *status quo ante bellum*: the victorious regime ought simply to re-establish the state of affairs which obtained before the war broke out. Restore the equilibrium disrupted by the aggressor, traditionalists advise. As Michael Walzer points out, however, this assertion makes little sense: we should not aim for the literal restoration of the *status quo ante bellum* ... because that situation was precisely what led to war in the first place![6] How is going back there going to improve things, or show the war was worth it? Also, given the sheer destructiveness of war, any such literal restoration is empirically impossible. War simply changes too much. For better and for worse, war remains a major generator of historical change. So the just goal of a just war, once won, must be *a more secure and more just state of affairs* than existed prior to the war. What might such a condition be?

The general answer is a *more secure possession of our rights*, both individual and collective. The aim of a just and lawful war, we know, is the resistance of aggression and the vindication of the fundamental rights of societies, ultimately on behalf of the human rights of their individual citizens. I have already argued that these deepest values revolve around the concept of a minimally just and hence legitimate community. Such a community is one which does all it reasonably can to: 1) gain recognition as being legitimate in the eyes of its own people and the international community; 2) adhere to basic rules of international justice and good international citizenship, notably non-aggression; and 3) satisfy the human rights of its individual members (to security, subsistence, liberty, equality and recognition).

With regard to this general principle—that the proper aim of a just war is the vindication of those rights whose violation grounded the resort to war in the first place—more detailed commentary needs to be offered. For what does such "vindication" of rights amount to: what does it include; what does it permit; and what does it forbid? The last aspect of the question seems the easiest to answer, at least in abstract terms: the principle of rights vindication forbids the continuation of the war after the relevant rights have, in fact, been vindicated. To go beyond that limit would itself become aggression: men and women would die for no just cause.[7] This bedrock limit to the justified continuance of a just war seems required in order to prevent the war from spilling over into something like a Crusade, which demands the utter destruction of the demonized enemy. The very essence of justice of, in, and after war is about there being firm limits and constraints upon its aims and conduct. Unconstrained fighting, with its fearful prospect of degenerating into barbaric slaughter, is the worst case scenario—regardless of the values for which the war is being fought.

This emphasis on the maintenance of some limits in wartime has the important consequence that there can be no such thing as a morally-mandated unconditional surrender. The principles vindicated successfully by the just state *themselves impose outside constraints* on what can be done to an aggressor following its defeat. This line of reasoning might spark resistance from those who view favourably the Allied insistence on "unconditional surrender" during the closing days of World War II. But we need to distinguish here between rhetoric and reality. The policy of unconditional surrender followed by the Allies at the end of that war was *not* genuinely unconditional; there was never any insistence that the Allies be able to do whatever they wanted with the defeated nations, as was, for instance, standard practice in ancient Greek and Roman times. Churchill himself said that "we are bound by our own consciences to civilization... [we are not] entitled to behave in a barbarous manner."[8] At the very most, the policy which the Allies pursued was genuinely unconditional *only* vis-à-vis the governing regimes of the Axis powers, but *not* vis-à-vis the civilian populations in those nations. Such a more discriminating policy on surrender may be defensible in extreme cases, involving truly abhorrent regimes, but is generally impermissible. For insistence on unconditional surrender is usually disproportionate and will prolong fighting as the defeated aggressor refuses to cave in, fearing the consequences of doing so. Walzer believes this was the case during the Pacific War, owing to America's insistence on Japan's unconditional surrender. Japan kept fighting because of this insistence, and eventually America resorted to atomic weapons to end the struggle. Walzer believes that the atom bombs would not have been necessary at all had America had a more reasonable policy regarding surrender in the first place.[9]

It is thus the responsibility of the victor to communicate clearly to the losing aggressor its sincere intentions for post-war settlement, intentions which must be consistent with the other principles of post-war justice here developed. This means that some serious planning must go into the post-war phase *right from the start*. Winners, like America over Iraq in 2003, should never find themselves in a position where they have won the war but they do not know what to do next, and so start making up post-war policy on the fly. That is irresponsible and the potential for bad decisions skyrockets in probability.[10]

What does the just aim of a just war—*namely, rights vindication, constrained by a proportionate policy on surrender*—precisely include or mandate? The following is a plausible list of principles regarding what would be a just settlement of a just war:

• The aggression needs, where possible and proportional, to be rolled back, which is to say that the unjust gains from aggression must be eliminated. If, to take a simple example, the aggression has involved invasion and taking over a country, then justice requires that the invader be driven out of the country and secure borders re-established, much as what happened regarding Iraq and Kuwait in 1990–91. The equally crucial corollary to this principle is that the victim of the aggression is to be re-established as an independent political community, enjoying political sovereignty and territorial integrity.

♦ The commission of aggression, as a serious international crime, requires punishment, in two forms: compensation to the victim for at least some of the costs incurred during the fight for its rights; and war crimes trials for the initiators of aggression. I will later argue that these are not the only war crimes trials required by justice in war's aftermath.

Why must there be punishment at all? Why can't we just cancel the aggressor's gains, and then live and let live? Three reasons suggest themselves. First, the obvious—yet powerful—one of deterrence. Punishing past aggression deters future aggression, or at least does so more than if we had no punishment at all. No punishment seems a lax policy which actually invites future aggression. Secondly, proper punishment can be an effective spur to atonement, change and rehabilitation on the part of the aggressor. Finally, and most powerfully, failing to punish the aggressor degrades and disrespects the worth, status and suffering of the victim.

♦ The aggressor state might also require some demilitarization and political rehabilitation, depending on the nature and severity of the aggression it committed and the threat it would continue to pose in the absence of such measures. "One can," Walzer advises, "legitimately aim not merely at a successful resistance but also at some reasonable security against future attack."[11] The question of forcible, forward-looking rehabilitation is one of the most controversial and interesting with respect to the justice of settlements.

Metaphorically, we have noted that a just war, justly prosecuted, is something like radical surgery: an extreme yet necessary measure to be taken in defence of fundamental values, such as human rights, against severe threats to them, like violent aggression. And if just war, justly prosecuted, is like radical surgery, then the justified conclusion to such a war can only be akin to the rehabilitation and therapy required after the surgery. This is in order to ensure that the original intent is effectively secured—namely, defeating the threat and protecting the rights—and that the patient is materially better off than prior to the exercise. The "patient" in this case is, in the first instance, the victim(s) of aggression. Secondarily, it refers to the international community generally—including even the aggressor(s) or, at least, their civilians.[12]

Sufficient comment has already been offered on what the first proposition requires and why: aggression, as a crime which justifies war, needs to be rolled back and have its gains eliminated as far as possible and proportional;

and the victim of aggression needs to have the objects of its rights restored. This principle seems quite straightforward and elemental, one of justice as rectification. The aggressor had an unjust gain and thus must lose that gain; whereas the victim had an unjust loss and thus must, where possible, be restored in that loss. But what about compensation, "political rehabilitation," and war crimes trials?

Compensation and Discrimination

Since aggression is a crime which violates important rights and causes much damage, it is reasonable to contend that, in a classical context of inter-state war, the aggressor nation, "Aggressor," owes some duty of compensation to the victim of the aggression, "Victim." This is the case because, in the absence of aggression, Victim would not have to reconstruct itself following the war, nor would it have had to fight for its rights in the first place, with all the death and destruction that implies. It has been said that the deepest nature of the wrong which an aggressor commits is to make people fight for their rights (i.e., to make them resort to violence to secure those things they have an elemental entitlement to in the first place, and which they should enjoy as a matter of course).[13] To put the compensation issue bluntly, Aggressor has cost Victim a considerable amount, and so at least some restitution is due. The critical questions seem to be: *how much* and *from whom* in Aggressor is the compensation to be paid out?

The "how much" question, clearly, will be relative to the nature and severity of the act of aggression itself, alongside considerations of what Aggressor can reasonably be expected to pay at war's end. Care needs to be taken not to bankrupt Aggressor's resources, if only for the reason that the civilians of Aggressor still, as always, retain their claims to human rights fulfilment, and the objects of such rights require that resources be devoted to them. There needs, in short, to be an application of the principle of proportionality here. The compensation required may not be draconian in nature. We have some indication, from the financial terms imposed on Germany at the Treaty of Versailles, that to "beggar thy neighbour" is to pick future fights.

This reference to the needs of the civilians in Aggressor gives rise to important considerations of discrimination in answering the "from whom" question: when it comes to establishing terms of compensation, care needs to be taken by the victorious Victim, and/or any third-party "Vindicators" who fought on behalf of Victim, not to penalize unduly the civilian population of Aggressor for the aggression carried out by their regime. This entails, for example, that any monetary compensation due to Victim ought to come, first and foremost, from the personal wealth of those political and military elites in Aggressor who were most responsible for the crime of aggression. Walzer seems to disagree, as he suggests that such a discriminating policy on reparations "can hardly" raise the needed amount. But he ignores the fact that, historically, those who launch aggressive war externally have very often abused their power internally to accumulate massive, sometimes obscene, personal fortunes. Saddam Hussein, for example, skimmed billions off Iraqi oil sales and used them to live lavishly, to secure the loyalty of his Republican Guard and to build up enormous foreign bank accounts in case things turned bad.[14]

In light of this supposed shortfall—between the fortunes of dictators and what their victims are owed—Walzer argues that, since "(r)eparations are surely due the victims of aggressive war," they should be paid from the taxation system of the defeated Aggressor. There ought to be a kind of post-war poll tax on the population of Aggressor, with the proceeds forwarded to Victim. In this sense, he says, "citizenship is a common destiny." I believe, however, that such a proposal probably fails to respect the discrimination principle during war termination. Though Walzer insists that "(t)he distribution of costs is not the distribution of guilt,"[15] it is difficult to see what that is supposed to mean here: why not respond by asking why civilians should be forced, through their tax system, to pay for the damage if they are not in some sense responsible for it? Respect for discrimination entails taking a *reasonable* amount of compensation *only* from those sources: 1) which can afford it; *and* 2) which were materially linked to the aggression in a morally culpable way. If such reparations "can hardly pay" for the destruction Aggressor meted out on Victim, then that fiscal deficiency does not somehow translate into Victim's moral entitlement to tax everyone left over in Aggressor. *The resources for reconstruction simply have to be found elsewhere.*

The one exception to this would be if Aggressor's destruction was of such magnitude that Victim can no longer afford to be a minimally just state, whereas Aggressor's post-war resources are clearly in a surplus over that threshold level. *Provided* that is the case, and *provided* the fortunes of the guilty in Aggressor were first exhausted, *then* we could justifiably talk about some kind of broader, Walzer-style transfer from Aggressor to Victim. Victim at least has the right to that level of post-war resources sufficient to provide minimally just governance to its people. If the reason it fell below that level was enormous wartime expenditures fighting off Aggressor, then it makes sense to say Aggressor owes it at least that. But if both Victim and Aggressor, after war, retain resources clearly above the minimal level, then the financial restitution coming from Aggressor to Victim must be limited to the assets of the guilty. That is what discrimination requires, and I believe such a more moderate policy would render the issue of compensation a lot less explosive than what it has been in the past.

One application of these thoughts to recent events can be seen by considering the following question: should America have levied a post-war poll tax on the citizens of Afghanistan, to increase the funds needed to compensate and care for those who lost loved ones during the 9/11 strikes, or else to rebuild New York's shattered financial district? The principles just developed argue *against* such a tax, since there is a serious question of its affordability to Afghanistan, and an even sharper one regarding responsibility, since the available evidence points to a collusion between the now-routed Taliban regime and the al-Qaeda terrorist network as the source of the attacks. Commendably, there has been virtually no talk of any such punitive measure on Afghanistan, and Americans have instead turned towards each other to raise the needed reconstruction resources. For example, right after 9/11, American celebrities and singers hosted a televised fundraiser for the widows and injured of the bombings.

Sanctions

A further implication of respect for discrimination in settlements is a ban on sweeping socio-economic sanctions. The reasoning is clear: sanctions which cut widely and deeply into the well-being of the civilian population are not only punitive, they surely end up punishing some—perhaps a great many— who do not deserve such treatment. When such treatment strikes at their vital welfare, such sanctions are properly condemned as inappropriately targeted and morally wrong-headed. People have argued over whether US-imposed sanctions on Iraq—following the Persian Gulf War in 1991 and lasting until 2003—counted as such morally-questionable sanctions or not. On the one hand, statistics show a sharp drop-off in Iraqi GDP during those years, as well as a sharp rise in indicators of poverty and preventable disease. On the other, supporters of the sanctions argue that Saddam Hussein's regime could have prevented any humanitarian damage by improving access to resources and giving his military and ethnic clique less, so that the majority could have had more and been alright. Saddam failed to do this for his own selfish reasons, and so he is the one to blame. We'll return to this debate when we focus on the Persian Gulf War settlement more broadly at the end of this chapter. In any event, for now, there is a vocal and growing community of thought which commends instead sanctions which target *only* the guilty elites, for instance by freezing their personal assets, banning their foreign travel and blocking any weapons trade. For example, the American assets of some organizations alleged to be involved in terrorism have been frozen since 9/11; it will be interesting to see whether further sanctions in the war on terror will be applied and, if so, what kind.[16]

Rehabilitation

MILITARY

We need to distinguish between military and political rehabilitation and note that the former is readily supported, while the latter is steeped in hot controversy. Under the military heading, we have the notion that, in the post-war environment, Aggressor may be required to demilitarize, at least to the extent that it will not pose another serious threat to Victim—and other members of the international community—for the foreseeable future. The appropriate elements of such demilitarization will clearly vary with the nature and severity of the act of aggression, along with the extent of Aggressor's residual military capabilities following its defeat. But they may, and often do, involve: the creation of a demilitarized "buffer zone" between Aggressor and Victim (and any Vindicator), whether it be on land, sea or air; the reducing and capping of certain aspects of Aggressor's military capability, be they troops, weapons or weapons-deployment systems; and especially the destruction of Aggressor's weapons of mass destruction (WMD). Why may an aggressor's WMD be destroyed, while those of other nations remain intact? As mentioned in Chapter 3, the key thing with WMD is *not* their mere possession so much as a responsible record of having such weapons *and* a stable recent history of non-aggression. By committing aggression, Aggressor has broken any trust— or, at least, tolerance—offered by the international community in this regard. Aggressor has shown itself to be capable of aggressive destruction and international criminality. It is simply too great a risk to allow it to keep WMD. Besides, from a more global point of view, the fewer WMD, the better. Non-proliferation seems the route to greater global security.

Proportionality must be brought to bear upon this general principle of military rehabilitation: the regime in Aggressor may not be so demilitarized as to jeopardize its ability to fulfil its function of maintaining law and order within its own borders, and of protecting its people from other countries who might be tempted to invade—for whatever reason—if they perceive serious weakness in Aggressor. The world, after all, has some rough neighbourhoods. Another way this requirement could be met would be for the victors to provide reliable security guarantees to the people of Aggressor, for instance by keeping military garrisons in the country.

POLITICAL

The imposition of political rehabilitation seems the most serious and invasive measure permitted a just regime, following its justified victory over Aggressor. This topic is so complex and topical that we have reserved all of next chapter for its thorough discussion. There I will argue that if the actions of Aggressor during the war were truly atrocious, or if the nature of the regime in Aggressor at the end of the war is still so heinous that its continued existence poses a serious threat to international justice and human rights, then— and only then—may such a regime be forcibly dismantled and a new, more defensible regime established in its stead. But we should be quick to note, and emphasize, that such construction necessitates an additional commitment *on the part of Victim and any Vindicators* to assist the new regime in Aggressor with this enormous task of political restructuring. This assistance would be composed of seeing such "political therapy" through to a reasonably successful conclusion—which is to say, until the new regime can stand on its own, as it were, and fulfil its core functions of providing domestic law and order, human rights fulfilment, and adherence to the basic norms of international law, notably those banning aggression. In other words, reconstruction must at least create a minimally just form of governance.

Apologies

We should also expect a formal apology by Aggressor to Victim, and any Vindicator, for its aggression. While it is right to agree with Walzer that "official apologies somehow seem an inadequate, perhaps even a perfunctory, way" of atoning for aggression,[17] this is no reason to rule such an apology out of the terms of the peace. Even though formal apologies cannot of themselves restore territory, revive casualties, or rebuild infrastructure, it is obvious that they do mean something real and important. If not, why do such formal apologies, and victim's campaigns to secure such apologies, generate considerable political and media attention? If not, why do informed people know that Germany has apologized profusely for its role in World War II whereas Japan has hardly apologized at all? (Indeed, there were riots in China as recently as 2005 protesting a Japanese history textbook downplaying Japan's occupation of Chinese territory during the 1930s and 1940s.) Walzer must concede that we expect wrongdoers eventually to admit their wrongdoing, and to express their regret for it. (The Japanese Prime Minister did indeed express a public apology to China following the 2005 riots.) We feel that victims of wrongdoing are owed that kind of respect, and that aggressors must at least show recognition of the moral principles they violated as part of their own rehabilitation. Apologies are an integral aspect of a complete peace treaty.

War Crimes Trials

This leaves the vexed topic of war crimes trials, perhaps the one issue of *jus post bellum* which has already received sustained and significant attention from many scholars. The normative need for such trials follows from Walzer's dictum that: "There can be no justice in war if there are not, ultimately, responsible men and women."[18] Individuals who play a prominent role during wartime must be held accountable for their actions and what they bring about. There are, of course, two broad categories of war crimes: those which violate *jus ad bellum* and those which violate *jus in bello*.

Jus ad bellum war crimes have to do with "planning, preparing, initiating and waging" aggressive war, as we have defined it throughout. Responsibility for the commission of any such crime falls on the shoulders of the political leader(s) of the aggressor regime. Such crimes, in the language of the Nuremberg prosecutors, are "crimes against peace."[19]

NUREMBERG

The Nuremberg trials, of course, refer to the very first set of modern war crimes trials, held right after World War II in the German city of that name. (There were Japanese war crimes trials, too, in Tokyo.)[20] In Nuremberg, much of what was left of the Nazi hierarchy was put on trial for both war crimes (i.e., starting an aggressive war) and crimes against humanity (i.e., The Holocaust). While every war crime is also a crime against humanity, the converse is not true, since crimes against humanity can be committed in peacetime and cover a broader range of terrible actions, such as torturing political dissidents.

While some complained that the Nuremberg trials were "victor's justice," it is hard to agree that that is all they were. The process, after all, was rigorous, open and fair. All those charged had lawyers, could cross-examine witnesses and experts, and present their own evidence. The trials operated on rules known to all. Consider also the raw numbers: 22 Nazi elites were tried over the course of a year, three were found innocent, nineteen guilty. Of the guilty, eleven were sentenced to death and eight to prison sentences of varying lengths. This conviction rate, of just over 86 per cent, is in line with the average rate of conviction for non-war-crimes in most developed societies.[21] (If that seems high, consider: 1) that prosecutors often drop charges against those they feel they cannot convict; and 2) there are many social and psychological factors—apart from the case's evidence—which incline judges and juries to convict.) Combine this percentage at Nuremberg with the variety of outcomes in sentencing there, and it looks like you have a fairly well-developed, reasonable judicial process looking at the evidence in each individual's case as opposed to one which sweepingly condemns and convicts them all because they happened to be on the losing side.[22] Plus, the first international war crimes trials had to happen *sometime*. The notion that the Nuremberg trials operated on principles just then being invented is silly: there had been talk since the 1800s of having post-war criminal tribunals, and the codes of proper military conduct, such as the Hague Conventions (1899–1907)—to say nothing of basic moral decency—were known to all who were charged. Whenever there is a new institution or innovation there is bound to be controversy, especially when something like war is involved. It was not perfect, but the Nuremberg trial process was decent and defensible. Decent, because it followed standard due process regulations. (Ironic and notable, indeed, that these Nazis, when in power, denounced the rule of law and due process and yet benefited from them during these trials.) And defensible, because the Nazis were culpable for horrendous crimes, and at the time the only people capable of running a trial for them were the winners of the war. It was a bold institutional move, for proper moral motives, which has resonated down to today.[23]

CONTEMPORARY TRIBUNALS

Resonated how, exactly? In a threefold sense. First, the Nuremberg trials directly inspired some future war crimes trials. After the brutal Bosnian civil war of 1992–95, and the near-genocidal Rwandan massacres of 1994, the international community decided to convene war crimes, and crimes against humanity, proceedings. The one regarding Bosnia is still ongoing and takes place at The Hague in Holland, long a place associated with international diplomacy and institutions. The other, regarding Rwanda, is situated in neighbouring Tanzania and is likewise still ongoing. Both tribunals actually confront huge back-logs in trials and workloads. These *ad hoc*—or "one-time"— criminal procedures feature the same commitment to rigorous due process as Nuremberg did. This is a partial reason for the backlog. They have also, unlike Nuremberg, tried some of the biggest fish—the ex-prime minister of Rwanda and the ex-president of Serbia/Yugoslavia, both seen as heavily complicit in the respective wars.

Partly to overcome the limitations of *ad hoc* trials, and to institute something more lasting, there arose in the late 1990s a movement to create a *permanent* international criminal court or ICC. In 1998, the Treaty of Rome was signed, paving the way for the ICC to be formed, also at The Hague. The court, a subsidiary of the United Nations (UN), is just now starting to get underway. Since it will be permanent, and fully international, accusations regarding revenge motives and victor's justice fail when applied to the ICC. Its permanence and global resources will also allow it to become a more experienced and efficient court process than, say, either the Bosnian or Rwandan efforts, which continue to be starved of resources. Although Americans continue to object to the ICC—fearing that it could be "politically hijacked" to feature "show trials" of US servicemen—it is going ahead anyway, and there are principled reasons to support the court.

First, there is the deterrence benefit. If all war crimes, in all wars, are prosecuted and punished by an impartial world court, then it stands to reason that future, would-be war criminals might well be deterred from committing their ghastly actions if they know that they will themselves pay a personal price for their crimes. Second, there is the war termination benefit. A permanent and non-partisan world court can assist nations in wrapping up their armed conflicts, punishing acts in an impartial manner. Third, there is the world system benefit. The global community has already witnessed the huge benefits of having an international system based on rules of law which are reasonable, impartial and applicable to all. The trade sector is the clearest and most recent example of this. The construction of a permanent world criminal court helps complete the international landscape, thereby adding to the existence of a global system which can run smoothly on a consistent and comprehensive set of shared values, notably human rights. History shows that specialist agencies of the UN (i.e., those manned by trained professionals and focusing on a specific task) enjoy a much higher success rate than the generalist and politicized agencies, such as the General Assembly and Security Council. Finally, there is the commitment benefit. The construction of a permanent war crimes court allows the world community to better keep its commitments to the core values of peace, security, and human rights. A world court enhances peace by punishing deeds which, if left unpunished, could sow the seeds of future wars. This augments global security more broadly. Finally, the existence of a world court for war crimes and crimes against humanity marks another much needed advance in the compelling cause of human rights protection around the world.

The third effect of Nuremberg—apart from the recent ad hoc trials and the ICC—concerns the much more active willingness of national armed forces, at least in developed nations, to investigate and prosecute members of their own services for alleged war crimes. The activity here is real and quite remarkable. Consider the American military prosecuting and punishing those of its own soldiers who engaged in the infamous My Lai Massacre during the Vietnam War. Frustrated by civilian support for, and hiding of, Viet Cong soldiers, one American unit—under Lt. William Calley—morally snapped and deliberately massacred the inhabitants of the village of My Lai. More recently, the Canadian Armed Forces prosecuted and punished some members of its Airborne Unit which served in the 1993 intervention in Somalia. Thuggish members of that Unit caught a Somali civilian stealing from their supplies, and beat him to death. Then there is the US reservists facing charges in the 2004 Abu Ghraib prisoner abuse scandal in Iraq. The first convictions came down in Spring, 2005. The list here can go on and on: the developed world's armed services drill their soldiers in the rules of engagement, and the ethics of war and peace, and they quite vigilantly oversee them. In some engagements, I have actually heard servicemen say, only half-jokingly, that they are more afraid of their own service's military lawyers than they are of the enemy. It should be noted, for those still anxious about the ICC, that it is empowered to act only when a given national armed service fails to act on and investigate an alleged war crime. It does not replace or supercede the national military justice systems.[24]

JUS AD BELLUM CRIMES

Enough about Nuremberg, and its sizable rippling consequences over time. Back to the ethical principles behind *jus ad bellum* war crimes. Subject to proportionality, the leaders of Aggressor are to be brought to trial before a public and fair international tribunal and accorded full due process rights in their defence. Why subject this principle of punishment to proportionality constraints? Why agree with one commentator who says that "it isn't always true that their leaders ought to be punished for their crimes"?[25] The answer is that sometimes such leaders, in spite of their moral decrepitude, retain considerable popular legitimacy and thus bringing them to trial could seriously destabilize the polity within Aggressor. The international community recently faced this situation twice. The first was in Somalia, in 1992–93, when attempt was made to arrest faction leader Mohammed Farah Aidid for war crimes, resulting in serious escalation in the conflict, which ultimately backfired and resulted in the international force withdrawing from the country. The second time was in Bosnia, in 1994–95, when charges against Bosnian Serb leaders Ratko Mladic and Radovan Karadzic seriously increased tensions and delayed the onset of a not unreasonable peace agreement. Care needs to be taken, as always, that appeal to proportionality does not amount to rewarding aggressors, or to letting them run free and unscathed despite their grievous crimes. Yet this care does not vitiate the need to consider the destruction and suffering which might result from adhering totally to what the requirements of justice as retribution demand.

One interesting and not unprincipled compromise position, with regard to Bosnia, has been not to move directly into Bosnian Serb lands to arrest Mladic and Karadzic—owing to the serious instability that would probably produce—but, rather, to pen the two of them into their narrow territory for the rest of their lives, by stipulating that, should they ever cross an international border, they will immediately be arrested and brought to trial. The two are, it is said, under a kind of house arrest. Another option is simply to wait until the wounds of war have healed somewhat, say around ten years, and then move in to arrest and try such figures. NATO in 2003 tried unsuccessfully to arrest Karadzic during a pin-point raid. In these cases, justice delayed need not be justice denied—a trial will be held but only after the political community has progressed enough to absorb its impact. Like murder in domestic legal regimes, there must never be a "statute of limitations" on when a case for war crimes, or crimes against humanity, can be brought.[26]

Should political leaders on trial for *jus ad bellum* violations be found guilty, through a public and fair proceeding, then the court is at liberty to determine a reasonable punishment, which will obviously depend upon the details of the relevant case. Perhaps the punishment will only consist of penalizing the leaders financially for the amount of compensation owed to Victim, as previously discussed. Or perhaps, should the need for political rehabilitation be invoked, such leaders will need to be stripped of power and barred from political participation, or perhaps even jailed. Some figures in the Bosnian Serb community, for example, have been prohibited from running in subsequent elections. It is clear that it is not possible, *a priori*, to stipulate what exactly is required with regard to such personal punishments. The point here is simply that the principle itself—of calling those most responsible for the aggression to task for their crimes—must be respected as an essential aspect of justice after war. The actual enforcement of this principle might constitute a non-trivial deterrent to future acts of aggression on the part of ambitious heads of state. If such figures have good reason to believe that they will themselves, personally, pay a price for the aggression they instigate and order, then perhaps they will be less likely to undertake such misadventures in the first place. The ex-prime minister of Rwanda was convicted and imprisoned for his large role in the 1994 civil war. The ex-president of Serbia/Yugoslavia, Slobodon Milosevic, was on trial at The Hague for his actions in the Bosnian civil war and the 1999 war with NATO over Kosovo. (But then he died of a heart attack in his cell.) The personal capture of Iraq's Saddam Hussein, in late 2003, and the start of his Iraqi trial in 2005, underlines the international community's commitment to increase *personal* punishment of aggressors and war criminals.

Heads of State

Walzer stresses that a head of state cannot escape judgment, at any such trial, by appealing to the function of his office. The fact that he "represents" his people on the world stage, and rationalizes his actions in terms of "reasons of state," can provide no exoneration for the crime of launching an unjust war. Why not? "Representative functions [far from exonerating representatives] are instead peculiarly risky ... because statesmen ... act for other people, and with wide-ranging effects." Heads of state covet power, actively seek it, enjoy its exercise, and exert enormous influence. If they "hope to be praised for the good they do, they cannot escape blame for the evil." Heads of state are as subject to blame—both moral and legal—as the rest of us, probably even more so since their actions have larger consequences. Walzer suggests that, when fishing for *jus ad bellum* war crimes, we cast our net wider than the head of state. No doubt, we must first look to the head of state but then should move down the chain of authority to see if other individuals are also decisively implicated. There will probably be others, such as the heads of the various armed forces, the head of national security, the head of intelligence gathering, the defence minister, certain top-level civil servants, and so on. It was also argued in Chapter 4, against Walzer, that some soldiers might meaningfully be included in this chain of authority. The general principle we are to apply in this regard is the following: *the greater a person's influence on his country's actions in wartime, the greater his responsibility for them.*[27]

Collective Democratic Responsibility

Some of Walzer's most interesting reflections in this regard concern the collective responsibility that citizens of a democracy face when their country launches an unjust war, as Walzer believes America did during Vietnam. Walzer suggests that we discern their responsibility by first considering what the responsibility of citizens in a perfect democracy would be. By such a "perfect democracy," Walzer means something like Jean-Jacques Rousseau's ideal society: a small participatory (or direct) democracy, peopled by enthusiastic citizens animated by the general will (i.e., a sincere regard for the common good of the community in which they are all equal members). Walzer asserts that in this idealized case, even though "it cannot be said that every citizen is the author of every state policy," it remains true that "every one of them can rightly be called into account." So who would be responsible for an aggressive war in this idealized instance? "(A)ll those men and women who voted for it and who cooperated in planning, initiating and waging it ... All of them are guilty of the crime of aggressive war, and of no lesser charge." Those who voted against the war are not to blame, whereas those who did not even bother to vote "are blameworthy, though they are not guilty of aggressive war." Why is this the case? Walzer suggests we recall the parable of the Good Samaritan, which illustrates our agreement that if it is possible for one to do good without great cost to oneself, then one ought to do it. Walzer says that when it comes to resisting aggressive war, "the obligation is stronger" than in the Good Samaritan story, because "it is not a question of doing good but of preventing serious harm, and harm that will be done in the name of my own political community—hence ... in my own name." An engaged citizen, in a perfect democracy which is waging an aggressive war, "must do all he can, short of accepting frightening risks, to prevent or stop the war." Presumably, political action, canvassing, arguing, organizing, protesting, running for office oneself, giving money to the cause, are all things on his mind here. In general, *the more one can do, the more one has to do* [my italics]."[28]

Very few of us, however, live in a perfect democracy. How then does this idealized model of democratic responsibility translate under conditions of an actual, imperfect, contemporary, representative democracy? Walzer believes it crucial to get the right description. Such a democracy has a fairly large, diverse and scattered population, and is "governed at a great distance from its ordinary citizens by powerful and often arrogant officials." While these officials are periodically endorsed through elections, "at the time of the choice very little is known about their programs and commitments" or, at least, their actual willingness to follow through on them. Active political participation is the rare exception rather than the regular rule, and knowledge about the justice of wars fought is "occasional, intermittent ... [and] partially controlled by these distant officials ... which ... allows for considerable distortions." One is reminded here of the ongoing controversy surrounding official US and UK intelligence estimates of Iraqi WMD, in 2003, as grounds for war.[29]

Under these normal conditions in an advanced Western democracy, the bulk of the burden for waging aggressive war will still fall most heavily on the governing elites and intelligentsia who support the war. We know this excuses those citizens who vote against the war and emphatically those who also protest against it, rally opposition to it, and so on. But does it completely excuse those citizens who support the unjust war effort? It does so, Walzer says, only if the information required to make a plausible judgment is seriously distorted by the elites, and correct information is exceedingly difficult for the citizenry to get their hands on. It does *not* excuse the citizenry if, with some effort, they could come across this information and make principled judgments. If citizens choose not to seek out such information, preferring either to "zone out" in front of the TV, or to endorse the war out of unreflective patriotism, then they are blameworthy, though *not* of the full charge of aggressive war. What they are guilty of, Walzer suggests, is "bad faith as citizens." The information about the war's injustice is available, say through credible media sources; it is critically important to do what one can to prevent serious harm (especially when it is being done in one's name); so failure to do so constitutes, at least, a failure to meet the moral requirements of decent democratic citizenship. Widespread bad faith, in Walzer's eyes, constitutes a searing indictment of the democracy in which it occurs. In reflects poorly on its system of education, on its media outlets, on its political system and representatives and, above all, on the very character of its people and their moral maturity.[30]

JUS IN BELLO WAR CRIMES

Jus ad bellum war crimes trials, we know, are not the only ones mandated by just war theory and international law. Attention must also, in the aftermath of conflict, be paid to trying those accused of *jus in bello* war crimes. Such crimes include: deliberately using indiscriminate and/or disproportionate force; failing to take due care to protect civilian populations from lethal violence; employing weapons which are themselves intrinsically indiscriminate and/or disproportionate, such as those of mass destruction; employing intrinsically heinous means, like rape campaigns; and treating surrendered prisoners of war in an inhumane fashion, such as torturing them. Primary responsibility for these war crimes must fall on the shoulders of those soldiers, officers and military commanders who were most actively involved in their commission. Officers and commanders carry considerable moral burdens of their own during wartime. They are duty bound *not* to issue orders which violate *any* aspect of the laws of war. Furthermore, they must plan military campaigns so that foreseeable civilian casualties are minimized, and they must teach and train their soldiers not only about combat but also about the rules of just war theory and the laws of armed conflict.[31]

A critical aspect to note here is that, unlike *jus ad bellum* war crimes, *jus in bello* war crimes can be—and usually are—committed by all sides in the conflict. It is fair to say that at least a few *jus in bello* violations are usually committed by every side in every armed conflict. So, care needs to be taken that Victim/Vindicator avoid the very tempting position of punishing only *jus ad bellum* war crimes. In order to avoid charges of having a "double-standard," or engaging in revenge punishment, the Victim/Vindicator—despite the justice of its cause in fighting—must also be willing either to try its suspected soldiers within its own military justice system or else to submit them to an impartially constructed international tribunal, such as the ICC. The exact kind of punishment for *jus in bello* war crimes, as for *jus ad bellum* violations, cannot be specified philosophically in advance of considering the concrete details of the case in question. It may involve such things as: disciplinary action within the service; demotion within, or expulsion from, the armed forces; jail time; perhaps the paying of personal restitution; and so on.

Let's consider the two defences soldiers most often employ in *jus in bello* war crimes cases: that of battle frenzy; and that of superior orders. The idea behind the first defence is that a particular battle, or even a whole war, is so intense, chaotic and brutalizing that, although it starts out measured and discriminating, it ends up escalating to the point where atrocities get committed. This was a line of defence taken by Calley and his comrades regarding the My Lai Massacre. We are right to be sceptical of this argument. Even in alleged cases of battle frenzy, other soldiers present at the scene seem to retain their control and combat savvy *under the exact same conditions* as those who fly off the handle and commit atrocities, like slaughtering civilians. Indeed, it was because some of these more sober soldiers were present, but non-participating, at the My Lai Massacre that Calley and his comrades were arrested, tried and convicted. The only plausible case for this implausible defence, as Walzer suggests, is when a senior officer actually encourages battle frenzy as a way of cementing the fighting spirit or unity of his troops. But this is at best *a mitigating factor in punishment*, not an excuse or justification for a finding of innocence. Walzer notes that such an officer is not only stupid—since soldiers fight best when they are disciplined and controlled, not wild and frenzied—he is issuing a blatantly immoral order; and the soldiers under him should not, and are usually taught not to, follow such an order.[32]

This ties into the second defence most frequently offered by soldiers in defence of *jus in bello* war crimes charges: superior orders. Such a defence strategy invokes savage scorn, almost automatically, owing to its extensive use by the Nazis at Nuremberg. But we should not indulge in such easy, black-and-white criticism. From the first day of induction into the armed forces, a soldier is literally drilled into obeying the orders of his commanding officers. This is the case in both just and unjust societies. Failure to obey *always* comes with punitive measures, some truly painful and serious. The very point of military training is to habituate soldiers to follow orders under the most hellish conditions of war, so that they can retain fighting coherence and achieve their objectives. Even so, ordinary soldiers, by common sense if not by training, know when they are confronted with a blatantly immoral order (such as massacring civilians), and they remain duty bound not to follow it. If they do follow it, they should be charged with war crimes. The only excuse here would be if the blatantly immoral order was *coupled with* a credible threat of execution for disobedience. Nazi officers, for example, would routinely shoot their own disobedient soldiers in front of their entire unit to enforce compliance. A soldier with a gun at his head, clearly, is a man acting under extreme duress and so cannot be held readily responsible for his actions. The person to be held responsible here would be the person who issued the immoral order and coupled it with the grievous threat as a matter of policy (i.e., the commanding officer). The excuse of superior orders will *only* hold if the penalty for disobedience is extremely severe, such as execution. There is always some penalty for disobedience, but not any old penalty will suffice as an excuse here. The threat of demotion in the ranks, for instance, is obviously not enough to excuse murder. It has to be something as grave as execution to count. And, again, it counts *only as an excuse or mitigation in punishment*, and never as a justification for a verdict of innocence.[33]

So officers and commanders are duty bound not to issue orders which violate any aspect of the laws of war, nor are they to threaten excessively severe penalties for failing to comply with an order. The orders they give, in other words, must all fit within the general structure of permissible action established by the laws of war and just war theory.

Publicity

Do the terms of the settlement, as thus far discussed, need to be public? On the one hand, war settlements often have a deep impact on people's lives. They are thus entitled to know the substance of peace settlements, and especially how they are likely to affect them. Kant, for one, was vehement about this publicity requirement in his famous writings on war.[34] But someone might challenge this publicity principle, for instance, by citing a counterexample. Consider the Cuban Missile Crisis of 1962. At the height of the Cold War, America discovered that the Soviet Union was installing nuclear-tipped missiles in Cuba at Fidel Castro's invitation. These missiles were thought to pose unacceptable first-strike capacities against the United States —since Cuba is so close—and US President John F. Kennedy demanded their removal. He even put Cuba under quarantine to ensure that more missiles were not on their way. We know that part of the reason why the Soviet Union backed down during this crisis was because of JFK's secret assurances that America would remove missiles from Turkey shortly after the Soviets removed theirs from Cuba.[35] But this "counter-example" does not deal with a full-blown war, much less a post-war period, and so it is not directly analogous. People who have suffered through a war do indeed deserve to know what the substance of the settlement is.

This does *not* mean that the people must explicitly and immediately endorse the proposed settlement, for instance through a plebiscite or referendum. Nor does it mean that the settlement must be drafted up in a formal treaty. Both things are clearly permissible, and perhaps desirable as well: a show of popular support for a settlement might bolster its endurance; and writing out the peace terms can enhance the clarity of everyone's understandings and expectations. But it seems needlessly strict to insist that both phenomena must be there for the settlement to be legitimate. We can imagine numerous and serious practical difficulties with running a referendum in the immediate post-war period. We can also imagine communities coming to an understanding on the settlement—even going so far as to adhere to it—without nailing down every possible contingency in a detailed legal document. After all, the 1919 Treaty of Versailles was a detailed legal document, and it did not work out all that well whereas the 1945 post-World War II settlement was left at an abstract level intentionally, lest too much fussing over each exact detail spoil the deal. In a sense, settlements are processes, and while on the one hand they represent the end of a war, in another sense they inaugurate transition and change. There needs to be a certain flexibility and sensitivity as one tries to fix and solidify the terms for moving on.[36]

Summary

Perhaps it would be helpful here, before considering an historical application in detail, to list the set of settlement principles discussed and defended. A state in the war termination phase ought to be guided by all of the following norms:

- Proportionality and Publicity. The peace settlement should be both measured and reasonable, as well as publicly proclaimed. To make a settlement serve as an instrument of revenge is to make a volatile bed one may be forced to sleep in later. In general, this rules out insistence on unconditional surrender.
- Rights Vindication. The settlement should secure those basic rights whose violation triggered the justified war. The relevant rights include human rights to life and liberty and community entitlements to territory and sovereignty. This is the main substantive goal of any decent settlement, ensuring that the war will actually have an improving affect. Respect for rights, after all, is a foundation of civilization, whether national or international. Vindicating rights, not vindictive revenge, is the order of the day.
- Discrimination. Distinction needs to be made between the leaders, the soldiers, and the civilians in the defeated country one is negotiating with. Civilians are entitled to reasonable immunity from punitive post-war measures. This rules out sweeping socio-economic sanctions as part of post-war punishment.

- Punishment #1. When the defeated country has been a blatant, rights-violating aggressor, proportionate punishment must be meted out. The leaders of the regime, in particular, should face fair and public international trials for war crimes.
- Punishment #2. Soldiers also commit war crimes. Justice after war requires that such soldiers, *from all sides to the conflict*, likewise be held accountable to investigation and possible trial.
- Compensation. Financial restitution may be mandated, subject to both proportionality and discrimination. A post-war poll tax on civilians is generally impermissible, and there needs to be enough resources left so that the defeated country can begin its own reconstruction. To "beggar thy neighbour" is to pick future fights.
- Rehabilitation. The post-war environment provides a promising opportunity to reform decrepit institutions in an aggressor regime. Such reforms are permissible—as I'll argue next chapter—but they must be proportional to the degree of depravity in the regime. They may involve: demilitarization and disarmament; police and judicial re-training; human rights education; and even deep structural transformation towards a minimally just society governed by a legitimate regime.

In short, there needs to be an *ethical* "exit strategy" from war, and it deserves at least as much thought and effort as the purely military exit strategy so much on the minds of policy planners and commanding officers. The terms of a just peace should satisfy all these requirements.

Any serious defection by any participant from these principles of just war settlement should be seen as a violation of the rules of just war termination, and so should be punished. At the least, violation of such principles mandates a new round of diplomatic negotiations—even binding international arbitration—between the relevant parties to the dispute. At the very most, such violation may give the aggrieved party a just cause—*but no more than a just cause*—for resuming hostilities. Full recourse to the resumption of hostilities may be made *only if* all the other traditional criteria of *jus ad bellum*—proportionality, last resort, etc.—are satisfied in addition to just cause.

Case Study: The 1991 Persian Gulf War Settlement

Let us consider, as helpful illustration, the justice of the post-war settlement with Iraq in 1991 following the Persian Gulf War. (We'll look at the justice of the post-war arrangements in the second, 2003, war next chapter.)

We argued, in Chapter 2, that the American-led Allies had a just cause in resorting to war against Iraq in 1991, following Iraq's invasion of Kuwait in 1990 and the subsequent plundering and brutality. Let us, to facilitate analysis, assume that the war on the part of the Allies also met the other criteria of *jus ad bellum*. And let us bracket in the meantime the question of how well *jus in bello* was fulfilled on both sides. Given these assumptions, how just and lawful was the termination phase of this otherwise justified war?

Consider first the aim of a just war: vindicating rights. When did the Allies terminate the war? The *de facto* (or actual) end to the war came on February 27, 1991, when American President George Bush Sr. ordered the Allied forces to adhere to a cease-fire, following the rout and flee of Iraqi forces from Kuwait. The *de jure* (or legal) end to the war came more than a month later, on April 3, 1991, when UN Security Council Resolution 687 proclaimed its end. Did the Allies have just cause to terminate the war when they did? It seems that the answer to this question is probably yes. It appears that the rights of the Kuwaiti people were reasonably vindicated, first and foremost by having the Allies stop the Iraqi aggression and, indeed, drive the Iraqi aggressors out of Kuwait entirely. Kuwait was then re-established as an independent community acknowledged by international society.

Between March and April 1991, terms of the cease-fire were hammered out under the auspices of the UN Security Council. These terms, which were publicly announced, included the following requirements of Iraq: 1) it had to cease hostilities and declare a formal end to them; 2) it had to rescind its claim to Kuwait, and return looted property; 3) it had to release immediately all prisoners of war (POWs); 4) it had to accept liability for loss, injury and damage in Kuwait which resulted from its invasion; and 5) it had to provide to the UN total disclosure of its program for making WMD and commit itself to that program's destruction, subject to verification by on-site UN inspectors.

Items 1–3 of these terms of the Persian Gulf War peace agreement are essential elements of agreeing to end a war: to stop fighting; to accept responsibility for aggression; to renounce unjust claims; and to release POWs. Article 4 provides for the kind of compensation for aggression that was defended in limited fashion above. The compensation was paid out in the following way. Following the war, the UN established a "compensation fund" that was financed by a gradual lifting of the oil embargo that was levelled on Iraq after its initial invasion of Kuwait. Under these terms, 30 per cent of the oil export sales of Iraq were allowed to be kept by its government, with the (purely verbal) stipulation that such monies be employed to provide for the humanitarian needs (foodstuffs and medicine) of its people. The remaining 70 per cent was split between: 1) the compensation fund for Kuwait; 2) a special fund designed to pay for the expenses of the on-site UN weapons inspectors; and 3) an escrow "incentive account," which was to be handed over to Iraq once full compliance with the terms of settlement was achieved. Such an account seems to have been an enlightened and sophisticated actualization of the compensation principle.

Article 5 of the ceasefire provided for that partial disarmament and demilitarization of the aggressor, defended above as part of the goal of achieving a more secure and peaceful international order than was the case prior to the war. In addition to the verifiable dismantling of Iraq's WMD program, the

Security Council also established demilitarized zones within Iraq, north of the 36th parallel (to greater protect Israel, Turkey and the Kurdish minority within Iraq) and south of the 32nd parallel (to greater protect Kuwait, Saudi Arabia and the Shiite community within Iraq). Iraq pledged neither to fly over nor to occupy those areas with military forces, for an indeterminate amount of time. It also acquiesced to Allied air patrols of the no-fly zones (NFZ) for enforcement purposes. It seems that such terms were also entirely in line with the criteria of *jus post bellum* defended above: Iraq was to be demilitarized not to the point of collapse but at least to the point where it could not pose a short-term threat to international peace and security within the region.

One criticism which might be levelled at this arrangement was that, because it was indefinite and open-ended, flare-ups were bound to occur. The first time was in January 1993, when Iraq tested the Allies by flying into both NFZs and quickly crossing the border into Kuwait to retrieve some weaponry it had abandoned during the retreat back into Iraq during February 1991. The US retaliated with three air attacks and missile strikes on military targets, albeit with at least one errant missile striking a residential section within Baghdad. Military fire was exchanged several times in 1996. Then, starting in late 1997 and moving into the summer of 1998, Iraq refused to comply with the UN weapons inspectors anymore. By December 1998 American President Bill Clinton ordered Operation Desert Fox.[37] British and American forces combined to bombard military targets in Iraq for four days. The "operation"—a serious military offensive—attempted to enforce compliance with the inspections regime and, in any event, to set back that part of Iraq's WMD program that had eluded inspection. The latter aim may have succeeded but not the former: Iraq as of 1999 absolutely refused to let any UN weapons inspectors back into its territory. This was, of course, cited as one major cause of war for the 2003 regime change.

One aspect of *jus post bellum* which clearly was not met was the failure to commit to holding any war crimes trials at all, on either side. There was nothing credible in the cease-fire agreement to this effect, nor was there any public commitment on the part of the Allies, particularly the USA.

Another region of controversy here concerns discrimination. When Iraq invaded Kuwait in August, 1990, much of the developed world responded with economic sanctions. These were substantially maintained by the peace treaty and, in fact, lasted until the very fall of the Hussein regime after the 2003 war, or 13 years in total. As noted before, soon after the war, the Allies partially eased the economic embargo on Iraqi oil exports, stipulating that the 30 per cent Iraqi benefit from such new sales be devoted to meeting the humanitarian needs of its people (foodstuffs, medicine and infrastructure repairs). However, it could be argued that this was too strict and indiscriminate a policy on the part of the Allies. After all, everything that everyone knew about the Hussein regime indicated that the funds would be used for

buttressing and benefiting its position, and there were no effective enforcement mechanisms built into the terms of Iraq's receiving this money. (The
Allies tried to change this somewhat in 1996 with the so-called "Oil-for-
Food" program, but that policy was deeply troubled—and, it turns out, deeply
riddled with corruption.) So perhaps it was disingenuous for the Allies simply
to leave the matter at that—particularly with regard to the damage that their
bombing had inflicted on part of the water treatment supply system in Iraq.
Perhaps effective enforcement mechanisms could have been built into the
receipt of that cash, and/or perhaps more could have been made available,
from the oil fund, to non-governmental aid and relief agencies. In the absence
of such measures, the Allies might have been guilty of some callousness with
regard to the post-war sufferings of the Iraqi people in the 1990s.

Of course, this is not at all to exonerate the Hussein regime, whose
truculence and indifference to the well-being of its own people must loom
large in any fair-minded account of why the Iraqi populace seemed to suffer
such deprivations during and after the war. It is to apportion only *some* of
the blame for this suffering: more should have been done for the Iraqi people
than to say "Look, we give Saddam 30 per cent of the oil revenue for you,
but he uses it for himself and his army." Funding international relief agencies
to go in with actual food and medicine seems an obvious way around this,
which should have at least been tried. To the extent to which this settlement
violated discrimination, it also raises issues of proportionality. In other
words, the strictness of the sanctions, and the widespread effects they had on
civilians, revealed that the treaty involved disproportionate punishment.[38]

Perhaps it might be said that the fact that the Allies created so-called "safe
havens"—protected by military force and liberally supplied with humanitarian
aid—within both demilitarized zones for the Kurdish and Shiite communities
does, in fact, indicate substantial adherence to the rule of discriminating
between the *people* of a given aggressor and the aggressive *regime* itself. And
so it does. However, the account cannot be left at this point. After all, during
the war Bush himself explicitly, and publicly, called on the Iraqi people to
overthrow Hussein. And the Kurds and Shiites heeded that call, but were
crushed in the immediate post-war period by the remnant of Hussein's armed
forces. I believe that such a call, and such a response, created an obligation
independent of the principle of discrimination on the part of the Allies, especially the United States, to create safe havens for those persecuted people in
the wake of war.

Despite these substantial difficulties, it needs to be admitted that the
majority of the post-war measures *were* directly targeted at the aggressor
regime: forcing it to abandon its claims; reducing its military capacity; limiting its resources and regional sway; and so on. So, the judgment with regard
to discrimination seems quite difficult and conflictual. It seems that, on the
whole, the Allies did indeed focus on punishing the regime—they clearly
intended to target the regime—but the extent and depth of Iraqi civilian

deprivation in the aftermath leaves one wondering whether the Allies could have done more to ease their suffering, without providing any comfort to the aggressor regime.

The big failing with the Persian Gulf War settlement concerns rehabilitation, in two senses. First, there was little attempt to reform Kuwait's political structure after its independence was re-established. Second, there was no attempt to reform the Hussein regime in Iraq. There are probably two reasons why this was the case. The first is the idea that the just cause for going to war was the invasion and brutality against Kuwait. Once the Allies reversed the invasion and restored the Kuwaitis to some security, the reasons justifying the war ended. It seems Bush Sr. sincerely believed in this, because many of his generals asked for permission to go into Baghdad to take out the Hussein regime, and he denied them. He had a quite conservative, cautious understanding of just war principles. The second reason for refraining from rehabilitating Iraq at that time was a belief that the various peace treaty terms would sufficiently contain the Hussein regime from further misadventures.

This choice not to rehabilitate was a mistake, and it is partly because of this Iraq experience that we have compelling evidence that forcible post-war rehabilitation can be, in some cases, a good long-term idea. This may be one reason why the mood in favour of rehabilitation is so much stronger today. Failing to rehabilitate Kuwait diminished the overall value of the war: while the war made Kuwaitis much better off than during the Iraqi occupation, did it make them better off than before the whole business? Not obviously so, and wars which fail to do this cannot be viewed very brightly. Failing to rehabilitate Iraq cost much more. First, the Kurdish and Shiite resistance to Hussein was betrayed. Second, the costs of the ongoing military containment programs were considerable. Third, the whole weapons inspection process could have happened much more quickly and effectively under a different regime instead of lasting for over a decade and escalating into a cause for another war. Fourth, all the fretting about Saddam supporting terrorism could have been avoided. Indeed, perhaps the whole second war could have been prevented. Above all, the Iraqi people would have been saved from: 1) the ravages of the sweeping sanctions; and 2) the rights-violating tyranny of the Hussein regime. What's morally the most striking about the Persian Gulf War settlement terms is the insensitivity to, and hence culpability for, the continued misery and rights-violation suffered by ordinary Iraqis. This experience, and in other cases throughout the 1990s, have rightly lessened concerns about undue interference and intervention, and instead strengthened the moral and even strategic case for progressive post-war rehabilitation measures.[39]

Now, it is very easy indeed to point out flaws and mistakes a long time after a serious decision has been made and we have been able to see the flow of history in-between. "Monday Morning Quarterbacks" always seem to know the right play *after* the results are in. We must resist this temptation. Wartime decision-making is incredibly pressured, the evidence often not as decisive as one wishes, the long-term consequences at times very difficult to see. We should not envy those whose job and responsibility it is to make such choices. Bush Sr. stuck to a cautious interpretation of just war theory and international law, and thus believed that the Allies had to stop after they drove Iraq out of Kuwait. He must have been anxious to stop the war, too—America's first major war since Vietnam. And the international scene was quite delicate at that time: the USSR and its Eastern European client states were all imploding and so Bush Sr. wanted to be prudent and cautious so as not to unwittingly spark something else far more severe. All very understandable and reasonable positions at the time. And that must really be our standard: *what was it reasonable to believe and do at the time?* At the time, perhaps regime change did seem incredibly risky, especially with the Vietnam quagmire looming large in memory and not wanting to convey to collapsing communist states that America favoured bold, Western-led social re-engineering around the world. But we have learned much since the 1990s, about regime change in general and about that regime in particular, and so perhaps the 1991 decision was a failure by history's harsh, long lights. This is not so much to criticize Bush Sr. as to learn from his example for the benefit of future decision-makers. It is not a personal criticism; it is a statement that the policy failed as a result of its effects. But, in my view, Bush Sr. can be more readily criticized for the maintenance of the sanctions. In spite of the safe havens, it was predictable at the time that Saddam's clique would always take care of itself, and thus nation-wide sanctions would bite into civilian well-being. There were mitigating factors, we have seen; even so, not quite enough effort was made in thinking that question through. And so the situation dragged on and on, the sanctions bit more and more severely, and serious problems were created for the Iraqi people and the Clinton and Bush Jr. administrations. It was also reasonable to see, in 1991, that if you let the weapons inspections process run indefinitely, that eventually Iraq would chafe and challenge it. Firm deadlines should have been given to prevent all the subsequent skirmishes and serious misunderstandings, which of course were partly responsible for sparking another war.

Notes

1. B.H. Liddell Hart, *Strategy* (New York: Random House, 1974), 338.
2. In *War and International Justice: A Kantian Perspective* (Waterloo, ON: Wilfrid Laurier University Press, 2000), pp. 218–23, I refer to some pieces of international law in the Hague Convention which *do* mention war termination, but such laws are: 1) very dated, almost 100 years old now; and 2) radically thin and lacking in substance. I suppose there are pieces of international human rights law which international lawyers would say also apply to post-war situations. Fair enough— and good—but it remains true that these pieces are not specifically designed to

guide states during that post-war phase, which is what I'm talking about here. There is the related issue of foreign occupation, and there is some international law on that, but we'll discuss it in the next chapter on regime change.

3. M. Boemeke, ed. *The Treaty of Versailles* (Cambridge: Cambridge University Press, 1998). However, we should not make the mistake of believing that the Treaty exonerates the German people from allowing Hitler to come to power. The Treaty may have been *a* factor in laying the groundwork for World War II but it can hardly be considered the only one. The failure of rival German elites to challenge Hitler, the ruthless thuggery of the Nazis, and the electoral appeal of simple solutions in a time of complex crisis were all important domestic factors in Germany. For an excellent study, see M. Macmillan, *Paris 1919* (New York: Macmillan, 2003).

4. D. Reiff, *Slaughterhouse: Bosnia and The Failure of the West* (New York: Simon and Schuster, 1995).

5. This is not to deny the existence, or the importance, of the robust conflict resolution literature. Much of that literature is relevant to the present concern, but not much of it is located within the explicitly *ethical* values and commitments of just war theory, whereas this chapter is. For more on conflict resolution in general, see: S.J. Cimbala, *Strategic War Termination* (New York: Praeger, 1986); P.R. Pillar, *Negotiating Peace: War Termination as a Bargaining Process* (Princeton: Princeton University Press, 1983); S. Albert and E. Luck, eds. *On the Endings of Wars* (London: Kennikat Press, 1980); and F.O. Hampson, *Nurturing Peace: Why Peace Settlements Succeed or Fail* (Washington, DC: US Institute of Peace, 1996).

6. M. Walzer, *Just and Unjust Wars* (New York: Basic Books, 3rd ed., 2000), 119, xx.

7. Walzer, *Wars*, 109–24.

8. Churchill, quoted in Walzer, *Wars*, 112.

9. Walzer, *Wars*, 109–24, 263–68: M. Walzer, in Symposium on the Bombing of Hiroshima, *Dissent*, Summer 1995, 330.

10. R. Scarborough, *Rumsfeld's War* (New York: Regnery, 2004); J. Carroll, *Crusade: Chronicles of an Unjust War* (New York: Metropolitan, 2004).

11. Walzer, *Wars*, 118.

12. This image of just war as radical surgery, and just settlement as the subsequent therapy, came to mind while reading N. Oren, "Prudence in Victory," in N. Oren, ed. *Termination of War: Processes, Procedures and Aftermaths* (Jerusalem: Hebrew University Press, 1982), 147–64.

13. Walzer, *Wars*, 113.

14. Walzer, *Wars*, 113, 119; E. Karsh and I. Rauter, *Saddam Hussein: A Political Biography* (New York: Grove, 2003) and C. Coughlin, *Saddam: King of Terror* (London: Ecco, 2002).

15. Walzer, *Wars*, 297.

16. R. Clark, *The Impact of Sanctions on Iraq* (London: World View Forum, 1996); A. Arnove and A. Abunimah, eds. *Iraq Under Siege* (London: South End Press,

2000); G. Simons, *The Scourging of Iraq* (New York: Macmillan, 2nd ed., 1996); A. Peirce, "Just War Principles and Economic Sanctions," *Ethics and International Affairs* (1996), 99–113; and the multi-essay exchange on the issue between J. Gordon and G. Lopez, from pp. 123–50, in *Ethics and International Affairs* (1999).

17. Walzer, in *Dissent*, 330.

18. Walzer, *Wars*, 288.

19. Walzer, *Wars*, 292–301.

20. Walzer, *Wars*, 319–22; M. Reisman and C. Antoniou, eds. *The Laws of War* (New York: Vintage, 1994), 337–50; T. Tanaka, *Hidden Horrors: Japanese War Crimes in World War II* (Boulder, CO: Westview Press, 1997); and T.P. Maya, *Judgment at Tokyo: The Japanese War Crimes Trial* (Lexington, KY: University of Kentucky Press, 2001).

21. Reisman and Antoniou, eds. *Laws*, 332–3.

22. Admittedly, however, there was a 100 per cent conviction rate in the Tokyo trials, which rightly raises eyebrows. There is no denying, looking at the events of 1945–6, that the Americans truly had it in for the Japanese.

23. Walzer, *Wars*, 292–6; Reisman and Antoniou, eds. *Laws*, 318–37; J. Persico, *Nuremberg: Infamy on Trial* (New York: Penguin, 1995) and M. Marus, *The Nuremberg War Crimes Trials 1945–6* (New York: St. Martin's Press, 1997).

24. Walzer, *Wars*, 309–16; Reisman and Antoniou, eds. *Laws*, 357–70; W. Schabas, *An Introduction to the International Criminal Court* (Cambridge: Cambridge University Press, 2001); S. Hersh, *My Lai 4* (New York: Doubleday, 1970); P. French, ed. *Individual and Collective Responsibility: The Massacre at My Lai* (Cambridge: Harvard University Press, 1972); S. Hersh, *Chain of Command: The Road from 9/11 to Abu Ghraib* (New York: HarperCollins, 2004).

25. Walzer, *Wars*, 123.

26. R. Regan, *Just War: Theory and Cases* (Washington, DC: Georgetown University Press, 1996), 172–212.

27. Walzer, *Wars*, 290–91, 298.

28. Walzer, *Wars*, 299–301.

29. Walzer, *Wars*, 301; US Congress, *The 9/11 Commission Report* (Washington, DC: US Congress, 2004).

30. Walzer, *Wars*, 301–3.

31. P. Christopher, *The Ethics of War and Peace* (Englewood Cliffs, NJ: Prentice Hall, 1994), 139–64; and Walzer, *Wars*, 304–28.

32. Walzer, *Wars*, 309–16, and Reisman and Antoniou, eds. *Laws*, 357–70.

33. Walzer, *Wars*, 305–16.

34. I. Kant, *The Metaphysics of Morals*, trans. M. Gregor (Cambridge: Cambridge University Press, 1995), 114–24; Orend, *Kantian Perspective, passim*.

35. M. Walker, *The Cold War: A History* (New York: Henry Holt, 1995), 160–83.

36. A. Arato, *Civil Society, Constitution and Legitimacy* (Lanham: Rowman and Littlefield, 2000).

37. Some were scandalized that Clinton ordered the operation on the night before the first scheduled vote on his impeachment in the US House of Representatives. Others noted the unhappy title of the operation, since "Desert Fox" was Nazi General Erwin Rommell's nickname during The Second World War.

38. See the sources in Note 16.

39. Information for this section on the Persian Gulf War has been drawn from the following sources: Regan, *Cases*, 172–79; L. Freedman and E. Karsh, *The Gulf Conflict: Diplomacy and War in the New World Order* (London: Farber and Farber, 1991); W. Danspeckgruber and C. Tripp, eds. *The Iraqi Aggression Against Kuwait* (Boulder, CO: Westview, 1996); US News and World Report, *Triumph without Victory* (New York: Random House, 1992); James Turner Johnson and G. Weigel, eds., *Just War and Gulf War* (Washington, DC: University Press of America, 1991); and A. Beyer and B. Green, eds. *Lines in the Sand: Justice and the Gulf War* (Louisville, KY: John Knox, 1992).

CHAPTER 7

Jus Post Bellum #2
Coercive Regime Change

*"They can only be made to accept a new constitution of a nature ...
unlikely to encourage their warlike inclinations."*
Immanuel Kant[1]

Last chapter we sketched out a general blueprint for post-war justice. While
we included the rehabilitation of illegitimate state structures, we need now to
explain and justify such assertions. What, if anything, justifies the deliberate
overthrow of a regime at war's end? Is setting out to do so from the start a
permissible war aim? What should the old regime be replaced with? What
are the relevant case studies? The questions keep coming in a torrent: how
should post-war reconstruction proceed? Who is entitled to do what, and
why? What are the rights and responsibilities of the overthrowing and occupying power, and what are those of the civil society which remains even after
the regime has been liquidated?

It is unclear whether anybody has satisfying answers to all these questions.
Yet we must consider them, not only out of intrinsic interest but also owing
to the press of current circumstances: Afghanistan, Bosnia, Iraq and Serbia
all feature ongoing processes of post-war reconstruction and regime change,
and on some of them hang regional and even global security issues—threats
of civil wars, border wars, failed states and terrorism—as well as concerns
over imperialism, sovereignty and human rights. The goal of this chapter is
to pose some sharp questions, and then to take a stab at some answers for
these tremendously difficult problems.

Historical Examples

Forcible regime change is not at all a new thing. It is, in fact, a frequent
occurrence in the history of warfare. This should not surprise us when we
recall that warfare does, essentially, aim at how a territory is governed. Most
of the wars of European colonial expansion, from 1500 to 1950, can be seen
as wars of coercive regime change. The Europeans found "new" territories
governed by locals (i.e., natives or aboriginals) and left them as lands ruled
by European appointees, with European-style state structures. Probably the

main moral controversy surrounding forcible regime change in our day is whether it is the old, offensive colonialism under new guise. Is post-war reconstruction a cover for neo-imperialism?[2]

Against such accusations, there are two preliminary replies. The first concerns historical counter-examples. Some prominent historians, like Niall Ferguson, are presently arguing that some of the old European empires were not so terrible. The ancient Roman Empire brought peace, prosperity, civilization and technological advance to the entire Mediterranean world for hundreds of years. And the British Empire—Ferguson's favourite example— likewise generated remarkable prosperity, political stability and cultural advance for its subjects. Indeed, some of the most developed and successful societies on earth are former members: America, Australia, Canada and the UK itself. And the benefits of the British Empire were not simply in terms of wealth and security but also, Ferguson says, important moral and legal values, such as individual liberty, free trade, the impersonal rule of law and parliamentary democracy. By population, the world's two largest democracies are ex-Empire members: India and America. The record is marred by flaws, of course: the Empire early on was involved in African slavery; it lost America to revolution; and there were sore spots of protracted violence, including Ireland and parts of the Middle East. Ferguson does not deny such realities; he merely wishes to point out the other, positive side of the ledger. The words sound strange but, historically, empire has had some advantages.[3]

The second response concerns the fact that forcible regime change has occurred in contexts completely devoid of European imperialism. Regime change is not logically connected, of necessity, to what the British used to refer to—in superior terms—as "The White Man's Burden." Consider two recent examples. In Chapter 3, during our discussion of humanitarian intervention, I mentioned that in the mid-1970s, the communist government of Vietnam invaded Cambodia and overthrew the Khmer Rouge regime. This regime, an extremely radical communist outfit, had come to power through force and was determined to reshape Cambodian society to accord with the most severe revolutionary principles. Accordingly, it sought to liquidate all opposed to this order. It did so by instituting "The Killing Fields" of organized mass slaughter: one million Cambodians were murdered, and tens of thousands fled as refugees out of the country and into Vietnam. So Vietnam decided that both for its own security and stability—as well as perhaps for humanitarian reasons?—it had to change the Cambodian regime by force. So it did, and while the regime it helped to install there did not, and will not, win any human rights awards, it is hard to argue that it is not a clear improvement over the Khmer Rouge.

The next example, also from the 1970s, occurred in Africa. Uganda suffered under the dictatorship of Idi Amin. A paranoid tyrant, he tortured and slaughtered some 300,000 of his own citizens. This eventually sparked an armed uprising against him. Amin thought he could prevail by invading neighbouring Tanzania and annexing a border province. The renegade ruler's strategy was to unite his own people behind him in the face of war with a foreign power—a war which, if won, would increase Uganda's size and resources. The plan backfired. Amin had wounded the people too much for them to support him. The president of Tanzania, Julius Nyerere, then decided to forge an alliance with Ugandan rebels, and together they forcibly over-threw Amin's regime. The resulting government was much as in the Cambo-dian case: not great but clearly morally better than an aggressive tyrant who was so brutally inhumane.[4]

America has also been deeply involved in forcible regime change—and not simply since World War II (much less Iraq). Indeed, the United States was founded in an act of forcible regime change during the Revolutionary War. It half-heartedly then, and again in 1812 (and even later in some circles), considered converting Canada by force into joining the republic. There was the bitter Civil War experience in 1861–65, which ultimately revolved around liquidating the Confederate regime and forcibly reconstructing it. The United States had many military entanglements in Latin America (especially Cuba and Mexico) as well as in Indonesia in the transition period from the 1800s to the 1900s, and several of those entanglements were attempts at forcing regime change. Some were successful, others not. The post-World War II experience gets almost all of the attention, and understandably so. It is the most recent era, and witnessed some spectacular successes as well as formi-dable failures. The reconstruction of Germany and Japan, from 1945 to 1955, probably count as the most successful and praiseworthy regime transforma-tions in recent world history. On the other hand, the Bay of Pigs invasion of Cuba in 1961—trying to oust Castro's communists by force—was a complete and embarrassing flop. Somewhere in-between reside such other examples as the Dominican Republic (1965), Grenada (1983), Panama (1989), Haiti (1994), Bosnia (1995) and Afghanistan (2001). There are also controversial cases—where US involvement in forcing regime change was real but indi-rect—such as Guatemala (1954) and Serbia (1999). And of course there is the current case of Iraq. Before considering it, however, let's take a closer look at the Germany and Japan cases, since they shed so much light on: 1) when forcible regime change might be justified; and 2) how it might be successfully realized.[5]

RECONSTRUCTING GERMANY AND JAPAN

The settlement of World War II was not contained in a detailed, legalistic peace treaty. This was, partly, because Germany and Japan were so thor-oughly crushed and had so little leverage. But World War II's settlement was sweeping and profound, with immense effects on world history. It was worked out, essentially, between America and the Soviet Union at meetings in Tehran and Yalta, but with participation from the UK, France, China and other of the "lesser" Allies. Both Britain and France kept control over their colonies, but everyone knew that powerful forces of anti-colonialism—abetted by the exhaustion of England and France—would soon cause those old empires to crumble. As for the new empires, it was understood that the USSR would hold sway in Eastern Europe, ostensibly to serve as a barrier between itself and Germany, preventing another Nazi-style invasion. (It also provided for the export and spread of communist tyranny, unfortunately.) The USA, by contrast, would get Hawaii, a number of Pacific Islands, and total sway over the reconstruction of Japan. As for Germany, America, Britain, France and Russia agreed to split it, into Western and Eastern halves. Ditto for the German capital Berlin, which was otherwise entirely within the Eastern Soviet sphere. Within the Soviet sphere, police-state communism came to dominate as readily as it did in Russia. But within the West, there was a concerted effort to establish genuine free-market, rights-respecting democracies. In Japan, the same experiment was undertaken, but there the US military, under the firm leadership of Douglas MacArthur, held more direct control for longer than it did in West Germany.

The Allies, genuinely working with nationals in both countries—more so in Germany than Japan, perhaps—first undertook a purging process, which in Germany came to be known as "de-nazi-fication." All signs, symbols, buildings, literature and things directly associated with the Nazis were destroyed utterly. The Nazi party itself was abolished and declared illegal. Surviving ex-Nazis—but not all of them[6]—were either put on trial, put in jail or otherwise punished and prohibited from political participation. The militaries of both Germany and Japan were utterly disbanded, and for years the Allied military became *the* military, and the direct ruler, of both Germany and Japan.[7]

After the negative purging process, the Allies in both countries established written constitutions or "Basic Law." These constitutions, after the period of direct military rule ended, provided for bills and charters of human rights, eventual democratic elections and, above all, the checks and balances so prominently featured in the American system. Since government had grown so huge and tyrannical in both Germany and Japan in the 1930s, it had to be shrunk down, and then broken into pieces, with each piece only authorized to handle its own business. Independent judiciaries and completely reconstituted police forces were an important part of this—and they went a long way to re-establishing the impersonal rule of law over the personal whims of former fascists. The executive branches, much more so than in the American system, were made more accountable to, and closely tied to, the legislative branch. The goal, of course, was to ensure that the executive could not grow into another dictator. By design, there were to be no strong presidents. So Germany and Japan became true *parliamentary* democracies, more in the European than American style.

Western-style liberal democracy was not the only change forcibly implemented. The education systems of both Germany and Japan were overhauled, since they played huge propaganda roles for both regimes and the content of their curricula had been filled with racism, ultra-nationalism and distorted ignorance of the outside world. Western experts redesigned these systems to impart concrete skills needed to participate in reconstruction, as well as to stress a more objective content favouring the basic cognitive functions ("the three Rs"), critical thinking and especially science and technology. The curricula were radically stripped of political content, though of course some lessons on the new social institutions and their principles were required.

The Americans quickly saw that their sweeping legal, constitutional, social and educational reforms would lack stability unless they could stimulate the German and Japanese economies. The people needed their vital needs met, as well as a sense of hope that, concretely, the future would get better. Otherwise, they might revolt, and the reforms fail. Here is where the really remarkable thing happened: instead of making the (World War I) mistake of sucking money out of these ruined countries through mandatory reparations payments, the Americans were the ones *who poured money into* Germany and Japan. America shunned the revenge paradigm and embraced the rehabilitative one. It was a staggering sum of money, too, channelled through the so-called "Marshall Plan." Money was needed to buy essentials, as well as to clear away all the rubble and ruined infrastructure. It was also just needed to circulate, to get the Germans and Japanese used to free market trading. Jobs were plentiful, as entire systems of infrastructure—transportation, water, sewage, electricity, agriculture, finance—had to be rebuilt. Since jobs paid wages thanks to the Marshall Plan, the people's lives improved and the free market system deepened. But it was not just the money. American management experts poured into Germany and Japan, showing them the very latest, and most efficient, means of production.[8] Within 30 years, Germany and Japan had not only rebounded economically, they had the two strongest economies in the world after America itself, based especially on quality high-tech manufacturing (e.g., automobiles).

The post-war reconstructions of Germany and Japan easily count as the most impressive post-war rehabilitations in modern history. Germany and Japan, today, have massive free market economies, and politically remain peaceful and stable liberal democracies. They are both very good "citizens" on the global stage. They are minimally just, and much more in fact. In addition, these countries are by no means "clones" (much less colonies) of America: they each have gone their own way, adding local colour and pursuing political paths quite distinct from those that most interest the United States—consider especially Germany's formative role in the European Union. So we have clear evidence that even massive forcible post-war changes need not threaten "a nation's character," or what makes it unique and special to its people. But such success *did* come at a huge cost in terms of time and treasure: it cost trillions of dollars; took trillions of "man-hours" in work and expertise; it took decades of real time; it took the co-operation of most of the German and Japanese people; and, above all, it took the will of the United States to see it through. It was American money, American security, American know-how, American patience and American generosity which brought it all into being. Such is the magnitude of commitment needed by any party bent on implementing substantial post-war rehabilitation.[9]

Connecting Start and Finish

I have stated repeatedly throughout this work that the three phases of war (beginning, middle and end) are interconnected, and so should be the three categories of just war theory (*jus ad bellum, jus in bello* and *jus post bellum*). In particular, when it comes to *jus post bellum* it is axiomatic that if there was no justice at the start of the war, there will be no justice at the end. In other words, the less just your start of war, the fewer your rights in the post-war phase. Coherence entails that injustice in the beginning *infects* both the middle and end of war. It is hard to imagine—logically, causally and historically—a war which X began unjustly yet, when X won and imposed its will, that justice was somehow ultimately served. In those three senses, it seems more accurate to quip that it is "garbage in, garbage out": decrepit inputs do not generate sublime outputs. So if we concern ourselves with justice after war, we must ensure we involve ourselves in a just war to begin with.

Some might ask: cannot we imagine a war unjustly begun, yet justly concluded? Some might say that America's 2003 Iraq attack was unjustly begun, yet it was fought quickly and with reasonable adherence to *jus in bello*. (The prison tortures came later, during the occupation.) And if America succeeds in reconstructing Iraq, that is just, is it not? Compared to the calibre of the Hussein regime? Well, justice is not just about results, though of course these *are* important. Justice is also about not violating rights, and about following a certain procedure. *Jus ad bellum* violations *are* violations of rights, and it has always been my contention[10] that we should understand each of the three just war categories coming together to form one long procedure which demands getting each step right before moving on to the next one. So, *jus ad bellum* failure corrupts the whole resulting project. We might therefore speak of Iraq being better off if—*if*—American-led reconstruction works, but not of it having been fully just if we seriously doubt, as I do, America's inauguration of that conflict. In other words, even if it all somehow turns out well, that still will not make the original decision just; it will simply mean that the post-war situation was not as bad as it might have been.

The connection between the categories means that the only party with post-war entitlements regarding regime change will be the one which fought on the side of justice to begin with. As Kant said, the raw fact of military victory only changes the power situation; it does not, and should not, change our *moral* assessment of the war, which is at the level of enduring principle and not merely of contingent power.[11] There is no guarantee the just side will actually win, of course, but it is quite another thing—surely, a mistaken thing—to interpret victory in war *as itself imbuing* the war or post-war measures with moral value. Nazi Germany won the Blitzkrieg phase of World War II, yet this hardly justifies what it subsequently did to Poland, Scandinavia, the Netherlands and France. The Communists, in the early- to mid-1900s, won their civil wars in Russia and China, but that does not justify how they later governed those territories. And so on.

As I argued in Chapter 3, the American-led war of regime change against the Taliban in Afghanistan satisfied *jus ad bellum*, whereas that against Saddam Hussein's regime probably violated it. Why? In the first war, in late 2001, strong evidence showed the Taliban provided state sponsorship—of resources, weapons and safe havens—to the terrorist group al-Qaeda, which had just committed aggression against America on 9/11. The Taliban did so because it shared al-Qaeda's radical Islamist ideology, which mandates the violent take-over of all governments in traditional Arab lands and their conversion into strict Islamic theocracies wherein there is a unification of church and state modelled after the Taliban's Afghanistan or, to a lesser extent, Iran. These groups despise the West because it is not Islamic and particularly target America because of its support for Middle Eastern regimes they would love to overthrow, in particular Saudi Arabia (the holy land of Islam) and Israel (which they claim is on traditional Arab land). Most just war theorists, and twenty-eight other countries, agreed with America that it was just to respond with force when the Taliban refused to hand over al-Qaeda suspects in November 2001. Owing to that large consensus on the justice of the start of that war, we can speak meaningfully of large post-war entitlements of the Allied force in Afghanistan.

Regarding Iraq, only seven countries agreed with America, and I think a majority of just war theorists disagreed with the war. International lawyers were perhaps the most incensed of all, since no clear Security Council vote was held. In Chapter 3, I argued that the main cause of the war—pre-emptive self-defence against an imminent WMD strike by Iraq or Iraq-supplied terrorists—was not proven to the degree it had to be. While I did admit that armed humanitarian intervention was the best cause for that war—Saddam's regime not being minimally just—it clearly was not the shot being called and, besides that, the attack ran afoul of issues of proper authority, last resort, probability of success and proportionality. So I must conclude that post-war entitlements in the Iraq case are much smaller than in the Afghanistan case. But even though I believe America has few if any rights in post-war Iraq, this does not mean I think America should just up and leave. That is because I endorse the much-publicized "Pottery Barn Rule": *if you break it, you buy it.* In March–May, 2003, America broke Iraq—there can be no doubt about that—and that act brought with it separate responsibilities to help put Iraq back together. In other words, America has few rights, but many duties, regarding post-war Iraq. This means that it still makes sense to hold America to standards, such as aiding the creation of a minimally just community in Iraq. Even if I think the Iraq war unjust, and thus cannot ever pronounce America's post-war policies fully just, I can—we have established—still pronounce them *better or worse*, according to the extent to which they would satisfy the ideal, had the inauguration of the conflict been different.

The Goal of Just Regime Change

Before considering in detail what is going on in Afghanistan and Iraq, let's speak of the goal of justified regime change in general. The goal of justified post-war regime change—whether permitted by rights or demanded by duties—is the timely construction of a minimally just political community. As we saw in Chapter 2, such a community makes every reasonable effort to: 1) avoid violating the rights of other minimally just communities; 2) gain recognition as being legitimate in the eyes of the international community and its own people; and 3) realize the human rights of all its individual members. We provided there a justification for having this standard, and we recall it here since the imposition of any standard in the post-war environment is such serious and controversial business. The ideal of a human rights-respecting, minimally just political community is a justified one because:

* It is in every individual's self-interest;
* It respects everyone's potential for autonomy and self-direction;
* It thus has universal appeal;
* It already enjoys very strong international consensus;
* It is based on thin, reasonable and accessible values like living a minimally good life;
* It generates good consequences, especially in terms of average quality of life; and
* It promotes long-term international peace and stability.

It is these values—their strength and moral resonance—which ground regime changing measures in a post-war environment. These are not extreme, narrow, "Crusading," or "imperialistic" values; they are modest, secular, widely accepted and based on appeal to the first principle of respecting individual rights as well as to after-the-fact considerations of generating concrete beneficial consequences for everyone. Let's now examine in some detail how well the ongoing reconstruction processes in Afghanistan and Iraq are faring, relative to these standards and goals.

Afghanistan and Iraq

Just as with Germany and Japan, American-led Allies in Afghanistan and Iraq have invoked the need for disarmament and demilitarization. This is consistent with the first criterion of making any newly reconstructed government one which will not commit aggression and will generally be respectful of its neighbours. But note that when you so demilitarize a country, this implies a duty on your part to fill in the gap and provide for that society effective military and police security from domestic as well as international threats. There are huge difficulties, at present, with satisfying this condition both in Afghanistan and Iraq.

In Afghanistan, its capital Kabul has been rendered fairly secure by the international force. But the same cannot be said of the rural parts of the country and emphatically the south-eastern portion near the Pakistan border. In that section, in fact, there is still something of a hot war—a live-fire armed conflict—between the remnants of the Taliban and al-Qaeda, on the one hand, and, on the other, the international Allies. Clearly, a country with a small-scale war within its borders is not entirely demilitarized and secure. Plus, there is the issue of the "warlords." Afghanistan is a society strongly structured on the basis of ethnicity and clan (or extended family). The warlords are heads of clan, who jealously guard their family's traditional territory with their own private, family-manned armed militias. These groups have not been disarmed either and could, if they all got together, challenge the power and authority of the new Afghani government. Thus, there is some, but little, success on the security front so far in Afghanistan.

That would be a huge overstatement in connection with Iraq, where security threatens to become a black hole into which every other post-war issue gets sucked and lost. Saddam's regime collapsed in May, 2003—much more quickly than the Americans predicted. US Defense Secretary Donald Rumsfeld ordered the disbanding of the Iraqi military a month later, when the US stepped in to provide direct military rule. The armed insurgency—or guerrilla war—started a month after that and is ongoing. Who are the insurgents, and what do they want? There are different groups, and they want different things. First, there are the "Hussein hold-outs," remnants of Saddam's regime who want the Americans out and some form of traditional Sunni clan dominance re-established in Iraq. Next are the radical Islamists who oppose US-led reconstruction because it will not let them institute a strict Islamic theocracy in Iraq. Finally, there are some foreign fighters, especially from Iran and Syria, who do not want to see the Americans succeed in structuring a pro-Western regime on their borders, lest it undermine their own authoritarian rule back home. Most of the insurgents fall into the first category, and as a result the most dangerous place in Iraq is the so-called "Sunni triangle" in the middle of that country, centred around Baghdad.

Some background: Iraq is mainly made of three groups: the Kurds in the north; the Sunni Arabs in the middle; and the Shi'ite Arabs in the south. Shi'ites form the majority and they tend to be more conservative and strict in their religious beliefs than Sunnis. Sunnis, while a minority, have traditionally held power in Iraq. Saddam was Sunni, for instance. The Kurds have always considered themselves their own people, and would prefer their own state to continued life in Iraq. The Kurds thus welcomed the US invasion, and the Shi'ites (while not fans of America) view the post-war situation as an opportunity to pull power back from the Sunnis. But the Sunnis see themselves as having the most to lose, and thus deeply resent the American war and occupation. So they form the bulk of the insurgency and their territory is rife with severe post-war violence (if indeed we can even call it "post-war"). Thousands have been killed, and tens of thousands injured, in the continuing Iraq insurgency.

The daily attacks and bombings shred to bits any claim that post-war Iraq is secure. Most military experts say it is a problem of insufficient force size on the part of the Americans—not enough "boots on the ground." This is partly because Saddam's regime collapsed so quickly, accelerating the transition from war to post-war before the Pentagon could catch up. But the Bush Jr. Administration's solution, thus far, has been to avoid increasing troop intake from back home—since that would be unpopular, and perhaps be perceived as a sign of weakness or error—preferring instead to train a new Iraqi army to fill the gap. This new-fangled Iraqi army and police force—many of them poor young country boys with few other job prospects—are the main targets of insurgent violence. This is smart strategy on the insurgents' part: they can cause the Americans to fail without actually attacking them. Here is where analogies to Vietnam actually become apt.

Vietnam became a long, bloody trap for America because it was confronted with an impossible dilemma: *it could not win, yet it could not leave.* Something similar may happen in Iraq. America may not be able to win because: 1) it cannot increase American troop levels, for domestic political reasons; and 2) it cannot train sufficient Iraqi troops and cops, because these get immediately targeted and taken out by the insurgents. So, the ongoing insecurity and violence prevents progress on all the other fronts (e.g., political and economic) and what you have is a recipe for an indefinite guerrilla war, which in Vietnam stretched for decades. But America cannot yet leave, either. Why? Because it rightly fears that, should it pull out of Iraq in the near future, what will result will be at least as bad as Saddam or quite possibly a lot worse—which would call into question the point and sense of the entire war. The situation in Iraq is so insecure that, should America leave too soon, the three groups might start fighting each other in a civil war over territory, religion, oil and ethnicity. Or a dictator just like Saddam could take over. Or religious zealots like the Taliban could come to power. Or any combination of the above. These are fearsome prospects, and not at all remote possibilities. America remembers that, when it left South Vietnam, the communists promptly took over—the very thing America went to war to prevent in the first place. America also knows it lacks clear, widespread popular support in Iraq, which is exactly the same as in Vietnam and totally unlike the German and Japanese cases.

What about the second criterion of a minimally just government: that it be recognized as legitimate by the international community and, above all, by its own people? International recognition is probably easier and clearer. Usually, it involves things like extending "diplomatic recognition" to the country, by sending and receiving ambassadors and by opening embassies. It also involves welcoming that country into international events and associations, in particular the United Nations. Finally, offering that country money for aid in reconstruction is another sign you recognize its legitimacy and wish to help it. There has been some obvious success here, both in Afghanistan and Iraq. Many countries have reopened their embassies there, and restaffed their diplomatic posts. Both countries continue as UN members, and have been welcomed back into such international events as the Olympics. Thankfully, both countries are also receiving reconstruction monies from around the world, both in the form of direct cash payments and indirect debt forgiveness.

Domestic legitimacy is more important, and trickier. In both Afghanistan and Iraq, the Americans launched similar processes of constitution-building, interim government formation, and subsequent popular elections. In Afghanistan, the clans came together to work out an interim constitutional and government formation, and the first elections were held in October, 2004. The interim president, Hamid Karzai, was reaffirmed as president in elections most international observers agreed were free and fair. Just as vital, the elections were not seriously challenged by rival clan leaders. In December 2005, a more enduring elected parliament was sworn in, and it features plural membership from different regions, clans, interests and genders. These are all real achievements, and we should not let the bleak security scene diminish them.

A similar policy was launched in Iraq—though America did have direct martial rule there between June 2003 and June 2004. The groups agreed on an Iraqi Provisional Authority, an interim constitution and elections. These latter, held in January 2005, produced a resounding defeat for the interim prime minister Allawi. Instead, the Shi'ites (as the majority) won the most seats in the National Assembly, followed by the Kurds and then the Sunnis. While there is no denying these real political achievements, serious challenges remain. Of particular concern is the role of the Sunnis, formerly the most powerful and currently the most aggrieved group. The Sunnis barely participated in the January election, for two reasons: 1) to withhold their consent deliberately; and 2) to avoid insurgent violence (in fact, six towns could not vote at all because they were controlled by insurgents). So how legitimate are elections when one major group barely participates?

The newly-elected, Kurd- and Shi'ite-dominated, government confronted the very difficult task of replacing the merely interim constitution with an enduring one, submitting it for referendum approval in October, 2005, which it achieved. Democratic elections were held in December 2005—popular turn-out was quite high—and, as of writing, the results are not in. While the

Sunnis *did* participate in these December elections—apparently out of fear of being frozen out entirely—there remain concerns that the new enduring constitution excludes them nonetheless.

The document enshrines federalism for Iraq, which seems sensible: the only way to keep the three groups together is not to have them be too close, and constructing a federal government which acknowledges strong regions and provinces with considerable autonomy fits the bill perfectly. But does the document create such strong regions that Iraq will eventually unravel into three separate states? And does that matter? Well, it does if the unravelling will lead to war. Another sore spot is the division of oil revenue, which the new constitution says should be done with an eye to giving more resources to "traditionally disadvantaged" regions of Iraq: the Kurd and Shi'ite parts. While that does seem historically fair, the Sunnis of the present day are unlikely to be satisfied and this is a definite flashpoint of anger. The big political issues in Iraq today are thus: how well will the newly elected federal government deal with these serious group rivalries, and will the constitution create unity or rather division and conflict?[12]

We come to the third criterion for a minimally just government: reasonable efforts at human rights realization. How well are things going in Afghanistan and Iraq, under the five major human rights headings of: security; liberty; subsistence; equality; and recognition? Of security, we have already seen plenty, and know that thus far it is a failure. Of liberty, some genuine advances can be reported. In both cases, there has been real political participation—elections—where previously there was none. In terms of free speech, new newspapers have sprouted in both Kabul and Baghdad, and satellite dishes (for accessing foreign media) can now be purchased. Freedom of religion, in Afghanistan especially, is much better now than under the repressive Taliban. But the more entrenched aspects of securing personal liberty—namely, the rule of law and due process rights in criminal matters—take decades to develop, and thus have not yet been realized in these countries.

In terms of equality and recognition, giant steps have been made for girls and women in Afghanistan compared to under the Taliban, when they were not even educated and were denied full legal personhood. Indeed, Afghanistan's new elected parliament contains many women. A possible recognition concern in Iraq, and I guess Afghanistan, too, concerns whether the various groups will continue to recognize each other as respected partners in constitution-building. Historically, in both countries the different groups and clans have had a difficult relationship, to say the least.

Subsistence poses challenges, especially for Afghanistan. War-torn since 1979, Afghanistan is one of the world's poorest countries, where average life expectancy is 46 and illiteracy runs at 65 per cent. Of particular concern is the rebirth of the narcotics economy, which the Taliban repressed for religious reasons. Afghanistan is the world's largest supplier of poppies, the main ingredient in opium. Now that the Taliban are gone, drug enforcement is lax, and impoverished farmers are growing poppies again, for which they can get much more money than legal crops like potatoes or beans. Figuring out how to suppress the drug trade—which actually strengthens the local warlords—is both an economic and security issue. Societies dominated by drugs (e.g., Colombia) are always crime- and gang-infested, and very violent.

Iraq has more resources than Afghanistan—notably, oil—and has a more sophisticated population, but there are subsistence problems here, too. As of writing, unemployment in Iraq is over 40 per cent, which is shockingly high. Iraq has also been at near-constant war since 1980, and faces massive and lingering reconstruction needs and costs. Recent foreign investment is encouraging, but is it enough? Experience shows that the people must feel a clear improvement in their economic situation comparing post-war to pre-war; if they do not, reconstruction will fail and war may erupt again. In other words, by about 2007–8 Iraqis must definitely feel they are better off than they were under Saddam, or the whole reconstruction project might end up in miserable failure.

The upshot is this: by the three criteria of minimally just communities, it is deeply unclear whether reconstruction in Afghanistan and Iraq is succeeding. It might be too early to tell but there have been some obvious failures, notably security. While there have been some successes, they have mainly been achieved in politics and personal freedoms. The reconstruction of the economies poses huge challenges going forward.

Back to the Ideal

It is important to consider these real-world—and very relevant and timely—cases of post-war reconstruction, and measure them up to our ideals and standards. But it must be stressed that the serious problems in Afghanistan and Iraq do *not* show that forcible, progressive post-war regime change cannot actually be done, and so we must abandon the effort. *Successful coercive post-war regime change was actually done in Germany and Japan, and so it is neither conceptually nor empirically impossible.* In fact, a review of the literature shows something of an ideal 10-point recipe for transforming a defeated aggressor into a minimally just regime.

Before sketching out this recipe, consider Kant's interesting and provocative opening quote. He clearly believed forcible regime change permissible. His moral test involved considering whether one's policies or actions would, if everyone else did the same thing, lead to contradiction or inhumanity. A brutal, rights-violating state obviously acts inhumanely, and if all states behaved like aggressors it would "make peace among nations impossible." Thus, states failing minimal justice forfeit rights of existence. Kant hastens to add, however, that other states should not simply carve up and "ingest" the offending state and its territory, since that would ignore completely the wishes and rights of the local population. The local population *does* have the right to exist as a people, but it *does not have* the right to establish an aggressive or rights-violating state. Kant concludes that the most reasonable, *middle-ground* solution is that the people stay together as a people but they must accept a new, "less war-like constitution." Forcible regime change is actually a sound compromise between the two extremes of conquest, on the one hand, and, on the other, letting terrible regimes exist and thrive.[13]

This puts the vital issue of entitlement nicely: regimes which are not minimally just have no right to govern, and so are in no position to complain should they be overthrown. But what about the right of the people there to be self-governing? National self-determination is not an end in itself; it is good only insofar as it results in a minimally just society. A people never have the right to establish an aggressive or human rights-violating regime, any more than a crook has the right to beat up people as a form of his "freedom of expression." We can imagine cases—indeed, know of cases—where a people lack the means for constructing a minimally just society. Perhaps they lack the resources and expertise, are deeply divided, have been exhausted by war, or flat out refuse out of blinkered nationalism or ideology. In all these cases, they can justly be forced to accept a new, minimally just regime in the post-war period *provided* the war was just. If the war was not just, they cannot be so forced but they should certainly be helped if they freely request it. Owing to the power of the idea of a minimally just political community, we should not be surprised to see locals clamouring for this option and for help. The new regime must then eventually get endorsement and show its local legitimacy—ideally through direct election—and then that effectively cements its right to govern. If the locals still do not like it, they can turf the government out and start again—but always within the confines of minimal justice.

So, and this is the heart of this chapter, forcible post-war regime change is permissible provided: 1) the war itself was just and conducted properly; 2) the target regime was illegitimate, thus forfeiting its state rights; 3) the goal of the reconstruction is a minimally just regime; and 4) respect for *jus in bello* and human rights is integral to the transformation process itself. The permission is then granted because the transformation: 1) violates neither state nor human rights; 2) its expected consequences are very desirable, namely, satisfied human rights for the local population and increased international peace and security for everyone; and 3) the post-war moment is especially promising regarding the possibilities for reform. And the transformation will be successful when there is: 1) a stable new regime, 2) run entirely by locals, which is 3) minimally just. The 2003 Dobbins Report, based on extensive historical evidence, suggests that this kind of success probably takes from seven to ten years to achieve.[14]

The Recipe

According to sound empirical research analyzing the cases,[15] the core
blueprint for transforming defeated, rights-violating aggressor regimes into
stable, peaceful, pro-rights societies is:

+ *Adhere diligently to the laws of war during the regime take-down and
  occupation.* This is morally vital for its own sake, as well as to help win
  the hearts and minds of the locals. America, of course, has notoriously
  run afoul of this principle in Iraq owing to the prisoner abuse scandal
  at the Abu Ghraib prison.

  (Speaking of the laws of war, there is a body of rules referred to as
  "occupation law" but it is much in dispute, even regarding whether it is
  still in force. As Simon Chesterman explains, occupation law demands
  that any occupation be temporary. It does allow occupation forces to
  defend themselves. And it requires that the occupier provide for civilian
  well-being, especially in connection with vital needs and basic infrastructure. But it stridently stipulates that the occupier *not* change any
  of the existing laws or structures within the occupied society. So,
  Chesterman observes, occupation law "provides little support for regime
  change." Thus, this 10-point recipe is in the domain of just war theory
  and political philosophy, not international law. Yet, not entirely so, since
  the UN Security Council has authorized recent regime-changing actions
  in Afghanistan, Cambodia, East Timor and Kosovo, so perhaps the principle is not completely foreign to international law. Additionally, what
  if the war causes the existing state structure to collapse? It seems irra-
  tional to suggest that the occupying power may not change such a condition of destroyed rubble: surely such change could only be for the
  better. And what about those cases of truly abhorrent regimes, like the
  Nazis or Khmer Rouge? The old ban on changing regimes seems pred-
  icated on a belief that the existing state structures do not have anything
  seriously, irredeemably wrong with them. But we know that is not
  always true. And so the clarity and utility of occupation law is much to
  be wondered at, and that is why here we focus on theory.)[16]
+ *Purge much of the old regime, and prosecute its war criminals.* Much,
  but not necessarily all. Clearly, anyone materially connected to aggression, tyranny or atrocity cannot be permitted a substantial role in the
  new order. They have lost the right to govern. But others—say, middle-
  ranking civil servants—might be kept on for their local knowledge and
  bureaucratic expertise. There always needs to be some continuity, even
  in the face of a sea change in institutions.
+ *Disarm and demilitarize the society.* The target military does need to be
  disarmed and demobilized—but then something needs to be done with
  them. Many critics of the American occupation of Iraq argue that a key
  decision which helped spark the ongoing insurgency was the US choice

to promptly disband the 400,000 strong Iraqi army—and then leave them to their own devices. Plans for employing these potentially dangerous men, providing them opportunity, should have been developed. Some of them—not so much the officer class as ordinary soldiers—might even be selectively re-mobilized under a reconstituted command structure.[17]

♦ *Provide effective military and police security for the whole country.* Most experts suggest a two-stage approach here: the successful "attack and overthrow" war divisions be replaced by other divisions *specifically trained* in post-combat peacekeeping and nation-building. Whether this latter force should be multinational, or UN-led, is taken up below. But the transition should be as seamless as possible, and the ratios are crucial. The nation-building research shows you need about 20 soldiers per 1,000 residents to stabilize and secure post-war populations. (Incidentally, both the Afghanistan and Iraq occupation forces are—as of writing—well short of this ratio.) The moral is to go in big, with plenty of "boots on the ground," boots tutored in what The Pentagon labels "stability operations." Show the locals strong—not hesitant—intentions to protect them and to provide a secure backdrop for the development of law and legitimacy.[18]

♦ *Work with a cross-section of locals on a new, rights-respecting constitution which features checks and balances.* Limited government is required to prevent regrowth of tyranny; legitimate government is needed both for moral fitness and for stability. The picture here is of a genuine political partnership between the war winner and the local civilian population. The facts show that *the meaningful participation and support of both is absolutely necessary*, and usually more extensive international participation is desirable as well. Constitution-making is a process, and so we cannot rationally expect perfection or closure the first time out. Even the most developed societies occasionally change their constitutions and/or take several tries before creating a workable one in the first place. So while the post-war atmosphere is pressured, and there is a desire to rapidly end foreign occupation, some patience is required on the part of everyone. Good things often take time. In terms of inclusion in the constitution-building process, Andrew Arato reminds us that every group must be included: 1) whose non-participation could ruin any subsequent arrangement; and 2) who is committed to the creation of a minimally just state. If these two conditions are met, all relevant groups—as guided by the war winner—are to develop an inclusive framework for limited, accountable and rights-respecting government.[19]

♦ *Allow other, non-state associations, or "civil society," to flourish.* Civil society associations refer to all groupings which do not involve the state. They range from chambers of commerce to little league sports associations and from churches to music societies to fan clubs for "The Simpsons." Research stresses how important such associations are, not only to enjoyment of life but also to people's commitment to their society. These groupings connect people to each other, provide satisfaction and promote non-political aspects of life. They serve to take pressure off the state (by providing diverse outlets for energy), they help to legitimize the society (by increasing participation and happiness) and they also indirectly limit state power (by showing there is more to life than politics). It is always the mark of a tyrannical government when there is little activity within civil society. Robust civil societies are thus an important ingredient in creating mature, legitimate social conditions.[20]

♦ *Forego compensation and sanctions in favour of investing in and rebuilding the economy.* In the last chapter we saw that many modern peace arrangements—notably the Treaty of Versailles and the terms ending the Persian Gulf War—unravelled, or created perverse consequences, when they included hefty compensation terms and sweeping sanctions.[21] Targeted compensation might still be justified but, beyond that and war crimes trials, punitive settlements do not seem to work. The goal of proper regime change is the creation of a stable, minimally just social condition. This is difficult enough as it is; trying to achieve it while sucking resources out of the target country becomes nigh impossible. Thankfully, in Iraq in 2003, the old punitive sanctions were dropped, and investment started to flow in. This need for funds is a strong argument for including international partners in reconstruction. Realistically speaking, though, such partners will probably volunteer their resources only if they believe the war was justified to begin with.

♦ *If necessary, re-vamp educational curricula to purge past propaganda and cement new values.* The fascists in the 1930s used school systems to warp future citizens so that they would subscribe to highly destructive doctrines of racial and national supremacy, with the flip-side being hatred and aggression against "Others." In Afghanistan under the Taliban, and elsewhere still in the Middle East, great controversy attaches to the teaching of Islamic extremism and its attitudes towards violence, Israel, the West and women in particular. Much development research powerfully shows the beneficial effects of massive commitment to the education of girls and women. Indeed, some have even pronounced this one of the few "silver bullets" in development, which correlates very strongly with such other desirable social outcomes as economic growth, life expectancy and internal political stability.[22]

♦ *Ensure that the benefits of the new order will be: 1) concrete; and 2) widely, not narrowly, distributed.* As Michael Walzer says, you have got to increase *everyone's* stake in the new, developing order. In particular, you must avoid a situation where it seems that the foreign occupier is favouring one group above the rest, giving that group most of the power. That group will soon be marked as traitors and foreign agents, and will lose legitimacy and popular support. This was frequently the case during the European colonial era—particularly with France and Belgium—when the colonizer would select an elite group to rule, creating bitter ethnic and communal rivalries which persist today. The reconstructions of Germany and Japan showed, by contrast, that there must be widespread concrete benefits distributed throughout the population to make reconstruction work. Political things like getting to vote and run for office where you could not before; civic things like having your daughter go to school where before she could not; social things like starting up reading clubs where they used to be banned; and, above all, economic things like an average rise in living standards within a reasonable time.[23]

♦ *Follow an orderly, not-too-hasty exit strategy when the new regime can stand on its own two feet.* This requires walking a fine line. On the one hand, the foreign occupier cannot stay forever—for that is conquest, not reconstruction. The locals must see that occupation will come to an end and they will return to full sovereignty. This knowledge should diffuse some tension. On the other hand, if you're going to do something as important as post-war rehabilitation, you should try to do it well. Plus there is a moral responsibility not to "cut and run." A botched reconstruction benefits no one, including impatient locals. While the Dobbins Report suggests seven years as a minimum timeline, that does not necessarily mean seven years of direct martial law. Room for creativity is possible, and that is the route chosen by the Americans in Iraq. Direct military rule lasted only for one year, and during that time a constitutional process was launched. Absolute US control ended by July, 2004, and has been replaced by a mixture of political sovereignty for the new Iraqi government combined with robust US military presence to guarantee security. Once the latest election results are in, we'll see what new negotiations take place between Iraq and the US on phasing out American presence entirely.

This ten-point recipe for reconstruction is only a general blueprint; clearly, in particular cases, some things will need to be emphasized over others. The best recipes always allow for individual variance and input depending on time and the ingredients at hand. We should also note the heavy interconnectedness of many of these elements. US Major-General William Nash is probably only exaggerating a bit when he declares: "The first rule of nation-building is that everything is related to everything, and it is all political."[24] Further, in spite of the variances among aggressive, rights-violating societies—different geography, history, language, economy, diet, ethnic composition—there has been striking similarity in the kind of regime here in view. Think of the major twentieth century aggressors and dictatorships: the USSR; Fascist Spain and Italy; Nazi Germany; Imperial Japan; North Korea; Communist China; Pol Pot's Cambodia; Idi Amin's Uganda; Saddam Hussein's

Iraq; the Taliban's Afghanistan. In spite of all the differences among them, the regimes shared large affinities: a small group of ruthless fanatics uses force to come to power; it keeps power through the widespread use of violence, both internally and externally; it engages in massively invasive control over every major sphere of life, with no other associations allowed to rival the state's prestige; the rule of law is jettisoned; the military, or "in-party," becomes all-important; human rights are trampled upon, and so on.[25] To a remarkable extent, in spite of all the other differences, *it has been the same kind of regime*. And this should not, in the end, come as so much of a surprise: they all learned from each other and sought to emulate what worked elsewhere. The modern police state only has so many precedents to draw upon, and might in fact be located ultimately in such early examples as Napoleonic France, or most probably Robespierre's Reign of Terror during the French Revolution.[26] So, then, we should not be all that shocked, surprised and sceptical if it turns out that one general recipe can, in fact, be found for transforming such regimes and societies away from rampant rights-violation into ones which are at least minimally just.

Knowing versus Doing

Al Pierce has noted that there is a difference between *knowing* what to do, and actually *being able* to do it. In other words, even if we do know the general recipe for pro-rights reconstruction, there is still the issue of whether we are able to implement that knowledge in particular instances. In Iraq, for example, there has been quite fierce armed resistance to both American and Iraqi attempts to implement the general recipe there. This does highlight the distance between the ideal and the real, which can never be ignored in international affairs. I agree with the moral logic of Pierce's position but it is hard to state what it finally means for the thesis advocated here. We cannot be overconfident of success; we must expect resistance and impatience; and we must meaningfully involve the local population in the reconstruction of its own regime. *But there have been actual cases of successful pro-rights, postwar reconstruction.* We think of Germany and Japan post-World War II especially. These cases have even occurred in social contexts—like Japan in 1945—with no appreciable background commitment to any of the needed attitudes, habits and values. So it *can* be done; there is no abstract, sweeping "can't." Perhaps it cannot be done in particular cases—but how are we to know without trying? Pierce's point is important, and rightly cautionary. But it does not show that post-war rehabilitation should not be tried at all, or that it is misguided in principle. We can still have it as our ideal plan, even if it turns out we can only partially realize it in particular cases.

Some also say that the process imagined here is only going to work in very rare cases, like Japan and Germany, wherein the target country was completely crushed during the war. In this sense, pro-rights reconstruction still "cannot be done" in the majority of cases, where there is less-than-total victory. The locals simply will not agree to it.[27] Fortunately, this view is sceptical speculation, with shaky empirical backing. Consider that right now there are ongoing pro-rights, post-war reconstruction processes underway in Afghanistan, Bosnia, East Timor, Kosovo and Iraq. None of these regimes—especially in Bosnia—were defeated as singularly as Nazi Germany and Imperial Japan. Yet they all find themselves on the same road to reconstruction. Now, there *are* real difficulties: the insurgency in Iraq and the lack of control over rural Afghanistan especially—and the group rivalries within both. But there have also been real successes, especially in Bosnia-Kosovo and East Timor. New institutions, based on human rights, are developing; there is relative stability and peace; there have been free elections and, in the case of Bosnia and East Timor, there is almost fully restored sovereignty. Bosnia and East Timor have been utterly transformed from societies bloodily battered by foreign invasion and civil war to peaceful, near-sovereign nations. Admittedly, there is a shorter timespan with these cases, so we cannot pronounce them successes on the order of a Germany or Japan, but they clearly offer support for the thesis that post-war rehabilitation is possible *even without* achieving crushing military victory, unconditional surrender and total sway over the local population. The locals in Bosnia and East Timor *did agree* to the values of post-war reconstruction here in view, and so again we see the incorrectness—the easy, fashionable pessimism—of the notion that the locals will not go for it, that it simply cannot be done. No one enjoys foreign occupation, to be sure. But most people can see that it is *the quality* of governance which matters most, not *the source of its genesis*. If a foreign source can help create a minimally just society where none existed before, it cannot rationally be rejected merely on grounds of foreign participation. Indeed, if you look back far enough, it is hard to think of any country which has not had some "foreign" contribution to its political structure. (Consider the USA itself, and the role that American Indians, British and French had on its founding structures—and waves of foreign immigrants have had on its society.) The point is that the process be *just*, not that it be "purely local" in its origins.[28]

Who's in Charge?

This leaves the large issue of who should be the main players in post-war reconstruction. The war winner? The international community? The locals? The Dobbins Report, interestingly, finds in repeated cases that the commitment, presence and investment of *the war winner* is most necessary to the success of post-war reform. That is apparently a fact of which we need to be mindful. There is also the value of the goal of minimal justice and our desire to see it actualized, which calls our attention to these power realities. Another fact is this: reconstruction needs to take place within a secure context, and the war-winner is clearly best positioned to provide this—at least initially. There is the relative responsibility argument, too: the war winner, after all, was the one who overthrew the regime. Having "broken it," the war winner "bought it" (i.e., shouldered the main responsibility for aiding the reconstruction of a replacement regime).

This is *not* a clarion call for triumphant unilateralism, much less "neo-imperialism." It is a judgment informed by: 1) the facts of who can secure the society; 2) who most bears responsibility; and 3) who can effectively leverage successful post-war regime change. Clearly, local involvement and endorsement is, eventually, a make-or-break deal. Given the good values of just reconstruction (compared with what went before), we should not worry about finding such support. Indeed, the cases show there are many locals to be found, in every society, who see the sense of minimal justice and who wish to take up leadership roles in the reconstruction process. It is more an issue of *when* and *how* to transfer reconstruction authority to a reconstituted and legitimate state structure, and that is clearly to be determined on a case-by-case basis. Local input—meaningful cross-sectional consultation—has to be there right from the start, and gradually grow to fully restored sovereignty, probably about ten years later. The war winner must always understand—as Chapter XI of the *UN Charter* (which deals with "Non-self-governing terri-tories") says—that it occupies a position of "sacred trust" in this regard. The war winner cannot ever forget, as the International Commission on Interven-tion and State Sovereignty (ICISS) says, that its reconstructive activities must be aimed at "putting itself out of a job." The war winner's authority lasts only as long as the trust remains earned and the rehabilitative task—as defined here by the recipe—keeps progressing in the direction of minimal justice.[29]

What role should the international community play? Both watchdog and junior partner. Watchdog, to ensure that the power enjoyed by the war winner does not corrupt. And junior partner, in that sensible war winners will want to reach out and receive additional resources as well as world wide expertise in the various fields of social reconstruction. The war winner should not have problems attracting such outside aid *if* the war itself was just. There is, for example, a large international presence in the reconstruction of Afghanistan. Nor should the international community hesitate to provide such aid, since it is not just a matter of charity but also of improving the peace and security of themselves and their own people. America, obviously, is having some problems in this connection with Iraq. Non-aid from erstwhile international allies is understandable—not wanting to reward and legitimize what they see as an unjust war. However, such allies cannot forget that the Iraqi people pay the price for such non-provision as well. I do not think non-aid violates a duty here but these consequences should still be kept in mind when making a decision whether to help a war winner engage in social reconstruction.

When it comes to United Nations involvement post-conflict, the UN does have much relevant, and recent, experience (e.g., in East Timor) which it would be wise to draw upon. Is such experience *needed* to confer legitimacy upon post-conflict reconstruction? I do not think so: the UN, while seasoned, has had some sour experiences as well, especially in African conflicts ranging from Congo to Somalia to Rwanda. The UN has also·recently been involved in serious corruption scandals, so there is no guarantee that multilateralism ensures integrity in the process.[30] The exclusivity of such UN bodies as the Security Council also raises questions regarding its political—as opposed to legal—legitimacy. There is also the probability of success issue. On the one hand, you do want lots of resources, support and diverse expertise; on the other, too many cooks can spoil the broth. Is the Afghani reconstruction— featuring the UN and many countries—going much better than the Iraqi? To those in the know, not obviously so. The Taliban are not in power but still exist, especially in rural Afghanistan; most of the reconstruction is centred only around the capital, Kabul; rival clan lords retain armed militias, posing security threats; and there has been a failure to develop the legitimate econ- omy, driving local farmers to poppy production, which feeds heroin addiction and provides illegal drug lords with resources and power.[31] Part of this check- ered record, of course, is the sheer difficulty of the enterprise—which we should never underestimate—but another part might be that responsibility so widely divided can leave actors with insufficient incentive for ensuring over- all success. In my view, fewer people worry about Afghanistan, despite its severe difficulties, because there is larger consensus on the justice of that war and accompanying regime change. Contrast this with the Iraq case, where the whole enterprise substantially rests on the shoulders of the Iraqis and the Americans. American prestige and possibly security are on the line, and the Iraqis have their very futures at stake. This illustrates, for me, that the key relationship in reconstruction always boils down to that between the war win- ner and the local population: they each bear big burdens, and the involvement of both is essential for enduring, successful reform.

Resistance

We should predict a rough ride, especially at the beginning. Regime hold- outs, fanatics of various stripes, criminal elements and foreign destabilizers might all actively resist forcible regime change, even if the initial war was clearly just. Assuming it was so, the war winner is entitled to combat the resistance, and embark on a "hearts and minds" campaign to win holdouts over. But if for some reason the resistance genuinely takes on the character of widespread public resistance and *uprising* to occupation, then careful con- sideration must be made of what to do next. Fact-finding is vital here: if the resistance is illegitimate—composed of those elements listed above—then it is legitimate to stamp it out, or at least control it through military and police measures. Social reconstruction is hugely difficult—but hugely worthwhile if successful. One cannot just turn tail and run in the face of some car bombings and kidnappings. That would, irresponsibly, create an incentive in favour of violent resistance and be a breach of faith with the interests of the majority of the local population. One also cannot allow the rebirth of a regime failing minimal justice—or else what was the point of the war? But if the resistance becomes deep, patterned and genuinely widespread—involving things like general strikes, commercial and political boycotts, and regular mass protests— then clearly a change of strategy is demanded, almost certainly including a stepped-up transfer of sovereignty. The devil here is truly in the details of the case, and none of us should envy policymakers who must decide when the resistance is rough but illegitimate, and when it becomes so serious that justice demands a radical policy shift. Much of how the resistance question plays out, in my view, will be affected by perceptions of the justice of the war to begin with. There is simply no escaping the interconnections, here as elsewhere.

Aiming at Regime Change from the Start

This perspective on rehabilitation—calling for disarmament, institutional reform, political transformation and infrastructure investments—brings into focus important questions. Does it follow from all the above that the imposition of rehabilitation on an aggressor is itself a legitimate war aim? In other words, may a state set out, from the start of the war, *not only* to vindicate violated rights but, *moreover*, to impose institutional therapy upon the aggressor? If so, Walzer asks, what does that imply in terms of the use of force *during* war, since being in a position to impose institutional therapy after the war is at least linked to, and may even depend on, the achievement of a certain degree of military superiority at war's end? The therapy requires the strength to see it through. My sense is that the imposition of institutional therapy on an aggressor is consistent with, even implied by, the overall goal of a justified war argued for last chapter, namely, rights vindication constrained by a proportionate policy on surrender. The therapy is justly invoked when required to prevent future aggression and to enable the defeated community to meet the requirements of minimal justice. In terms of war-fighting, having regime change and rehabilitation as a war goal does *not* somehow diminish the responsibility to fight in accord with the *jus in bello* rules of right conduct. The importance of the end does not lessen the constraints just communities face when they vindicate their rights by force. Will insistence on rehabilitation as part of war settlement itself prolong the fighting? While it might do so as a matter of fact—relative to a less stringent or unjust settlement offer—seeing it through is not wrong *provided* the fighting continues to respect *jus in bello*. The duty falls on Aggressor to agree to reasonable terms of rehabilitation, not on Victim/Vindicator to avoid seeking those means necessary to secure adherence to them. Besides, as previously noted with reference to cases, the bringing of rehabilitation does not demand the infliction of a crushing military defeat upon the Aggressor.

Containment Instead of Change?

What of those who suggest that, instead of all these dramatic post-war regime transformations, we should settle for "merely" defeating and *containing* aggressors? Let's not muck around with the very structures of their society; let's simply defeat the aggressor regime and de-fang it, so to speak, so that it cannot cause more problems in the foreseeable future. Note, as Walzer does, that this recommendation makes no sense with humanitarian intervention. For in such a case, it is precisely the depravity of the regime which invites the military manœuvres. It makes no sense to leave such a regime in place following its defeat: *regime transformation is needed to stop the very crisis in question*. So, the containment option only comes up in instances of cross-border aggression. How, in this regard, to compare and evaluate the merits of containment versus reconstruction and rehabilitation?

The core, defining difference between containment and reconstruction is this: with containment, one leaves the defeated regime in power whereas with rehabilitation, one ejects the regime and guides the process for creating a new one. A logically lesser distinction, but still a substantial one, is that containment is mainly concerned with preventing future *cross-border* aggression on the part of the defeated regime whereas rehabilitation is concerned not just with that *but also* with transforming the regime in a way which benefits the domestic citizenry. These further differences get us close to the Oxford English Dictionary definitions of the split in approach: containment means "to hold within itself, or to prevent from moving or extending" whereas rehabilitation means "to restore to effectiveness, or normal life, or proper condition by training, especially after prison or illness." Clearly, rehabilitation is a more ambitious policy. But is it more costly? Is it recklessly risky? Is it better?

Let us first note one large area of agreement between containment and rehabilitation. This is the need to disarm the defeated regime. This suits both aims of preventing future aggression by the regime as well as, quite often, breaking its main source of domestic power. There is thus widespread consensus on the need for such common post-war disarmament measures as: chopping the defeated regime's armed forces; capping future military capability; creating buffer zones between the regime and other countries; and cataloguing and destroying its weapons, especially those of mass destruction. We noted this last chapter.

It is after military disarmament where the models split. Consider that when a decision to contain is made, the question of war crimes trials goes out the window. This was, for instance, never brought up in the 1991 Persian Gulf War settlement. After all, you're leaving the regime in power, so you cannot insist that its top people surrender to a war crimes tribunal. Conversely, when you decide to rehabilitate, you keep this option open. We think of historical links between rehabilitation and war crimes (or crimes against humanity) tribunals, whether at Nuremberg, Tokyo or The Hague. This morally marks one up for rehabilitation over containment: containment sacrifices some justice for what it thinks is expediency. While war crimes trials can cause pain within a political community, so too can a failure to have them. Trials also de-legitimize unjust regimes in a way that inaction, obviously, never can.

There is a huge difference between the two models regarding the treatment of the defeated country's economy. The logical goal of the containment model is to cut, or at least to limit, the target regime's resources so as to clip its capabilities for future aggression. Thus, some form of economic punishment, or at least non-engagement, is called for. The 1991 settlement terms of the Persian Gulf War left intact the sweeping socio-economic sanctions levelled after Iraq's original invasion of Kuwait in 1990, and they also required Iraq to pay compensation to Kuwait, out of future Iraqi oil sales. The result of the sanctions was a humanitarian disaster for the Iraqi people throughout the 1990s. This disaster was the result not just of poor treaty drafting, but of the logic of containment itself. The treaty drafters, of course, should have known that civilian welfare was not a priority for Saddam, and so leaving it up to him was either naïve or callous. The deeper point is that, because containment's focus is on preventing cross-border aggression, it is much more *insensitive* to local civilian suffering than many people want to admit. Since containment wishes to cut the regime's resources, this will necessarily leave less for civilians. And if nothing is done to change a regime which does not much care for its civilians, then material deprivation amongst the civilian population is *a predictable consequence of containment*. It is not just Iraq: there is no doubt, for instance, that American containment during the Cold War contributed to real economic hardships in such communist countries as Cuba. With containment resources are essentially sucked out of the regime, whereas with rehabilitation the resources flow the other way: *into* the defeated country to aid in reconstruction and to ensure that the new regime can enjoy popular support without threat of backsliding into injustice and illegitimacy. This, we noted, is what is currently happening in Iraq and Afghanistan—though whether the amount of resources is sufficient might be wondered at—and of course it also happened, to great success, with Germany and Japan in the post-1945 period.

Another myth about containment is that it is non-violent, or at least relative to rehabilitation. The Iraq experience casts a cloud of doubt over this. First, the sanctions arguably *were* violent—inflicting physical harm—and in an indiscriminate way. Say what you will about forcible regime change, but taking out a regime with force is much more discriminating than slowly starving a country of resources. Now, there obviously is *more* military force involved in rehabilitation over containment, *but* it can be more discriminating. And even the military equation is not entirely obvious. There were over two dozen military clashes, and one major combat operation, between America and Iraq during the containment phase from 1991 to 2003. These episodes generated scores of casualties, including some civilians. The violence and casualties can be predicted because the terms of containment, to be effective, need to be enforced. In Iraq's case, the no-fly-zones and the weapons inspection process both required repeated military enforcement.

Military clashes during containment can also be predicted out of frustration with what are often *open-ended*, long-lasting containment procedures. The recent containment of Iraq lasted twelve years, and only ended because America decided to attack instead. The reconstruction of Germany and Japan, by contrast—enormous undertakings—lasted about ten years each. Containment is open-ended because its end is "negative"—merely preventive—as opposed to the "positive" goal of reconstruction in rehabilitation's case. *How do you know when to stop the containment?* The only sure answer seems to be: when the regime has changed. But that is precisely what rehabilitation seeks to do directly right from the start. As Walzer puts it perceptively, and concisely, "(l)egitimacy and closure are the two criteria against which we can test war's endings."[32]

Some people suggest that containment is more respectful of state rights to political sovereignty and territorial integrity than is rehabilitation. But consider that permissible reconstruction gets rid of an illegitimate, rights-violating regime, thereby enabling *greater* political participation and thus expression of national sovereignty. Illegitimate regimes, we have established, have no right to govern, and their removal enables all kinds—even democratic kinds— of expressions of national sovereignty. There are also the human rights of individuals to account for, too, and in that regard the containment model must answer for its insensitivity to continued civilian suffering under the illegitimate regime which it allows to continue. Trading human rights violations for respecting state rights is not exactly a bargain to be bragging about.

Other people worry that rehabilitation is more costly and risky: *cost* in the form of overthrowing the regime and rebuilding the economy; and *risk* in the form of possibly botching reconstruction, leading to backsliding into illegitimacy or perhaps even civil war. These admittedly real risks of rehabilitation—bitingly real in Iraq—are somewhat mitigated by the fact that we *do* know the basic recipe for sound rehabilitation, discussed above. And we cannot forget that containment *has its own costs and risks*: the *cost* of enforcing containment, both financially and militarily; the *risk* that civilians will continue to suffer material deprivations and rights violations, perhaps even more so under the straightened circumstances of containment; the risk that containment will be needed indefinitely; or the risk that containment will be ineffective and that armed conflict and forcible regime change will be needed anyway, as clearly seems to have been the case recently with the Taliban in Afghanistan and with Milosevic in Serbia. Was the containment of Saddam a success? It may have stripped him of WMD, and Iraq did not seem to commit international aggression during those years—real achievements. But it did nothing to help the Iraqi people, and may have actually hurt them. If Iraq's containment was a success, clearly it was of a checkered kind.

Now, I'm *not* an apologist for Bush Jr. and the 2003 Iraq attack. *I have already raised real doubts about the justice of his Iraq intervention, and I fear he will pull out of Iraq and Afghanistan* instead of seeing them through on the seven to ten year scale the Dobbins Report establishes. And I'm *not* saying America's post-war policy in Iraq is just. In Afghanistan, it has the chance of being just because the war to begin with was just. But the war in Iraq was probably unjust, and so the best the USA can hope for is to leave Iraq better off than how it found it. (Recall our discussion last chapter that, to be fully just, post-war reconstruction must not only produce good results but also have violated no rights and to have respected procedural rules of fairness. But, since it was an unjust war, it violated those rules and rights, and so the best that can be hoped for is some good consequences—better institutions, etc.—but never complete justice.) America still has to be held up to the standards of post-war justice in Iraq—and it *can* do better or worse by them—but it *cannot ever fully* satisfy them because of how the war started.

My point here is this: the rewards for good rehabilitation are *greater than* those of good containment, and so the greater risk can be reconceived as a more promising investment. We all know greater returns can only be had by assuming greater risks. And the return on good containment is, so to speak, merely negative: there is *no more* cross-border aggression. But with good rehabilitation you get not only that *but also* a better life for the civilians, greater rights realization and a more secure international order.

In the end, our attitudes about containment versus rehabilitation boil down to two issues: war and governance. These are intimately connected, both historically and because war *is* ultimately about governance (i.e., about who gets to decide what goes on in a given territory). Defenders of containment are willing to tolerate an illegitimate and rights-violating regime *in exchange for* the avoidance of war. But there are moral reasons, sometimes, to doubt this tolerance. First, it is quite easy, perhaps smug, to tolerate *somebody else's* terrible regime. Second, there are good reasons to believe that terrible regimes eventually produce war anyway, and so containment merely postpones the inevitable. Which good reasons are these? First, historical ones: there is heavy empirical evidence that rights-violating regimes go on to attack others. Think of Mussolini, Hitler, Hirohito, Stalin, Kim Il Sung, Pol Pot, Idi Amin, Saddam and Milosevic. Second, conceptual reasons. As Kant noted, if regimes are willing to violate the rights of their own citizens, why would they hesitate to do the same with foreigners, as soon as they are capable and willing? *It is the regime which needs changing and rehabilitation recognizes this, whereas containment does not.* At best, containment recognizes this but somehow views the tools of containment as better at achieving this than the tools of rehabilitation. *This might, admittedly, be the case when the regime in question has nuclear weapons, as in the Cold War.* I do not deny that containment *sometimes* makes great sense, for instance when the probability of success for regime overthrow and reconstruction are minimal or when the quantum of force needed to break the regime is simply too great, as in any nuclear case. But when these obstacles do *not* hold, I have suggested here that containment's tools are dull and slow, whereas those of rehabilitation are sharper and quicker. Containment's tools are not cheap, nor are they risk-free. They are not even non-violent. They probably also avoid justice for mere expediency. Above all, containment's measures are more indiscriminate and insensitive to civilian suffering.

This all suggests that, in *some* cases of defeating an illegitimate regime in war, reconstruction is preferable to mere containment. I'm *not* going so far as to say it is a duty to choose the former over the latter—I believe it is an option, and contingent upon the opportunities circumstances make available. There are the other just war rules to consider, too, notably probability of success and proportionality: is the regime really that bad? And will rehabilitating it likely achieve minimal justice? All I'm saying here is that there are strong *general* reasons for preferring reconstruction over containment, reasons which might be defeasible in *particular* instances.

Summary

There have been successful pro-rights, post-war regime changes, and these make us mindful of an important option when wars end. Forcible regime change is permissible when the war itself was just, when it violates no rights, and when it promises the good consequences of instituting a minimally just regime. To that extent, aiming to impose rehabilitation right from the start of a just war is permissible, too. Without excluding the international community, the key reconstruction relationship is that between the war winner and the local population. The war winner occupies a position of enormous power and therefore trust, and is duty bound to follow the recipe and to work with and nurture local leadership. The locals, for their part, must commit themselves to peace, to good faith interaction with each other and, above all, to the development of a minimally just regime. Some resistance should be expected and the huge difficulties acknowledged—perhaps only partial realization of the ideal is possible. That is still better than nothing—or worse, not even trying—and in fact might be a reasonable definition of progress in such difficult circumstances.

Notes

1. I. Kant, *The Metaphysics of Morals*, trans. H.B. Nisbet in H. Reiss, ed. *Kant: Political Writings* (Cambridge: Cambridge University Press, 1991), p. 170.
2. D. Abernathy, *The Dynamics of Global Dominance* (New Haven: Yale University Press, 2001); I. Eland, *The Empire Has No Clothes* (Oakland: The Independent Institute, 2004).
3. N. Ferguson, *Empire* (New York: Basic Books, 2002); N. Ferguson, *Colossus* (New York: Basic Books, 2004).

4. B. Kiernan, *The Pol Pot Regime* (New Haven: Yale University Press, 1998); J. Holzgrefe and R. Keohane, eds. *Humanitarian Intervention* (Cambridge: Cambridge University Press, 2003).

5. J. Dobbins, et al, *America's Role in Nation-Building: From Germany to Iraq* (Washington: RAND, 2003); R. Regan, *Just War: Principles and Cases* (Washington: Catholic University of America Press, 1996).

6. Some especially useful ex-Nazis were provided safe havens in the West, particularly those who were working on Hitler's rocket program.

7. Only very gradually and cautiously was the construction of a German and Japanese military undertaken. Even today, it is extremely controversial domestically when the German or Japanese military is called into action. The constitution of each country forbids its participation in offensive wars, and generally confines any military participation to a purely defensive, or at most peacekeeping, role.

8. Of course, the Germans and Japanese were already acquainted with advanced industrial—especially wartime—production. But the Americans aided economic growth vastly with the new business theories of the 1950s, informed by best practices discovered during the war.

9. L.V. Segal, *Fighting to the Finish: The Politics of War Termination in America and Japan* (Ithaca: Cornell University Press, 1989); H. Schonberger, *Aftermath of War: Americans and The Remaking of Japan* (Ohio: Kent State University Press, 1989); M. Schaller, *The American Occupation of Japan* (Oxford: Oxford University Press, 1987); and E. Davidson, *The Death and Life of Germany: An Account of the American Occupation* (St. Louis: University of Missouri Press, 1999).

10. B. Orend, *War and International Justice: A Kantian Perspective* (Waterloo, ON: Wilfrid Laurier University Press, 2000).

11. Kant, *Metaphysics*, 169–71.

12. A. Arato, "Imposing a Constitution on Iraq," *Ethics and International Affairs* (2004), 25–50.

13. Kant, *Metaphysics*, with both quotes at 170.

14. Dobbins, et al, *Nation-Building, passim*.

15. Dobbins, *Nation-Building*; R.S. Jennings, *The Road Ahead* (Washington, DC: United States Institute of Peace, 2003); A. Donini, ed. *Nation-Building Unravelled?* (New York: International Peace Academy, 2004); and J. Dobbins and S. Jones, eds. *The United Nations' Role in Nation-Building* (Forthcoming from the RAND Corporation).

16. S. Chesterman, "Occupation as Liberation: International Humanitarian Law and Regime Change," *Ethics and International Affairs* (2004), 51–64 with quote at 54.

17. International Commission on Intervention and State Sovereignty, *The Responsibility to Protect* (Ottawa: International Development Research Institute, 2001), 40–1; K. Annan, *The Causes of Conflict and The Promotion of Durable Peace in Africa* (New York: United Nations, 1998); R. Scarborough, *Rumsfeld's War* (New York: Regnery, 2004).

18. J. Traub, "Making Sense of the Mission," *New York Times Magazine* (April 11, 2004), 36.
19. A. Arato, "Constitution-Making in Iraq," *Dissent* (Spring, 2004) 32–6; A. Arato, *Civil Society, Constitution and Legitimacy* (Lanham, MD: Rowman Littlefield, 2000).
20. R. Putnam, *Bowling Alone* (New York: Simon Schuster, 2000).
21. M. Boemeke, et al, eds., *The Treaty of Versailles* (Cambridge: Cambridge University Press, 1998); A. Arnove and A. Abunimeh, eds. *Iraq Under Siege* (London: South End, 2000).
22. See, e.g., <*www.unicef.org/girlseducation/index.html*>.
23. M. Walzer, *Arguing About War* (New Haven: Yale University Press, 2004), 164–5.
24. W. Nash, quoted in Traub, "Making Sense," 35.
25. J. Glover, *Humanity: A Moral History of the 20th Century* (New Haven, CT: Yale University Press, 2001).
26. L. Hunt, ed. *The French Revolution and Human Rights* (London: Bedford, 1996).
27. T. Dodge, *Inventing Iraq* (New York: Columbia University Press, 2003).
28. Dobbins, *Nation-Building*; Dobbins, *United Nations*; Traub, "Making Sense," 32–62.
29. ICISS, *Protect*, 44–5; UN Charter, Articles 73 and 74.
30. R. Dallaire, *Shake Hands with the Devil* (Toronto: Random House, 2003); K. Cain, et al, *Emergency Sex and Other Desperate Measures* (New York: Miramax, 2003).
31. Traub, "Making Sense," 32–62.
32. Walzer, *Arguing*, 20.

PART TWO

The Alternatives

CHAPTER 8

Evaluating the Realist Alternative

> "The general inclination of mankind is a perpetual and restless desire of power after power that ceaseth only in death."
>
> *Thomas Hobbes*[1]

Last section was a large one, devoted to explaining and mainly defending contemporary just war theory and, to a lesser extent, the current international laws of armed conflict. (The one exception was *jus post bellum*, where new efforts were and remain required.) But there are two large and influential rivals to just war theory which must be explored in a comprehensive text on these issues. They are realism and pacifism: the first is taken up in this chapter, the second in the next.

Realism in General

The core propositions of realism express a strong suspicion about applying moral concepts, like justice, to the conduct of international affairs. Realists believe that moral concepts should be employed *neither* as descriptions of, *nor* as prescriptions for, state behaviour on the international plane. Realists emphasize power and national security issues as well as the need for a state to forward its own self-interest. Above all, realists view the international arena quite darkly. They see it as a kind of anarchy—an ungoverned condition—in which *the will to power* enjoys primacy amongst the players. The drive for augmenting one's own security, power and resources is the prime mover in the realist's reality. (Hence the above quotation from Hobbes.) Referring specifically to war, realists believe that it is a completely predictable part of an anarchical world system; that it ought to be resorted to *only if* it makes sense in terms of national self-interest; and that, once war has begun, a state ought to do *whatever it can to win*. So if adhering to the rules of just war theory and international law hinders a state in this regard, it should disregard them and stick steadfastly to its fundamental interests in power, national interest and security.[2] Classical realists include the ancient Greek historian Thucydides and the medieval Italian diplomat and writer Machiavelli. Modern realists include the likes of professors Hans Morgenthau

223

and Hedley Bull, civil servant George Kennan, theologian Reinhold Niebuhr and former US National Security Advisor Henry Kissinger.[3]

Realists, Michael Walzer notes, view war as "a world apart," where "self-interest and necessity prevail. Here men and women do what they must to save themselves and their communities, and morality and law have no place." "(R)ealism," he observes, "imposes no moral requirements," either in war or more broadly in international affairs. Just war theory, designed to limit war's destructiveness and to protect rights during armed conflict, is viewed by realists as mere "idle chatter, a mask of noise with which we conceal ... the awful truth." This truth is that we are essentially "fearful, self-concerned, driven, [even] murderous" and war brings all these ugly traits to the surface and gives them free reign. Much of morality is rank self-deception (and self-glorification), and probably no more so than during wartime, when states and people are pushed to their very limits. Just war theory is, then, quite unrealistic in the literal sense of not applying meaningfully to the facts. If realists endorse any rule at all with regard to wartime behaviour, it is something like the old saying, "all is fair in love and war." In war's desperate circumstances, *anything goes*.[4]

Thucydides' *Melian Dialogue* offers a frank expression of realism. This memorable, well-known piece describes an historical meeting between ancient Athenian generals and the leaders of Melos, a Greek island. The expansionist Athenians want to annex Melos and supplement their power, whereas the Melians wish to preserve their independence and protect their own way of life. The generals propose that "all fine talk of justice" be put aside, and that everyone stare reality square in the face. This reality is that "they that have odds of power exact as much as they can, and the weak yield to such conditions as they can get." It is rule or be ruled in our rough-and-tumble world. The Melians refuse to play ball, citing their right as an independent and peaceful community not to be invaded, and subsequently get invaded and crushed by the Athenians. Just war theory would view this as classic aggression, whereas realists simply view it as the way of the world.[5]

Descriptive Realism

CHARACTERIZATION

We should at this point distinguish, importantly, between *descriptive* or factual realism and *prescriptive* or normative realism. Descriptive realism is the doctrine according to which states, the primary actors in the international arena, *are in fact* motivated by considerations of power, security and national interest, and not at all by those of morality or justice. *States simply do not care about morality and justice; they only care about their own interests.* They might—and often do—pay lip-service to ethics but, in the end, they act to benefit themselves. These benefits reside not in ethical ideals but, rather, in basic material things like survival, security, economic growth, natural resources, power and prestige.

The starting point for descriptive realism is an understanding of the nature of the international arena as one of anarchy. There is no reliable international government. The United Nations (UN) *does* exist, but it is *neither* reliable *nor* does it have much power or resources. Indeed, as its name shows, the UN is merely an association *of* nations, not a government *over* nations. Indeed, the UN is largely at the mercy of powerful countries, or blocs thereof. We think here, in particular, of the five veto-holding permanent members of the Security Council and, especially, the USA. The UN does not come close to having the same power over its "subjects" that national governments have over theirs.

Since there is no reliable international authority, all states are fundamentally insecure: they are always vulnerable to the attacks and encroachments of others. At the very least, they have no reliable assurances from the others that they will not attack or interfere in a damaging way in their affairs. This so-called "assurance problem" makes states fearful and insecure. Fundamentally, they cannot trust, or count on, other countries. The lack of central authority means that, in the final analysis, states can rely on no one other than themselves to secure their interests. So self-help is the order of the day. It follows that each state will be, and is, concerned—first and foremost— with its own power and security vis-à-vis other states. Each state will, and does, act so as to maximize what it takes to be its own enlightened self-interest, and this involves relying on armed force, trying to assert and forward its own power and security, and in general doing the best it can vis-à-vis other states in terms of cultural, commercial, political and military competition.

In light of this, Morgenthau for one argued that we cannot speak meaningfully of state behaviour in terms of moral concepts and judgments. The only meaningful kind of discourse surrounding international relations is that centred on power, interests and security. *Moral concepts are literally inapplicable* to the realm of foreign affairs. To appeal to moral judgment in international relations—like saying a certain war is unjust—would be to commit what is sometimes called a "category mistake." It would be like trying to apply the rules of baseball to football. It simply does not fit. The rules which make sense in one context (i.e., interpersonally) fail to make sense in a completely different one (i.e., internationally). Werner Jaeger concurs, and opines that "the principle of force forms a realm of its own with laws of its own" which are unique and separate from the rules of ethics applicable amongst people living ordinary lives in developed, settled societies.[6]

Indeed some realists, like Edmund Wilson, even argue that the international arena is not actually a place wherein free choice—including morally responsible choice—plays a meaningful role at all. These realists frequently speak of the "necessity" of state action in the global context: states have no meaningful choice but to act on the basis of power and interest *if they are to survive at all*, much less thrive. The one thing that looms large, in all such accounts, is the bleak and dangerous picture of the international arena. On this view, war is seen as an entirely predictable, even inescapable, reality of the interstate system; it is a simple fact that the clash of national self-interest will sometimes spill over into armed conflict. It is another simple fact that states will do whatever they can, in the midst of war, to win. To hope otherwise—as just war theory does—is to engage in wishful thinking about the brutal facts on the ground in the international arena. So attempting to limit or constrain warfare—for instance with a set of just war rules and laws—is, as Carl von Clausewitz contended, at odds with its very nature and the very animating force behind state action. Wars are rather like storms that just naturally break out every now and then. No one can influence them and they just have to be left alone to exhaust themselves, as it were, and blow over. US Civil War General W.T. Sherman once said that "[w]ar is cruelty, and you cannot refine it ... You might as well appeal against the thunderstorm as against these terrible hardships of war."[7]

CRITICISM

The first criticism which can be made of descriptive realism—on behalf of just war theory—concerns the deep ambiguity of its appeal to the "inapplicability" of moral concepts to international affairs. This claim seems false. States, at least sometimes, really do seem to act on the basis of moral commitments, *even when* such actions seem manifestly at odds with their national interests. Although such examples are always complex and open to controversy, some have contended that Britain's efforts in the 1800s to outlaw the international slave trade constitute one such example, since its actions: 1) greatly increased the price of its imports of such basics as sugar and cotton; and 2) aggravated its relations with America. But the British people, especially as inspired by Protestant preachers, simply would not stand for it anymore. They rejected the practice morally, and forced their government to act accordingly. Jack Donnelly cites American participation in World War I as another case of moral motivation at odds with national interest. America intervened to pacify Europe—"to make the world safe for democracy"—not because its own territory or sovereignty was threatened.[8] Someone might argue the same thing with regard to the international interventions in Somalia and Bosnia in the early 1990s, discussed in the book's first part.

Even if it is controversial to say that states sometimes adhere to their moral beliefs before, or above, their national interests, at the very least it seems true to say that *among a state's interests are its moral and political ideals*. States want to see their moral and political beliefs realized in the world as much as individuals do—indeed, states *must* want this because they are, after all, composed of individual persons. If this is true, and it seems obviously so to me, then mixing moral talk with international affairs cannot be an "inapplicable" category mistake. Indeed, the category mistake would be to leave moral matters *out* of international issues like war and peace, and simply let states and peoples do whatever they want without fear of criticism or punishment.

A second criticism is that these realist accusations—regarding the "inapplicability" of morality—fly in the face of common, long-standing practice. We have had a very long history, indeed, of utterly coherent ethical thought about international relations in general and warfare in particular. Just war theory is only one example in this regard, and it is centuries old. *We all understand* what someone is trying to say when they assert that a war is unjust, or that trade should be free, or that more aid should go to Africa—and we frequently make similar judgments ourselves. So if we all understand and participate in such talk—talk which evaluates international affairs ethically—how can it be systematically mistaken? How likely is it that, all this time, the realists have been right (as they condescendingly assert) and the rest of us have not known what we were doing? Not very likely, I'd say, especially since ethical evaluations of international affairs and war simply seem so meaningful, and they attract so much passion and engagement in response.[9]

Further evidence, of the weakness of realism's claim that moral talk in wartime is meaningless, concerns the similarities between morality and military strategy. Both discourses are devoted to evaluating the same course of action—the deployment of armed force in foreign affairs—and to enabling both justification and criticism of it. Both discourses offer firm, action-guiding rules, such as (in morality) "Do not directly attack civilians" and (in strategy) "Do not launch a frontal attack on a protected position." Both discourses presuppose a shared vocabulary, they appeal to public evidence for support, and they recognize the risks attending alternative courses of action. Both discourses presuppose that the alternatives in question are real and not merely apparent: the actors are genuinely confronted with free choices. Both offer norms for action. And though these norms can be ignored on the ground during the heat of battle, this does not detract from the intelligibility of the norms, nor even (perhaps) the overall commitment to adhere to them. In light of these profound similarities between morality and strategy, how can the realist completely ignore and even mock the one while emphasizing the importance of the other? How can the realist consistently exalt the importance of smart strategy during wartime while shouting down those who dare to forward moral arguments about military conduct?[10]

And what of all this realist talk about the "necessity" of state self-regard? It appears, upon reflection, to be quite misleading and ill-founded. As Walzer says, rarely is a state credibly threatened with extinction; and so the day-to-day reality of international affairs is *much more a matter of probability and risk than it is of strict necessity* and of adhering to the fierce requirements of survival. States, it seems, are much freer to choose between alternative courses of action than realists contend. This means that states are free, in a very clear sense, to choose to act on the basis of moral commitments and conceptions of justice, as well as upon considerations of their own national interest.[11]

It seems straightforwardly true that states do, indeed, act upon the basis of both national interests and moral commitments. This is perhaps clearest in democratic, representative regimes where the people simply insist that their governments take seriously the moral beliefs of the nation. Perhaps these states do not always listen, but they do so at their own peril, since the discipline of the ballot box remains. It follows from these thoughts that the ancient Athenian generals, for example, were not actually forced to "rule or be ruled"; rather, they carried out a deliberate policy of aggressive expansion that was authorized by the Athenian assembly. The crushing of the Melians was not a "necessity of nature"—an "ingurgitation" of a small state by a big one— but rather the brutal outcome of a free collective decision by a group of Athenians giddy with power and lusting for more. Walzer notes that Thucydides omits these prior debates and decisions in his storied *Dialogue*. Walzer then rightly concludes that war is the inevitable product *neither* of the structure of nature *nor* of the international system; rather, war is "a human action, purposive and premeditated, for whose effects someone is responsible."[12]

The upshot is that descriptive realism seriously misunderstands the nature of moral discourse, particularly with regard to war. War is an *intentional* human activity: states *choose* whether or not to take the dramatic step of embarking down the road of war. They *deliberately decide* whether it is in their best interests to do so, and whether they think it is right to do so. It is an important fact about moral discourse that *any* intentional, deliberate human activity is one which *can* be subjected to moral scrutiny. Of any prospective choice in the realm of human action, we can always meaningfully ask: "What ought the agent to do?" Furthermore, war is not just *any* intentional human activity: it is one of the most extreme and destructive activities there is. The very activity inherent in warfare—namely mass killing and destruction for political purposes—is so serious and far-reaching in its impact on our lives that it clearly *demands* moral judgment. Wars are *not* like storms spontaneously breaking out on the horizon, to be weathered with strength and luck. Wars, rather, are acts of mass violence deliberately set in motion by those empowered with the war authority. It follows that we can, we ought, and we actually do make meaningful moral judgments with regard to international relations in general and war in particular.

Walzer has a fascinating further point to consider here. He claims that a state with only self-preservation and self-assertion (i.e., realism) as its policy would not last long. It would fail to inspire its people enough to keep the partnership alive. A collective association can endure, he says, only if there is a shared "commitment to the kind of belief or value that might inspire and sustain a common life and lift it out of mere existence." In other words, humans are much more complex and demanding than realists picture them: we want more out of our community than mere animal survival and economic growth. We are not simple creatures, even though we do have straightforward material needs. You cannot reduce the complexity of human action and motivation into simplistic slogans, like Friedrich Nietzsche's "will to power." "It isn't really prudent," Walzer suggests, "to assume the malign intent of one's neighbours; it is merely cynical, an example of the worldly wisdom which no one lives by or could live by." We must, of course, tend to our elemental claims to physical security. We have human rights to such security, and in a very rare supreme emergency this must, as I admitted in Chapter 5, be our objective. But this is not all we want, nor all we can expect under normal conditions. Our fuller desires and hopes reside in inhabiting a community in which our values are reflected, in which we enjoy equal membership, recognition and even some fellow-feeling. We do not merely desire personal security, or political and economic expansion; we also want a place we can call our own and feel comfortable in, a political home. And we want our political home to make serious efforts at being just as opposed to unjust, ethical as opposed to evil. In other words, no one wants to live in a realist paradise; no one—not even an ancient Athenian—ultimately wants to live in a world dominated by the cynical, imperialistic generals of Athens.[13]

Prescriptive Realism

Prescriptive realism is the view that states *should* only care about maximizing what they take to be their own enlightened national interest. (Note that prescriptive realism need *not* be based on descriptive realism; it is its own doctrine and that is why we must examine it separately.) This leads to one more important distinction, namely, that between a *prudential* and a *moral* prescriptive realism.

THE PRUDENTIAL FORM

Characterization

Prudential prescriptive realism stipulates that nation-states ought, *prudentially*, to be motivated in their international relations only in terms of national interest. The bottom line here is that basing a foreign policy solely on an informed and sober understanding of national interest is simply the smartest and most advantageous thing to do. Why? There is a self-interested reason, and a more universal one. The self-interested reason runs like this. Even if moral considerations can *in principle* be relevant to international affairs, most of the time what we *actually* see, for lack of a better phrase, is states behaving badly. Even if it is not a strict necessity, it is a norm to witness most states behaving in a realist kind of way—trying to maximize resources, looking out for Number One. In light of this reality, you do not want to get suckered by behaving too nicely. *If you're too moral, you'll be treated like a doormat, taken advantage of, exploited.* But that is not smart; what is, is to behave like a realist. Behave like a realist, and you'll do better for your own people than if you behave like a moralist.

The more universal grounding offered for prudential prescriptive realism is the notion that all states should be motivated solely in terms of prudence in their international relations because *everyone would thereby be better off*. If only every state minded its own business from a purely hard-nosed prudential perspective the world would be a much better place. Why? Because people get hot and bothered about their moral beliefs. They care deeply about their vision of justice, and are very reluctant to change their views about it. Think of how many past wars were (arguably) created by fanatical moralism: the Crusades; the Wars of Religion between Catholic and Protestant; the French Revolutionary Wars; and perhaps even World War II, owing to Hitler's conviction that it was just for the Germans to rule Europe because of their supposed racial superiority. The prudential realist will thus suggest that we would all be better off leaving our different moralities at home, and deal with each other internationally *only in terms of interests all states share*, such as sovereignty, secure territory, developing the economy and tending to their people's well-being.

There is a version of this argument which realists make special use of against just war theorists. They accuse them of having a Crusading mentality, and of actually *increasing* the destruction of war by linking it to passionately contested beliefs about justice. Just war theorists fill people's heads with talk of aggression, and dreams about securing justice through violence. And the result? Much more death and destruction than there would be if we de-linked warfare and morality. We should only link warfare to strategy, and leave all hot-blooded appeals to justice to the side (or simply confine them within our nation's justice system or our interpersonal relations).[14]

So the view of war, on this realist understanding, is this: war is to be undertaken only if it is clearly in the nation's best interests to do so. Generally speaking, since war is such a momentous, costly and risky undertaking, war should be considered *only in the most serious cases* where the nation's fundamental interests are demonstrably at stake. Furthermore, once a war has begun, the only principle which is to guide a nation's actions is again one of prudence: one should do *whatever* will maximize one's interests in terms of the war. Whether that involves adhering to just war rules constraining wartime action or not *depends entirely* on whether the nation in question sees such behaviour contributing to its end of victory. But there is here no question of adhering to a set of restrictions or rules as a matter of principle or right; the guiding light emanates solely from the notion of protecting and enhancing national security and power. Indeed, the understanding here is that *we should be cynical about warfare*. War is not a moral business; it is a brutally violent thing which should be resorted to only when vital interests are genuinely, and severely, threatened. When we're cynical like this, fewer mistakes will be made, passions will be held in check, fewer people will die and the war will be over more quickly.

Criticism

This is a challenging and provocative doctrine, and just war theory must respond. Consider first the argument about being suckered. I do agree that it *can* be relevant to one's behaviour what most others around one are doing. If most other states are behaving badly, this does give grounds for being extra cautious, and for not forgetting to tend to one's fundamental interests. I demonstrated, in the supreme emergency chapter, an affinity with *some* aspects of realism: if the risk to oneself is truly terrible and mortal, then prudentially one must tend to one's survival. That being said, in the absence of such extreme conditions—which are very rare—I do not agree that the *mere risk* of being suckered and exploited justifies jettisoning moral beliefs and behaving in a completely egoistic way. First, one's moral beliefs *are a part of* one's fundamental interests, and one selfishly wants to see them realized as readily as one's interest in becoming more secure and wealthy. So it is not so easy to simply carve out, and dump, one's moral interests in favour of one's prudential interests. Often, moral beliefs are a crucial part of one's identity, be one a person or a nation. Second, *under normal, non-emergency conditions*, the moral defection and badness of others is *not* a sufficient reason for one to behave amorally or immorally oneself. If, for example, "everyone else" is looting during a city-wide blackout, this does not justify—or make it smart— to engage in looting oneself. We could even understand such moments as testing one's moral character and integrity, rather than as providing one license to set them aside. One might find it more valuable to preserve one's integrity than to betray one's moral convictions, even under conditions of real risk. At the least, then, it is not at all so obvious that the risk of being exploited renders it clearly better to behave like a realist than not.

Additionally, there is no reason why prescriptive realism should be thought to be more peaceful, or stabilizing, or advantageous, than alternative understandings of the imperatives of foreign policy. For every state, according to this view, is to be a self-regarding egoist. It does not take much imagination to see how having each state behave in a completely self-regarding way would, eventually and inevitably, lead to conflict. Indeed, one can easily imagine realism recommending *more* aggressive foreign policies—perhaps even more wars—than, say, a justice-based account of foreign policy. *This is especially the case for a powerful state*, which has less to lose and more to gain by exercising its influence, perhaps even by resorting to armed force.

This is not just an idle thought experiment. Even the most cursory glance at the historical record shows the bad consequences of states basing their mutual dealings solely on the basis of national egoism and the strategic struggle for power. The fundamental reason is that *it makes trust between states*

very difficult to come by, and then the realist view of global anarchy and
conflict becomes a self-fulfilling prophecy. We should all behave ruthlessly
and selfishly—thus disintegrating any trust between us—and *then* the collapse of that trust causes all of us to behave *that much more* ruthlessly and
selfishly. There is a downward spiral of mistrust, paranoia and eventually
conflict. If we all adhered to realist advice, I do not think the result would
be peace and prosperity. The result is more likely to be bitterness and suspicion, eventually paranoia and then conflict over natural resources, territory
and perhaps even over the mere fear that one's neighbours are getting too big
for their own britches. Indeed, that used to be the famed "balance of power"
thinking which dominated European foreign policy, permitted preventive war
and culminated in the two World Wars.

To be sure, if we look more closely at the history of war (as the realist
invites us to do) it is clear that, as often as morality has sparked wars, the
clash of national interests has done so as well. Think of all the wars, from
the 1400s to the 1900s, between the European powers regarding their various
empires and struggles over colonial territory and resources.[15]

Consider also that, in addition to his insane "racial" beliefs, Hitler invaded
Poland in 1939 to get more territory so that populous Germany could have
more "living room." In 1914, a previous generation of Germans invaded tiny
Belgium to get more land, show their power, and because they thought they
could get away with it. And in 1870, an even previous generation of Germans
—led by a master practitioner of *realpolitik*, Otto von Bismarck[16]—provoked
the French into war so that he might win land and cement newly-formed
German unity. Elsewhere in the world, Saddam Hussein invaded Kuwait in
1990 to capture its waterfront territory and oil supply, partly to help pay off
his massive war debt from the Iran-Iraq war. Indeed, it is a common realist
tactic to go to war externally not to resist any outside aggression but, rather,
because it "solves"—or at least distracts attention from—some domestic
problem one is having, like a sluggish economy. It is not at all clear, to say
the least, that widespread adherence to realism would be better for the peace
and prosperity of the world, compared to a justice-based account that has
firm rules against this kind of aggressive behaviour.

This point is quite separate from whether morality can plausibly be seen
as the source of conflict which realism contends it is. There are real differences, of course, but also real similarities, between the world's many moral
codes. Moreover, the similarities seem to focus around a growing international consensus in favour of respecting human rights. In other words, not all
moral beliefs give rise to the kinds of tensions, threats and insecurities that
are endemic to the purely prudential approach. Indeed, as Thomas Pogge has
argued, shared moral commitments serve *as more promising bases of a
secure international system*, in that they are by no means as prone to change
and renunciation as are those resulting from the latest cost-benefit calculation
of interests. Generally speaking, people keep their moral commitments, even

when doing so leads to a sub-optimal result in terms of their personal interests. Just think of how many times you have made some sacrifices in order
to keep your commitments, especially to friends and family. *This might even
be part of what it truly means to have a moral commitment: that one sticks
with it even in the face of temptation.* So moral motivation in foreign policy,
provided that it is universally accessible and minimally conceived—limited,
say, to respecting human rights—need provide no grounds for worry about
stoking the fires of interstate conflict. Indeed, consensus around such moral
beliefs can make international trust and rewarding co-operation possible,
even strong and predictable, over time.[17]

What about the particular shot at just war theory? It is important, I admit,
to consider whether "the justice motive" causes wars, and/or causes them to
be especially destructive. The first thing to note, as I have stressed several
times, is that the clash of subjective moral opinion over a war *is not enough*
to shatter just war theory. Just because belligerents *say* they have justice on
their side *does not make it so*. Just war theory is designed to reduce such
subjective clashes and passions by explaining and enumerating *more objective grounds* for morally judging warfare. Besides, it seems a very severe
"solution" to suggest that, because moral opinions can differ and are often
strongly held, that we should ditch all of morality itself when it comes to
judging warfare! Secondly, the notion that realism would allow wars to be
better fought, with less killing and shorter duration, is pure speculation.
Heads of state can make severe prudential mistakes about their national
interests, too. Consider Saddam's 1990 invasion of Kuwait: was that a smart
move? Did his realist motivation prevent a destructive conflict? Did the realist motivations of the European empires render the colonial era war-free?!
*Just war theory is not pro-violence and pro-destruction any more than real-
ism is.* Moreover, being cynical about warfare can lead decision-makers to
be casual about it, with horrible death and destruction following. World War I
is an example of this, both in its beginning and often in its conduct.
Historians have depicted the comedy of errors, ruthless scheming and
mindless nationalism that set the war into motion. People actually thought
it would be "a lovely little war." And generals on both sides have been
roasted by historians for the ease and callousness with which they ordered
their own men to their deaths.[18] People who believe that war can be *sometimes* morally justified are not fans of warfare and violence; if sane, they
believe wars are just as dangerous and destructive as any realist or pacifist.
Third, just war theorists need not have a Crusading mentality.[19] Some unfortunately may, but there is nothing *essential* to the theory which calls for this.
Just war theory does *not* commit us to fighting unlimited Crusades in pursuit
of Pure Justice. Just wars, Walzer stresses, "are limited wars; there are moral
reasons for the statesmen and soldiers who fight them to be prudent and
realistic."[20] Such moral reasons include, perhaps above all, the need to
minimize human suffering.

Another deep flaw with prescriptive realism—indeed, realism in general— is that it is incapable of ruling out from consideration state actions which are blatantly immoral. To that extent, realism seems at odds with some of our deepest commitments, which do indeed levy definitive prohibitions. As Donnelly says, there is nothing in realism which would be at odds with, say, colonialism or imperialism—or even slavery, torture, killing the innocent and genocide—*provided* the right conditions and calculations were met. The familiar point here is that the recommendations of realism are always *contingent and subject to change*; there are no rules which states are to adhere to *on unchanging moral principle*, as in just war theory or international law. This feeds back into the instability which realism, contrary to its self-image, fuels and furthers. If a state's foreign policy is always malleable (because it is based on the latest conditions and calculations of self-interest), then this can only add to the insecurity which all other states feel in wondering about its motives and future manœuvres, and what they ought to do next to forward their own power and security against it. In the most literal and biting sense, realism is an *unprincipled* perspective. This is clearest in its "anything goes" advice regarding warfare.[21]

Realism also favours and legitimizes the actions of the most powerful states in the interstate system. Realism benefits and buttresses—*is biased towards*—the actions and interests of the most powerful, which is perhaps one unfortunate reason why so much realist literature and thought comes out of the United States.[22] If states ought to do what it is in their best interests to do, and if the most powerful states have the greatest capability of doing what they want to do, then the result is a legitimation of the fact that powerful states are able to exert such incredible power over the interstate system in general and smaller states in particular. But this bias in favour of the powerful is at odds with our other values (e.g., democracy, sovereignty and the self-determination of political communities). Also, if the only standard for praise and blame in the realm of foreign policy is a prudential one, this all-too-conveniently deprives smaller, less influential states of what is often their most powerful claim for international reform: moral criticism. In other words, realism is a doctrine powerful states—from ancient Athens to contemporary America—advance to render themselves immune from criticism. But we all know that, often, it is precisely the most powerful who deserve the most scrutiny.

THE MORAL FORM

Characterization

There is one last form of realism to consider: morally prescriptive realism. This might sound paradoxical, and perhaps it is, but the idea runs as follows: *morally*, nation-states ought to be motivated, in their international relations, only in terms of national interest. Morality itself demands realistic prudence on the international stage. There are two prominent grounds for morally prescriptive realism, just as there were for prudentially prescriptive realism. The first ground is impersonal or universal. The notion here is that all states ought to be animated internationally only in terms of self-regarding prudence because moral animation makes states intolerant, inflexible, arrogant and disrespectful of the autonomy of other peoples, particularly those committed to a different set of moral values.[23]

The second grounding is more particularist or nationalist in nature. This nationalist form is based on the notion that there are no global moral duties. *Moral demands alter radically along national borders*; indeed, they alter so radically that only norms of prudence ought to be adhered to internationally. Why? First, a legitimate national government is a trustee, or advocate, or agent representative of its people and, as such, its overwhelming and overriding duty is to look out for the well-being of its people, and only its own people. Secondly, individual identity is very closely tied to national membership. Shared values, languages, historical experiences and customs tie together a moral community based on mutual recognition and regard—a kind of mutuality which is simply not present (at least not yet) at the international level. In other words, morality itself is rooted in community, and communities only exist nationally. People talk loosely about "the international community" but it is not a genuine shared culture, which is what you need to ground authentic moral duties. Whether universal or particular in terms of its grounding, morally prescriptive realism, in terms specifically referring to war, counsels that it is *not only prudent but fully moral* to base decisions to go to war on a calculation of national interests. And in the conduct of war, the best that a national government can do, morally, is to do the best it can by its own citizens, namely, by winning the war as quickly as it can, with as little cost to itself and its people as possible.[24]

Moral realism, regardless of the way it is grounded, is a clever, sophisticated and influential doctrine. Kennan, one of the chief architects of Cold War foreign policy in America, repeatedly contended that "the primary obligation" of a national government "is to the interests of the national society it represents ... its military security, the integrity of its political life, and the well-being of its people." And Kissinger has repeatedly claimed that it is morally offensive for states to be "morally charged" in terms of their foreign policy, contending that the world is thereby made worse off. Strong moralism invites strong moralism in return, and this passionate process can easily create an insecure, threatening situation, as both sides dig in their heels over their clash of ideals.[25] Yet a contemporary just war theorist will reject such a view. On what grounds?

Criticism
The first thing to note is that, as a form of prescriptive realism, moral realism shares a number of fatal flaws with prudential realism—flaws we have

already diagnosed. These include: 1) refusing to rule out atrocious actions, especially in war; 2) recommending a doctrine which, if widely adhered to, would result, and has resulted, in serious international instability and conflict; and 3) being biased in favour of the most powerful nation-states. In fact, moral realism is perhaps more offensive than prudential realism, with regard to this last remark, since it grounds pure national self-regard morally, as opposed to merely prudentially. It therefore offers *moral* cover and justification for the dominance of the most powerful and privileged states. The reasoning is: it is moral that states base their foreign policies on national self-interest; and the most powerful states have the most capability to pursue their self-interest; thus, it is morally legitimate that the most powerful states have the most capability to shape the interstate system to their own benefit. A quite dubious inference, and conclusion, indeed.[26]

Consider now the impersonal, universalist grounding for moral realism. The core claim is that moral motivation in international affairs is a source of arrogance and intolerance. Since there is radical moral diversity in our world, states ought not to base their dealings with the rest of the world in terms of their own (presumably provincial) morality. A contemporary just war theorist will object to this argument on grounds that it offers an excessively balkanized, fragmented conception of morality, hardly allowing for the existence of any shared moral values between admittedly diverse ethical traditions. Yet clearly there *is* considerable overlap amongst the world's most influential moral codes, at least in terms of their most basic propositions. Very rare, indeed, is the moral system which approves of murder, torture, cruelty, aggression, deception and betrayal. Equally rare is an ethics code which does not, in some way, recommend honesty, courage, wisdom, friendliness and respect for human dignity.[27] And consider human rights. Nearly every state on earth has ratified the United Nations' Charter, which mandates commitment to human rights. Human rights have thus been endorsed, in a substantial sense, by representatives of every major ethical tradition on the globe. Furthermore, the grounds typically offered for respecting human rights are utterly non-provincial, invoking the vital needs of the human person and the very widespread norm not to do serious harm to persons without just cause. There are thus grounds for believing that an international morality *limited* to respect for such human rights—such as that advocated in this book—will successfully avoid this realist accusation. In sum, it seems false to argue that a human rights-based foreign policy, and accompanying set of war actions, will produce or express intolerance.[28]

So much for the impersonal grounds of moral realism. What of the particularist or nationalist ones? The first particularist claim, recall, is that a legitimate national government is one which is a trustee or agent of its people and, as such, has an overriding moral duty to look after the interests and well-being of those it represents. There is obviously an important political truth in this claim, especially if one subscribes to values like democracy and the self-determination of communities freely and legitimately organized into minimally just states. The real question here is *not* whether such a claim is morally compelling; it is, rather: *what does its truth actually justify*? In particular, does its truth justify the supposed non-existence of cosmopolitan duties? To what extent does its truth allow national governments to put the interests and well-being of their own citizens over those of foreigners, especially in wartime?

By way of response, consider that a trustee or agent of any X is not morally entitled to do something which X may not himself do. A defence lawyer, for example, is neither morally nor legally entitled to do *anything and everything* on behalf of his client. He is not permitted, for instance, to bribe the judge or to murder a damaging witness. The lawyer has to maintain a set of rules; but within the parameters established by those rules, he is entitled to argue vigorously on behalf of his client. Analogously, we might say that, within a minimal set of fair and just standards applicable to all, the agent or trustee is entitled to be partial to the interests of his client. Are there any such minimal standards operative at the international level?

Following ideas developed throughout this book, it seems defensible to say that human rights establish the minimal set of rules and principles of justice which states are duty bound to uphold on the international level. Such rights are, as John Rawls has said, the baseline requirements of political reasonableness and just conduct in our era. And human rights are crystal clear commitments mandated by international law. With respect to war, I suggest that just war theory—itself connected to human rights protection—serves as a set of minimal and universal rules, applicable to all, within which states are to operate on behalf of their citizens. These notions put paid to any ignorance, or degradation, of cosmopolitan duties. All national governments are duty bound *not* to violate human rights, *regardless* of the nationality of the rights holder. They are not to violate any human rights because to do so is to do severe harm to human beings without just cause, something which no one is morally entitled to do. *National governments may not do something which their own citizens may not themselves do.* In Chapter 2, we established that state rights are legitimized, and delimited, by human rights. There are thus real, powerful and principled limits on the degree of national partiality which moral realism can plausibly justify.[29]

It is important to note that this just war, or international law, claim is compatible with *one aspect* of the realist claim that national governments owe some degree of partiality to their own citizens. Just like the case of the defence lawyer, it seems cogent to contend that, *above and beyond* the minimal, universal threshold of human rights fulfilment required by international justice, national governments may feel free to do the best they can for those they represent. Above and beyond respect for human rights, and the rights of minimally just states, national governments need not treat all claims of foreigners on par with those of their own citizens, for instance with regard to tax treatment, access to government subsidies, social programs and welfare benefits, participatory rights, and so on. *National governments may offer their own citizens much more than they offer foreigners but they cannot treat foreigners with less than the minimum respect established by human rights principles.*

But what of the second nationalist claim often advanced by moral realists, namely, that moral duties are created out of a sense of moral community and belongingness which only obtains at the national level? It needs to be admitted, in response, that the global community obviously does not constitute a community in any way nearly as strong as that of a nation-state. It also seems as though a considerable part of an individual's self-understanding is shaped by her cultural and historical membership and thus that our communities enjoy a privileged position in our political thinking, especially when it comes to the international plane. But, that being granted, there are serious limits and ambiguities to this grounding of moral realism.

The first thing to note is that individuals can also feel quite alienated from, and disillusioned with, their own communities—and can place greater personal value on leaving them behind rather than on preserving their traditions and customs. Furthermore, it is very difficult to speak consistently about a shared, coherent national culture or identity which is worthy of the exalted status often claimed by nationalists (or "communitarians"),[30] given that *no national culture is homogeneous.* The reality on the ground is that almost every so-called "nation-state" is actually a multi-national state, with majority-minority dynamics and tensions, differences of language, gender, region, race, custom, interest, historical perception, political ideology and so forth. In fact, we know from the historical record that most "shared cultures" have come to be that way through very questionable practices, such as wars of genocide, persecution of minorities and dissidents, propaganda campaigns, and so on. So, *even if* there were a truly "shared national culture," and *even if* it did play an enormous role in individual self-understanding, it would seem to be (at least somewhat) morally tainted by the way it came into being historically. At the very least, *such knowledge cautions us from claiming too much on behalf of the nation-state.* It certainly seems to prevent us from agreeing with the realist claim that such is the exalted moral status of the nation-state that, internationally, it ought only to act to forward its own power and interests vis-à-vis neighbouring communities. That is one reason why I prefer, in my work, to speak only of *minimally* just societies, and the need to secure *minimal* justice. Too many people think far too highly of their own society and believe that it serves as a blueprint for mankind. Far better, I suggest, to leave such delusions behind and focus on the less narrow, more universally acceptable standard of minimal justice, and then let communities differ as they wish.

Pogge has come up with a telling point in this regard. Consider the human association which seems, obviously, to be most constitutive of self-identity, namely, the family. Even though we acknowledge many special measures on behalf of families in our social structures, we do not think that family ties justify *any* act on behalf of the family. We do not think that moral duties radically alter, perhaps to the point of dissolution, as soon as one walks out the front door of the house or apartment. We do not encourage families to think in terms of a desperate struggle of "us versus them," of doing the best they can amongst themselves without any regard to how their acts impact upon their neighbours. And if we are not inclined to extend such permissive privileges to the family, why should we believe we ought to do so when it comes to the less influential nation-state?[31]

Another dubious aspect of moral realism is that, as Charles Beitz has contended, it seems to constitute another kind of groundless discrimination. Membership, on a moral realist account, is all-important: a state is *only* duty-bound to look after the interests and well-being of its own members, let the interests of others fall where they may. But what is political membership based on? In the vast majority of states, and for the vast majority of the world's people, membership is based on the place of one's birth. And yet no one had a choice where or when they were born, just as no one had a choice what sex or race into which they were born. And we do not argue on principled grounds in favour of racism or sexism. So how can we argue on principled grounds that political membership is to be absolutely determinative of how one gets treated in the contemporary world, especially during times as dangerous as those of war? Membership, by and large, is an arbitrary, unchosen characteristic for which no one can be held responsible; so how can so much turn on it, morally, in terms of what governments may and may not do to human beings?[32]

We see these issues in bold relief when it comes to what realism recommends in times of war: namely, an efficient victory, with minimal costs to one's own citizens. In the illustrative words of Michael Gelven: "The value we place on the concerns of peace ... are challenged by those of war, which make up our communal meaning and allow us to posit the worth of what is ours against the challenge of what is alien." He makes an even stronger claim, that "war [is] grounded in the existential concern for the priority of the We over the They."[33] This red-blooded communalism—literally "us versus them"—implies the existence of only voluntary restraints upon the conduct of war with regard to foreigners. As with prudential realism, there are here *no firm principles*, such as rules of just war, restraining a nation's conduct during war. There is nothing which might be called the employment of intrinsically heinous means: everything is thought to be entirely contingent upon the situation and wishes of the nation in question. But surely this is morally dubious, and violates our other values. The employment of mass rape campaigns, for example, or weapons of mass destruction, are usually actions we want to level non-contingent (i.e., firm, fierce, unchanging) prohibitions against. These are not idle thoughts: realism, with its emphasis on ending the war as quickly and as favourably as possible, would seem *to recommend and endorse* the employment of dirty means against the enemy state. For what quicker and more thorough way to crush an enemy, and minimize the total costs to one's own people, than by rapidly deploying overwhelming, disproportionate and indiscriminate force? Quick, dirty, ugly and despicable wars are the predictable result of state adherence to moral realism.

Summary

Communities are to adhere, as a minimal condition of justice, to human rights. Even during times of war, human rights form the bedrock of cosmopolitan moral duties. Indeed, just war norms are designed to secure human rights as best they can be secured amid the grim circumstances of war. But above and beyond the threshold level of minimal justice established by human rights, states may justifiably pay much more attention, and give greater weight, to the interests of their own citizens. It does not, in other words, seem defensible to support national partiality all the way down, as realism does. There remains a residual, yet stubborn and real, threshold level of moral universality and cosmopolitanism. Compatriots may well owe each other *more* than they do foreigners, but they are not utterly free of all obligations with regard to even the most distant of strangers. Community, fellow-feeling, and even the maintenance of a part of one's sense of self, do not justify doing severe harm and grievous injury to other human beings.

While this amounts to an on-the-whole rejection of realism, it needs to be admitted that *some* aspects of realist thought have already been accommodated and integrated. Recall, from our Introduction, that we stressed that each of the three traditions has something important and enduring to share. We have just mentioned the maintenance of *some* national partiality on the part of a nation's government and even its people's affections and affiliations. We also note that, while the international arena is not quite a bloody anarchy, it clearly does lack sufficient ordering; in the final analysis, it is true that states must rely on self-help and be vigilant about protecting their rights and interests. Indeed, acknowledgement of this "realistic" fact *is built into* the just war argument in favour of permitting armed self-defence in the face of aggression (see Chapter 2).

Realism also makes us mindful of the current limits of international institutions, like the UN, and prevents us from putting too much faith in their capacity to resolve severe disputes pacifically. On the other hand, it might also drive us to improve such institutions, in the expectation that more developed and effective global governance can lessen the self-help strain too often left upon the shoulders of national statesmen.

Realism highlights the fact that statesmen, and their states, very often succumb to temptation and behave badly, or at least greedily, insecurely and short-sightedly. We need to know this as we reflect upon our own foreign policy choices and, again, to check any tendency towards naïve optimism. We want not only to be just but also smart. Realism, however, does *not* show that morality should not be a part of a nations' foreign policy, much less that it is an illusion. It might be rare, but states *can* act with moral motivation and be fair and reasonable in their actions. They are at least capable of such; we should hold them to some standards and not merely let them do whatever they want. Governments unbound by principles are among history's most frightening creatures.

Realism, I believe, is best thought of as a healthy and needed antidote to those who—whether out of a secure upbringing, little contact with distant strangers or blinkered ideology—simply expect too much of flawed people behaving in an insecure environment. Against such utopians, realism offers a bracing tonic, a needed "negative" purging of their surreal optimism and lack of worldliness. Such utopians can sometimes actually be damaging do-gooders. But as a "positive" doctrine of foreign affairs, realism has far too many flaws—as shown throughout this chapter. With the exception—again, very rare—of a genuine supreme emergency, realism should not be the ruling doctrine of foreign affairs in general, much less wartime in particular. Indeed, when it comes to wartime, just war theory *already incorporates* much realist wisdom in the *jus ad bellum* rules of: last resort; probability of success; and proportionality. Each of these rules urges a sober caution regarding war, a clear calculation that it is probably going to be worthwhile and a realistic appraisal that the problem is really so severe that war seems a fitting solution. Each of these rules is designed to make us mindful of the expected consequences of going to war and, as such, is consistent with realism's insistence that we look reality square in the face and make smart decisions about war within an accurate, not fanciful, context.

Notes

1. T. Hobbes, *Leviathan*, ed. A.P. Martinich (Peterborough, ON: Broadview Press, 2004), Chapter 11, 79–80.

2. J. MacMahan, "Realism, Morality and War" (78–92) and D. Mapel, "Realism and the Ethics of War and Peace" (180–200), both in T. Nardin, ed. *The Ethics of War and Peace: Religious and Secular Perspectives* (Princeton, NJ: Princeton University Press, 1996); S. Forde, "Classical Realism" (62–84) and J. Donnelly, "Twentieth Century Realism" (85–111), both in T. Nardin and D. Mapel, eds. *Traditions in International Ethics* (Cambridge: Cambridge University Press, 1992). See also R. Keohane, ed. *Neorealism and Its Critics* (New York: Columbia University Press, 1986).

3. H. Morgenthau, *Politics Among Nations* (New York: Knopf, 5th ed., 1973); G. Kennan, *Realities of American Foreign Policy* (Princeton, NJ: Princeton University Press, 1954); R. Niebuhr, *Christianity and Power Politics* (New York: Charles Scribner's Sons, 1940); H. Bull, *The Anarchical Society: A Study of*

Order in World Politics (New York: Columbia University Press, 1977); K. Waltz, *Man, The State and War* (Princeton, NJ: Princeton University Press, 1978); H. Kissinger, *Diplomacy* (New York: Harper Collins, 1995).

4. M. Walzer, *Just and Unjust Wars* (New York: Basic Books, 3rd ed. 2000), 3–4, 117.

5. Walzer, *Wars*, 5.

6. Morgenthau, *Politics*, 16–22; W. Jaeger, *Paideia*, trans. G. Highet (New York: Random House, 1949), 402. Thanks to Christian Barry here.

7. Wilson cited in Walzer, *Wars*, 3–21; C. von Clausewitz, *On War*, trans. A. Rapoport (New York: Penguin, 1994). Quote from W. Sherman, *From Atlanta to the Sea* (London: Folio Society, 1961), 121–22.

8. Donnelly, "Realism," 85–111.

9. Walzer, *Wars*, 3–20.

10. Walzer, *Wars*, 13–16.

11. Walzer, *Wars*, 3–21.

12. Walzer, *Wars*, 5–10, 15.

13. M. Walzer, "Nation and Universe," in G.B. Peterson, ed. *The Tanner Lecture on Human Values* (Salt Lake City, UT: Utah University Press, 1990), 537–40.

14. T. Franck, *The Power of Legitimacy Among Nations* (Princeton, NJ: Princeton University Press, 1990), Appendix; D. Welch, *Justice and The Genesis of War* (Cambridge: Cambridge University Press, 1988).

15. D. Abernathy, *The Dynamics of Global Dominance: European Overseas Empires 1415–1980* (New Haven, CT: Yale University Press, 2001).

16. T. Hamerow, *Otto Von Bismarck* (London: Heath, 2nd ed., 1972).

17. T. Pogge, *Realizing Rawls* (Ithaca: Cornell University Press, 1989), 211–81.

18. J. Keegan, *The First World War* (New York: Vintage, 2000).

19. Is a Crusading mentality present in my own defence, last chapter, of forcible regime change? I do not think so: a Crusading mentality denotes a narrow-minded, absolutist, simplistic and probably religious world view which perceives itself as entirely righteous and the other side as completely unjust and to be demonized and vanquished. The last chapter does not display such traits: what is defended there is an idea of *minimal* justice—not pure or maximal justice—which is rooted in modest, reasonable, secular values like individual human rights and the good consequences of greater international peace and the ability of everyone to lead a minimally good life. Please note again the difference between a *just* war and a *holy* war discussed in Chapter 1. Moreover, the conception of coercive post-war regime change endorsed last chapter was assuming that the target regime was the aggressor: the permission to start the war comes from the target regime's act of aggression, not from its rooting in different values. Further, my defence of forcible regime change was quite guarded, with many careful distinctions, exceptions and noted needs for checks-and-balances: especially the constraints imposed by the ten-point recipe for regime reconstruction. Believing that clear improvements can and should be made in a defeated aggressor post-war is not the same thing, surely, as calling for a crusade against infidels.

20. Walzer, *Wars*, 122.
21. Donnelly, "Realism," 85–111.
22. There are other reasons why Americans show a predilection for realist thought. Their being "top dog" in the international arena has led them to be inordinately concerned with their own status and influence in the international system. Being top dog also makes one a target of those who wish to dethrone and replace the dog, or just to rough it up a bit. Either way, you can see how the top dog is going to view the world in a very conflict-ridden way, always watching his back. *But there is nothing essential or universal about that experience.* If one neither is the top dog nor intends to harass or replace the top dog, then one is not very likely to be impressed in any way with the realist view of international relations. This is probably why so few "middle power" countries—like Canada, Australia, the Scandinavian countries—talk or behave like realists.
23. Kissinger, *Diplomacy, passim*.
24. Morgenthau, *Politics, passim*; Niebuhr, *Power, passim*.
25. Kennan, *Realities*, 48; Kissinger, *Diplomacy, passim*.
26. Donnelly, "Realism," 85–111.
27. M. Walzer, *Thick and Thin* (Notre Dame: University of Notre Dame Press, 1994).
28. This is not to say that a foreign policy animated by more provincial values than human rights satisfaction would not run afoul of this criticism. It may well—but it is not a claim advanced here.
29. J. Rawls, *The Law of Peoples* (Cambridge, MA: Harvard University Press, 1999), *passim*; T. Pogge, "The Bounds of Nationalism," in J. Couture, et al, eds. *Rethinking Nationalism* (Calgary, AB: University of Calgary Press, 1998), 463–504.
30. W. Kymlicka, *Liberalism, Community and Culture* (Oxford: Clarendon, 1988); M. Sandel, *Liberalism and The Limits of Justice* (Cambridge, MA: Harvard University Press, 1982); A. Etzioni, *The Spirit of Community* (New York: Touchstone, 1994).
31. Pogge, "Bounds," 463–504.
32. C. Beitz, "Cosmopolitan Ideals and National Sentiment," *Journal of Philosophy* (1983), 591–600.
33. M. Gelven, *War and Existence* (Notre Dame, IN: University of Notre Dame Press, 1994); 12.

CHAPTER 9
Evaluating the Pacifist Alternative

> But I tell you not to resist an evil person. Whoever slaps you
> on your right cheek, turn the other to him also.
> *Jesus*, Matthew 5:39

> "He shall judge between many nations, and rebuke strong
> nations afar off; they shall beat their swords into ploughshares,
> and their spears into pruning hooks; nations shall not lift up
> sword against nation, neither shall they learn war anymore."
> *Micah*, 4:3

There are many kinds of pacifism. It is not my task here to diagnose and describe all of them. Different pacifists define pacifism differently, and offer various kinds of justification for their beliefs. But it seems that what unites all forms of pacifism—the basic proposition, or lowest common denominator—is opposition to warfare. The logical core of pacifism, as Jenny Teichman says, is "anti-war-ism."[1] No matter what kind of pacifist you are, you believe that *war is always wrong*; there is always some better approach to the problem than warfare. So, unlike realists, pacifists believe that it *is* possible and meaningful to apply moral judgment to international affairs. In this, they agree with just war theorists. But they disagree with just war theorists regarding the application of moral judgment to warfare. Just war theorists say war is *sometimes* morally permissible, whereas pacifists say war is *never* morally permissible.

Jim Sterba has attempted to mesh just war theory and pacifism into what he calls "just war pacifism,"[2] and he has collected some support in this regard. But I don't buy it. It is a strange kind of pacifist, after all, who can endorse warfare. If they do endorse warfare under just war conditions, then I suggest that ... they are just war theorists! Sterba's proposal does not integrate, so much as assimilate, pacifism into just war theory. The conceptual kernel of both theories, in my view, cannot be reconciled—the one says warfare *can* be permissible, and then defines those conditions, whereas the other says, *regardless* of the conditions, war *cannot* be morally justified. Quite literally and straightforwardly, a pacifist rejects war in favour of peace. It is not violence in all its forms to which the most challenging kind of pacifist objects; rather, it is the specific *kind and degree of violence that war involves* to which the pacifist objects. A pacifist objects to killing (not just violence) in general and, in particular, he objects to the mass killing, for political reasons, which is part and parcel of the wartime experience. So, a pacifist rejects war; he believes that there are no moral grounds which can justify resorting to war. War, for the pacifist, is always wrong.[3]

Having come to a working definition of pacifism as anti-war-ism, we can now consider some of the reasons offered in its favour. Many such reasons have been offered but not all of them are appropriate to our concern. For example, many pacifists are so for religious reasons. Christians and Buddhists, in particular, have vibrant pacifist sects, such as the Quakers. They base their beliefs on sacred scriptures and a drive to be more like the divine, whom they view as essentially peaceful. Christians, for example, point to Jesus' life and teachings as disclosed in the New Testament. These do indeed, at first glance, seem to recommend something very much like pacifism. Consider the quote above, and the other important imperative to love even your enemies.[4] Jesus also says that he is "gentle and humble in heart" and he refuses to use force to resist his arrest, telling his disciples: "Put your sword back into its place; for all who take the sword will perish by the sword."[5] But this—like much else in religion—is hotly contested. For example, we saw in Chapter 1 that just war theory has historically been associated with, and supported by, the Catholic Church—so clearly the Church doesn't think pacifism is mandated by the New Testament. I will not delve further into religious justifications for pacifism because they rest on beliefs—about God and Scripture, souls and the afterlife—which simply are too personal, speculative, contentious and even exclusionary. I direct the reader to the relevant literature for more on the religious perspective.[6]

This book will stick to secular justifications for pacifism, which try to appeal to *any* rational person *regardless* of religious affiliation. The most relevant pro-pacifist arguments here include the following: 1) a more "teleological" form of pacifism (or TP), which asserts that war and killing are at odds with human excellence and flourishing; 2) a more "consequentialist" form of pacifism (or CP), which maintains that the benefits accruing from war can never outweigh the costs of fighting it; and 3) a more "deontological" form of pacifism (or DP), which contends that the very activity of war is intrinsically unjust, since it violates foremost duties of morality and justice, such as not killing other human beings. Most common and compelling amongst contemporary secular pacifists, such as Robert Holmes and Richard Norman, is a mixed doctrine which combines, in some way, all three.[7]

Before describing in detail—and ultimately overthrowing—TP, CP and DP, mention should be made of a very popular criticism of pacifism which will not here be employed. This criticism is that pacifism amounts to an indefensible "clean hands policy." The pacifist, it is often said, refuses to take the brutal measures necessary for the defence of himself or his nation for the selfish sake of maintaining his own inner moral purity. It is argued that the pacifist is thus a kind of free rider on the rest of us, gathering all the benefits of citizenship while not sharing all its burdens. The pacifist is not willing to fight, yet gains security from those who are. Not only is the pacifist ungrateful for this, he actually looks down his nose, morally, at those who have provided him with his security. The picture is of a rather unlikeable, holier-than-thou, selfish free rider. A related inference drawn is that the pacifist can actually be an internal threat to the overall security of the state, because his non-participation and objection diminishes the state's resources and resolve in fighting.

This "clean hands" argument is easily, and frequently, overstated. It is important to note that, to the extent to which *any* moral stance will commend a certain set of actions deemed morally worthy, and condemn others as being reprehensible, the "clean hands" criticism can be so malleable as to apply to any substantive moral and political doctrine. *Every* moral and political theory stipulates that one ought to do what it deems good or just, and to avoid what it deems bad or unjust. The very point of morality itself, we might say, is to help keep one's hands "clean." So this popular just war criticism of pacifism is not especially appealing. Besides, the very idea of a selfish pacifist simply does not ring true: many pacifists have, historically, paid a very high price for their pacifism during wartime (through severe ridicule, job loss, ostracism and even jail time), and their pacifism seems less rooted in regard for inner moral purity than it is in regard for constructing a less violent and more humane world order.[8] So, this argument against pacifism seems to fail; but others, now to be discussed, succeed in questioning the plausibility of its core principles, at least relative to those of just war theory.

Describing and Criticizing TP

Teleology is a perspective on the nature of morality itself. Literally meaning "the study of purpose," teleology often now gets referred to as a form of "virtue ethics." Virtue ethicists, such as Aristotle, believe that human beings must live their lives trying to develop their faculties to the fullest extent. This, for them, is the purpose (or *telos*) of life. Of course, we have many faculties to develop: intellectual; physical; social; moral; and so on. What does it mean to develop one's *moral* capacity to the fullest? It is to pursue ethical excellence, which is displayed by the virtues (hence "virtue ethics"). What are the virtues? They are freely-chosen character traits which we praise in others. We praise them because: 1) they are difficult to develop; 2) they are corrective of natural deficiencies (e.g., industriousness is corrective of our tendency to be lazy); and 3) they are beneficial both to self and society.[9]

There are many virtues, and a moral person is one who develops them and consistently displays them over time. The ancient Greeks listed four "cardinal virtues," namely, wisdom, courage, moderation and justice, and Christian teaching is well-known for its recommendation of faith, hope, charity and love. Other prominent virtues include honesty, helpfulness, forgiveness, pleasantness, consistency, tolerance, modesty, thoughtfulness, and so on. For the human vices, simply negate the above.

The essence of TP is this: when we think of warfare and war-fighting, we see that none of this is praiseworthy activity. Violence, killing and blood-shed are not virtuous activities; they seem clearly at odds with the kind of ideal life—a fully realized and excellent human life—which is the focus of virtue ethics. War is not part of any sane person's idea of a flourishing life. Warfare causes terrible pain and suffering, and the infliction of violence brutalizes the victim and corrupts the character—making it hard and insensitive—even of the inflictor. A TP pacifist would also suggest that, although some aspects of courage might, admittedly, be called upon in war, just as common is the experience of post-traumatic stress disorder, which reduces the formerly strong soldier to a broken shell. Moreover, which is truly more courageous: fighting, or refusing to fight in spite of the danger? There are a number of sharp questions here: is war truly a wise choice? A moderate and humane one? One expressive of hope and charity, instead of hatred and malice? Doesn't war, as a destroyer, seem the opposite of creativity and life? How can war be consistent with love? Indeed, doesn't all this show that *peace itself is a virtue*—part of the human ideal—and that, although it might be very difficult, it is in pursuit of peace that we must orient our thoughts and actions?

There *is* something to TP, just as there is something in every major doctrine on the ethics of war and peace. But there are problems. The major one is whether the commitments of the pacifist are utopian (i.e., excessively unrealistic). War might be a nasty business which, ultimately, calls forth more vice than virtue. But it might also simply be needed to defeat an aggressor who is not moved by pacifist ideals. A world where aggressors are allowed to triumph, and then to inflict rights-violating brutality, is not part of any sane person's idea of the best life, either. And there is something to be said, in the case of a just war, for: the virtues of defending one's people (or fellow citizens) from aggression; the courage it takes to confront an aggressor; the self-discipline it takes to fight justly; and the strength and ingenuity it takes to formulate and execute a successful war plan. More generally, *justice is also a virtue*, and a major one at that. Much of the dispute has to do with different perspectives on what to do when the world puts us in situations where the virtues of peace and justice are in conflict, and cannot both be realized. Where just war theorists differ from pacifists is that they suspect that there can be cases where justice does not include peace or, more precisely, where peace includes or creates injustice. Consider that just war theorists, like Michael Walzer, argue that, by failing to resist international aggression with effective means, pacifists end up *rewarding* aggression and *failing* to protect people—fellow citizens—who need it.[10]

Pacifists reply to these just war arguments by contending that we do not need to resort to war in order to protect people and to punish aggression effectively. In the event of an armed invasion by an aggressor state, an organized and committed campaign of non-violent civil disobedience—perhaps combined with international diplomatic and economic sanctions—would be just as effective as war in expelling the aggressor, with much less destruction of lives and property. After all, the pacifist might say, no invader could possibly maintain its grip on the conquered nation in light of such systematic isolation, non-co-operation and non-violent resistance. How could it work the factories, harvest the fields, run the transportation network, staff the stores and banks, when everyone would be striking, refusing to comply or quietly sabotaging orders? How could it maintain the will to keep the country in the face of crippling economic sanctions and diplomatic censure from the international community? And so on. Jack DuVall and Peter Ackerman have detailed many actual, historical cases of non-violent resistance around the world; Robert Holmes and Gene Sharp, amongst others, have developed the abstract non-violent tactics which pacifists might rely on.[11] Consider the following list of tactics offered by Sharp:

> ... general strike, sit-down strike, industry strike, go-slow and work to rule ... economic boycotts, consumers' boycott, traders boycott, rent refusal, international economic embargo and social boycott ... boycott of government employment, boycott of elections, revenue refusal, civil disobedience and mutiny ... sit-ins, reverse strikes, non-violent obstruction, non-violent invasion and parallel government.[12]

Though one cannot exactly disprove this pacifist proposition—since it is (conveniently?) a counter-factual thesis—there are powerful reasons to agree with John Rawls that this is "an unworldly view" to hold. For the effectiveness of these campaigns of civil disobedience *relies on the standards and scruples of the invading aggressor.* But what if the aggressor is utterly brutal and ruthless? What if, faced with civil disobedience, the invader "cleanses" the area of the native population, and then imports its own people from back home? It is hard to strike, or sabotage orders, if one is dead. And what if, faced with economic sanctions and diplomatic censure from a neighbouring country, the invader decides to invade *it,* too? We have some indication from history, particularly that of Nazi Germany, that such pitiless tactics are effective at breaking the will of even very principled people to resist. The defence of our lives and rights may well, against such heartless invaders, require the use of political violence. Indeed, under such conditions, as Walzer says, adherence to pacifism might even amount to a "disguised form of surrender." He thinks that, in such instances, if one truly believes in values like "resisting aggression effectively" and "protecting oneself and fellow citizens from aggression," then one should be willing to fight for them—because, in such cases, *fighting holds the only realistic prospect of actually defending these values.* Unwillingness to fight here means non-support for these values. But how can you not want to protect people, and resist aggression effectively?[13]

Pacifists respond to this accusation of "unworldliness" by citing what they believe are real world examples of successful non-violent resistance to aggression. Examples most often mentioned include: 1) Mahatma Gandhi's campaign to drive the British Imperial regime out of India in the late 1940s, leading to the independence of modern India; and 2) Martin Luther King Jr.'s civil rights crusade in the 1960s on behalf of African-Americans.[14] Walzer replies curtly that there is no evidence that non-violent resistance has ever, *of itself*, succeeded. This may be a bit rash on his part, though it is clear, for example, that Britain's own exhaustion, financial and otherwise, after World War II had much to do with the evaporation of its Empire and the independence of India. Walzer's main counter-argument, against these so-called counter-examples, is that *they only illustrate his point*: that effective non-violent resistance depends upon the scruples of those it is aimed against. It was only because the British and the Americans had some scruples and standards, and were in the end moved morally by the determined idealism of the non-violent protesters, that they acquiesced to their demands. *But aggressors will not always be so moved.* It might seem unthinkable to us, but a tyrant like Hitler, for example, might interpret non-violent resistance as disgusting weakness, deserving contemptuous crushing. "Non-violent defence," Walzer suggests, "is no defence at all against tyrants or conquerors ready to adopt such measures."[15]

To those pacifists who retort that even Hitler was faced with his own non-violent resistance, namely in Scandinavia after he conquered those lands in 1940, the point must be made that the problems that the Swedes, Norwegians and Danes put in his way because of their strikes, sabotage and protest cannot really, in my view, be considered *successful* acts of pacifist resistance to aggression. They happened, after all, *after* Hitler had already conquered those lands—so how were they helpful in resisting the aggressive take-over of their territory and political systems? Second, perhaps the reason why the Nazis didn't crush these Scandinavian protest movements were: 1) they had already conquered Scandinavia and didn't consider these protests a serious threat to their control; and 2) they now had bigger fish to fry, like England, Russia and America. Thirdly, and speaking of the major powers, *they* were the ones who beat Hitler—with force—resulting amongst other things in the liberation of Scandinavia. It was not home-grown pacifist protest which got the Nazis out of Stockholm, Oslo and Copenhagen; it was the decisive military defeat of Germany by the remaining Allies. This is not to deny the fact that Scandinavian resistance *did* cause problems for the Nazis, that it did bolster the spirits of the locals, and that the co-ordination required was impressive and the acts often ingenious. It is, rather, to put them into their proper perspective as smart and bracing tools of resistance but not, ultimately, as tools successful in rolling back aggression.[16]

Walzer puts the whole issue persuasively when he says that the idea of an effective "war without weapons," much less a world without war, is (for now) a "messianic dream." For the foreseeable future, and in the real world we all inhabit, it is better to follow just war theory, which is committed to an effective yet principled use of defensive armed force in the face of aggression.

The constraints on violence established by just war theory are, in fact, the necessary conditions for the more peaceful world which pacifists mistakenly believe is already within sight. "The restraint of war," Walzer concludes, "is the beginning of peace."[17]

Describing and Criticizing CP

Consequentialism is another fundamental world view regarding ethics. As the name indicates, the core focus of consequentialism is on the concrete results of one's actions. This tradition is sceptical of the value of focusing on personal character traits, as teleology does, or on abstract universal rules, as we'll see deontology does. The key, ethically, is whether the world ends up better as a result of one's actions. The proof is in the pudding: the right thing to do, in every instance, is to perform that action which is going to have the best contribution to the world's welfare. So consequentialism involves a serious attempt to predict the costs and benefits of one's options, and then a mandate to act in accord with the one promising the highest "payoff"—in terms of pleasure, happiness or welfare—to the world at large.[18] The CP element of contemporary pacifism, accordingly, is the notion that the costs of war always outweigh the benefits from undertaking war. One does not need to be a military historian to get the point, namely, that war is incredibly destructive, brutal and often deeply inhumane. And the benefits, if any, of wars are often seriously unclear and are soon overtaken, in any case, by the flow of historical events. As the famous song asks: "War, what is it good for?" The CP pacifist agrees with the next line, "Absolutely nothing!"

The first critical question to raise here, by way of response, is: what kind of costs and benefits are being appealed to here? Short-term or long-term costs and benefits, or both? Prudential or moral costs and benefits, or both? And costs from whose point of view? And so on. There is a lack, in the literature, of a detailed breakdown of war's costs and benefits; pacifists prefer instead to gesture towards very general—almost clichéd—understandings of war's destructiveness, such as those just offered in the last paragraph. Could this tendency towards sweeping generality and abstraction exist due to a lack of confidence in the results of a more finely grained analysis?

One important element to note, in this regard, is that we have to consider not only the explicit costs of war action (i.e., both military and civilian casualties, the costs of deployment, and the destruction of property), but also the implicit costs of war *inaction*: not resorting to war to defend political sovereignty and territorial integrity may well be tantamount to rewarding aggression in international relations. The lack of armed resistance and forceful punishment allows the aggressor state to keep the fruits of its campaign, thereby augmenting the incentives in favour of future aggression. To what extent can we have a well-functioning and stable—much less a just—international system in which aggression between nations is thus rewarded? Call this the "macro-cost of war inaction": the rewarding of interstate aggression, which leads to the long-term weakening of the interstate system of peaceful dispute-resolution. The thought experiment becomes more grim for pacifism when we think not just of classical cross-border wars but of potential humanitarian interventions. The costs of inaction here—as we tragically witnessed in Rwanda in 1994—are not simply sovereignty and land but literally hundreds of thousands of lives.

We must also talk of the "micro-costs" of not resorting to war to defend one's own populace from an aggressive invader. Such a pacifist strategy seems, at the very least, to run enormous risks with the safety and well-being of one's people, not to mention their right to be self-governing and not subject to a conquering regime. In light of this, we should ask: does pacifism make sense at the level of collective agents, like states, *especially* if those collective agents are charged with the responsibility of protecting and serving their citizen members? Is there too great a reliance, by the pacifist, on the intuitive appeal of the interpersonal case (of not killing another individual), as opposed to the analogous, yet different, inter-national case? In other words, pacifism at the level of the individual—the conscientious objector, for instance—seems much more plausible and principled than advocating that an entire state be geared along pacifist lines, *especially given the status quo of the international arena* (as the realist would remind us). Again, the risks to one's people would be huge, and so it is deeply unclear whether a prudent, or moral, government ought to adhere to such a view. Just war theorists believe that it should *not* do so: one of the core functions of the state, after all, is to provide reliable protection from serious, standard threats to our human rights, one of which is armed invasion by an aggressor regime. It is compelling to conclude that states ought to be prepared to enforce that protection, through armed force if necessary.[19]

The combination of both the macro- and the micro-costs of *failing* to resort to war (in situations otherwise well-defined by just war criteria) are sufficient at least to cast doubt on whether war-fighting can *only* result in greater negative, than positive, consequences. It is very simple to cluck one's tongue and shake one's head at the destruction of warfare—"War is bad!"— and quite another to *think through the costs of pacifism* and what they might involve relative to just war theory. Being against war, after all, can be like being in favour of motherhood—a "no-brainer" that no one in her right mind would disagree with. But it is different for those with responsibility to protect their people, especially when threatened by a terrible aggressor who relishes warfare and conquest.

We might also, in our consideration of CP, consider the historical record. I am fully prepared to concede that many—perhaps even most—historical wars can be questioned, very forcefully, by the CP aspect of contemporary pacifism. World War I seems a fitting example of the futility, waste and sheer human tragedy of many wars our ancestors fought. But not all wars seem to fall neatly under this objection. World War II, for instance, is much more debatable. Many thoughtful people, including participants who actually made the sacrifices, have argued—appealing to both prudential and moral costs—that defeating ultra-aggressive regimes like Nazi Germany, Fascist Italy and Imperial Japan was worth the costs of fighting the war, as enormous as those admittedly were. Can we, they ask, imagine and endorse what our world would currently look like had the Nazis been allowed to conquer Europe and rule it, had Mussolini spread his "New Roman Empire" beyond Ethiopia, and/or had Imperial Japan been allowed to subdue most of East Asia? George Orwell's searing image of a soldier's boot stomping on a human face comes to mind. World War II didn't create a wonderful world—the world of our dreams—but it did prevent a truly terrible world from coming into being. It also ushered in many international improvements—the spread of democracy, the creation of the United Nations, the growth of international law and respect for human rights—which have made the modern world a more humane place.[20]

A third issue to raise, with regard to CP, focuses on the relationship between consequentialism and the denial of killing, especially on the level which is endemic to warfare. Pacifism places great, perhaps overriding, value on respecting human life, notably through its usual injunction against killing. But this core pacifist value seems to rest uneasily with the appeal to consequentialism in CP. For there is nothing to a *consequentialist* approach to the ethics of war and peace which would *always* outlaw killing. There is here no firm principle that one must never kill another person, or that nations ought not to launch military campaigns which kill thousands of enemy soldiers. With consequentialism, it is always a matter of considering the latest costs, benefits and circumstances. Consequentialism was actually first designed, quite explicitly, to be flexible in a way in which teleology and deontology are not. (Note the difference between consequentialism and realism: while both appeal to cost-benefit utilities, consequentialism remains an ethical doctrine focused on the world's overall improvement whereas realism is a doctrine sceptical of ethics and thus featuring strong commitments only to one's own selfish benefit.)

When considering whether or not one should kill another human being, consequentialism will typically appeal to the pain and suffering such killing will cause both the victim and her friends and family—not just in terms of the loss of life but also in terms of the loss of further, future life experiences. Appeal will also be made to a more universal (or legislative) point of view, and contention made that permitting or mandating killing is a bad precedent which might lead to loss of respect for human life, and thus to serious insecurities within the community, and so on. These are all excellent and powerful points to be made against killing another human being. The remaining problem, though, is that a consequentialist approach to the injunction against killing and war does not seem to come with *the kind of firmness* which the pacifist needs to ground his categorical contentions. The pacifist isn't just committed to saying that, *usually*, killing and warfare are a bad idea; he wants to say, much more strongly, that killing—or at least war—is *always* wrong. Can consequentialism deliver that kind of absoluteness?[21]

Since it is always a matter of choosing the best option amongst feasible alternatives, consequentialism clearly leaves conceptual space open to the claim that under *these* conditions, at *this* time and place, and given *these* possible alternatives, killing and/or war seem(s) permissible. There can be particular counter-examples, some offered above, wherein the calculations may well come out the other way. After all, what if killing 3,000 people (say, some members of an invading army) seems necessary to save the lives of 9,000 people (say, people of one's nation who would die from the rights-violating activities of the unchecked invader, as it sought to consolidate its rule)? It is at least possible to conceive that a quick and decisive resort to war can be employed effectively to prevent even greater suffering, killing and devastation in the future. Indeed, military and political historians often engage in this thinking, and sometimes claim things like "Had the Allies confronted Hitler after Austria, it wouldn't have taken so long, later, to defeat Germany. Appeasement made the war longer and more destructive." To put it plainly, it seems rather bizarre for the *consequentialist* pacifist, whose principles exhibit a profound abhorrence for killing people, to be willing in such a scenario to allow *an even greater number of people to be killed* by acquiescing in the violence of others less scrupulous. Two related points are being made here: 1) the general point that the CP element of pacifism does not, of itself, seem to ground the categorical rejection of killing and war which is the very essence of pacifism; and 2) the particular point that CP seems open to counter-examples (like World War II) which question whether consequentialism would even reject killing and war at all in certain conditions. Consequentialism might actually *recommend* warfare, if the circumstances were dark enough and the other options limited enough.[22]

Describing and Criticizing DP

Deontology is yet another major world view regarding morality. We discussed it, without using the word, when we spoke in Chapter 5 of supreme emergencies and Kant's "strict respect for the rules" option. Deontology has, as its core intuition, the notion that the concept of duty is at the foundation of morality. Ideas like duty, obligation and responsibility are uniquely moral ones—indeed, the most uniquely and clearly moral ones. There might be confusion between morality and mere personal prudence when we talk, like teleologists, about beneficial character traits or when we speak, like consequentialists, about costs and benefits. But there is no mistaking that we are talking about morality when we consider duty and obligation. So these ideas, and not the others, must be the very essence of ethics. Doing one's duty is what is central in ethics. And by "duty," deontologists usually mean that one's behaviour is permitted, or demanded, by a first principle or general rule regarding morality, such as "Thou shall not lie," or "Honour your father and mother." How does deontology get used by pacifists? The exact nature of the DP element varies from thinker to thinker, but the core notion is that *the very activity of fighting a war violates a foremost duty of morality*. Thus, undertaking such activity can never be justified by appealing to the aims or consequences of the action in question. War, as a means to an end, is thought to be intrinsically unjust. The supposed "justice" of the goal sought, through war, does not redeem the injustice of the means used to pursue it. There must be consistency between means and ends. War ought never to be resorted to: there is always some vastly superior option with regard to international dispute-resolution, such as diplomacy, sanctions or organized campaigns of non-violence.

NOT KILLING PEOPLE

Much has been left unsaid in this terse characterization of DP. Depth and detail must be added: *why* does war-fighting violate *which* foremost duty of morality? In my view, the best pacifist consideration of these matters has been offered by Robert Holmes. Holmes deals with this consideration initially by stating that the foremost duty of morality violated by fighting a war is *the duty not to kill other human beings*.[23] But the obvious objection to this claim is that such a duty—though crucially important under normal conditions of life—does not seem to override all other considerations under special, very threatening circumstances. Consider the most obvious example: A brutally attacks B, thereby posing a severe threat to B's life. Provided that A attacks without justification, many people would respond that B may retaliate against A in self-defence, with lethal force if needed. Consider another example: are we not to kill a dangerous terrorist who is credibly threatening the lives of many innocent civilians? Say, one of the 9/11 hijackers while he was in the act? It seems defensible to assert that we may, so that we protect the lives of the innocent.

The essence of this objection has been stated very forcefully by G.E.M. Anscombe, who lambastes pacifism for not distinguishing between "the blood of the innocent" and "the blood of the guilty." The question, as Anscombe would pose it, is: why should we respect the duty not to kill the terrorist when he is guilty of a seriously immoral act, namely, credibly threatening and endangering the lives of many innocent civilians? Do we not also owe the duty of protection, by lethal force if necessary, to those who are being so seriously threatened? After all, if we do nothing, then severe harm, or even death, will befall all these innocents. The terrorist will get his way, even though his way is the morally wrong one. In short, Anscombe's claim is that we have weightier moral reasons to side with the civilians instead of the terrorist, even if that means killing him.[24]

There is a raft of complex issues, addressed in the rhetorical questions above, which requires a much fuller development. The first concerns the permissibility, perhaps even the right, to kill a person who presents a severe threat either to oneself or to others. Why exactly is this permissible? Does it not, for instance, violate the human rights of the person presenting the threat?

The employment of lethal force against an aggressor is permissible because the victim of the aggression would lose too much if she were not permitted to kill the aggressor. Indeed, the victim could literally lose everything. But perhaps it will be objected that the aggressor, if killed in response to his attack, would also lose everything. So, why may the victim kill the aggressor? The answer seems to be that the aggressor is responsible *for* forcing the victim to choose between her life and that of the aggressor, and it would be not only unreasonable but unfair to bar the victim from choosing her own life.

An agent A is an aggressor when A uses force to violate the human rights of another person, victim V. In violating the human rights of V, A reveals himself to be a severe threat to V, since human rights serve to protect vital human needs. It is an important claim of this book, defended throughout, that the commission of aggression by A against V: 1) justifies V in responding to A with lethal force, if needed; and 2) justifies any third party, T, in employing needed lethal force against A in order to protect V. The key principle at work here—dubbed the "Core Principle on Aggression" (or CPA) in Chapter 2— is thus the following: *the commission of aggression by A against V entitles V, and/or any third party T acting on behalf of V, to employ all necessary means to stop A including lethal force, provided such means do not themselves violate human rights.* Let us briefly remind ourselves of the elements of this complex principle.

Consider the first element, namely, the entitlement of either V or T to respond with the required force against aggressor A. Jan Narveson seems to put this point well when he notes that it is a matter of moral logic that if V has a human right HR to X (say, personal security), then V also has title to employ those means necessary to secure X from serious, standard threats, such as the violent aggression of others. This is required for us to speak of V's truly having HR at all.[25] Thus, if the employment of lethal force against A reasonably seems required to make A desist from committing aggression against, or even killing, V, it follows that V is at least permitted to do so. But how does this first-person permission get extended to the third person?

The extension proceeds on the basis of *the wrongness* of the aggression and *the intent* of the third party to protect the victim from the wrongful aggression. Sometimes victims, for whatever reason, lack the wherewithal to defend themselves effectively from aggression. In such cases, are we to say that their factual deficiency undermines their normative claim that the aggressor either stop or be stopped? The answer, clearly, is no. It is crucial to stress that the normative essence of the victim's claim is that *the aggressor stop or be stopped*, and not more narrowly that only she (the victim) be allowed to stop him. This moral reality grounds a third party's intervention in the case, and we applied this reasoning to humanitarian intervention in Chapter 3. It is clear, however, that to be justified the third party's intent can only be protection of V from A.

Consider now more precisely the second element of the principle, namely, the permission to employ *lethal* force against A if required. Many thinkers will be quick to pronounce on the need for a proportionality of force in response to a threat from an aggressor. And this claim is undeniable. But it may be worth stressing how we ought not to succumb readily to pious delusions about first trying to disarm the aggressor and then, *only if* that fails, be allowed to up the ante, perhaps to the point of killing. In situations where such a measured escalation of violent defence is reasonable, obviously it must be employed. But many situations wherein violent aggression occurs are ones which require a very swift and effective response. We cannot hold victims to excessively stringent interpretations of proportionality in such cases: they are, after all, under an immediate, grievous threat to their lives and rights.

NOT VIOLATING RIGHTS

Let us now turn to the crucial third element of our principle, namely, that the violent response of V to A's aggression violates no human rights. The obvious, and important, question here is: why would V's killing A, in response to A's aggression, not violate A's human rights? As the DP pacifist would say: doesn't the above principle CPA actually compound the wrongness of the tragic situation by permitting V to kill A if required? Isn't this all just the delusion that "two wrongs make a right"? There is a new slogan bandied about in this regard: "An eye for an eye leaves us all blind." The response of just war theorists is *no*: V does no wrong whatsoever—violates no rights—by responding to A's aggression with lethal force if required.

The reason grounding this just war claim is that the commission of aggression by A causes A to *forfeit* his human right not to be dealt with violently, or even killed. It must be understood that rights are reasons. *They are not properties of persons, rather, they are reasons to treat persons in certain ways.* From this conception, it involves no great conceptual leap to point out that *reasons to treat persons in certain ways can change*, depending on the circumstances and what they are doing. Provided that one has a non-absolutist, and thus reasonable, conception of human rights as claims no stronger than their justifying reasons,[26] forfeiture appears to pose no considerable difficulties. It amounts to nothing more than the claim that *the weight of reasons* in the situation informs us that V does nothing wrong in responding to A's aggression with lethal force if necessary.

Why does V do nothing wrong? What exactly constitutes "the weight of reasons" in this regard? We have already mentioned this, in Chapter 2, while defining aggression, but let's introduce a quick reminder, since it is vital for our encounter with DP pacifism. First, it is A who is *responsible* for forcing V to choose between her own life and rights and those of A. We can hardly blame V for choosing her own. For, if she does not choose her own, she loses an enormous amount, perhaps everything. Second, it is simply *not reasonable* to expect creatures like us to intentionally suffer catastrophic loss. Third, consider the question of *fairness*: if V is not allowed to use lethal force, if necessary, against A in the event of A's aggression, then V loses everything while A loses nothing. Indeed, A gains whatever object he desired in violating or killing V. Such is a patently unfair reward of deeply objectionable behaviour. Finally, V's having rights at all provides V with an *implicit entitlement* to those means and measures necessary to secure her rights, such as the use of force in the face of a severe threat. These four powerful considerations of *responsibility, reasonableness, fairness* and *implicit entitlement* all unite together in supporting the just war claims that: 1) V *may* respond with lethal force to A's aggression; 2) V *does no wrong* in doing so; 3) it would be *wrong to prohibit* V's doing so; and 4) A *bears all of the blame* in the situation.

Once A has stopped his aggression, and poses no imminent threat of renewed aggression, his full set of rights spring forth intact, save for those still deemed forfeit for legitimate reasons of appropriate punishment and restitution for his act of aggression. The notion of "springing forth" is nothing more puzzling or magical than the claim that now the weight of reasons with regard to how we should treat this person has changed. Since he is no longer a clear and present danger to another's vital needs, for example, he may no longer be killed—though he may, perhaps, still be jailed, fined and/or rehabilitated as appropriate punishment.

INNOCENT AGGRESSORS?

One related topic, which gets mentioned in conjunction with these issues, is that of the so-called "innocent aggressor." Say, for instance, that C and D are in an elevator together. Unbeknownst to C, D suffers from a very serious mental disorder, which suddenly causes him to attack C. Is C thereby justified in employing lethal force against D? A number of thinkers have denied this, claiming that at best C has an excuse. This is to say that C has done something which is not morally permitted (namely, killing an innocent) yet C ought not to be punished for it because he has an excuse. This excuse is the fact that C could in no way be expected to know what was wrong inside of D's head, which caused him to attack C.[27]

These abstract thoughts, on this curious figure of the innocent aggressor, should be applied to a more relevant case. Sometimes pacifists will contend that soldiers are innocent aggressors—they are not to blame for the wars they fight and many are conscripts; they go further and deny even the excusability of intentionally killing them.[28] At the very least, they will assert, there is no moral permission to kill them: the just war theorist still does not have *morality* on his side.

The first thing to be crystal clear about, in response, is the uncontested fact that soldiers *are* aggressors, *regardless* of whether they are conscripts and *regardless* of their own personal attitude regarding the justice of the war they are fighting. They do indeed present themselves as severe threats against the lives and rights of those to whom they are opposed. They are armed with deadly force, and trained to kill for political reasons.

This first fact establishes, at least, a strong *prima facie* (or initial) case in favour of the notion that targeting soldiers with lethal force is morally justified and not merely excusable. After all, it is not as though soldiers can be thought of as being no different from unarmed civilians who do not present themselves as lethal threats.

The only plausible objection to this *prima facie* case is that there can be times when soldiers do disagree profoundly with the cause of their own state in fighting and yet still fight on its behalf for reasons which are outside of their control. But there are complicated issues to be resolved in this regard: if the soldier in question does have these personal objections, why does he continue to fight? Is the raw fact of his conscription (assuming that were the case) sufficient to exonerate him from his culpability as an aggressor? Or does some further story have to be told about what punishments he would have risked by resisting conscription? I do not pretend to have ready answers to these questions, only to insist that the realities at play in this case are considerably more complex than those in the highly contrived case of C and D in the elevator. The burden of proof is on those who would insist that soldiers are innocent aggressors. "Innocent" in what salient sense? It seems a category mistake to say combatants can be innocent, since just war theory and international law *define innocence precisely as non-combatancy*.

My view is that only rarely, if ever, do we come across a genuinely "innocent aggressor" in the heat of battle. Many soldiers are only too glad to fight on behalf of their own country, for good or ill. Conscription does nothing, one way or the other, to shed evidential light on their interior innocence or guilt. And the external fact remains that *they are aggressors*. Thus, states possess an on-the-whole justification in responding to aggressive armed force with forces of their own, for the reasons of reasonableness, fairness and implicit entitlement described above. There may well be exceptional cases where this will mean targeting an innocent aggressor (i.e., a soldier involved in the war, somehow, through no fault of his own) with lethal force. I think, as opined by Helen Brocklehurst, that the closest to an "innocent aggressor" in real life would be a child soldier. Some civil wars in developing countries—especially in Central Africa—have recently conscripted child soldiers as young as nine or even eight.[29] They remain aggressors because they are combatants deploying armed force, yet they are also innocent in the sense that they have been grossly manipulated by cruel adults and have probably not developed intelligent free will and moral capacities. Now, I still think such child soldiers are legitimate targets—you cannot ask them their age while they're shooting at you—even though the whole affair becomes imbued with tragedy. I understand the problem of child soldiers to boil down to this: they are *not* a case for pacifism, rather, they are a case for creating a new category of *jus in bello* war crime. Generals and officers caught using child soldiers to execute their will should be arraigned on severe charges for it after the war.

NEVER KILLING THE INNOCENT

DP pacifists, however, are not at this point out of options. Holmes, for instance, offers another argument which contends that the foremost duty of morality which is violated by fighting a war is *not* the duty not to kill *aggressive* human beings, but rather the duty not to kill *innocent, non-aggressive* human beings. What is the relevant sense of "innocence" now being employed? To be innocent here means the regular sense of: to have done nothing which would justify being harmed or killed; in particular, it means not constituting a serious threat or harm to other people. It means not being an aggressor. It is primarily in this sense, we have seen, in which civilian populations are thought, by traditional just war theory, to be "innocent" of war and thus morally immune from direct attack during wartime. Even if civilians support the unjust war effort politically, or simply in terms of their personal attitude towards the war effort, they clearly are *not* armed and dangerous aggressors. Only armed forces, and the political-industrial-technological complexes which guide them, constitute serious threats against which threatened people may respond in kind. Civilian populations are morally off-limits as targets.

Holmes contends that this just war criterion of discrimination, with its crucial corollary of non-combatant immunity, *can never actually be satisfied*. For all possible wars in this world—given the nature of military technology and tactics, the heat of battle, the proximity between legitimate and illegitimate targets, and the limits of human knowledge and self-discipline—involve the killing of innocents, thus defined. We know this to be true from history, and have no good reason for thinking otherwise. There simply has never been a war, nor will there ever be a war, without at least some civilian casualties. But the killing of innocent non-aggressive civilians, Holmes says, is always unjust. Therefore, just war theory's claim that resort to war can be mandated, or at least permitted, by justice conflicts with the supposed moral fact that the very acts constitutive of war in our world are unjust. So, for a pacifist like Holmes, *no war can ever be fought justly, regardless of the ends* (such as self- or other-defence) *supposedly aimed for*. This is a strong pacifist argument because it does not contest the ends in question: it does not argue whether self-defence, or the defeat of the Nazis, might be morally legitimate causes for killing. It says that, *even if* the cause or goal of the war is just, consistency demands that it *only* be pursued through just means. *But there are no just means*, since they all involve killing at least some civilians who are innocent and non-aggressive. How is a just war theorist to respond to this pointed pacifist challenge, in my view probably the sharpest there is?[30]

A number of thinkers have sought to defeat this pacifist argument by casting doubt on the utility of employing the concept of innocence in wartime. But a just war theorist subscribing to the *jus in bello* rule of discrimination, with its corollary of non-combatant immunity, will neither want, nor logically be at liberty, to argue in this fashion. It seems that, despite all the residual ambiguities which remain regarding who exactly is "innocent" during wartime, just war theorists are correct to maintain this concept. It is hard to see, for example, how infants could be anything other than innocent during a war, and as such entitled to immunity from direct and intentional lethal force. It is only those who are involved in harming us (i.e., those who are committing aggression against us) that we can justly target in a direct and intentional fashion during wartime.

We know, from Chapter 4, that the way in which traditional just war theory has dealt with this pacifist objection has been through the Doctrine of Double Effect (or DDE). The DDE, recall, is based on the following scenario: assume agent X is considering performing an action A, which will have both good effects G and bad effects B. X is permitted to perform A *only if*: 1) A is otherwise permissible; 2) X only intends G and not B; 3) B is not a means to G; and 4) the goodness of G is worth, or is proportionate to, the badness of B.[31] Assume now that X is a country and A is war. The government of X, which is contemplating war in response to an unjustified armed invasion by country Y, knows that, should it embark on war, such activity will result in civilian casualties (both in X and Y), even if X manages to vindicate its rights of political sovereignty and territorial integrity. The DDE stipulates that X may still launch such a justified war provided that: 1) this war is an otherwise permissible one of resisting aggression; 2) X does not intend any resulting civilian casualties (but, rather, aims only at vindicating its rights); 3) such casualties are not themselves the means whereby X's end (namely, vindicating its rights) is achieved; and 4) the importance of vindicating X's rights is proportionately greater than—or, at least, equal to—the badness of the resulting civilian casualties.

The key just war notion, we saw in the *jus in bello* chapters, is that civilians are *not* entitled to some kind of absolute, or fail-safe, immunity from attack; rather, they are owed neither more nor less than what Walzer has called "due care" from the belligerent government(s) that they not be made casualties of the war activity in question. Civilians are not entitled to such absolute immunity because the effect of allowing for such absolute immunity would be, essentially, to outlaw warfare altogether—and it is neither reasonable nor fair to require a political community to stand down in the face of an aggressive invasion which threatens the lives and rights of its member citizens.[32]

But this is precisely the nub of the DP pacifist's argument. The DP pacifist wants to say that the moral principle of never killing innocents throws a true blanket of immunity over the civilian population. Since just war theory doesn't likewise throw this blanket—but, rather, the thinner, threadbare fabric of "due care"—it does not really believe in civilian immunity. This is true: just war theory *only* endorses due care and *not* complete immunity. Due care means the belligerents must fight in accord with *jus in bello* rules as we have previously defined them and, if indirect and unintended civilian casualties still result, they are justifiable *provided that jus ad bellum* is also met. Here we see that, ultimately, the moral difference between DP pacifism and just war theory remains the "big picture" difference of opinion whether war can ever be justly begun. Just war theory says that, since some causes of war—like resisting aggression—are morally just, this means that *some civilian casualties must be permitted*, provided they happen unintentionally after *jus in bello* gets satisfied. DP pacifism, by contrast, says that *because* civilian casualties cannot ever be permitted—because of the wrongness of killing innocents—this shows that *no causes of war* can be sufficiently moral to start the murderous process. Here, just war theory moves from the top-down, whereas pacifism moves from the bottom-up. How can we adjudicate this vital, central debate?

I believe this is the strongest pacifist challenge to just war theory—war cannot be justly fought, therefore the cause doesn't matter. The injustice of the conduct corrupts the cause and infects the entire war and, indeed, all wars. The only thing for the just war theorist to do is: 1) stress the importance of the cause as *providing the moral context for* the conduct issues; and 2) argue that due care for civilians is morally enough, given the stringency with which it is defined by just war theory, and the remaining need to defeat aggression. In other words, *the cause does matter*, and it affects our evaluation of fair conduct. My perspective is: how else are minimally just states, in our world, to defend themselves, to protect their people, and to vindicate the international system of law and order, save through armed force and the resort to war? And why should states surrender their rights to political sovereignty and territorial integrity? Above all, why should they fail to protect their own people from aggression? *Provided* that the other criteria of just war are fulfilled, then the defence of rights, the protection of people, and the punishment of aggression seem worth the cost of incidental, indirect civilian casualties. It is worth it because, as contended above, it is unreasonable and unfair either to require or expect people not to resist an aggressive invasion of their country by force if required. They would lose too much, perhaps everything, if they capitulated. And it is not morally compelling that a government fail to perform one of its core functions: to protect its citizens, by force if necessary, from severe threats to their lives and their human rights.

Whereas the DP pacifist wants to insist on the absolute duty never to kill innocent human beings, the just war theorist must disagree—because otherwise the pacifist will win. But how to disagree, since the principle seems so strong? By substituting for the pacifist's simplistic rule another one more responsive to war's complexity, namely, that we must never kill innocent human beings unless: 1) we have just cause to do so; *and* 2) the killing is unintentional and indirect. This is a more complex rule, but we cannot side with simplicity for simplicity's sake. This new rule does preserve a prohibition on killing the innocent, which is very important for any plausible system of ethics. But it can allow genuinely unintended and indirect killing. (We know the DDE and *jus in bello* define indirection and non-intent for us more specifically, as discussed in Chapter 4.) Moreover, this new rule does bring in the reference to the larger context and the issue of the justice of cause, whereas the pacifist principle refuses to do so (perhaps out of concern for what it might introduce). Having more information informing one's rules and principles clearly seems better than less. So, I argue that even DP ultimately isn't good enough to overthrow just war theory because: 1) it is too simple in comparison; 2) it is inflexible and absolute; 3) it ignores the issue of just cause; and 4) it deliberately and irresponsibly prefers less to more information. What DP gains in clarity, it loses in plausibility upon analysis. The operative rule should *not* be "never kill innocent people" but, rather, "never kill innocent people directly, deliberately and without just cause."

A notable consequence of these reflections is that they support the theoretical point made throughout this book, namely, that the categories of just war theory *must* ultimately be tied together into a coherent whole. Here we see another strong reason why: if they're not so tied, they cannot fend off the strongest pacifist challenge. That challenge focuses on *jus in bello* and, to be overcome, the connection between *jus in bello* and *jus ad bellum* must be made. Those denying this connection are thus seriously vulnerable to defeat at the pacifist's hand.

This has been a difficult and challenging section, raising some of the most profound issues of moral theory itself. That's why it was saved until the end of the book. To summarize this section, DP raised a number of important duties, and alleged that just war theory violates them all. But:

1 The duty not to kill another person seems questionable, in light of compelling cases of self- and other-defence.
2 The duty not to violate rights is not broken by just war theory, which stipulates that war may be fought only in response to aggression. Once aggression has been committed by a state, it forfeits its state rights not to be attacked, for reasons of responsibility, reasonableness, fairness,

and implicit entitlement. Although the people in the aggressor state retain their human rights, these will not be violated, provided that the · victim state fights its just war in accord with the laws of war.

3 The duty not to kill innocent human beings is likewise not violated by just war theory, owing to its appeal to the doctrine of double effect. The foremost duty just war theory should seek to substitute and enshrine, in this regard, is the duty never to kill innocent human beings directly, deliberately and without just cause.

Summary

The goal of this chapter was to discuss and evaluate the pacifist alternative to just war theory. We described various pacifist arguments with considerable care and charity. But the arguments for TP, CP and DP are, in the final analysis, not as strong as those of just war theory. Pacifism, while well-intentioned, seems, in effect, to reward aggression and to fail to take measures needed to protect people from aggression. Pacifism is also premised on an excessively optimistic view of the world. It does offer an alternative to armed resistance, but the success of this method historically seems deeply questionable. The method of systematic civil disobedience in the face of aggression remains essentially untried, for it has worked only in cases where the target was morally sensitive to begin with. When the target or aggressor is not sensitive, the result of this method is pure speculation. Pacifists hope it will work—and hope is a virtue—but this ultimately makes me wonder very seriously whether pacifism can actually be divorced from religion. It would seem that only under the warm blanket of religious faith could pacifism's prospects, in our rough-and-tumble world, seem promising.

Perhaps that is insightful, but too quick. As in the last chapter, we should remind ourselves not just of pacifism's weaknesses but also of its strengths. Even though I believe pacifism too optimistic to be practical in the realities of our world, I do agree that it is still important to hold on to ideals and do what you can to work towards them. It seems persuasive to say that, ultimately, we'd like to see a peaceful world and for disputes to be resolved without violence and, certainly, without war. Who could disagree with that, at the level of pure ideals? Having that as a long-term ideal can help shape our judgments and guide our actions in the present. While it probably does not trump just war theory—so long as the world remains so insecure and violent—it helps us resist realist pessimism that it is all a hopeless cycle of violent power-seeking. This is one reason why just war theory seems so attractive as a middle-ground option: it is not so optimistic that it is utopian and unresponsive to aggression yet it is not so pessimistic that it refuses to hold communities to a standard higher than their own national interests. In my own efforts at improving just war theory—notably through trying to articulate *jus post bellum*—I must confess to having been motivated by

pacifism's insistence that we shouldn't take war for granted and that we must
do something to make the international system more peaceful, such as pro-
rights post-war transformation and the evolution of better global governance.

So pacifism can be incorporated into just war theory, just as parts of
realism were. Pacifism and *jus post bellum* can find many common causes
and support for reform, and pacifism reminds us of ultimate ideals most
reasonable people would like to see realized. The other thing pacifism provides, in the meantime, is a rich source of material regarding the last resort
rule in *jus ad bellum*. The traditional interpretation of last resort, we saw in
Chapter 2, is that after you have tried diplomacy and sanctions, force remains
as the final option. Pacifism calls that small triad into question, and offers us
many more tools within the anti-aggression tool-box. Some of these tools
and tactics of non-violent resistance (general strikes, mass protest, systematic
un-co-operation, etc.) may well be smartly deployed in several instances,
even though we cannot count on them working against the most ferocious
aggressors, like the Nazis. Non-violent tactics, in some instances, *hindered*
the Nazis but they didn't *defeat* them. What did was armed force. I see this
illustrating the main conclusion here: that pacifism (like realism) does substantially contribute to the ethics of war and peace but it does not—at least,
not yet—dislodge just war theory from its central position.

Notes

1. J. Teichman, *Pacifism and the Just War* (Oxford: Basil Blackwell, 1986), 3.
2. J. Sterba, "Reconciling Pacifists and Just War Theorists," *Social Theory and Practice* (1992), 21–38.
3. For more on defining pacifism, see: R. Holmes, *On War and Morality* (Princeton, NJ: Princeton University Press, 1989), 19–49; J. Narveson, "Pacifism: A Philosophical Analysis," in R. Wasserstrom, ed. *Morality and War* (Belmont, CA: Wadsworth, 1970), 63–77; J. Narveson, "Violence and War," in T. Regan, ed. *Matters of Life and Death* (Philadelphia, PA: Temple University Press, 1980), 109–47.
4. *Matthew* 6:44.
5. *Matthew* 11:29 and 26:52.
6. The works of John Howard Yoder (e.g., *When War is Unjust: Being Honest in Just-War Thinking* (Minneapolis: Augsburg, 1984)) offer a good example of a religious justification for pacifism. See also: J.P. Burns, *War and Its Discontents: Pacifism and Quietism in the Abrahamic Traditions* (Washington: Georgetown University Press, 1986); L.S. Cahill, *Love Your Enemies: Discipleship, Pacifism and Just War Theory* (Minneapolis: Fortress, 1994); M.C. Cartwright, "Conflicting Interpretations of Christian Pacifism," 197–213, and T.J. Koontz, "Christian Nonviolence: An Interpretation," 169–96, both in T. Nardin, ed. *The Ethics of War and Peace: Religious and Secular Perspectives* (Princeton: Princeton University Press, 1996); D. Dombrowski, *Christian Pacifism* (Philadelphia: Temple

University Press, 1991); and S. Hauerwas, *Should War be Eliminated? Philosophical and Theological Investigations* (Milwaukee: Marquette University Press, 1984). On just war theory as part of official Catholic catechism, see <www.vatican.va/archive/catechism> as well as the works of Augustine and Aquinas cited in Chapter 1.

7. R. Holmes, *On War and Morality* (Princeton: Princeton University Press, 1989); R. Norman, *Ethics, Killing and War* (Cambridge: Cambridge University Press, 1995).

8. P. Roots, *A Brief History of Pacifism from Jesus to Tolstoy* (Syracuse: Syracuse University Press, 1993); P. Brock and N. Young, *Pacifism in the 20th Century* (Syracuse: Syracuse University Press, 1999).

9. Aristotle, *Nichomachean Ethics*, trans. W.D. Ross (Oxford: Oxford University Press, 1998); P. Foot, *Virtues and Vices* (Berkeley, CA: University of California Press, 1978); A. MacIntyre, *After Virtue* (Notre Dame: University of Notre Dame Press, 1984).

10. M. Walzer, *Just and Unjust Wars* (New York: Basic Books, 3rd ed., 2000), xvi.

11. Walzer, *Wars*, 329–36; Holmes, *War*, 260–96; Norman, *Ethics*, 210–15; P. Ackerman and J. DuVall, *A Force More Powerful* (New York: St. Martin's, 2000). This last book was also blended into an extended PBS documentary special by the same title.

12. G. Sharp, "The Technique of Nonviolent Action," in R. Holmes and B. Gan, eds. *Nonviolence in Theory and Practice* (Long Grove: Waveland, 2nd ed., 2005), 254.

13. J. Rawls, *A Theory of Justice* (Cambridge: Harvard University Press, 1971), 370–82; Walzer, *Wars*, 329–36.

14. J. Brown, *Gandhi and Civil Disobedience* (Cambridge: Cambridge University Press, 1977); D. Dalton, *Mahatma Gandhi: Nonviolent Power in Action* (New York: Columbia University Press, 1993); A. Fairclough, *To Redeem the Soul of America* (Athens: University of Georgia Press, 1987); A. Morris, *The Origins of the Civil Rights Movement* (New York: Free Press, 1984); Ackerman and DuVall, *Force*, 61–113 and 305–35.

15. Walzer, *Wars*, 330–35.

16. Ackerman and DuVall, *Force*, 207–41; E. Schwarz, *Paths to Freedom Through Nonviolence* (Vienna: Sensen-Verlag, 1959); R. Petrow, *The Bitter Years* (New York: Morrow, 1974); L. Bergfelt, *Experiences of Civilian Resistance* (Uppsala: University of Uppsala Press, 1993); J. Thomas, *The Giant Killers* (New York: Taplinger, 1976).

17. Walzer, *Wars*, xxii, 330–35.

18. J. Bentham, *The Principles of Morals and Legislation* (Indianapolis, IN: Hackett, 1981); J.S. Mill, *Utilitarianism* (Indianapolis, IN: Hackett, 1987).

19. M. Walzer, "The Moral Standing of States: A Response to Four Critics," *Philosophy and Public Affairs* (1979/80), 209–29; T. Nagel, "Ruthlessness in Public Life," in his *Mortal Questions* (Cambridge: Cambridge University Press, 1979), 75–90.

20. J. Keegan, *The Second World War* (New York: Vintage, 1990); M. Walzer, "World War II: Why was this War Different?" *Philosophy and Public Affairs* (1970/71), 3–21; W.V. O'Brien, *The Conduct of Just and Limited War* (New York: Praeger, 1981), 35–65; G. Orwell, *1984* (Harmondsworth: Penguin, 1989).

21. Norman, *Ethics*, 80–93.

22. Narveson, "Pacifism," 62–77.

23. Holmes, *War*, 146–213, esp. 183–213.

24. G.E.M. Anscombe, "War and Murder" in R. Wasserstrom, ed. *War and Morality* (Belmont: Wadsworth, 1970), 41–53.

25. Narveson, "Pacifism," 63–78; Narveson, "Violence and War," 109–47; H. Shue, *Basic Rights* (Princeton: Princeton University Press, 2nd ed., 1996); A. Gewirth, *Human Rights: Essays in Justification and Application* (Chicago: University of Chicago Press, 1982), *passim*.

26. B. Orend, *Human Rights: Concept and Context* (Peterborough, ON: Broadview, 2002).

27. G. Fletcher, "Proportionality and the Psychotic Aggressor," *Israel Law Review* (1973), 367–90.

28. M. Otsuka appears to support this claim in his "Killing the Innocent in Self-Defense," *Philosophy and Public Affairs* (1992), 74–94. It is also present in Holmes, *War*, *passim*.

29. H. Brocklehurst, "Kids 'R' Us? Children as Political Bodies," *International Journal of Politics and Ethics* (2003), 79–92.

30. Holmes, *War*, 146–213.

31. The DDE, thus defined, cannot solve the innocent aggressor/child soldier problem discussed above. Say soldier S is considering shooting soldier T, who under some description is an innocent aggressor. S cannot appeal to the DDE here because, while he might say that he intends only to defeat the aggression and not kill an innocent, and while he might contend that the defeat of the aggression is worth the price, he *cannot* plausibly contend that killing the innocent is not means to his end of defeating the aggression, since the innocent and the aggressor are (by hypothesis) one and the same person. Innocent aggressors, if such there be, must thus be dealt with differently from innocent non-aggressors. Hence my further arguments above.

32. Walzer, *Wars*, 152–59, 257, 277–83, 317–21; Norman, *Killing*, 73–118 and 159–200.

Conclusion

Reflecting on the ethics of war and peace can be tough, and is fraught with dangers both conceptual and moral. We have seen this, in spades, throughout this book. Yet reflect on war's morality we must, as responsible individuals actively engaged in our world.

Active engagement, the press of events, and the weight of the stakes all make wartime decision-making doubly difficult. We thus appreciate, in its full force, the observation that rigorous contemplation of the justice of war—in all its phases—must be given *before* the decision to go to war is made. Contemporary wars tend to be fought much more quickly than prior wars—think of Iraq in 2003 versus Vietnam, or Afghanistan in 2001 versus the World Wars. Advances in technology and technique mean that the damage can now be done in weeks, as opposed to years. As decent people, citizens and decision-makers, we must examine all we can, and formulate firm, sensible and humane policies which cannot and will not be dislodged during someone's rush to war. Quick action may indeed be necessary, but it cannot be informed by rash decisions based on shoddy evidence, superficial values and temporary fears.

I have argued, throughout this text, that the best aid to contemplation of these issues is just war theory and, to a somewhat lesser extent, international law. My conviction here at the end remains the same, in spite of the substantial contributions of realism and pacifism. Just war theory is more *detailed* and *comprehensive* than either of its rivals, and it is *neither* too pessimistic *nor* too optimistic. Just war theory is *less extreme* and sweeping in its conclusions and *it bases its views on deep and sincerely considered values*, such as those of human rights, minimally just communities and the need to protect both from aggression. Aggression, sadly, is a common failing in human beings and the societies they form. Lots of people love telling other people what to do. When that desire for dominance becomes coupled with physical violence, it must be resisted for the sake of our rights and the integrity and quality of our lives. Just war theory realizes this, and recognizes its moral importance. It is for all these reasons that just war theory is already so deeply ingrained in international law, as well as in our daily discourse and debate about the ethics of war and peace.

Today, those who we should, perhaps, be most suspicious about are those who argue that a new age has dawned—with the events of 9/11—and that we must now do without time-tested values and fight with an unprecedented ferocity and lack of restraint. As in other spheres of life—think of the high-tech economic bubble in the 1990s—these self-appointed gurus of "a brand new era" are all too often wrong. And what they are here proposing and allowing is too extreme, far too dangerous and verging at times even on savagery. Just war theory and international law remain hugely useful and insightful—indeed, unparalleled—aids to reflection and decision-making in connection with war, including the very latest and even future challenges. Until the advent of a genuinely more peaceful world, they will be in one form or another irreplaceable.

APPENDIX A

Sources on the Laws of Armed Conflict

Primary Sources

The best websites are below, where most of the major international laws and treaties on war can be down loaded for free and in full. Go to:

Air War College:
  <www.au.af.mil/au/awc/awcgate/awc-law.htm>
Avalon Project at Yale Law School:
  <www.yale.edu/lawweb/avalon/lawofwar/lawwar.htm>
Fletcher School at Tufts University:
  <www.fletcher.tufts.edu/multi/warfare.html>
International Humanitarian Law Research Institute:
  <www.ihlresearch.org.ihl>
University of Minnesota Law of Armed Conflict:
  <www1.umn.edu/humanrts/instree/auoy.htm>

Thematic and Chronological Organization of the Primary Sources

2.1 *Jus ad Bellum*

Hague Convention I & III (1907)
The Kellogg-Briand Pact (1928)
Charter of the United Nations (1945) especially Articles 1, 2, 5, 6, 23–7 and 33–54.
United Nations General Assembly Definition of Aggression (1974)
Decision of the International Court of Justice on *Nicaragua vs. The United States of America* (1986)
(Chapters 1 and 3 of Reisman and Antoniou, eds. *Laws*. See section 3 for full citation.)

2.2 *Jus in Bello*

United States' Field Army Manual (or "Lieber's Code") (1863)
Hague Conventions (1899–1907)
Convention Regulating Poisonous Gases (1925)
Convention Regulating Genocide (1948)
Geneva Conventions (1949)
Additional Protocol to the Geneva Convention (1977)
Convention Regulating Cultural Property and Sites during Wartime (1954)
United Nations General Assembly Resolutions Prohibiting Nuclear Weapons
   (1961 and 1973)
Convention Regulating Aircraft Offences (1963), including Aircraft Seizure
   (1970) and Civil Aviation Safety (1971)
Convention Regulating Biological Weapons (1972)
Convention Regulating Diplomatic Agents during Wartime (1973)
Convention Regulating Weapons Which Modify the Environment (1976)
Convention Regulating Hostages (1979)
Convention Regulating Excessively Injurious or Indiscriminate Weapons (1980)
(Chapters 2, 4 and 6 of Reisman and Antoniou, eds. *Laws*.)

2.3 *Jus post Bellum*

Hague Convention IV (1907)
United Nations Charter (1945) especially Articles 73–85 and 92–6.
Nuremberg Judgments (1946)
Tokyo Judgments (1946)
Geneva Convention IV (1949)
Treaty of Rome Establishing the International Criminal Court (1998)
(Chapters 5 and 7 of Reisman and Antoniou, eds. *Laws*.)

Secondary Sources (include some primary documents, usually with editing and sometimes commentary)

I prefer, and have extensively used, W. Reisman and C. Antoniou, eds. *The Laws of War: A Comprehensive Collection of Primary Documents Governing Armed Conflict* (New York: Vintage, 1994). See also:

Bailey, S. *Prohibitions and Restraints in War* (Oxford: Oxford University Press, 1972).

Benvenisti, E. *The International Law of Occupation* (Princeton: Princeton University Press, 1993).

Best, G. *War and Law since 1945* (Oxford: Clarendon, 1994).

Brownlie, I. *International Law and The Use of Force by States* (Oxford: Clarendon, 1963).

Chesterman, S. *Just War or Just Peace? Humanitarian Intervention and International Law* (Oxford: Oxford University Press, 2001).

Detter Delupis, I. *The Law of War* (Cambridge: Cambridge University Press, 1987).

Dinstein, Y. *War, Aggression and Self-Defence* (Cambridge: Cambridge University Press, 1995).

Henkin, L. *How Nations Behave: Law and Foreign Policy* (New York: Columbia University Press, 2nd ed., 1979).

Higgins, R. and M. Flory, eds. *Terrorism and International Law* (London: Routledge, 1997).

Howard, M. *The Laws of War: Constraints on Warfare in the Western World* (New Haven: Yale University Press, 1994).

Lauterpacht, H. *International Law, Vols. 3 and 4: The Law of War and Peace* (Cambridge: Cambridge University Press, 1977–8).

Miller, R. *The Law of War* (Lexington: Lexington Books, 1975).

O'Brien, W.V. *The Law of Limited Armed Conflict* (Washington: Georgetown University Press, 1965).

Nardin, T. *Law, Morality and The Relations of States* (Princeton: Princeton University Press, 1983).

Roberts, A. and R. Guelff, eds. *Documents on The Laws of War* (Oxford: Oxford University Press, 1999).

APPENDIX B
Sources on Just War Theory

Website sources

"War" by Brian Orend for the Stanford Encyclopedia of Philosophy:
<plato.stanford.edu/entries/war>
Just War Theory.com by Mark Rigstad:
<www.justwartheory.com>
"Just War Theory" by Mark Rigstad for Wikipedia:
<http://en/wikipedia.org/wiki/Just_war>
"Just War Theory" by Alex Moseley for the Internet Encyclopedia of Philosophy:
<www.iep.utm.edu/justwar.htm>
"Resources in Just War Theory" by Larry Hinman:
<http://ethics.acusd/applied/military/justwar.html>

Text Sources

Anscombe, G.E.M. "War and Murder," in R. Wasserstrom, ed. *War and Morality* (Belmont, CA: Wadsworth, 1970), 41–53.

Aquinas, *Summa Theologiae* (London: Christian Classics, 1981), 2–2, Qs 40 and 64.

Aristotle, *Politics*, trans. C. Lord (Chicago: University of Chicago Press, 1984), Book 1, Chaps. 3–8.

Augustine, *The City of God*, trans. R. Ryson (Cambridge: Cambridge University Press, 1998).

—. *The Political Writings*, ed. and trans. H. Paolucci (Chicago: Regnery, 1962).

Axinn, S. *A Moral Military* (Philadelphia: Temple University Press, 1989).

Christopher, P. *The Ethics of War and Peace* (Englewood Cliffs, NJ: Prentice Hall, 1994).

Cicero, *De Officiius*, trans. W. Miller (Cambridge, MA: Harvard University Press, 1961), 1, XI, 35–39.

—. *De Re Publica*, 3, XXIII, trans. C. Keyes (New York: Putnam, 1928), 211–15.

Deane, H. *The Political and Social Ideas of St. Augustine* (New York: Columbia University Press, 1963).

De las Casas, B. *In Defence of the Indians*, trans. S. Poole (Chicago: Northern Illinois University Press, 1992).

Elshtain, J.B. *Just War Against Terror* (New York: Basic Books, 2003).

Elshtain, J.B., ed. *Just War Theory* (Oxford: Blackwell, 1992).

Eppstein, J. *The Catholic Tradition of the Law of Nations* (Washington, DC: CAIP, 1935).

Evans, M., ed. *Just War Theory: A Reappraisal* (London: Palgrave Macmillan, 2005).

Ford, J. "The Morality of Obliteration Bombing," *Theological Studies* 5 (1944), 261–309.

Fullinwinder, R. "War and Innocence," *Philosophy and Public Affairs* (1975), 90–7.

Grotius, H. *The Law of War and Peace*, trans. L.R. Loomis (Roslyn, NY: WJ Black Inc., 1949).

Hartle, A. *Moral Issues in Military Decision-Making* (Kansas City: University of Kansas Press, 1989).

Ignatieff, M. *The Lesser Evil* (Princeton: Princeton University Press, 2004).

—. *Virtual War* (Toronto: Viking, 2000).

Johnson, J.T. *Can Modern War Be Just?* (New Haven, CT: Yale University Press, 1984).

—. *Ideology, Reason and The Limitation of War* (Princeton: Princeton University Press, 1975).

—. *The Just War Tradition and The Restraint of War* (Princeton: Princeton University Press, 1981).

Kant, I. *Political Writings,* trans. H. Nisbet and ed. H. Reiss (Cambridge: Cambridge University Press, 1995).

Lackey, D. *The Ethics of War and Peace* (Englewood Cliffs, NJ: Prentice Hall, 1989).

Langan, J. and W.V. O'Brien, eds. *The Nuclear Dilemma and The Just War Tradition* (Lexington, MA: Lexington, 1986).

Locke, J. *Two Treatises of Civil Government* (Cambridge: Cambridge University Press, 1988).

Luban, D. "Just War and Human Rights," *Philosophy and Public Affairs* (1979/80), 160–81.

Melzer, Y. *Concepts of Just War* (Jerusalem: Hebrew University, 1975).

Nagel, T. "War and Massacre," *Philosophy and Public Affairs* (1971/72), 123–43.

O'Brien, W.V. *The Conduct of Just and Limited War* (New York: Praeger, 1981).

Orend, B. "Justice After War," *Ethics and International Affairs* (2002), 43–56.

—. *Michael Walzer on War and Justice.* Co-published, 2000, by McGill-Queen's University Press and the University of Wales Press.

—. *War and International Justice: A Kantian Perspective* (Waterloo, ON: Wilfrid Laurier University Press, 2000).

Osgood, R. and R. Tucker, *Force, Order and Justice* (Baltimore: Johns Hopkins University Press, 1967).

Phillips, R. *War and Justice* (Oklahoma City: University of Oklahoma Press, 1984).

Ramsey, P. *The Just War* (New York: Scribners Sons, 1968).

Regan, R. *Just War: Principles and Cases* (Washington, DC: Catholic University Press of America, 1996).

Russell, F. *The Just War in the Middle Ages* (Cambridge: Cambridge University Press, 1975).

Ryan, J.K. *Modern War and Basic Ethics* (Milwaukee, WN: Bruce, 1940).

Scott, James Brown, ed. *Classics of International Law.* (Washington, DC: Carnegie Institute, 1917). Contains Grotius, Vattel, Vitoria and Suarez.

Sepulveda, J.G. *Democrates Alter*, trans. S. Poole in *Contemporary Civilization Reader* (New York: American Heritage, 6th ed., 1997), 39–51.

Sterba, J. *The Ethics of War and Nuclear Deterrence* (Belmont, CA: Wadsworth, 1985).

Teichman, J. *Pacifism and The Just War* (Oxford: Blackwell, 1986).

Temes, P. *The Just War* (New York: Ivan Dee, 2003).

Tooke, J.D. *The Just War in Aquinas and Grotius* (London: SPCK, 1975).

Tucker, R. *The Just War* (Baltimore: Johns Hopkins University Press, 1960).

Vitoria, F. *Political Writings*, ed. A. Pagden and J. Lawrence (Cambridge: Cambridge University Press, 1991).

Walzer, M. *Arguing About War* (New Haven, CT: Yale University Press, 2004).

—. *Just and Unjust Wars* (New York: Basic, 1977).

Wasserstrom, R. ed. *War and Morality* (Belmont, CA: Wadsworth, 1970).

Zupan, D. *War, Morality and Autonomy* (London: Ashgate, 2004).

INDEX

from the publisher

A name never says it all, but the word "broadview" expresses a good deal of the philosophy behind our company. We are open to a broad range of academic approaches and political viewpoints. We pay attention to the broad impact book publishing and book printing has in the wider world; we began using recycled stock more than a decade ago, and for some years now we have used 100% recycled paper for most titles. As a Canadian-based company we naturally publish a number of titles with a Canadian emphasis, but our publishing program overall is internationally oriented and broad-ranging. Our individual titles often appeal to a broad readership too; many are of interest as much to general readers as to academics and students.

Founded in 1985, Broadview remains a fully independent company owned by its shareholders—not an imprint or subsidiary of a larger multinational.

If you would like to find out more about Broadview and about the books we publish, please visit us at **www.broadviewpress.com**. And if you'd like to place an order through the site, we'd like to show our appreciation by extending a special discount to you: by entering the code below you will receive a 20% discount on purchases made through the Broadview website.

Discount code: **broadview20%**

Thank you for choosing Broadview.

Please note: this offer applies only to sales of bound books within the United States or Canada.

Using 3037 lb. of Rolland Enviro100 Print instead
of virgin fibres paper reduces your ecological footprint of:

Trees: 26
Solid waste: 3,176lb
Water: 25,125gal
Air emissions: 8,256lb